# In a New Land

# In a New Land

*A Comparative View of Immigration*

Nancy Foner

NEW YORK UNIVERSITY PRESS
*New York and London*

NEW YORK UNIVERSITY PRESS
New York and London
www.nyupress.org

Library of Congress Cataloging-in-Publication Data
Foner, Nancy, 1945–
In a new land : a comparative view of immigration / Nancy Foner.
p.  cm.
Includes bibliographical references and index.
ISBN 0-8147-2745-X (acid-free paper)
ISBN 0-8147-2746-8 (pbk. : acid-free paper)
  1. Emigration and immigration—United States.  2. Emigration and
immigration—Europe.  3. Emigration and immigration—New York
(State)—New York.  4. Emigration and immigration—-England—
London.  5. Emigration and immigration—Cross-cultural studies.
I. Title.
JV6465.F66 2005
304.8'73—dc22          2005004863

Manufactured in the United States of America

c 10 9 8 7 6 5 4 3 2 1
p 10 9 8 7 6 5 4 3 2

# Contents

# Acknowledgments

In the course of working on this book, I have acquired many debts. As the Lillie and Nathan Ackerman Professor of Equality and Justice in America at Baruch College's School of Public Affairs during 2002–2004, I was given precious time to work on this project. I am grateful to the Engelman family for funding the professorship and to my colleagues at Baruch for providing an intellectually stimulating environment. Also at Baruch, many students helped me to better understand what it means to be an immigrant, or the child of an immigrant, in New York today.

As I was writing this book, I benefited from opportunities to present my work in progress at the Gotham Center Seminar in Post-War New York City History at the City University of New York; the University of Amsterdam; the workshop on Paths of Integration at the Institute of Migration Research and Intercultural Studies, University of Osnabrueck, Germany; and the Derek Gordon Research Seminar at the University of the West Indies. I want to thank Leo Lucassen for organizing a session on my work on immigration to New York, past and present, at the 2002 Social Science History Association meetings, and Caroline Brettell, Carmel Chiswick, Brian Gratton, as well as Leo Lucassen, for their comments at the session, which led me to rework and expand on some of my arguments.

A great many friends and colleagues in the immigration field have been a source of insights and ideas. It is not possible to name them all here, for there are so many and I would not want to leave anyone off the list. I do, however, want to acknowledge my debt to two organizations with which I've been involved. The Social Science Research Council (SSRC), specifically the Committee on International Migration and its program director, Josh DeWind, have supported a growing interdisciplinary field of immigration studies in the United States and sponsored numerous programs, conferences, and working groups that have enriched my own work. Most recently, I had the opportunity to collaborate with George Fredrickson on a SSRC working group on historical and contemporary perspectives on immigration, race, and ethnicity in the United States, and I learned a great deal from him as well as the other participants. I also owe a debt to the Russell Sage Foundation, where I began to work on the comparative-historical study of migration as a visiting scholar in the early 1990s, and to Eric Wanner, the foundation president, who has played a role in developing immigration research in the United States.

Ilene Kalish, editor at New York University Press, was an enthusiastic backer of the book project from the beginning, made valuable suggestions as I was working on it, and guided the manuscript through the publication process with great expertise and good humor. I feel fortunate to have had the opportunity to work with her. Thanks to Caroline Brettell and Steven Gold, who generously revealed their names as reviewers for New York University Press, for their comments on the manuscript.

Last but certainly not least, I want to thank members of my family, who, as usual, offered advice and encouragement at every step of the way. Once again, my mother, Anne Foner, read the manuscript with a keen critical eye and was a much-valued sounding board. My daughter, Alexis, now a professional writer in her own right, has made me sensitive to the need for clear and lively writing, although I am sure that I do not live up to her high standards. My husband, Peter Swerdloff, spent hours talking over ideas with me, provided critical insights, and, perhaps most important, was a constant source of support.

# Introduction

## Migration in Comparative Perspective

By now, it is almost a cliché to say that immigration is trans forming the United States. At the time of the last census in 2000, more than 10 percent of U.S. residents were foreign-born; together with their American-born children, this group constituted one-fifth of the nation's population. Not surprisingly, the massive recent immigration has given rise to a growing scholarly literature as academics in different disciplines try to grapple with the complexity of the subject.

This book is based on the premise that a comparative perspective can yield new insights into the nature and impact of the new wave of immigration to the United States. A product of my own long-standing engagement with comparative research, in this book I look at migration in terms of multiple dimensions. I focus on three types of comparisons: comparisons of migrants across cities or regions within the United States, across nation-states, and across different periods of time.[1] The analysis centers on three main themes that are fundamental to understanding the migration process: race and ethnicity, gender, and transnational connections.

The constant, or base-line, in virtually all the comparisons is New York—America's quintessential immigrant city, that in 2000 was home to 2.9 million immigrants or 9 percent of the nation's foreign-born. This book compares today's Latin American, Asian, and Caribbean newcomers in New York City with eastern and southern European immigrants a century ago, as well as with immigrants in other major U.S. receiving cities in the current period. Looking beyond the United States, it compares the experiences of a major group in New York City—West Indians—with their cousins in London. More generally, it views the dynamics of immigration in the United States, in the past as well as present, against those in western Europe.

To some degree, of course, virtually all migration research is comparative.[2] Any study that follows migrants from their country of origin to their new destination is, in effect, comparative in a "before-and-after" sense, even if the comparison is not made explicit.[3] In anthropology, ethnographies of migrants from different cultures are also implicitly comparative in that they entail analyzing and representing activities and relations among people from one culture for audiences in another.[4] More explicit types of comparisons are also common. Sociologists, political scientists, and economists of migration routinely compare immigrants in large samples through quantitative techniques to gauge the effect of age, gender, race, country of birth, and other variables on a broad range of outcomes; historians and social scientists have employed what Nancy Green calls "convergent comparisons" that contrast different immigrant groups in one setting—Jews and Italians in New York City in the past or Dominicans and Jamaicans in the present, to mention just two possibilities.[5]

In this book, the comparisons are explicit. And they are at the core of the enterprise. I look both "across time" and "across space," with an emphasis on what happens in the place of destination after migration. Surprisingly few full-length works on U.S. immigration focus on these kinds of comparisons. None, as far as I know, brings together the three kinds of comparisons—of different historical eras, among different cities, and across national boundaries—that are examined here.[6]

The comparisons in the chapters that follow are qualitative comparisons rather than statistical analyses of large data sets. In the discussion of West Indian migrants, I draw on my own ethnographic research in New York and London. Much of the volume, however, is an interpretive synthesis that pulls together strands from the literature on immigration, including individual case studies of particular times, groups, and places as well as material from broader analyses and overviews. The sources I use are extremely varied. They range from historical accounts of immigration a hundred years ago to contemporary ethnographic studies and statistical material, from census reports to surveys collected by social science researchers and governmental bodies.[7]

## Why Compare?

Whether across time or space, a comparative perspective has, I believe, much to offer to the study of the immigration experience. We now have a mass of information in the form of myriad monographs and studies on particular immigrant groups in particular periods or places. It is time to bring these materials together into a comparative framework. A comparative analysis can deepen our understanding of migration by raising new questions and research problems and help to evaluate, and in some cases modify, theoretical perspectives and formulate explanations that could not be made on the basis of one case—or one time period—alone.

Much of the scholarly material on immigration is fairly narrowly drawn, focusing on a specific group or groups of immigrants in one location and specific aspects of their experiences at one period of time. A comparative approach provides a broader view. Comparisons often bring fresh perspectives to old problems; they have the special quality of calling attention to—or bringing into sharper focus—dynamics that might have been missed or minimized if focusing on only one case. Also, by acquainting us with what has gone on before or in other places, a comparative approach can inspire a critical awareness of what is taken for granted in our own era, city, or society. The experiences of each group, whether it is West Indians in New York today or Russian Jews a hundred years ago, may be more fully understood in light of the experiences of others in different locations or different eras. As Reinhard Bendix put it in another context, comparative studies "increase the 'visibility' of one structure by contrasting it with another."[8]

A comparative approach, as George Fredrickson has observed, can undermine two contrary but equally damaging presuppositions—the illusion of total regularity and the illusion of absolute uniqueness.[9] Or to put it another way, it enables us to see what is unique to a specific situation and what is more general to the migration experience. Of course, to some degree it is a matter of emphasis. Or of finding what you are looking for. If you look for similarities across time you find them, if you look for differences across time, you also find them. The same can be said about similarities and differences across space. And then there are disciplinary predilections. As Green notes, historians are more inclined to emphasize historical parallels in understanding today's migrant and settlement patterns than sociologists who see contemporary detail with disciplinary eyes that emphasize newness.[10] Indeed, in emphasizing what is distinctive today, social scientists often give insufficient weight to similarities with the past. Frequently, there is only a brief nod to the past—usually to emphasize how different it is from the present —before proceeding to an analysis of the current era. For their part, historians, according to Gary Gerstle and John Mollenkopf, have not "risen to the challenge" of applying lessons from the past to the present immigration.[11]

Regardless of discipline, one of the great benefits of comparisons is that they bring out *both* the similarities and differences between past and present and between migrations to different cities and societies. What comparisons force us to do is to try to account for the similarities and differences—a process which is useful "in enlarging our theoretical understanding of the kinds of institutions and processes being compared, thereby making a contribution to the development of social scientific theories and generalizations."[12] Comparing present-day immigrant New Yorkers with their predecessors a century ago can show whether, and in what ways, we have been there before—whether we are currently witnessing variations on long-standing themes that characterize the immigrant experience in the United States or in particular cities like New York. Comparing West Indians in New York City with their counterparts in London broadens our understanding of the West Indian experience in both places and sheds light on both the structural constraints and cultural choices framing their migration experience.[13]

A comparative perspective can push forward our ability to understand and theorize processes associated with immigration because it leads us to step back and examine what are often time-bound, culture-bound, and even city-bound assumptions. If, as Alejandro Portes notes, theoretical advances arise out of the ability to reconstitute a perceptual field and to identify connections not previously seen, then comparisons across time and space may be productive in bringing new perspectives to bear on familiar issues and promoting the kind of "distance from reality" that Portes argues is important "in order to identify patterns lost at close range."[14] Comparisons across time raise questions about whether theoretical perspectives elaborated in light of today's immigration, such as transnationalism, are unique to the current period or whether they also pertain to the past; comparisons across space allow us to see if models and concepts, such as segmented assimilation, designed with the United States in mind make sense to apply to other societies.

There is another benefit to comparisons across time and space: they bring together literatures that have often flowed in separate streams. Until recently, the literatures on past and present immigrations to the United States have been quite unconnected, with historians and sociologists often "discovering" what has been acknowledged and treated in the other's discipline for some time. Insights from historical studies—for example, on the question of "whiteness" among earlier immigrants—can enrich our understanding of contemporary immigration. In much the same way, sociological research on such topics as transnationalism can shed light on the past. U.S. migration research has also often proceeded without much awareness of work on migration in Europe, and certainly the chapters on West Indians show that scholars on this side of the Atlantic can profit from a closer acquaintance with research on the Caribbean community in Britain.

## Overview

The plan of the book is as follows. The four chapters in Part I focus on a comparison across time, or immigration to New York City, then and now. The "then" in this case is the period between 1880–1920 at the time of the last great immigration to New York; the "now" is the past few decades when several million immigrants have arrived in the city. I begin the past-present comparison in chapter 1 with the subject of race. Among the central questions are how immigrants were seen, in racial and ethnic terms, in the two immigration eras and the relevance of understanding how Jews and Italians were transformed into racial insiders for analyzing changing ethnoracial dynamics in the twenty-first century. In this sense, chapter 1 is not just a "then and now" comparison but also examines processes that have taken place over time.[15]

A comparative lens can also bring into sharper focus the complex connections between immigrants and African Americans in New York City. These connections are the subject of chapter 2, where I explore the consequences for today's immigrants of living in a city with a large African American population compared to a century ago when there were only a tiny number of black New Yorkers. In general, migrant inflows in one period change the context that greets the next wave, and the analysis makes clear that the huge African American influx from around the First World War to 1960 created a new racial order that had an enormous effect on the immigrants who arrived in the post-1965 era.[16]

In chapter 3, the then-now comparison focuses on transnationalism: whether, and in what ways, the transnational ties of today's first- and second-generation immigrant New Yorkers are a new development —and the consequences for them and their communities. Immigrant women are on center stage in chapter 4, which considers how changes in their work roles have affected their experiences today as compared to the past.

Part II of the book puts the spotlight on one group, West Indians, and in one era, the post–World War II period. The comparisons of West Indians in New York and London are what Green has labeled "divergent comparisons" in that they contrast the experiences of a particular immigrant group in different destinations.[17] What they show, in a dramatic fashion, is the important role of the racial context in shaping the West Indian migrant experience—the central theme in chapter 5. Why does being black mean something different on the two sides of the Atlantic? How does this affect the lives of migrants and their children in terms of identity construction as well as actual social relations? The dynamics of race in Britain and the United States have influenced the very questions posed and explored by scholars about the fate of the West Indian second generation. Why, for example, does the literature on West Indians in New York (and indeed the United States more generally) focus so heavily on segmented assimilation, while no comparable concept has emerged or been adopted in Britain?

Chapter 6 pushes the comparative discussion further by looking at other ways that place makes a difference for West Indian migrants in New York as compared to London. In addition to the character of race and ethnic relations, other contextual features matter, from the structure of the urban labor market to the nature of the welfare state. So do characteristics of the migration stream as well as the timing of the migration, the legal context in which it occurs, and distance from the home society. The analysis also branches in yet another direction as it compares West Indians in New York and those who have settled in other American cities, thereby bringing a cross-city as well as cross-national perspective to the analysis of the West Indian migrant experience.

In chapter 7, I take up questions pertaining to Jamaican migrant women in New York and London, with special emphasis on their work and family lives. It is a case, in many ways, of parallels on both sides of the Atlantic in terms of the benefits and burdens of work in the context of economic opportunities, gender divisions in the labor market, gender roles in the household, and the stresses of transnational motherhood. Yet there are also differences, and among the questions the chapter explores are why Jamaican women in New York were more likely to be pioneers in the move abroad and to work in private homes than their cousins in London.

Part III offers yet another set of comparisons across space. Moving beyond the particular case of West Indians, chapter 8 looks more generally at the issue of New York exceptionalism: How special is New York as an immigrant destination compared to other American gateway cities? Race and ethnicity are at the center of the discussion. How have New York City's peculiar features—its history, institutions, and immigrant flows—affected perceptions of race and ethnicity and the dynamics of intergroup relations? What makes the city unique as a place for immigrants today? And what features does it share with other immigrant destinations in the nation?

The book concludes, in chapter 9, with comparisons across space *and* across time. The taking-off point is the United States rather than New York and the comparisons are, very broadly, with western Europe. One theme is popular myths about immigrants in the past that color contemporary discussions of immigrants on both sides of the Atlantic. Another has to do with race. Comparing the United States and western Europe underscores the particular impact of the American racial structure—and the legacy of slavery and segregation—in shaping responses to immigration, the experiences of immigrants, and the way scholars themselves analyze the new arrivals.

In their introduction to a volume on migration theory, Caroline Brettell and James Hollifield note that comparisons have resulted in some of the most innovative scholarship in the migration field—most of the work they cite involving cross-national comparisons within Europe.[18] This book takes the comparative approach a step forward through a series of essays that view the recent immigration to the United States in a multiplicity of dimensions: making comparisons across time periods, cities and regions, and nations, and focusing on issues pertaining to race, gender, and transnationalism. Comparisons of course are impossible without detailed studies of particular groups, places, and time periods. But as we seek to make sense of how the huge recent immigration is changing American society and the lives of the immigrants who have moved there we need to go beyond these individual case studies. Comparisons of immigration that look back in time, to different cities, and to different societies can, as this book suggests, help us to see not only whether we have come to a genuinely new place—but also to better understand the complex dynamics of immigration today and the implications for where we are headed in the future.

# PART I

# Comparisons Across Time
*Immigrants in New York's
Two Great Waves*

# 1

## The Social Construction of Race
## in Two Immigrant Eras

The racial difference between today's nonwhite immigrant New Yorkers and their white European predecessors seems like a basic —and obvious—fact. Yet much is not obvious about racial matters then and now. At the turn of the twentieth century, when nearly all New York City residents were of European descent, recently arrived Jewish and Italian immigrants were seen as racially distinct from and inferior to those of Anglo-Saxon or Nordic stock. Today, although immigrants from Latin America, Asia, and the Caribbean are often referred to as nonwhite or people of color, these blanket terms oversimplify the nature and impact of race among them.

The comparison of past and present brings out, in an especially dramatic way, how race has been socially constructed among immigrants in different eras. And it raises questions about the way conceptions of race have changed, and are likely to continue to change, as a result of immigration. The focus in this chapter, as in the three that follow, is on what I have called New York's two great waves of immigration: between 1880 and 1920, close to a million and a half immigrants, mostly Jews and Italians, arrived and settled in the city and, since the late 1960s, more than two and a half million immigrants—mainly from Asia, the Caribbean, and Latin America—have moved to New York City.

Race is a highly problematic—and highly charged—concept, partly because there are so many scholarly definitions of the term, partly because it has taken on particular meanings in popular discourse that differ from academic understandings, and partly because of a concern that using the term could be taken as an endorsement or legitimation of the very inequalities that it describes. Although there is no one agreed-upon definition of "race," a definition recently offered by George Fredrickson would, I think, find broad acceptance: race refers to "the belief that socially significant differences between human groups or communities that differ in visible physical characteristics or putative ancestry are innate and unchangeable."[1]

Racial differences may seem permanent and immutable—as if they are natural and inevitable—but in fact race is a changeable perception. Indeed, the awesome power of race is related to its ability to pass as a feature of the natural landscape. Races are not fixed biological categories, and dividing human populations into "races," as physical anthropologists have shown, has no basis in genetics. Regardless of its dubious roots in biology, however, race is "real because, to paraphrase W. I. Thomas, people act as though it is real and thus it has become real in its social consequences."[2] Race, in short, is a social and cultural construction, and what is important is how physical characteristics and/or putative ancestry are interpreted within particular social contexts and are used to define categories of people as inferior or superior. Race, as Fredrickson notes, is commonly used as a criterion to justify a dominant and privileged position—"accompanied by the notion that 'we' are superior to 'them' and need to be protected from real or imagined threats to our privileged group position that might arise if 'they' were to gain in resources and rights. Here we have 'racism' in the full and unambiguous sense of the term."[3] As the historian Gary Okihiro puts it, race is a "conjuring," but it "acquires a searing reality through the weight of history, through the nation's laws and institutions, through popular culture and everyday practices."[4]

In discussing the way race is—and has been—constructed in New York, it may be helpful to think in terms of a series of questions raised by sociologists Stephen Cornell and Douglas Hartmann in their attempt to clarify conceptual issues in the study of race, ethnicity, and immigration.[5] Which groups, they ask, have the freedom to construct themselves? Which groups, and why, find themselves caught in inescapable categories constructed by others? Which groups, and why and how, are moving from one situation to another? How do both our definitions of groups and the groups themselves change when populations are moving to the United States—who gets combined together, who is seen as separate and distinct?

## When Jews and Italians Were Inferior Races

It may have become a cliché in academic circles to speak of race as a social construction, but even when racial categories are acknowledged as social constructions that vary across time and place, they have often been used, as Victoria Hattam has recently put it, in transhistorical terms.[6] Many accounts in the scholarly as well as popular literature speak of "nonwhite" immigrants today in contrast to "white" immigrants in the past as if the term white meant the same thing as it does now. It does not. Race today is basically a color word, but it was not that way in New York a hundred years ago. Then, Jewish and Italian immigrants in New York were seen as racially different from—and inferior to—people with origins in northern and western Europe. They were believed to have distinct biological features, mental abilities, and innate character traits. They looked different to most New Yorkers and were thought to have physical features that set them apart—facial features often noted, for example, in the case of Jews, and "swarthy" skin, in the case of Italians. These stereotypes were used to describe a significant proportion of New Yorkers at the time. Owing to the overwhelming predominance of Russian Jews and Italians in the immigrant flow, they defined what was then thought of as the new immigration. In 1910, Russian and Italian immigrants were almost a fifth of the city's population; by 1920, with their children, Italian Americans numbered over 800,000 and the Jewish population had soared to over 1.6 million, or, together, about 43 percent of the city's population.

Did this mean that Jews and Italians were not considered "white"? I had not realized I was getting into a historical minefield when I first wrote about this subject in *From Ellis Island to JFK* and grappled with the way to describe immigrants who, in many contexts, were seen as white, but, in other contexts, as an inferior kind of white or sometimes even distinguished from whites, who were defined as Nordic, Anglo-Saxon, or northern and western Europeans.[7] Much of the recent literature on the racial status of early twentieth-century immigrants focuses on this "whiteness" question. Some scholars, like Karen Brodkin, argue that Jews a hundred years ago were not considered fully white; David Roediger and James Barrett suggest the term "inbetween people" as a way to describe Jews' and Italians' ambiguous racial status—seen as above African and Asian Americans yet below "white" people; Matthew Jacobson refers to "probationary whites"; and Michael Topp now adds "inconclusively white."[8] Others emphasize that southern and eastern European arrivals were, to use Thomas Guglielmo's phrase, white on arrival—that they suffered from their racial undesirability but also, simultaneously, benefited from their privileged color status as whites. In line with this approach would be a decision to speak of inferior races of whites and hierarchic gradations of white people.[9] As one historian puts it in his critique of whiteness studies, Americans have had many ways of looking down on people without questioning their whiteness.[10] Clearly, we need fine-grained historical research that explores what terms were employed to describe racial differences among Jews and Italians in New York a century ago and the contexts in which they were used, what "white" actually meant then, and the role of considerations other than race—most significantly, religion—in stigmatizing Jews and Italians as inferior and legitimizing discrimination against them.[11]

There may be debate about eastern and southern Europeans' color status—whether, as Guglielmo puts it, they were racial outsiders and color insiders—but it is clear that race in early twentieth-century New York was not the kind of color-coded concept that it is today. And historians would agree that when it came to southern and eastern Europeans, characteristics other than color—believed to be innate and unchangeable—were involved in defining them as separate races. American scholarship, as Matthew Frye Jacobson, writes, "has generally conflated race and color, and so has transported a late twentieth century understanding of 'difference' into a period . . . [when] one might be both white *and* racially distinct from other whites."[12]

From the start, Jews and Italians were recognized as whites in terms of legal and political rights. They were allowed to naturalize as U.S. citizens at a time when American naturalization laws only gave "free white persons" or "persons of African nativity or African descent" the right to naturalize, and when the courts repeatedly denied Asian immigrants access to American citizenship because they were not, in Ian Haney Lopez's phrase, "white by law."[13] In fact, Guglielmo points out that, at the turn of the twentieth century, the naturalization application asked immigrants to provide both their race and color and expected different answers for each; Italians were often listed as southern or northern Italians—for race—and white for color.[14] Jews and Italians were allowed to vote in states that restricted the suffrage to whites, and miscegenation laws were never enforced to prevent their marriages to other Europeans.[15]

Yet if Italians and Jews were white, at the same time they were also, as Jacobson aptly puts it, viewed as "racially distinct from other whites." Whereas today, in Jacobson's words, "we see only subtly varying shades of a mostly undifferentiated whiteness," a hundred years ago, Americans saw "Celtic, Hebrew, Anglo-Saxon or Mediterranean physiognomies." Jews and Italians, in Cornell and Hartmann's formulation, were caught in categories constructed by others, although the emphasis needs to be put on the constraints owing to the *way* the categories were constructed by others. Most Jewish New Yorkers, after all, chose to identify as Jewish (and had done so in Europe as well); most Italian immigrants eventually came to see themselves as Italian in America, even if town and regional loyalties remained supreme.[16] The problem was being racialized as Italians and Jews—seen as inherently inferior on account of their Italianness or Jewishness and caught in the negative images and connotations associated with these categories.

Far from being on the fringe, full-blown theories about the racial inferiority of eastern Europeans and southern Italians were well within the mainstream of the scientific community at the turn of the twentieth century. Openly propounded by respected scholars, such views were also propagated and given the stamp of approval by public intellectuals and opinion leaders and the press.

The most influential of the books proclaiming a scientific racism was *The Passing of the Great Race,* written by Madison Grant, a patrician New Yorker and founder of the New York Zoological Society. The book set forth the notion that people of inferior breeding from southern and eastern Europe were overrunning the country, intermarrying, and diminishing the quality of the nation's superior Nordic stock—and sweeping America toward a "racial abyss."[17] This theme was picked up by figures of the stature of soon-to-be president Calvin Coolidge, who wrote in a popular magazine in 1921 that "America must be kept American. Biological laws show . . . that Nordics deteriorate when mixed with other races."[18]

Edward A. Ross, one of the most race conscious of American social scientists, was also troubled that newcomers, with their inborn deficiencies, would dilute America's sturdier Anglo-Saxon stock. He condemned Jews for their inborn love of money, and southern Italians for their volatility, instability, and unreliability. Steerage passengers from Naples "show a distressing frequency of low foreheads, open mouths, weak chins, poor features, skew faces, small or knobby crania, and backless heads. Such people lack the power to take rational care of themselves." Ross spoke of the "dusk of Saracenic or Berber ancestors" showing in the cheeks of Italian immigrant children. "One sees no reason," he wrote, "why the Italian dusk should not in time quench what of the

Celto-Teutonic flush lingers in the cheek of the native American."[19] Interestingly, in stressing the racial inferiority of southern (as opposed to northern) Italians, Ross, like other early twentieth-century writers, echoed arguments of Italian positivist anthropologists who, in the context of nation-building efforts in Italy and concerns about the destitute and disorganized South, wrote studies "proving" that northern Italians were descended from superior Aryan stock, while southerners were primarily of inferior African blood.[20]

Articles in the press and popular magazines echoed racial views of this kind. Articles with titles like "Are the Jews an Inferior Race?" (1912) and "Will the Jews Ever Lose Their Racial Identity?" (1911) appeared in the most frequently read periodicals. The "marks of their race," said *Harper's* of Lower East Side Jews, "appear in the formation of the jaw and mouth and in the general facial aspect."[21] Jewish racial features, the *New York Sun* (1893) argued, made them unassimilable: "Other races of men lose their identity by migration and by intermarrying with different peoples, with the result that their peculiar characteristics and physiognomies are lost in the mess. The Jewish face and character remain the same as they were in the days of the PHARAOH. . . . Usually a Jew is recognizable as such by sight. . . . After a few generations other immigrants to this country lose their race identity and become Americans only. Generally the Jews retain theirs, undiminished, so that it is observable by all men."[22]

Jews were thought to have visible physical characteristics that marked them off and made them "look Jewish."[23] The Dillingham Commission's Report on Immigration, A Dictionary of Races or Peoples, had this to say about Jews: "The Jewish nose and to a lesser degree other facial characteristics are found well nigh everywhere throughout the race."[24] To refute the racial stereotypes, Dr. Maurice Fishberg, a professor of medicine at New York University and Bellevue Medical College and a Russian Jewish immigrant himself, actually classified the noses of 2,836 Jewish men in New York City, finding that "only 14 percent had the aquiline or hooked nose commonly labeled as a 'Jewish' nose."[25]

In everyday life, there was a racial vocabulary to describe—and abuse—the new immigrants, and the language of color was sometimes involved. Italians were often described as "swarthy," and a common epithet for them, guinea, connected them to Africa. Although Guglielmo argues that there was never a systematic or sustained challenge to Italians' position as whites, he cites evidence that their color status was often contested. In the Chicago press, which he studied in detail, crime stories frequently marked Italians as racially distinct and problematic by continually stressing their dark skin, and many commentators also racialized Italian criminals by describing them as savage—sometimes simian—beasts more akin to animals than human beings.[26] Although the attempt was unsuccessful, in 1903 the Democratic Party sought to exclude Italians (and Mexicans) from voting in their "white primaries" since they did not qualify on color grounds:

> Eight years later, the U.S. House Committee on Immigration and Naturalization openly debated and seriously questioned whether one should regard "the south Italian as a full-blooded Caucasian"; many representatives did not seem to think so. And a range of Americans shared such suspicions. From the docks of New York to railroads out west, some native-born American workers carefully drew distinctions between themselves—"white men"—and foreigners like Italians. In 1891, for instance, a West Coast construction boss testified before a congressional committee that an Italian was "a Dago" not a "white man."[27]

As late as the 1930s, an American history textbook asked whether it would be possible to absorb the "millions of olive-skinned Italians and swarthy black-haired Slavs and dark-eyed Hebrews into the body of the American people."[28] Trying to capture the way others saw her Italian-born grandmother in the 1930s and 1940s, Louise DeSalvo says she was viewed as a darker shade of white—"Dark White."[29]

Not only was it acceptable to speak about the inferiority of Jews and Italians in newspapers, magazines, and public forums, but also discrimination against them was open and, by and large, legal. Elite summer resorts made no bones about shutting out Jews. In the 1880s, many in upstate New York set up placards: "No Jews or Dogs Admitted Here." When a 1913 New York State law forbade places of public accommodation from advertising their unwillingness to admit anyone because of race, creed, or color, more subtle means were employed. When resorts and private clubs announced that they served "restricted clientele," it was understood that Jews were not allowed.

"Restrictive covenants," clauses in real estate titles that limited the sale or transfer of property to members of certain groups, kept Jews out of some of New York City's most desirable suburban neighborhoods. Toward the end of the 1920s, apartment-house owners in Jackson Heights, Queens advertised that their buildings were "restricted" and prohibited Catholics, Jews, and dogs. A legal battle over the exclusion ensued, but the court upheld the rights of the property owners to choose their own tenants. It was not until a 1948 Supreme Court case outlawed restrictive covenants that such agreements became unenforceable in the courts of law.[30]

There were various forms of open discrimination in employment, too. At the end of the nineteenth century, for example, pay rates for common laboring jobs could vary by racial group. In 1895, a public notice recruiting laborers to build the Croton Reservoir listed the daily wage schedule of three groups: common labor, white, $1.30 to $1.50; common labor, colored, $1.25 to $1.40; common labor, Italian, $1.15 to $1.25. For Jews, the bars were felt higher up the job scale.[31] In 1917, the U.S. Army inserted ads in the *New York World* blatantly stating its need for "Christian" carpenters, although after objections from the president of the American Jewish Committee, a directive was issued forbidding such bigotry. After World War I, as more Jews sought white-collar jobs with private firms, newspaper advertisements indicating a preference for Christians proliferated.[32]

Also in the post–World War I years, many colleges, universities, and medical schools adopted quota systems that set limits on Jewish admission. Although in 1922 President Lowell of Harvard University openly recommended limiting the number of Jewish students, the allotments there, as elsewhere, were covert, and institutions developed discreet ways to achieve their objectives. Sarah Lawrence College, for example, asked about strict Sunday observance; Columbia College wanted to know the student applicant's religious affiliation, whether his parents had ever been known by another name, the parents' place of birth, the mother's full maiden name, and the father's occupation. It was not until 1946 that New York's City Council passed a resolution threatening the tax-exempt status of nonsectarian colleges and universities that used racial or religious criteria in selecting students; in 1948, New York State (soon followed by New Jersey and Massachusetts) forbade discrimination on grounds of religion and race in higher education.[33]

## Race and the Newest New Yorkers

Today, there are a new set of racial issues on the table in New York. In a time when race is largely coded as color, the issue is not the ambiguity

TABLE I.I
*Population of New York City by Race and Hispanic Origin, 1970–2000*
(percentages)

|  | 1970 | 1980 | 1990 | 2000 |
|---|---|---|---|---|
| Non-Hispanic White | 63.0 | 51.9 | 43.2 | 35.0 |
| Non-Hispanic Black | 19.3 | 24.0 | 25.2 | 25.6 |
| Hispanic | 16.2 | 19.9 | 24.4 | 27.0 |
| Asian | 1.5 | 3.3 | 7.0 | 10.6 |

*Source*: Mollenkopf 1993; Logan and Mollenkopf 2003.

of the term "white" but the complexities underlying the terms "non-white" and "people of color." In the wake of the huge immigration of the past few decades, a new racial/ethnic hierarchy is evolving in New York City—in broad strokes, white/black/Hispanic/Asian, although in reality it is much more complex than this. The black-white dichotomy, which dominated New York race relations for so much of the twentieth century—owing to the mass inflow of African Americans from the South between World War I and the 1960s—remains central, but it is proving inadequate in light of the growing number of not-black and not-white Asians and Hispanics.

## A White Minority

The days when New Yorkers spoke of Jewish or Italian races are long gone. So is the numerical dominance of what are now called non-Hispanic whites, who, in demographic terms, are a decided minority—only 35 percent of the city's population in 2000, down from 63 percent only thirty years before (see Table 1.1).

The impact of the last great wave of immigration lingers on in the significant, although shrinking, number of Jews and Italians in the five boroughs—an estimated 972,000 Jews in 2002 and somewhat below 700,000 Italian Americans in 2000.[34] Ethnic distinctions based on European ancestry have not disappeared; most Italian Americans continue to identify with their Italian origins; Jews typically identify (at least some of the time) as Jews. Yet these ethnic distinctions have, as Richard Alba argues, "become so faint as to pale beside other racial/ethnic boundaries," and a common identity has emerged among "Euro-americans" as whites in opposition to other racial groups in the city.[35]

New Yorkers of European descent have a wide latitude in how they

TABLE 1.2
*Ten Largest Foreign-Born Groups in New York City, 2000*

| Country of Birth | Number |
|---|---|
| Dominican Republic | 369,186 |
| China | 261,551 |
| Jamaica | 178,922 |
| Former Soviet Union | 162,322 |
| Guyana | 130,647 |
| Mexico | 122,550 |
| Ecuador | 114,944 |
| Haiti | 95,580 |
| Trinidad/Tobago | 88,794 |
| Colombia | 84,404 |

*Source*: Beveridge 2002a, based on U.S. Bureau of Census 2000.

can construct their identities—what Mary Waters calls "ethnic options." In other words, they have the option of whether to claim any specific ancestry or just be "white" or American.[36] This freedom is not available to the vast bulk of the newcomers, who are defined as—or, to put it another way, assigned the designation—"nonwhite." It is, however, extended to immigrant New Yorkers from Europe, who are seen by others as "white," and, it should be noted, are a sizable group; in 2000, more than a quarter of non-Hispanic white New Yorkers were foreign-born, including substantial numbers of Russians and Poles.[37] Indeed, in that year former Soviets were the fourth largest foreign-born group in the city (see Table 1.2). A modern anomalous case is that of Arab Americans—and in 2000 about 71,000 New Yorkers claimed Arab ancestry on the census. They have recently been classified as white by the census, although a number of scholars have noted that the media regard Arabs as nonwhite and, particularly in the wake of the events of September 11th, many Arab Americans have faced discrimination on the basis of their Muslim identity and national origins.[38]

## Black Immigrants

As people of African descent, West Indian and African immigrants are clearly on the black side of the racial divide. And they are a growing proportion of New York's black population. By 2000, more than a quarter of New York City's non-Hispanic black population was foreign-born. After a decade of heavy in-migration, there were nearly 70,000 Africans (born in a sub-Saharan African country) in New York City or

3.4 percent of the black population; Afro-Caribbeans (people of Afro-Caribbean ancestry) numbered about 524,000 or a quarter of the black population.[39] Because West Indians are the much larger group—and because, by now, there is a fairly extensive literature on their reactions to New York's racial order—the focus here is on them.[40] The term West Indian refers here to people of African descent from the English-speaking Caribbean, although what I say about race also pertains to immigrants from Haiti, who are also considered black. I do not include the growing number of Trinidadian and Guyanese immigrants of East Indian descent, whose ancestors were brought to the Caribbean as indentured laborers to replace slaves after emancipation. East Indians, as they are called in the Caribbean, are a separate, and fascinating, case, since they typically attempt to establish an Asian identity in New York as a way to avoid being labeled "black."

West Indians of African descent cannot avoid this designation. No matter how light their skin tones, immigrants (like the native-born) with known African ancestry continue to be delineated as black. Although legally in retreat, the peculiarly American "one-drop rule" that defined as black a person with as little as a single drop of black blood has had an enduring legacy. West Indians are increasingly visible in New York now that they are an ever-growing proportion of black New York, but they still often find themselves lumped with African Americans. Even when other New Yorkers recognize Caribbean immigrants as West Indian, as foreign, or, as many whites say, "from the islands," West Indians are seen as an ethnic group within the larger black population. Their racial status, in other words, is always salient.

Being viewed as black, and being identified with black Americans, has enormous consequences for their lives. Certainly it is true, as many studies show, that in the aftermath of the civil rights revolution, American whites are more racially tolerant and less likely to voice racist sentiments in public. A series of laws and court decisions have banned discrimination, and new agencies and systems are in place to enforce them. Still, racial stereotypes, prejudice, and discrimination against blacks have had a tenacious hold—and persist in a variety of forms.

At one extreme, blatant interpersonal racism—physical attacks or threats, denials of housing or employment specifically for racial reasons, and harassment by the police—is unfortunately still with us. Less dramatic, but still painful, West Indians tell of an accumulation of racial slurs, insults, and slights, and of their sense that whites do not want to associate with them. Young black men, whom many whites see as potentially dangerous, have an especially hard time. It is not unusual for white women to cross the street or clutch their handbags when they see a young black man approach—and they do not stop to wonder whether the man is West Indian or African American. West Indian teenagers describe being followed in stores because they are suspected of shoplifting and having whites recoil from them in fear on the street, in the subway, and in parks. "Because when you go to the stores . . . people follow you around; you go on the bus and people hold their pocketbooks," one fourteen-year-old West Indian girl explained. "They don't discriminate against you because you're West Indian. They are discriminating against you because you're black."[41] Mary Waters notes that the teenage boys (from West Indian families) in her study reported far more racial harassment from whites and the police than did the girls, and they also felt less at ease when they left their all-black neighborhoods.[42]

Race is a primary factor in determining where West Indians live. Choice plays a role: like other newcomers, West Indians gravitate to areas with kinfolk and friends, where they find comfort and security in an environment of familiar institutions. Yet racial discrimination and prejudice put severe constraints in their way. West Indians are as segregated from whites as American blacks (see chapter 5). Real estate agents often steer West Indians to black neighborhoods or withhold information on housing availability elsewhere, and West Indians themselves often prefer communities where they can avoid racism and rejection. "Some neighborhoods," observed one West Indian New Yorker, "are not yet ready for black people. And I don't want to be a hero."[43] Those who have braved open hostility and branched out from West Indian areas in Brooklyn and Queens to adjacent white communities find that their new neighborhoods become increasingly black. Antiblack prejudice tends to fuel a process of racial turnover as whites begin to leave and no new whites move in; at the same time, the growing number of black families makes the neighborhood seem more welcoming to West Indians (and native blacks) looking for homes. The result is a pattern of segregation in which West Indian residential enclaves are located in largely black areas of the city and the suburbs. Calculations of segregation indices based on 2000 census data indicate that Afro-Caribbean neighborhoods overlap substantially with those of African Americans in the New York metropolitan area, although interestingly Afro-Caribbeans are highly segregated from Africans.[44]

West Indians' lack of access to white neighborhoods—and the inevitable turnover that occurs when middle-class "pioneers" move into white communities—confines the majority to areas with inferior schools, high crime rates, and poor government services and limits their informal contacts with white Americans. Outside of work (and sometimes at work as well), most West Indians find themselves moving in all-black social worlds. This is fortified, it should be noted, by patterns of marriage, which are another indication of continuing racial prejudice and the distinctive social distance separating whites and blacks in America. Census figures show that white Americans who intermarry are far more likely to wed an Asian or Hispanic than a black person—whether West Indian or African American (see chapter 5 on West Indian intermarriage rates).[45]

The sting of racial prejudice in New York is especially painful because West Indians come from societies with different racial hierarchies and conceptions of race. This, as well as West Indians' relations with African Americans, is something I discuss in more detail in chapter 5. Suffice it to say at present that African ancestry carries far more serious consequences in the United States than it does in their home societies, where people of African ancestry are the overwhelming majority (the exceptions are Trinidad and Guyana, with their enormous East Indian populations), where there are hardly any whites or Europeans, and where social class, occupation, wealth, ancestry, and education outweigh skin color in defining social status. A person with dark skin who is highly educated, wealthy, and holds a prestigious occupation is recognized for these characteristics—and is not stigmatized on the basis of his or her skin color. Indeed, one of the most profound adjustments to America is coming to terms with the fact that their skin color has such negative impact on their daily lives and aspirations.[46]

## Hispanic Newcomers

Where Hispanic immigrants fit in is much more complicated. The very category Hispanic is open to contention—some who are labeled this way prefer to be called Latino, and others argue that the category is a statistical fiction that bears little relation to reality. The census treats Hispanic as an ethnic category, since it asks people who say they have Hispanic origins to indicate their race as well. But read nearly any New York newspaper or hear people talk on the street, and it becomes clear that Hispanic stands for something more than ethnicity. There has been a gradual racialization of Hispanics—a belief that physical characteristics, particularly skin color, are involved. Indeed, by treating Hispanics as a group equivalent to blacks in antidiscrimination and affirmative action policies, the federal government has contributed to raising Hispanic to the status of a racial category—what some journalists call a racialized demographic race.[47]

Forty years ago, New Yorkers spoke of Puerto Ricans as one of the city's two minority groups (the other was blacks), but today, in public discourse, the term Hispanic is commonly used. This is not just because the term is a fairly recent creation, coined by U.S. census takers as a way to count the Latin American population. The ethnic composition of New York City's Spanish-speaking population has undergone a sea change. Puerto Ricans first started arriving in large numbers after World War II, the migration peaking in the 1940s and 1950s; since 1970, more Puerto Ricans have left than entered the city. Moreover, the number of Dominicans, Mexicans, Colombians, Ecuadorians, and other Latin Americans in New York continues to rise so that by 2000, Puerto Ricans were only a little more than a third of the city's Hispanic population, down from 61 percent in 1980.[48] (Altogether in 2000, Hispanics were 27 percent of New York City's population.) In public discourse, Hispanics are generally thought of as belonging to a "brown" or "mixed race," but they include people of remarkable racial diversity, ranging from phenotypically white Hispanics who claim strong European heritage to those with dark skin and visible African ancestry.

The label "Hispanic" carries a stigma in New York, often conjuring up images of people who are brown- or tan-skinned, foreign in speech and manner, and unable or unwilling to adapt to U.S. laws, culture, and norms of hygiene.[49] A Cuban-born stock broker, whose only contact with clients was on the phone, described how he changed his surname (Gonzalez) so that when he solicited new clients they would "listen to me and trust me more than they would with a Hispanic name." (In fact, he was phenotypically white and had no accent, having moved to the United States as a small child.)[50] New Yorkers generally are not sensitive to the differences among immigrants from the Dominican Republic, Cuba, Ecuador, Colombia, Mexico, and Ecuador. And they often lump the most recent Spanish-speaking arrivals with Puerto Ricans, who are still New York City's single largest Hispanic group, have extremely high rates of poverty and are imagined, by many New Yorkers, as an underclass mired in crime and drugs. No wonder that Spanish-speaking immigrants from the Caribbean and Latin America often make efforts to distinguish themselves by nationality from Puerto Ricans. Robert Smith, for example, tells of how Mexican immigrants define themselves as neither black nor Puerto Rican, emphasizing their strong community institutions, tightly knit families, and solid work ethic.[51]

If Hispanics are increasingly thought of as a race in popular discourse, do they identify themselves this way? Immigrants with origins in Latin America and the Spanish-speaking Caribbean, after all, prefer to be known by their group of national origin, not as Hispanic or Latinos; although they share linguistic and cultural roots, they do not comprise a single, coherent community, and are divided by, among other factors, class, color, and generation.[52] Many second- or third-generation Latinos do not even speak Spanish. The category Hispanic can be seen, in many ways, as being imposed from above by dominant groups. Yet by treating Latinos/Hispanics as a single group, José Itzigsohn argues, the census and government agencies allocating resources, charities and nonprofit groups, and the media and their marketing techniques have combined to foster a sense of panethnic Hispanic/Latino identity. Indeed, Itzigsohn contends that the Latino or Latina label has a racial meaning, designating a racial position different from white and black. At the same time, he also notes that Hispanics adopt and use this label to construct their own personal and collective identities and projects, particularly when there is a common political advantage to cooperation. Panethnicity, in Itzigsohn's words, becomes part of the language of self-identification used by Latinos and Latinas and can be invoked or put aside in different moments for different purposes.[53]

Ongoing cross-national exchanges and interactions in daily life can also promote a sense of Hispanic or Latino identity. This is what Milagros Ricourt and Ruby Danta say has happened in the multiethnic Queens neighborhood of Corona they studied, where no single national group predominates in the Latino population and immigrants of diverse Latin American origins regularly interact in their daily lives on the streets and in apartments, houses, stores, workplaces, and churches. Shared language is a powerful unifier that makes communication and shared experiences possible. National identities remain primary, but a new overarching Hispanic or Latino identity has also emerged among Spanish-speaking immigrants from the Caribbean and South and Central America that can be mobilized by Latino panethnic leaders and organizations.[54]

If daily interaction, political mobilization, and cultural and linguistic commonalities can foster a sense of panethnic identity, another factor behind the desire to identify as Hispanic or Latino is the wish to avoid association with blackness and to be positioned in the racial classification system as nonblack.[55] This denial of blackness may help explain why so many Hispanic New Yorkers—nearly half of the people in the New York metropolitan area who checked off Hispanic on the 2000 census—identified, in the race question, as "some other race."[56]

And this leads to the question of color. On one end, are white Hispanics of European ancestry who, if self-identification is anything to go by, are a substantial number. In the 1990 census, a quarter of New York City's Dominicans and over half of the Colombians and Cubans described themselves as white.[57] In 2000, in the wider metropolitan area, about two-fifths of those who checked off Hispanic in the census identified as white.[58] White Hispanics often cannot escape the stigma associated with the Hispanic label. The remark by one Puerto Rican New Yorker, recorded in Oscar Lewis's *La Vida,* would doubtless strike a familiar chord with many new arrivals. "I'm so white," the respondent said, "that they've even taken me for a Jew, but when they see my Spanish name, they back right off."[59] According to sociologist Clara Rodriguez, regardless of color, knowledge of a person's "Hispanicity" often leads them to be thought of as "other," and "even an accent is heard when it was not before."[60]

Yet there are obvious advantages to being white. One study found that Dominicans who are perceived as white have lower poverty levels than, and enjoy advantages in the labor market over, their darker skinned compatriots. "When I got my job in the laundry," said one extremely fair-skinned Dominican, "the owners said that even though I spoke Spanish, they would hire me because they didn't want any Blacks working for them."[61] An analysis of residential patterns based on 2000 census data found that Hispanics in the United States who described themselves as white were less residentially segregated from non-Hispanic whites than other Hispanics.[62] Presumably, many of the Hispanics who marry non-Hispanic whites—nationwide, in 1990, nearly half of the white men who intermarried wed Hispanics—are white or very light-skinned.[63]

As one might expect, the reality of the American color line creates special problems for dark-skinned or black Hispanics. (This has a significant impact in the New York metropolitan area where, according to

the 2000 census, 9 percent of Hispanics identified as black, and the figure is considerably higher for Dominicans.)[64] In the United States as a
whole, Hispanics who described themselves as black (as opposed to
white or "some other" race) in the 2000 census were the most segregated from non-Hispanic whites and the least segregated from non-
Hispanic blacks.[65] Apart from residence, there are the day-to-day hu-
miliations. A dark-skinned young New York-born man of Dominican
descent explained, "When I was jumped by whites, I was not called a
spic but I was called a nigger."[66] Or consider the experience of another
dark-skinned Dominican who tells of waiting in a corporate office for a
job interview: "A woman wandered out into the room I was sitting in,
looked at me, looked around, and returned to her office. A few minutes
later she did the same thing again. After the third time, she finally
asked, 'Are you Luis Rodriguez?' I replied 'Yes,' as the woman tried to
explain her way out of the blunder she had just made. 'I was looking
for someone who looked different, I mean Hispanic, I mean.'"[67]

Dominicans with African features and dark skin find it especially
unsettling to be confused with African Americans since they come from
a society where the category black is reserved for the highly disdained
Haitians and where to be partly white (the case for most Dominicans)
is to be nonblack. In the Dominican Republic, Dominicans of mixed
phenotype tend to discount their African heritage and say they are
"indios," seeing themselves as descendants of the Spanish and indigenous populations.[68] Dark-skinned immigrants from other Latin American countries experience a similar clash of racial orders in New York.
Although each country in Latin America has evolved its own racial context because of its unique history, race is generally thought of as a continuum from black to white, with a large number of terms to describe
those in-between. Moreover, income and education can have a lighten-
ing effect so that a "person who is called *negro* or *prieto* when he is
poor and uneducated will almost always be described by some more
flattering term, such as *trigueno*, if he rises in status."[69]

Where does this leave the many Hispanic immigrants in New York,
whose skin color and other physical features do not qualify them as
white but who tend not to be considered black either? In many ways,
very much in the middle. These are the people New Yorkers usually
have in mind when they use or hear the term Hispanic. On occasion,
"not white, not black" Hispanic immigrants may find that they are
taken for "light skinned blacks." But on the whole they have avoided

the presumptions of inferiority associated with Africa and slavery and have been able to put a visible distance between themselves and black Americans.

Class distinctions add further complexity to the way Hispanic immigrants are seen. Whereas West Indians find that race remains a barrier whatever their class status, for white or light-skinned Hispanics, income, education, and occupation enhance and solidify the advantages they already enjoy. White or light-skinned Hispanic New Yorkers who enter the upper reaches of the middle class, become fluent English speakers, and adopt Anglo-American ways are able to move fairly easily in a native non-Hispanic white social world, and my own observations suggest that such people are increasingly accepted as "white."[70] Less happily, lower-class status reinforces and intensifies racial prejudice against mixed race and black Hispanic immigrants. Outside of New York City, in suburban areas, Hispanic immigrants from poor backgrounds who hold menial jobs—and who out of necessity often live in overcrowded quarters—have often found themselves the victims of animosity from white residents, who see the newcomers as eroding the quality of suburban life. In 2000, two Mexican day laborers were beaten, nearly to death, in Suffolk County; in 2003, in another racially motivated incident, several white teenagers were charged with firebombing a Mexican family's home in Farmingville.[71]

## Asians: The Elasticity of Race

Asians have undergone a contemporary metamorphosis. The very term Asian is a new one in popular discourse, increasingly used since the post-1965 influx of immigrants from different Asian countries and now that the Chinese are less than half of the city's Asian population. (In 2000, the Chinese were just over 40 percent of the Asian total, followed by Indians, 23 percent, Koreans, 10 percent, and Filipinos, 7 percent.[72] In that year, Asians represented 11 percent of the city's population, up from about 2 percent in 1970. See Table 1.1.) Once looked down on as the yellow peril, East Asians are now touted as the "model minority"—or as one sociologist has put it, "the best of the 'other' [than black or white] category."[73]

In the past, Asian groups were subject to blatant exclusion and discrimination on racial grounds. Until the recent immigration, Asian in New York meant Chinese. Not black, and not white, they were often portrayed as "slanty-eyed" and belonging to the "yellow race." One reason that Chinese immigrants huddled together in Chinatown was fear of racism in the world outside.

Racial prejudice against Asians was enshrined in restrictive immigration and naturalization laws. The Chinese Exclusion Act of 1882 singled out the Chinese as the first and only group to be excluded from the United States on the basis of race, ethnicity, or nationality, and by 1917, Congress had banned the immigration of most other Asians as well.[74] For much of the nation's history, Asian immigrants were denied the right to become citizens. After Congress passed a statute in 1870 expanding naturalization to include persons of African descent, legal measures were taken to deny this right to Asian immigrants. The 1882 Chinese Exclusion Act decreed that the Chinese were "aliens ineligible for citizenship"; over the next few decades the rule was extended, through a series of decisions in state and federal courts, to all other immigrants from east and south Asia. The judgment of a 1921 Federal District court stated that Congress required someone to be white for naturalization because "color [is] . . . evidence of a type of civilization which it characterizes. The yellow or bronze racial color is the hallmark of Oriental despotisms."[75] It was not until 1943 that Chinese immigrants gained the right to become citizens and that the discriminatory immigration laws affecting Asians began to be relaxed. Only in 1952, with the passage of the McCarran-Walter Act, was naturalization eligibility extended to all Asians.

On the West Coast, where anti-Asian sentiments were particularly virulent, several states adopted laws prohibiting intermarriage between Asians and whites. A 1913 California law, targeting Japanese farmers, barred Asian immigrants from owning land. When a California court held, in 1885, that the public schools had to admit Chinese children, the state legislature passed a bill allowing school districts to set up separate schools for "Mongolians."[76] Most devastating of all, during World War II more than one hundred thousand Japanese Americans who lived on the Pacific Coast were forcibly evacuated and moved to internment camps.

Today, over fifty years later, it is hard to imagine that Asians, as "aliens ineligible for citizenship," used to be cast, as Yen Le Espiritu puts it, as "almost blacks but not blacks." Now the model minority stereotype renders them "almost whites but not whites."[77] New York's Asians rank just below non-Hispanic whites in the city's ethnoracial hierarchy—and they generally meet with greater acceptance from middle-class white New Yorkers than other racial minorities.

As compared to blacks and Hispanics, Asians are the least residentially segregated from non-Hispanic whites in the New York metropolitan area. Especially striking is the growing number of affluent suburban communities, like Scarsdale, where small numbers of Asians live in the midst of large white majorities.[78] Nationwide, there is a high rate of intermarriage between the children of Asian immigrants and non-Hispanic whites.[79] Moreover, a growing number of affluent white families in New York have adopted Asian children. By 1997, about eighteen hundred families belonged to the Greater New York chapter of Families with Children from China; by one account, there were, in that year, at least one thousand adopted Chinese orphan girls under the age of five in the New York area.[80]

What accounts for the greater acceptance and changed perceptions of Asians today? Partly it is the class composition of the recent Asian immigration and the successes of their children. A large number of the new arrivals from Korea, the Philippines, Taiwan, Hong Kong, Japan, and India come with college degrees, ready to compete for middle-class careers, able to afford homes in middle-class areas, and intent that their children advance through education. Many of their children have done extraordinarily well. National figures show that native-born Asians are substantially more likely to complete college than whites and other groups.[81] In New York, Asian students are overrepresented at the top of the academic ladder. They make up about half of the student body at Stuyvesant High School, the city's most selective public high school, where entrance is based on notoriously difficult exams.

Views of Asian immigrants' home countries have changed—and this is another factor behind the new racial perceptions. In the past, Americans saw Asia as a backward region. Now, Japan is a modern advanced nation and a world economic power; Singapore, Taiwan, South Korea, and Hong Kong emerged in the postwar period as important modern economies; and China is a major player in world politics and markets.

Asians may now seem *almost* white to some New Yorkers, but, as some have put it, yellow is not white.[82] Asians are still viewed as racially distinct, marked off by physical features and, even when born in the United States, often assumed to be newcomers or, in Mia Tuan's phrase, thought of as "forever foreigners."[83] In terms of skin color, Koreans,

Japanese, and Chinese "tend to register rather mildly on screens of 'white' American color sensitivity."[84] The darker skin color of many Indian immigrants puts them at risk of being mistaken for African American, and they emphasize their ethnic identity and distinctive history, customs, and culture as a way to avoid such mistakes.[85]

Asians still confront prejudice and discrimination. Indeed, a number of Asian-American scholars note that a downside of the model minority stereotype is that it diverts attention away from the existence of continued racism against Asians.[86] There are reports of racial slurs and insults—Korean immigrants, for example, being faced with "go back to China" or "no chinks allowed."[87] Although Asian New Yorkers often live in communities with substantial numbers of whites, they have sometimes met with resistance, especially when they have begun to move into lower-middle-class white areas. This happened in the late 1980s in Brooklyn's Bensonhurst neighborhood, when anti-Asian flyers were distributed urging residents to boycott those who sold property to Asians, and in 1995, in Bellerose, Queens, where real estate agents were reported to be trying to drum up business by contacting white residents with what seemed to be tips that more Indian and Pakistani residents were moving into the neighborhood.[88]

On occasion, Asians have been victims of racial attacks, and South Asians have been particularly vulnerable. In 1987, troubling attacks took place in a New Jersey town where large numbers of Indians had moved. Groups of young white and Hispanic hoodlums, who called themselves dotbusters, pushed, shoved, and insulted Indian housewives who walked down the street wearing *saris* and *bindi* (the cosmetic dot on the forehead of Hindu women). Dotbusters beat up Indian students at a nearby technical college, and eventually two young Indian men were set upon and brutally beaten; one suffered permanent brain damage, and the other was fatally injured.[89] In the wake of the September 11th attack on the World Trade Center in 2001, South Asian Muslims (and Sikhs mistaken for Muslims) have faced a backlash. A study of South Asian taxi drivers (mainly Muslims from Pakistan and Bangladesh), conducted in the year following the attack, found that many reported verbal abuse from passengers, and some even spoke of experiencing physical threats. One driver was called "terrorist" by young men in his neighborhood, who threw eggs at him; another said that his children received hate mail at school.[90] In the summer of 2003, three Indian immigrants (one wearing a Sikh turban) were attacked outside their

Woodside (Queens) home by white men who cursed, spat on, and punched them, saying "bin Laden family, go back to your country."[91]

Incidents like these may well foster a sense of pan-South Asian identity among Indians, Pakistanis, and Bangladeshis in New York. The development of a broader Asian identity movement also owes much to discriminatory practices in the United States—as Espiritu puts it, "to the racialization of Asian national groups by dominant groups as well as . . . responses to these constructions by Asian Americans themselves."[92] White Americans are often insensitive to ethnic differences among Asian populations. Virtually all of the second-generation Chinese and Korean Americans in Nazli Kibria's recent study had, at one time or another, been called *chink* or *Jap*: "By their very nature as racial slurs, these names are . . . generalized Asian designations; they are used against all Asians, regardless of ethnicity, as expressions of hostility, and those who use them are for the most part unconcerned about making distinctions between Asians."[93] The census classifies Asians as one of the six major racial categories; the media constantly refer to "Asians," often oblivious to nationality distinctions. Moreover, Asian Americans, like Hispanics, are treated as a homogeneous group administratively in distributing economic and political resources, thereby imposing a pan-Asian structure on persons and communities dependent on government support.[94] Indeed, Asian Americans are most likely to come together in situations where cooperation offers the ability to exert political influence to the common advantage.[95]

If these forces, as well as efforts by Asian American legislators, community leaders, and organizations, provide a potential basis for Asian American panethnic identity, countervailing forces, including ethnic, generational, and socioeconomic diversity within Asia America, work in the opposite direction. Like Hispanics, Asians are strongly attached to their more specific ethnic or national identities, which are revitalized and energized by continuing immigration and transnational networks. In New York, where South Asians are so numerous, they, and others, tend to equate Asian with East Asians or the "yellow" race, despite political efforts to include Asian Indians and other South Asians in a pan-Asian category.[96]

Unlike Hispanics, no common home-country language provides a basis for unity and communication among Asian Americans, and the cultural practices (including religion) of different national (and subnational) Asian groups are widely divergent. Indeed, research shows that ethnonational identities continue among second-generation Asian Americans. As Nazli Kibria argues, Chinese and Korean American, as well as many other Asian-origin, communities are institutionally and culturally dense, with "a rich and well-defined cultural tradition, in which members feel and experience a deep and extensive sense of belonging and support, as well as distinction and pride."[97] In contrast, a pan-Asian American ethnicity is "thin—something that organizes their existence in only sparse ways."[98]

## Will the Descendants of Today's Immigrants Become White?

And so we come to the future which, paradoxically, requires us, once again, to look back to the past. At the heart of any discussion of immigration and race in America is how today's Latino, Caribbean, and Asian immigration will affect the future of the color line. The notion that dark skin color will impede the progress of the current second and third generation rests on the assumption that today's racial views will continue to be dominant. This may not be the case. If the historical literature teaches us anything, it is that racial categories are highly changeable—and there has been a radical change in the meaning of race in the last hundred years. It is a measure of how dramatic the transformation has been that most Americans have forgotten that Jews and Italians were ever seen as separate races and an inferior kind of European. How did Jews and Italians become racial insiders and unambiguously "white"? Will any of the new groups repeat this pattern? Or will entirely new racial categories and divisions emerge in the wake of the recent immigration?

It may well be misleading to speak of Jews and Italians becoming white or of the whitening process since Jews and Italians were at the outset, in many contexts, recognized as white. But they did, eventually, become part of an all-encompassing white community; they were increasingly referred to (and thought of themselves) as white; and they were no longer viewed as races in the popular mind. It is in this sense that in *From Ellis Island to JFK* I wrote of Jews and Italians becoming "full-fledged whites," "unquestionably," or "fully" white, although perhaps it is preferable to speak, in more general terms, of racialization processes by which groups once disparaged as racial outsiders have become part of the racial majority. Whatever one calls the process, the insights of whiteness studies have helped focus our attention on it, understand it, and capture the dynamics involved. A full history of how Jews and Italians, each in their own way, came to be thought of, and to see themselves, as members of a unified white race remains to be written, yet it is possible to sketch out the underlying factors involved.

One was the economic successes of Jews and Italians and their increased intermingling with other European groups. With postwar prosperity, as well as generous GI housing and educational benefits, the children, and later grandchildren, of turn-of-the-century Jewish and Italian arrivals did well. As members of the groups climbed the socioeconomic ladder and mixed residentially with people of northern and western European descent, "their perceived distinctiveness from the majority faded. . . . Intermarriage both marked the shift and accelerated it."[99]

Obviously, climbing the socioeconomic ladder and adopting the dominant society's ways were not enough to guarantee racial inclusion into the white mainstream. Other immigrant groups in this same period —the Chinese or Japanese, for example,—who also became economically successful and assimilated to American ways remained outside the pale of whiteness. Jews and Italians, as I have emphasized, shared a safe haven of legal whiteness with other European groups from the very beginning—and they were not subject to the same kind of systematic, legal, and official discrimination that faced black and Asian immigrants. That the law declared southern and eastern Europeans white—and fit for naturalization—was a powerful symbolic argument in their favor. Indeed, in early twentieth-century America, politicians often tailored their thinking about the desirability of new European immigrants in the context of campaigns in which the foreign vote counted.[100]

Italians and Jews may have ranked lower than northern and western Europeans but, in the racial continuum of the time, they were a step above Asians who, in turn, were relatively more desirable than blacks.[101] African Americans, it is well to recall, had only just been released from slavery when the last great immigration wave began— and not until the civil rights revolution of the 1960s would the structures of segregation in the American South begin to be dismantled. The racial notions underlying the response of whites toward blacks, as Stanley Lieberson has written, were both deeper and more pervasive than toward European immigrants, wherever they came from. Despite notions of the inherent inferiority of Jews and Italians, it was believed they could become more acceptable by abandoning their strange cultures and becoming more "American."[102]

The fact is, too, that many Jews and Italians physically resembled members of the older European groups, something that was particularly relevant when color-coded race became increasingly decisive in mid-twentieth-century New York. It was often possible for children of Jewish and Italian immigrants to blend into the majority population ("to pass") if they shed their distinctive dialects, dress, and other cultural features; this was not an option for Chinese or West Indian immigrant children of the period, who were more visibly distinct.[103] In his study of second-generation Italians in New Haven in the 1930s, Irvin Child described a young man who passed as non-Italian. "I don't hear it [derogatory epithets]," the young man explained, "except from people I know because the others don't guess that I'm Italian."[104] In my own family history, my mother tells me that when she applied for a job on Wall Street in the 1940s, friends advised her not to reveal her Jewish identity (she didn't), and quite a few Jews tried to hide their Jewishness by changing their surnames. Among movie stars, Betty Joan Perske became Lauren Bacall, and Issur Danielovich was transformed into Kirk Douglas. But the ability to hide one's identity was impossible for the vast majority of African Americans, whose skin color made them more visible. The emphasis on skin color had different results for European immigrants and African Americans who intermarried. An Italian or Jewish woman who intermarried and took the surname of her husband would be less identifiable as Italian or Jewish; a black woman who married a white man, by contrast, would still be labeled black. Similarly, when Jewish and Italian women married husbands of "old European stock," their children bore their fathers' surnames; if a black woman had a child with a white man, the child was socially defined as black.[105]

Other factors, of course, also helped to erode the once salient racial differences among New Yorkers of European origin. Of critical importance was the end of the massive influx of eastern and southern Europeans in the wake of restrictive legislation in the 1920s. The dramatic decrease in the flow of new arrivals reduced the fears of old-stock Americans about the deluge of "racial inferiors"; it also facilitated assimilation by depriving Jews and Italians of constant, large-scale reinforcements.[106] Indeed, by the time World War II ended, most of New York's Jews and Italians were American born. The Nazi genocide made anti-Semitism less respectable, and in the scientific world, theories of nurture and culture eclipsed theories of nature and biology. A spate of books in the 1930s and 1940s, from Ashley Montagu's *Race: Man's Most Dangerous Myth* to Franz Boas's *Race and Democratic Society*, challenged the view, championed by earlier advocates of eugenics and scientific racism, that race determined character, customs, and behavior; new views that argued for the primary role of environment and culture became dominant in intellectual circles.[107] Whereas formerly the literature of race discussed "capacities," "traits," "characters," and "deficiencies," the rising literature on race relations now spoke in a language of "equality," "justice," "discrimination," and "prejudice."[108]

Then there was the massive influx of African Americans from the South that dramatically altered the city's racial composition, adding large numbers of people who were below Jews and Italians in the racial hierarchy. Matthew Guterl argues that the Great Migration of African Americans into the urban North after the First World War was a principal factor behind the change from a racial order marked by the multiplicity of white races to one focused on race as color, and almost solely on whiteness and blackness.[109] As immigrant New Yorkers and their children increasingly confronted "Negroes" at close range, in face-to-face situations, and in unprecedented numbers, they grew more concerned about color boundaries and had a growing sense of belonging to a "white race." Indeed, Jews and Italians themselves made efforts to distance themselves from African Americans: they did this by stressing their whiteness.[110]

Admittedly, Jews' history of persecution and exclusion in Europe led them to sympathize and identify with the plight of African Americans, yet, at the same time, they were eager for inclusion in America and acceptance as whites.[111] As blacks poured into Harlem in the 1920s, Jews left in part, Eric Goldstein argues, to firmly establish their position as whites. In the interwar years, as their mobility brought them greater expectations of social recognition in the non-Jewish world, New York's Jews worried more about their insecure racial position and sought to demonstrate their status as whites. In the years following the Depression, Jewish women asserted a distinctiveness from black women by hiring African American domestic workers to clean their homes.[112] For their part, American-educated Jewish intellectuals developed a notion of ethnicity that underscored Jews' position as whites. Victoria Hattam contends that one reason Jewish thinkers like the philosopher Horace Kallen and the educator Isaac Berkson began to refer to "ethnic groups" in the period around World War I was to legitimate difference without running the risk of being put on the wrong (nonwhite) side of the racial divide.[113]

World War II also encouraged Jews and Italian Americans to publicly identify as whites. As Gary Gerstle argues, the war invigorated the idea that America was "first and foremost a white nation" through popular culture's lily white representations of U.S. soldiers, the internment of tens of thousands of Japanese and Japanese Americans, riots and hate strikes at workplaces, in neighborhoods, and on army bases, and the segregation of the armed forces.[114] Exemplifying  and reinforcing  the growing importance of color-coded race, by the beginning of World War II, the naturalization application no longer asked immigrants to provide both their race and color with the expectation of different answers for each; now there was just a race question, and the only acceptable answer for Jews and Italians was "white."[115]

And finally, we should not forget the struggles of the groups themselves to eliminate exclusionary barriers. Following the end of World War II, Jewish organizations like the Anti-Defamation League waged campaigns to curb discrimination in housing, employment, higher education, resorts, and social clubs; they stressed the undemocratic and un-American nature of anti-Semitism and emphasized cooperation with Gentile groups to promote tolerance. These campaigns bore fruit and played an important role in the passage of laws in New York and elsewhere in the late 1940s prohibiting racial and religious bias in employment and higher education.[116] Paradoxically, the struggle over civil rights for African Americans between the 1930s and 1950s helped create and sustain a black-white social calculus that indirectly benefited southern and eastern Europeans. By putting black-white issues on center stage in the national agenda, the movement for African American civil rights reduced the salience of racial distinctions among European groups, thereby allowing Jews and Italians, in Jacobson's words, to "vanish into whiteness."[117]

What, then, can we learn from the dynamics of the changing construction of race in the past? If the transformation of Jews and Italians into members of an all-encompassing white community had a lot to do with their starting-off points, their economic achievements, and their attempts to distance themselves from African Americans, will these factors play a role in the future? Of course, some of today's immigrants, like Russians, Poles, and other Europeans, are already recognized as white. But what about those who are now labeled nonwhite?[118] Will any of the immigrant groups currently thought of as not-white but not-black come to be seen as white? Or is it misleading to pose the question this way? Just as "white" meant something different a hundred years ago than it does today, so, too, the very category white may become outmoded in the future as new ways of thinking about racial and ethnic differences, and new racial divisions, emerge. Whereas in the past, Jews and Italians were transformed from races into white ethnics without undergoing any physical change, today, when the language of color is so prominent in racial discourse, intermarriage and the blurring of physical differences among mixed-race offspring are often predicted to be the key agents of change.

Already, the centrality of the black-white divide, which dominated New York race relations for much of the twentieth century, is being challenged and changed by the growing number of Asians and Hispanics who do not fit clearly into either category. Indeed, given high Hispanic birthrates and the prospect of continued Asian and Hispanic immigration, the proportion of Asian and Hispanic New Yorkers will surely rise. High rates of intermarriage—and the growing number of multiracial offspring—are also an indication that we are moving toward a new kind of racial order. Intermarriage, as Joel Perlmann and Mary Waters observe, both reflects the lowering of racial divides that have already occurred and indicates that those divides will decline still further—as a result of intermarriage itself. Second-generation Hispanics and Asians commonly marry people in other ethnoracial groups, most often whites.[119] According to Zhenchao Qian's analysis of 1990 census data, nearly two-thirds of young U.S.-born Asians married non-Asians, the great majority of them whites; and nearly 40 percent of their Latino counterparts married non-Latinos, again the majority of them white.[120] Looking ahead, it is possible that the fourth or fifth generation descendants of the Hispanic and Asian immigrants of our time will be almost all of mixed origin, and almost all will also be the descendants of non-Asians and non-Hispanics.[121]

One scenario for the future suggests that there will be a shift in the way people are assigned to—and in the very meaning of—the category white. In this scenario, the lighter of the multiracials will join whites of European ancestry and light-skinned Hispanics to constitute an expanded white group. The white category, in other words, will be widened to include some new strands, perhaps even successful Asians as well. Of interest in this regard is the large number of immigrants who chose "white" as their racial identity in the 2000 census. Of the 28 million foreign-born counted, two-thirds said they were white, a significant increase over 1990, when half the foreign-born population checked white as their race. "White," suggests Kenneth Prewitt, will perhaps become the catch-all category for most new immigrants and their children, who may treat it as a synonym for opportunity and inclusion as it was for the southern and eastern Europeans a century ago.[122]

In another scenario, the category white will cease to be salient, and the current white-nonwhite division will give way to a new black-nonblack dichotomy. In this scenario, a white-Asian-Hispanic melting pot will be offset by a minority consisting of those with African ancestry—African Americans, Afro-Caribbeans, and African immigrants, and Hispanics of visible African ancestry. There have been speculations that the black category itself could expand, as the most unsuccessful portions of some immigrant groups (presumably darker in skin color) assimilate into the black population.[123] Several sociologists have also offered qualifications to the black/nonblack binary. Herbert Gans foresees a third "residual" category for groups that do not fit into the basic dualism, likely to include less affluent members of today's Asian, Hispanic, and Filipino, Central and South American Indian, and mixed Indian-Latino populations; Frank Bean and Gillian Stevens write that the black-nonblack line may operate more strongly in the case of blacks with lower levels of education than among those with higher education.[124] Whatever the qualifications, whiteness, in this forecast, would be much less meaningful than it is today; indeed, a new term might emerge, as Joel Perlmann and Roger Waldinger note, to "replace white—a term that can include Asians and Hispanics easily enough and that essentially means 'native born, and not black.'"[125] The black category, however, would not lose significance.

A shift to a black-nonblack—or as Michael Lind has put it, a black-beige—racial order is a troubling forecast, for it sees the boundary dividing blacks from other Americans as the most intractable in the nation, and blacks being consigned, once again, to racial exclusion.[126] It is based, unfortunately, on some hard realities. Although black-white intermarriages in the United States rose from a reported 65,000 in 1970 to 328,000 in 1995, the intermarriage rate is dramatically lower than for Hispanics and Asians.[127] Residential segregation patterns show a similar trend: people of African ancestry, native and immigrant alike, continue to be highly segregated from the white majority—much more so than Asians and lighter-skinned Latinos.[128] Just as the salience of the "Negro question" helped Jews and Italians fuse with Anglo-Americans into a unified white race, so today's immigrants often make efforts to distance themselves from African Americans as a way to gain acceptance and assert claims to equality with whites. Moreover, as I have emphasized, Asians and most Hispanics start out in an in-between status, neither black nor white. As such, they could easily become part of a new nonblack or beige majority.

Some may say that the physical characteristics distinguishing Asians and many Hispanics will make it impossible for them to blend into one racial category alongside whites. In Shawn Wong's novel, *American Knees,* the thoroughly Americanized, third-generation Chinese American hero, Raymond Ding, can never forget that he is Chinese because others classify him as Chinese or Asian when they see his color and physical features. "Don't you know in America skin color is your identity?" he says. "This is a racist country. You can't be invisible."[129] Yet race, as I have shown, is in the eyes of the beholder—and conditioned by cultural understandings of difference. Perceptions of, and social values attached to, different physical features have changed over time.[130] The Chinese are no longer stigmatized the way they were in the early twentieth century, and if a black-nonblack order does emerge, the Chinese and other Asians would become, if not invisible, than less visible as part of a new racial majority. Presumably, whiteness would then no longer be the metonym for power and inclusion the way it is now.

If the nonblack-black scenario is a worrisome prospect for blacks, yet another forecast sees black-white relations evolving in a different way. In this scenario, increasing intermarriage and intermingling will reduce the salience of current racial and ethnic boundaries, including the black-white divide. "In a society characterized by increasing rates of movement, mixing, and intermarriage, and by growing numbers of persons who assert their multiplicity," write Cornell and Hartmann, "boundaries become less obvious, less potent, and far more difficult to maintain."[131]

One argument is that rates of intermarriage between blacks and whites, though low, are rising and many children of these marriages are demanding social recognition of their mixed ancestry. A hundred years from now, Stanley Crouch predicts, "Americans . . . will find themselves surrounded in every direction by people who are part Asian, part African, part European, part Indian. . . . The sweep of body types, combinations of facial features, hair textures, eye colors, and what are now unexpected skin tones will be far more common."[132] If many Asians and Hispanics are brought into the racial majority, this expansion could "dissolve the transparency of racial distinctions and thus impact upon the distinctions that set African Americans racially apart."[133]

In the aftermath of the civil rights revolution, there has been a remarkable growth in the black middle class as well as an expansion of black college enrollment. The more whites mix with blacks at work, on campus, and other social settings, the more their assumptions about the social meanings attached to skin color are apt to erode. This is especially likely in the upper-middle class, where class may end up trumping race as common school ties, elite occupational status, and various social connections and interests begin to blur ethnic and racial boundaries.

Already, as Gerald Jaynes notes, middle-class blacks often can avoid stigmatization by whites in everyday interactions by making their class position clear. He predicts that as the number of poor Asians and Latinos grows, the tradition of "confounding poverty and dependency with being African American" will die. At the same time, the growing presence of middle-class and elite minorities of color will render "African American and black too imprecise to be sustained as synonyms for 'underclass.'"[134]

Pressure for change may also come from the new multiple race option on the census. Although this option was not heavily used in 2000 —only 2.4 percent of the people counted reported themselves as being of two or more races—this is likely to change. By expanding the racial classification system, the multiple race option may call into question the idea of a fixed number of discrete categories. Another possibility is an increase in the number of hyphenated groups that try to step outside the racial taxonomy altogether: "This strategy echoes how American Jews positioned themselves early in the twentieth century, when they resisted being racialized as nonwhite but also refused to become 'Anglo' and thereby lose their cultural identity."[135]

Perhaps, as Alba and Nee suggest, America might evolve in the direction of Latin American racial systems in which race/ethnicity "will lose some of its clear-cut categorical character; it will become more like a spectrum on which an individual's location will be determined by a number of social and physical characteristics and may shift from one social setting to another." Even if this happens, however, Alba and Nee argue that such a development would not eliminate a racial and ethnic stratification system, and placement in it would matter for the life chances of individuals.[136] In countries like Brazil, as David Hollinger points out, physical mixing of blacks and whites has "failed to achieve social justice and to eliminate a color hierarchy." Nor are racial inequalities the only kind of inequalities. As he notes, the "diminution of racism could leave many members of historically disadvantaged ethnoracial groups in deeply unequal relations to whites simply by virtue of class position. Even the end of racism . . . would not necessarily ensure a society of equals."[137]

Just how the future will unfold, and which scenario will triumph is hard to say. These scenarios are, after all, just that—possibilities that allow us to see some of the variables that might shape what happens in the years ahead. Indeed, it may well be that something altogether different will come to pass, involving an amalgam of some of the forecasts outlined above. The process of change is likely to be gradual, though it is bound to involve struggles and divisions, as some groups attempt to alter or widen existing racial categories while others resist. It seems a safe bet, however, that the racial order will look very different in thirty or forty years from the way it does now and that the changes will have enormous implications for the children of today's immigrants as well as for the immigrants of tomorrow. A hundred years ago, New Yorkers would never have imagined that Jews and Italians would be thought of, in racial terms, the same way as old-stock, White-Anglo-Saxon Protestants. As unforeseen economic, demographic, and political changes take place in the years to come, there will, no doubt, be equally astonishing surprises that lie ahead.

# 2

# Immigrants and
# African Americans

.

New York's immigrants and African Americans are, inevitably, connected. The African American presence has had a significant impact on the lives of immigrants as well as on the scholarship about them. These interconnections become particularly clear when we compare present-day immigrant New Yorkers with those in the past.

A look back in time to the city a hundred years ago, when African Americans were a small fraction of the population, highlights—by comparison—how important the African American community is today in shaping the experiences of immigrants and the way they are viewed. At the time of the last great wave of immigration to the city, the African American community was numerically insignificant, and the total black population did not even reach a hundred thousand. By the time of the next great wave of immigration, the city had been on the receiving end of a massive internal migration flow of African Americans from the South that began around World War I and continued until the 1960s. Today, African Americans are a major component of New York's population and key players in the political, cultural, and social life of the city. They shape, among other things, debates about immigrants' impact on the economy and outlooks for the second generation, and play a more significant role than they did a century ago in the way racial and ethnic identities are formed among immigrants and the way intergroup relations have developed. Black immigrants also come into the equation. The latest immigration has greatly added to the total number of black residents in the city—and this, too, marks a difference from the past, when a much smaller proportion of immigrants themselves had African ancestry.

## Immigrants and African Americans in the Last Great Wave

In 1910, New York was a city of European immigrants and their descendants. Only about 80,000 African Americans resided in the city—a little under 2 percent of the population. (The total black population was 91,709, with 87 percent native-born. See Table 2.1.) Most African Americans were southern-born, giving New York's black community a southern flavor.[1] Although an appreciable West Indian migration had begun at the start of the twentieth century—and continued until the mid-1920s—the numbers were small: in 1910, 12,000 foreign-born blacks lived in New York City; by 1920, the figure was 37,000, representing 24 percent of the city's black population.[2] There were very few Hispanics—only 22,000 in 1916.[3]

What did the relatively small number of blacks mean for the hundreds of thousands of Jewish and Italian immigrants who were pouring into New York City? For one thing, at the beginning of the twentieth century, questions about race were much more focused on the new southern and eastern European immigrants than on African Americans. In 1910, after several decades of heavy immigration, foreign-born Italians and Jews were nearly a fifth of the city's population; ten years later, Italian Americans and Jews (including the American-born children of immigrants) numbered around 2.4 million, or 43 percent of the city's population. (By way of contrast, blacks were less than 2 percent of the city's population in 1910, a little under 3 percent in 1920. See Table 2.1.) The huge numbers of Italians and Jews made them a highly visible presence in the city—and a threat to the existing ethnic/racial order. Indeed, the main race issue in New York a century ago was the influx of what were then seen as inferior white races, who were polluting the nation's Nordic or Anglo-Saxon stock (see chapter 1).

If old-stock New Yorkers focused their anxieties about race on Jewish and Italian newcomers, this does not mean that they looked positively on blacks. Far from it. As Frederick Binder and David Reimers observe, New York blacks confronted a "virulent racism in the late nineteenth and early twentieth centuries." In the racial continuum of the time, blacks were at the very bottom; racial notions underlying the response of native whites to blacks, as I noted in the previous chapter, were both deeper and more pervasive than toward European immigrants, wherever they came from.[4]

TABLE 2.1
*New York City's Black Population, 1900–2000*

| Year | Black Population | % of NYC Total | % Black Population Foreign-Born |
|---|---|---|---|
| 1900 | 60,666 | 1.8 | NA |
| 1910 | 91,709 | 1.9 | 12.8 |
| 1920 | 152,467 | 2.7 | 24.0 |
| 1930 | 327,706 | 4.7 | 16.7 |
| 1940 | 458,444 | 6.1 | 10.6 |
| 1950 | 747,608 | 9.5 | 7.2* |
| 1960 | 1,087,931 | 14.0 | 6.2* |
| 1970 | 1,525,745 | 19.3 | NA |
| 1980 | 1,694,127 | 24.0 | 23.2 |
| 1990 | 1,847,049 | 25.2 | 22.6 |
| 2000 | 2,050,764 | 25.6 | 28.3 |

* Estimated percentages; in 1950, foreign-born blacks were not enumerated by locality within states, and in 1960, the census reported nativity data for all "nonwhites" together, not reporting data for individual races by state or locality (Kasinitz 1992: 41).
*Source*: Kasinitz 1992: 41; Logan and Mollenkopf 2003; Mollenkopf 1993: 93.

The second-class status of the city's blacks—or, perhaps more accurately, third-class status below native and immigrant Europeans—is illustrated by the August 1900 riot in the Tenderloin District, where tensions between blacks and the white (mostly Irish) residents of the area had existed for a number of years. The riot had its origins in the killing of a plainclothes policeman by a black man in a scuffle and, several days later, another fight between a black and a white. For two days, white residents in the district ranged through the streets and beat blacks who crossed their path. "Negroes were set upon wherever they could be found and brutally beaten," one journalist observed, and the *New York Times* noted that "every car passing up or down Eighth Avenue . . . was stopped by the crowd and every negro on board dragged out. . . . The police made little or no attempt to arrest any of [the] assailants."[5] It was reported that policemen often led the mobs attacking African Americans, some even dragging blacks off streetcars and beating them. African American community leaders demanded that white rioters and policemen be brought to justice. They were not. The police department set up its own investigating board which dismissed the charges against the police.[6] While some white newspapers criticized police brutality, there was "little chance . . . that the city government controlled by Tammany Hall's Democrats would move against the police department . . .

and blacks had no influence whatsoever in Democratic party politics. Clearly racial hatreds ran deep, but blacks, constituting less than two percent of the city's population, could find few politicians willing to offer their support."[7]

Interestingly, two years later, when Irish workers attacked a Jewish funeral procession on the Lower East Side and the police joined in assaulting the mourners—"Kill those Sheenies! Club them right and left!" shouted the police inspector in charge—protest rallies led Mayor Seth Low to appoint a commission that produced a devastating indictment of the police (despite the recommendations of Low's committee, the guilty policemen were exonerated by their peers).[8] Because Jews were a much larger proportion of New York's population than blacks—and had larger numbers of regular voters in concentrated areas—they were able to win political influence and office not long after arrival.[9] Indeed, Jews had helped to elect Mayor Seth Low. As early as 1900, a Jew won a seat in Congress from the Lower East Side; in 1913, the East Side's Aaron Jefferson Levy became the Democrats' majority leader in the state assembly; and in 1914, the Lower East Side elected Meyer London as the first Socialist congressman from New York.[10] A Republican, Isaac Siegel, the son of Russian Jewish immigrants, represented East Harlem in Congress from 1914 to 1922, defeating Jewish rivals supported by Tammany and the Socialist Party.[11] Blacks' access to political power in the first decades of the twentieth century was stymied in part by their lack of demographic strength, and it was not until they were heavily concentrated in Harlem, toward the end of the First World War, that the first black was elected to the state legislature (in 1917), followed by five others in the 1920s, also representing Harlem.[12] It took until 1944, when Harlem's political boundaries were redrawn, for New York City to send its first black, Adam Clayton Powell, Jr., to Congress.[13]

Unfortunately, we know little about relations between African Americans and the new Italian and Jewish arrivals in New York at the time of the last great wave of immigration. In the pre-1915 years, before the massive black migration to northern cities, Jews and blacks, as Hasia Diner observes, did not really have much contact. Generally, in this pre-World War I period, blacks and Jews did not meet in the world of work since they occupied different niches in the economy.[14] Nor did they live in the same neighborhoods.

In terms of residential separation, it is true that blacks were less segregated from native whites than they are today. Given the small black population in 1910, only one census tract in Manhattan, in the West 50s, had a black majority. Yet black New Yorkers generally lived in neighborhoods—and, within neighborhoods, on particular blocks— with large numbers of other blacks. This is borne out by an analysis of the 1910 census using microdata, which calculated the level of segrega- tion of major ethnic/racial groups in the city. The analysis revealed high levels of group isolation for native blacks—as well as for Jews and Ital- ians. Members of each of the three groups rarely had neighbors in any other group.[15]

In 1910, most blacks lived in Manhattan—and, within Manhattan, in the areas then known as the Tenderloin and San Juan Hill, which stretched on the west side from around Twentieth Street to Sixty-fourth Street. Harlem was still more Jewish and Italian than black—home, in 1910, to some 100,000 Russian Jews, 72,000 Italians, and 22,000 blacks.[16] Each group in Harlem had its own well-defined areas. As they moved in, blacks clustered in the newly built northwest section. Already by 1901, the *New York Times* referred to 130th Street between Amster- dam Avenue and Broadway as "Darktown."[17] At the time of the 1910 census, more than two-thirds of Harlem's black residents had settled in a neighborhood roughly bordered by 133rd and 140th Streets and Park and Lenox Avenues.[18] Several thousand Jews lived in Harlem's black enclave, among them businessmen who wanted to be near their shops and others who owned private homes in the area.[19] There is also evi- dence of some friction between Jews and blacks (showing up in the black press as early as 1908) as blacks made incursions into predomi- nantly Jewish sections of Harlem. By and large, however, Jews did not respond violently to the increasing black presence in Harlem.[20] In any case, as the black influx increased after the First World War and as rents rose, the Jewish exodus grew; by 1930, as the historian Jeffrey Gurock puts it, the Jewish evacuation of Harlem was almost complete.[21]

Italians and blacks also tended to live apart, with Italians heavily concentrated in the "Little Italies" of lower Manhattan and East Har- lem. Evidence suggests that there may have been more contact between blacks and Italians in other venues. Italian "pick and shovelmen," one historian writes, often "occupied a disquieting position between their black fellow workers and their 'white' supervisors and union leaders."[22] In churches, according to Rudolph Vecoli, Italians were often turned away or "seated in the rear with Negroes."[23] Still, African Americans and Italians in New York City basically moved in separate worlds, and it is unclear whether the interactions that occurred at work or at church led to a willingness to sympathize and fraternize with African Americans or to tensions and distancing in this early period.[24]

As for immigrants' racial or ethnic identities, in the pre–World War I era, distancing strategies from African Americans were not a significant component in Jews' and Italians' self-images. Granted, the word commonly used to describe Italians—"swarthy"—had such strong emotive power (and negative meaning) mainly because it linked Italians with blacks; an epithet for Italians, "guinea," had long referred to African slaves. Yet it was not until later decades—after the immigrant influx came to a halt, after a growing number of Jews and Italians moved up the socioeconomic ladder, after a huge second generation was entering adulthood, and, significantly, after a sizable African American population was present in the city—that a noteworthy element in eastern and southern Europeans' claims to membership in the racial majority was setting themselves apart from blacks.[25] Thus historians have noted that as Jews acculturated in the 1920s, 1930s, and 1940s, they marked themselves off as different from African Americans to attain the status of full-fledged whites, although at the same time their history of persecution in Europe led them to identify with the plight of African Americans. A posture of sympathy for blacks, as Eric Goldstein argues, fulfilled Jews' emotional need to distinguish themselves as "whites of another kind."[26]

Finally, the tiny size of New York City's African American population in the early twentieth century—along with intense discrimination against African Americans and their lack of political influence—help to explain why questions of black-immigrant economic competition were not major public issues and lacked the urgency that they have today. Not that such competition did not happen. It has been argued that the immigrant influx resulted in African Americans' eviction from trades where they had previously been accepted, and their confinement to the most menial, least attractive jobs, such as janitors, elevator operators, and domestic servants.[27] According to Suzanne Model, black barbers and caterers in nineteenth-century New York were serving a white population, but by 1910, immigrant competitors had captured most of the white market for these services. Roger Waldinger writes that blacks in New York City had a well-established role in the domestic production of clothing at the turn of the twentieth century, but the huge immigrant influx crowded them out of the industry.[28]

Yet to the extent that immigrant competition in the labor market was an issue at the time, it was Irish laborers' resentment that took center stage as they were displaced by Italians on the docks and in unskilled construction work. The special hatred that the Irish harbored for Italians, writes one scholarly observer, was displayed in the job market. The "Irish workers struck back by attempting to intimidate the Italians and drive them away from the work sites." In one of the more serious incidents, at a worksite in Mamaroneck (Westchester County), about two hundred Irishmen attacked a group of Italian workers who were receiving their monthly pay; the Irish injured several Italians and forced them and their families to abandon their homes and flee south to the Bronx.[29]

## *Immigrants and African Americans Today*

Today, New York's African American population has a much greater impact on the new immigrants, and the effects of immigrants on African Americans are of much greater public policy concern.

A substantial proportion of the latest arrivals are themselves of African ancestry; in 2000, close to 600,000 black New Yorkers were born abroad.[30] Also, the current immigration takes place in post–civil rights America, in which blacks have made enormous social, economic, and political gains. Institutional change dismantling the formal rules of racial separatism during the civil rights era of the 1960s, as Victor Nee has noted, has shaped a new institutional environment for immigrants of non-European ancestry.[31] And, as I have stressed, African Americans are a significant segment of New York City's population. A massive inflow of African Americans from the South between World War I and the 1960s transformed New York's racial dynamics. The city's black population first passed the million mark in 1960, a more than tenfold increase since 1910 (see Table 2.1). In 2000, despite the heavy inflow of black immigrants, more than half (58 percent) of New York City's black population were natives with native-born parents—1.1 million people, or one out of seven New Yorkers.[32] Bear in mind that these figures refer to "non-Hispanic blacks"—a category that did not exist a hundred years ago at the time of the last great immigrant influx, and that has only become relevant in recent decades with the enormous growth in the nation's Hispanic population and the creation of the Hispanic category by the U.S. census. A sizable number of New York Hispanics—

especially Dominicans—check off "black" as their race on the census, but for official purposes they are counted as "Hispanics" rather than blacks.

African Americans' numerical strength in contemporary New York—in combination with their residential concentration and the creation of minority legislative districts under the mandate of the Voting Rights Act —has given them considerable political clout. By the 1990s, as Mollenkopf notes, blacks, in a nontrivial sense, had become part of New York City's political establishment, with relatively high rates of voter registration and turnout and electing representatives in proportion to their population size.[33] In 2000, native blacks formed the second largest electoral bloc (second to native whites in the city).[34] In the early 1990s, New York City had a black mayor (David Dinkins) as well as numerous elected black officials in Congress and state and city legislative bodies.

## Economic Issues

In this context, the issue of whether immigrants are hurting African Americans economically is of much greater concern to public commentators, scholars, and policymakers than it was a hundred years ago. Measuring the impact of immigrants on natives, as Roger Waldinger and Michael Lichter observe, is an endeavor fraught with dilemmas, including the best way to identify competing skill groups, and the appropriate areal unit in which competition might take place.[35] What is clear is that low-skilled native black New Yorkers are lagging behind their foreign-born peers in nearly every nationality group. (Despite gains in the past few decades and the growth of the black middle class, large numbers of native black New Yorkers are low skilled and poorly educated.) Census data for 1990 show native blacks in New York City trailing immigrants on the bottom rungs of the labor market. Among those without a high school diploma, the foreign-born, as a whole, earned a third more than native blacks; their unemployment rates were half what they were for native blacks.[36]

Why are native blacks lagging behind immigrants this way? In explaining the disparity in earnings and unemployment between low-skilled immigrants and native blacks, their attitudes come into play. Immigrants are more willing to tolerate harsh conditions, low pay, and dead-end jobs because even rock-bottom wages look good compared to what they can earn back home. Also, many see their stay in the United States as temporary: they are here to save money with the intent of improving their status upon return. Native-born blacks (and Puerto Ricans), particularly those who have come of age in post–civil rights America, have different expectations. To them, menial, minimum wage jobs that offer no possibility for upward movement and require deference to better-off, often white, supervisors and customers are decidedly unattractive. They are less likely than immigrants to seek out these kinds of jobs in the first place, and when they do, they have less motivation to stay. According to a Chicago study, inner-city black men have a heightened sensitivity to exploitation, which fuels their anger and gives rise to a tendency to "just walk off the job"; although recent immigrants also feel exploited, this "somehow . . . comes with the territory."[37]

But it is not just a question of attitudes and expectations. The immigrant influx has contributed to making low-level jobs more unattractive to native minority workers by lowering wage rates—thereby having a modest but identifiable negative effect on segments of the African American population in the labor market.[38] The National Academy of Sciences report on the economic impact of immigration concluded that, in the United States as a whole, 44 percent of the decline in the real wages of high school dropouts from 1980 to 1995 resulted from immigration. In New York City, one analysis found that an increasing share of recent immigrant workers in jobs between 1979 and 1989 had a strong negative effect on native-born blacks' earnings.[39] Hypothesizing about "what might have been" in the absence of large-scale immigration is highly speculative, but it is possible that had there been no massive immigration, employers might have made greater effort to recruit native minorities for jobs that could not be moved elsewhere—and, in the process, may have improved wage rates and working conditions as a way to attract them.

A growing number of studies also reveal employers' preferences for hiring immigrants, whatever their race or ethnicity, over native blacks and Puerto Ricans for low-level jobs. Employers often see immigrants as willing to work hard and long for low wages, as reliable and pliable, and likely to stay on the job; they often view native blacks and Puerto Ricans as a bad risk, fearing that native minorities will be less productive, less reliable, and less tractable than immigrants—that they will be more likely to openly voice complaints, make claims on the firm, or contest managerial decisions.[40] In their Los Angeles study, Waldinger and Lichter found that employers of low-skilled labor had a strong dislike for American workers of African descent, blending traditional antiblack stereotypes with new views disseminated in the discourse surrounding the "black underclass." Employers saw native blacks not only as expecting more than is usually possible at the bottom of the labor market, but also as out-group members whose alienation increased the likelihood of their making a fuss. The employers, Waldinger and Lichter note, gave African Americans "bad marks" because they would not quietly accept subordination in low-level jobs: "African Americans have the temerity to expect good wages for hard work, when employers have no difficulty finding immigrants who are happy (as far as the employers can tell) to work hard at an unpleasant job for low wages."[41]

Once immigrants become a dominant presence in particular firms, network hiring ends up perpetuating their advantage—and excluding native blacks and Hispanics. In this sense, too, one can say that immigration has come at the expense of native blacks. When private-sector employers rely on referrals from current workers—which saves time and money, is efficient, reduces the risks in hiring new personnel, and brings in workers who feel obliged to perform well as a result of social obligations owed to their sponsors—native minorities are out of the loop. They often do not hear about openings, which are rarely advertised, and when they do, they often lack a sponsor on the job. Moreover, once a particular ethnic group penetrates a workplace, employers are often reluctant to bring in native minorities for fear of interethnic conflict. And if the language on the shop floor is, say, Chinese or Spanish, native English speakers will not be able to communicate or fit in.[42]

This gloomy picture for African Americans needs to be balanced by a positive side to the balance sheet. For one thing, the absence of large-scale immigration might have led to a different "what if" scenario than the one I mentioned earlier. Rather than (or in addition to) stimulating an upgrading of conditions in low-level jobs to attract native minority workers, there might have been a relocation of more investments abroad and, where possible, extensive outsourcing of "immigrant jobs" to cheaper wage regions outside the United States.[43] The out-migration of jobs may well have had negative ripple effects for many African Americans.

The addition of immigrants to the city's population base also has had positive consequences for African Americans in public employment.

Without the huge immigrant influx, New York City's population would almost certainly have shrunk—and there would have been a reduced demand for public services, from health care to schooling, and thus less need for public sector workers. In this way, immigration has bene-fited the more skilled segments of the African American population who entered government employment in large numbers in the 1970s and 1980s. One of the big stories of the post–civil rights era has been Afri-can Americans' significant gains in public sector employment. To the extent that immigrants swelled the demand for public employment, "the inflow of immigration may have generated distinctive benefits for native-born African Americans, whose dependency on public sector jobs has grown over the years."[44]

Still, caution is in order in speaking about public sector employ-ment since recent developments suggest that African Americans will face stiffer competition for a smaller number of jobs in the municipal work force. In the 1970s, African American New Yorkers were gain-ing access to public service jobs that native whites were leaving—and that immigrants generally found hard to obtain. Now, government is a declining enterprise and immigrants—and if not immigrants, their descendants—increasingly want access to these jobs.[45] A recent analysis shows that African Americans in New York City experienced serious losses in public-sector jobs in the 1990s in the face of retrenchment in public employment—with other groups, particularly certain immigrant groups, gaining public sector jobs.[46]

## Racial/Ethnic Identity and Intergroup Relations

Modern-day demographic realities—the size of the African American population as well as the large numbers of immigrants of African ances-try—have also affected racial/ethnic identity formation and intergroup relations in a way that did not happen in the past. Today, the presence, and the continued stigmatization, of New York's huge African Ameri-can community invariably shape the identities of the foreign-born. The city's ethnoracial hierarchy has undergone a sea change in the last hun-dred years, and the once salient distinctions among white races are long forgotten. In recent decades, in the wake of the "new" immigration, New Yorkers, as I noted in chapter 1, have increasingly come to think in terms of a four-race framework of white, black, Hispanic, and Asian.

Yet blacks remain on the bottom and, despite remarkable progress since the civil rights revolution, still suffer from discrimination and prejudice. Black New Yorkers—native and foreign-born—continue to be highly residentially segregated from whites and other groups, thereby limiting informal social contacts at the neighborhood level. According to national figures, blacks have much lower rates of intermarriage with whites than Hispanics or Asians.[47]

What does this mean for immigrants? For West Indians, it is in many ways a case of déjà vu. I discuss West Indian ethnic and racial identities more fully in later chapters, but a few points are worth noting here. Today, as in the early twentieth century when there was a significant West Indian influx, black West Indian immigrants develop new racial and ethnic identities in the New York racial context, where they confront racial discrimination of a sort unknown in their home countries, are defined as black ("Negro" a hundred yeas ago) on the basis of their African ancestry, and are lumped with African Americans. Now, as in the past, West Indians' relations with African Americans, whom they often live among and work beside, are a complex combination of conflict and cooperation and of distancing and identification.[48]

Today, however, these processes and dynamics affect a much larger proportion of the city's population: the African American community is more than fifteen times the size it was in 1910, and the West Indian community is about fifty times the size it was then. (The astounding growth of the West Indian population is one factor behind the rise of a distinctly West Indian ethnic politics, something that did not exist in New York in the early twentieth century, when identification with African Americans was the key defining factor of West Indian public activities.)[49] Today as well, there are new black immigrants—most notably, a growing number from Africa—who are subject to many of the same cross pressures that West Indians experience in their relations with African Americans.

The impact of the African American community on immigrants' identities and relations is most deeply felt by immigrants who share a common African ancestry with African Americans and who are closest in phenotype to them—particularly Africans and West Indians. But the significant African American presence affects other immigrants as well. Dark-skinned Hispanic immigrants, who find it unsettling to be confused with African Americans, often engage in distancing strategies to avoid prejudice and discrimination. Mexicans in New York City, Robert

Smith reports, make clear that they see themselves as "not black" and "not Puerto Rican."[50] The case of Dominicans is especially interesting since a significant proportion identify (at least in part) as black; on the 1990 census, a quarter of New York City's Dominicans said they were black in response to the question about race. About half, however, checked off "other" rather than "black" or "white." And other often means "Hispanic" or "Latino." Indeed, in their study of racial identities among a sample of Dominicans, José Itzigsohn and Carlos Dore-Cabral argue that one reason many chose the Hispanic or Latino label as a form of racial identification was in order to position themselves as non-black in America's racial classification system.[51]

Distancing strategies operate among some Asian groups, too. Asian Indian immigrants, whose darker skin color puts them at risk of being confused with black Americans, emphasize their ethnic identity and distinctive history, customs, and culture as a way to avoid such mistakes.[52] Many South Asians, writes Margaret Abraham, have sought "identification with the dominant group by drawing the color divide between themselves and African Americans . . . [and] used avoidance and disassociation strategies toward other minorities whom they perceived as unsuccessful."[53] Or as Vijay Prashad puts it in *The Karma of Brown Folk,* although South Asians in the United States "realize they are not 'white,' . . . there is certainly a strong sense among most . . . that they are not 'black.' In a racist society, it is hard to expect people to opt for the most despised category."[54]

Quite apart from distancing, middlemen minority groups in New York, especially Koreans, often confront racial hostility from African American (and Afro-Caribbean) customers that occasionally has led to boycotts of Korean stores and even arson.[55] The roots of the animosity, Jennifer Lee argues, stem from the way racial differences infuse merchant-customer relations and the fact that Korean-owned businesses in black neighborhoods have come to symbolize black economic subordination to other racial and ethnic groups.[56] This has a familiar ring, not unlike the hostility that Jewish shopkeepers and landlords in Harlem experienced in the past. Black hostility to Jewish entrepreneurs was mainly an issue after the Great Migration from the South, when the "mid-belly of Harlem had become predominantly black" and a "Negro world unto itself," rather than in the pre-World War I period that I focus on in the historical analysis in this chapter.[57]

## Debates about the Second Generation

The presence of the enormous African American community—and large numbers of African Americans who are doing poorly in school—has shaped debates about the second generation in a different way from the past. In 2003, over a third of New York City's public school students were non-Hispanic blacks, and as a group they were not faring well academically.[58] A common concern in the social science literature is that the children of immigrants will be influenced by the negative attitudes said to prevail among native minority youth in inner-city schools. Pertinent here is the notion of segmented assimilation, a term developed and elaborated by Alejandro Portes and his colleagues, which implies a diversity of outcomes among today's second generation. According to "segmented assimilationists," some members of the second generation will move rapidly upward due to their parents' high human capital and favorable context of reception; others will do well because of their parents' dense networks and solidary ethnic communities; and still others, whose parents have fewer resources and who are exposed to the life styles and outlooks of inner-city schools and neighborhoods, will experience downward assimilation.[59] It is this last possibility that is relevant here.

A hundred years ago, scholars and educators were not worried that the children of immigrant New Yorkers would experience downward assimilation through "contamination" by native black minorities. To be sure, there was concern about the school progress of the second generation, particularly Italians, who had especially high dropout and truancy rates and were stereotyped by teachers as irresponsible and difficult to discipline. In the 1930s and 1940s, when high schools had become mass institutions, an oppositional culture flourished among Italian American working-class boys, involving a cynicism and hostility to school and teachers. Indeed, as Joel Perlmann and Roger Waldinger note, a comparison with the past reminds us that an oppositional culture can emerge from the working-class experience without exposure to a "proximal host" comprised of visible, stigmatized, native-born minorities.[60] There was no concern, however, in the early part of the twentieth century that the children of the "new" European immigrants were absorbing the values of African Americans. Policymakers and educators in those days were worried about Italian Americans'—not blacks'—attitudes to education. (The Jews, of course, were another story; they were viewed as committed to education as a path to mobility.)

Today something different is going on. Many second-generation immigrants attend schools in inner-city neighborhoods with native black (and Hispanic) minorities with whom they share a bond of race or ethnicity. (The native minority children in New York City schools, it should be noted, are themselves the children, grandchildren, and sometimes great-grandchildren of internal migrants from the South and Puerto Rico.) And in this context, a common theme in the scholarly literature is that segmented assimilation will spell disaster for many second-generation youth as they adopt the peer culture of "downtrodden" native black and Hispanic ghetto schoolmates.

This peer culture in inner-city ghetto neighborhood schools is portrayed as rooted in the structure of opportunities and constraints facing native minority teenagers, including racial inequality, poverty and crime in their communities, and overcrowded, unsafe, poorly equipped, and often "out of control" schools with low academic standards. Whatever its origins, the peer culture is described as devaluing educational achievement and encouraging behavior, including opposition to school rules and authorities, that impedes academic success. This is especially worrisome given the structure of occupational opportunities in the current era. In the past, the oppositional culture that flourished among Italian American working-class boys was less of a problem; despite not doing well in school, they could enter the unionized blue-collar labor force through the help of friends and relatives and earn enough to support a stable and secure middle-class life style.[61]

In today's economic and occupational context, an oppositional ethos —and doing badly in school—have much more dire occupational consequences. The decline of well-paid industrial jobs and increasing educational requirements in a technology-driven economy will, it is argued, consign those without much education to unskilled and low-paid service employment. And the kind of tough-guy and anti-authoritarian stance that was acceptable, indeed encouraged, in the work culture of the factory floor is a problem, to put it mildly, in most service jobs that dominate the contemporary landscape.

Whether these pessimistic predictions about the fate of many of today's second generation, and the impact of exposure to the peer culture of native blacks and Puerto Ricans, are correct is an open question. One issue is how extensive really *is* an oppositional outlook or ethos among native minority—and immigrant—youth today. Assumptions about the pervasiveness of an oppositional ethos that devalues academic

achievement have, to date, been based on only a few ethnographic studies in various American locations.[62] Moreover, it has been argued that
the discussion of oppositional culture among the children of immigrants
may confuse style for substance: listening to hip-hop music and affecting a "ghetto" presentation of self should not be taken as evidence of
joining a subordinated "segment" of society that engages in self-defeating behavior.[63] And there is yet another matter. Because, in the present
era, oppositional behaviors are so closely associated in public—and
academic—discourse with native minorities, their presence among native whites is generally ignored. This is a point that Philip Kasinitz and
his colleagues bring out in their New York study of second-generation
young adults that also included comparison groups of native whites,
blacks, and Puerto Ricans. What they found is that white youth who
exhibited oppositional behaviors and made mistakes—native whites
had arrest levels equal to or surpassing all of the second-generation
groups—often ended up recovering. The very same behaviors left minority group members with lasting disadvantages, and they suggest that
this is because minorities were branded by negative stereotypes tied to
race and had families and social networks with fewer resources to help
them overcome youthful errors.[64]

As to what will happen when members of the second generation
enter the work force, it is hard to tell. It is still early. The current second
generation is just beginning to enter the labor force in significant numbers; the majority are still children or adolescents or at the start of their
work careers. It is as if we were trying to measure the progress of the
children of immigrants from southern and eastern Europe in 1920.
Some tentative patterns can be observed, but the full picture will not be
evident for several decades.[65] In this regard, one recent national study
suggests that the segmented assimilation perspective is too pessimistic
regarding the fate of the second generation whose parents belong to
racial and ethnic minorities. Using pooled Current Population Survey
data from the 1998 and 2000 surveys, the study indicates that the bulk
of the second generation (including those of Afro- and Spanish Caribbean and Central American origin) is doing better than their first-generation parents in educational attainment, occupational achievement, and
economic status—and in many comparisons, second-generation groups
do better than third- and higher-generation whites and African Americans.[66] The New York study of second-generation young adults shows

much the same thing: most (including West Indians and Latinos) did not indicate any signs of the second-generation decline that distressed some analysts in the 1990s.[67]

In stressing how becoming a native minority can lead to a negative path of assimilation for the second generation, the segmented assimilation model also overlooks the possible benefits. As Kasinitz and his colleagues observe, being classified as a native minority can provide access to institutions that promote success:

> The civil rights movement, along with the minority advancement in mainstream institutions, has created a legacy of opportunity for new members of old minority groups. The struggle for minority empowerment has established new entry points into mainstream institutions and created many new minority-run institutions.[68]

Becoming part of the black (or Latino) community in New York can give the second generation contacts in and entry into institutions dominated and controlled by native minorities—for example, labor unions and political groups—that can facilitate their upward movement. Moreover, there is now a considerable African American middle class; incorporation into the African American middle-class "minority culture of mobility" provides resources for upward mobility, including black professional and fraternal associations and organizations of black students in racially integrated high schools and universities.[69] And we should not forget that many black and Hispanic immigrants from the Caribbean and Latin America have benefited from affirmative action programs originally designed to help black Americans; some high-achieving black and Hispanic immigrants and their children have gained admission to and been offered scholarships by private colleges and universities in the New York metropolitan area and elsewhere.

Whatever the positive or negative effects, what is clear is that the experiences of many of the children of today's immigrants in New York City are deeply colored by their interactions with African Americans. Quite apart from issues of economic and occupational mobility, there is the cultural influence of African Americans as well. The children of today's immigrants are exposed to, and often adopt, the styles of African American youth culture, including music, dress, and speech patterns.[70] Certainly, this was not the case among Jews and Italians a century ago.

## Conclusion

One benefit of a comparison of immigrants in two different eras is that it brings out, in a particularly dramatic way, how features of the host society—or, in this case, host city—shape the reception and incorporation of immigrants. In this chapter, I have focused on one particular contextual feature in New York: the presence—and demographic weight—of the African American community. In many ways, this analysis is an artificial exercise, since obviously much more has changed in the New York context than the number and proportion of African Americans, as I have indicated along the way. Among other things, New York City's economy has undergone a radical transformation, as have a host of institutions, including schools and municipal services, and, on a national level, legal changes in the wake of the civil rights revolution which have reduced exclusionary barriers and opened up opportunities for racial minorities.[71] Yet, for analytic purposes, there is virtue in considering what difference the size of the city's African American population has made for the immigrant experience, especially in understanding ethnic and racial identities and relations in the current period.

Although African Americans have long been central in the dynamics of race in the United States, at the beginning of the twentieth century, before the Great Migration from the South, African Americans were a tiny proportion of New York City's population. After decades of heavy internal migration, this was no longer the case, and the huge numbers of African Americans in New York have had a significant impact on the way that contemporary immigrants experience life in the city, as well as on scholarly analysis of these experiences. Put more generally, changes that have occurred since the last great immigration wave have dramatically altered the context in which contemporary new arrivals work out their identities and social relations and come to make their place in New York.

Demography is not destiny, and numbers alone are not what make the African American presence so significant. Attitudes and policies toward people with African ancestry—and the continuation of the color line in American society—are what set African Americans apart and underpin conceptions by others, and by African Americans themselves, that they are a stigmatized racial group. Also of relevance is the composition of the immigrant flows in the two eras. In early twentieth-century New York, people with African ancestry made up a miniscule proportion of the total immigrant population, which was overwhelmingly European in origin. Today, about one in five immigrants is non-Hispanic black, and given the enduring realities of racial prejudice and residential segregation in the city, immigrants who are labeled "black" are most acutely affected by New York's large African American community. In fact, the children of black immigrants, born in the United States, are often defined—and define themselves—as African American, an issue I consider when I look more closely at West Indian New Yorkers in later chapters.

If immigrants today often try to distance themselves from African Americans, this is owing to the wider society's views of African Americans. Although some immigrants bring negative views of blacks with them from their home countries, many acquire these prejudices in the United States.[72] Whatever immigrants' attitudes on arrival, part of the process of becoming American is learning America's culture of race and learning that identification with African Americans is something they may wish to avoid.

Of course, as I discussed in the previous chapter, the racial order in the United States—and New York—is currently in a state of flux, and the kind of stigma now attached to African ancestry may become less marked (or even disappear) over time. Indeed, the very category "black" may become a relic of the past. Less happily, there is the possibility that people of African ancestry will continue to be set apart from others and find themselves losing out as descendants of Asian and Latino immigrants leapfrog over them and achieve greater success and inclusion in American society.[73] No matter what happens in the future, we can say with certainty that the city's ethnoracial landscape today bears little resemblance to what it was in the past—and one factor behind this is the enormous growth in the African American population, which makes becoming a New Yorker far different for contemporary immigrants than for Jewish and Italian arrivals a century ago.

# 3

# Transnationalism Old and New

> The conception of citizenship itself is rapidly changing and we may
> have to recognize a sort of world or international citizenship as
> more logical than the present peripatetic kind, which makes a man
> an American while here, and an Italian while in Italy. International
> conferences are not so rare nowadays. Health, the apprehension or
> exclusion of criminals, financial standards, postage, telegraphs and
> shipping are today to a great extent, regulated by international
> action. . . . The old barriers are everywhere breaking down. We
> may even bring ourselves to the point of recognizing foreign "col-
> onies" in our midst, on our own soil, as entitled to partake in the
> parliamentary life of their mother country.

Sound familiar? This reflection on the globalizing world and
the possibility of electoral representation for Italians abroad describes
issues that immigration scholars are debating and discussing today. The
words were written, however, in 1906 by Gino Speranza, the secretary
of the Society for the Protection of Italian Immigrants.[1] They are a powerful reminder that processes that scholars now call transnational have
a long history. Contemporary immigrant New Yorkers are not the first
newcomers to live transnational lives. Although their transnational connections reflect many new dynamics, there are also many parallels with
the past.

The term "transnationalism" encompasses processes by which immigrants "forge and sustain multi-stranded social relations that link together their societies of origin and settlement. . . . An essential element
. . . is the multiplicity of involvements that transmigrants sustain in both
home and host societies."[2] Transnational migration refers to the way
ordinary individuals live their everyday lives across borders and the
consequences of these activities for sending- and receiving-country life.[3]
It is not just a question of political ties that span borders of the kind

that Speranza had in mind. In a transnational perspective, the focus is on how contemporary immigrants maintain familial, economic, cultural, as well as political ties across international borders, in effect making the home and host society a single arena of social action.[4] Migrants may be living in New York, but, at the same time, they often maintain strong involvements in their communities of origin which, tellingly, they continue to call home.

Since the early 1990s, a virtual academic industry has developed on transnationalism, giving rise to debates on a variety of topics, including the very definition of the term itself. Some scholars prefer to speak of transnational practices or networks; others of transnational communities or villages; still others of transnational social spaces or social fields.[5] Whatever the term, by now, there is general agreement that transnationalism is not a new phenomenon—an argument I made in the late 1990s, when there was just beginning to be an awareness that early claims of transnationalism's "newness" were exaggerated.[6] To say that transnationalism is not completely new, however, does not invalidate its importance as a conceptual framework.[7] I want to emphasize this point. Indeed, one of the benefits of a transnational perspective is that it can shed fresh light on the past, highlighting connections and processes that have been overlooked or minimized in the study of immigration in earlier eras—just as it can bring new insights to the study of immigration in the present.

What follows is a closer look at transnationalism past and present. By narrowing the field of analysis to one context—New York City—and comparing contemporary immigration with one period—the turn of the twentieth century—we can begin to specify the kinds of social, economic, and political relationships immigrants have established and maintained with their home societies in different eras. Many transnational patterns, as it turns out, have a long history—and some of the sources of transnationalism sometimes seen as unique today also operated in the past. At the same time, much is distinctive about transnationalism today not only because earlier patterns have been intensified but also because new processes and dynamics are involved.

## *Transnationalism: Parallels Between Past and Present*

Like contemporary immigrants, Russian Jews and Italians in early twentieth century New York often established and sustained familial, economic, political, and cultural links to their home societies at the same time as they developed ties and connections in their new land. They did so for many of the same reasons that have been advanced to explain transnationalism today. There were relatives left behind and ties of sentiment to home communities. Many immigrants came to the United States with the notion that they would eventually return. If, as one anthropologist notes, labor-exporting nations now acknowledge "that members of their diaspora communities are resources that should not and need not be lost to the home country," this was also true of the Italian government of the past.[8] Moreover, lack of economic security and full acceptance also plagued these earlier immigrants and may have fostered their continued involvement in and allegiance to their home societies. Of the two groups, Italians best fit the ideal type of transmigrant described in the contemporary literature; many led the kind of dual lives said to characterize transmigrants today.[9]

Many Russian Jews and Italian immigrants in New York's past, like their modern-day counterparts, continued to be engaged with those they left behind. What social scientists now call "transnational households," with members scattered across borders, were not uncommon a century ago. Most Italian men—from 1870 to 1910 nearly 80 percent of Italian immigrants to the United States were men—left behind wives, children, and parents; Jewish men, too, were often the pioneers who later sent money to pay for the passage of other family members. Those who came to New York sent letters to relatives and friends in the Old World —and significant amounts of money. Jake, the young Jewish immigrant in Abraham Cahan's story *Yekl*, was following a common pattern when he regularly sent money to his wife in Russia. Whenever he got a letter from his wife, Jake would hold onto his reply "until he had spare United States money enough to convert to rubles, and then he would betake himself to the draft office and have the amount, together with the well-crumpled epistle, forwarded to Poveodye."[10] The New York Post Office sent 12.3 million individual money orders to foreign lands in 1900–1906, with half of the dollar amount going to Italy, Hungary, and Slavic countries.[11] In those same years, for the United States as a whole, immigrants sent $69 million in money orders to Russia and Austria-Hungary.[12] Gino Speranza claimed that "it was quite probable that 'Little Italy' in New York contributes more to the tax roll of Italy than some of the poorer provinces in Sicily or Calabria."[13]

There were organized kinds of aid, too. New York's Jewish *lands-manshaftn,* or home town associations, sent millions of dollars to their war-ravaged home communities between 1914 and 1924. The societies' traditional activities concerts, balls, banquets, regular meetings, and Sabbath services—all became occasions for raising money. Special mass meetings were held as well. In one week in December 1914, more than twenty rallies took place in New York, raising between seventy-five and fifteen hundred dollars each for the war victims of various towns.[14] After the war, many Jewish immigrant associations sent delegates who actually delivered the money. A writer in one Jewish daily wrote: "The 'delegate' has become, so to speak, an institution in the Jewish community. There is not a single *landsmanshaft* here in America . . . which has not sent, is not sending, or will not send a delegate with money and letters to the *landslayt* on the other side of the ocean."[15]

Putting away money in New York to buy land and houses in the home country is also another long-term habit among immigrants who intend to return. In the last great wave, many Italian immigrants invested in projects back home. "He who crosses the ocean can buy a house" was a popular refrain celebrating one goal of emigration.[16] An inspector for the port of New York quizzed fifteen entering Italians who had previously been to the United States. "When I asked them what they did with the money they carried over, I think about two-thirds told me they had bought a little place in Italy, a little house and a plot of ground; that they had paid a certain sum; that there was a mortgage on it; that they were returning to this country for the purpose of making enough money to pay that mortgage off." It was not unusual for Italians in New York to send funds home with instructions about land purchases. An Italian told of his five years of backbreaking construction work in New York. Each day, he recalled, "I dreamed of the land I would one day buy with my savings. Land anywhere else has no value to me."[17]

Many did more than just dream of going back—they actually returned. Nationwide, return migration rates are actually lower now than they were in the past. In the first two decades of the twentieth century, for every one hundred immigrants who entered the United States, thirty-six left; between 1971 and 1990, the number had fallen to twenty-three.[18] Return migration, as Glick Schiller observes, should be viewed as part of a broader pattern of transnational connection. Those who have come to America with the notion of going back truly have their "feet in two societies." To organize return, Glick Schiller argues, necessitates the maintenance of home ties. And plans to return entail a continuing commitment to the norms, values, and aspirations of the home society.[19]

Russian Jews in New York were unusual for their time in the degree to which they were permanent settlers. Having fled political repression and virulent anti-Semitism, the vast majority came to the New World to stay. Even then, there was more return migration than is generally assumed. Between 1880 and 1900, perhaps as many as 15 to 20 percent who came to the United States returned to Europe.[20]

Many Russian Jewish migrants planned to return only temporarily in order to visit their home towns, although "not a few turned out to be one-way visits." Some had aged relatives whom they longed to see; others sought brides, young Jewish women being in short supply in the United States; still others went home merely to show off, to demonstrate that they had somehow made good; and in a few cases immigrants returned home to study. Jonathan Sarna tells us that a few "enterprising immigrants employed their knowledge of English and Russian to engage in commerce. In 1903, according to Alexander Hume Ford, there was 'a Russian American Hebrew in each of the large Manchurian cities securing in Russia the cream of the contracts for American material used in Manchuria.'" Altogether, Russian statistics indicate that 12,313 more U.S. citizens entered Russian territory from 1881 to 1914 than left. According to U.S. government investigators, "plenty of Jews living in Russia hold United States passports, the most famous being Cantor Pinchas Minkowsky of Odessa, formerly of New York."[21]

After 1900, however, events in Russia led immigrants in New York to abandon the notion of return. With revolutionary upheaval and the increasing intensity of pogroms, the return migration rate among Russian Jews fell off to about 5 percent.[22] In the post-1900 period, there were also few repeat crossers. Of the Jews who entered the United States between 1899 and 1910, only 2 percent had been in the country before, the lowest rate of any immigrant group in the United States in this period.[23]

Many more Italians came with the expectation of returning home. Large numbers engaged in circular or recurrent migration, as much commuters as many contemporary immigrants. Many were "birds of passage" who went back to their villages seasonally or after a few years in the United States. Italians called the United States "the workshop"; many arrived in the spring and returned to Italy in the winter when layoffs were most numerous.[24] They flitted "back and forth," writes Mark Wyman, "always trying to get enough for that additional plot, to pay off previous purchases, or to remove the load of debt from their backs."[25] By the end of the nineteenth century, steamships were bigger, faster, and safer than before; tickets for the sixteen- or seventeen-day passage in steerage from Naples to New York cost fifteen dollars in 1880 and twenty-five dollars in 1907 and could be paid for in installments. Prefiguring terms used today, one early twentieth-century observer of Italian migration wrote of how improved methods of transportation were leading to the "annihilation of time and space."[26] Overall, between the 1880s and World War I, of every ten Italians who left for the United States, five returned. Many of these returnees—*ritornati* as the Italians called them—remigrated to the United States. According to reports of the U.S. Immigration Commission, about 15 percent of all Italian immigrants between 1899 and 1910 had been in the United States before.[27]

If economic insecurity, both at home and abroad, now leads many migrants to hedge their bets by participating in two economies, it was also a factor motivating Italians to travel back and forth across the Atlantic. The work Italian men found in New York's docks and construction sites was physically strenuous and often dangerous; the pay was low and the hours long; and the seasonal nature of the building trades meant that laborers had many weeks without work at all. During economic downturns, work was scarcer and, not surprisingly, Italian rates of return went up during the financial depression of 1894 and the panic years of 1904 and 1907.[28] Many Jews in the late nineteenth century, according to Sarna, returned to Russia because they could not find decent work in America—owing to "the boom-bust cycle, the miserable working conditions, the loneliness, the insecurity."[29] Fannie Shapiro remembers crying when her father returned from a three-month stay in America since she had wanted to join him. (She later emigrated on her own in 1906.) In Russia, she explained, her father "put people to work; . . . he was the boss," but in New York "they put him in a coal cellar."[30]

Lack of acceptance in America then, as now, probably contributed to a desire to return. Certainly, it fostered a continued identification with the home community or, among Jews, a sense of belonging to a large diaspora population. Because most current immigrants are people of color, it is argued that modern-day racism is an important underpinning of transnationalism; nonwhite immigrants, denied full acceptance in the United States, maintain and build ties to their communities of origin to have a place they can call home.[31] Unfortunately, as recounted in chapter 1, rejection of immigrants on the basis of race has a long history, and in the days before "white ethnics," Jews and Italians were thought to be racially distinct from—and inferior to—people with origins in northern and western Europe.

Whether because they felt marginalized and insecure in America or maintained ethnic allegiances for other reasons, Italians and Jews then, like immigrants today, often avidly followed news of and remained actively involved in home-country politics. As Matthew Jacobson puts it in his study of "the diasporic imagination" of Irish, Polish, and Jewish immigrants, the homelands did not lose their centrality in "migrants' ideological geographies." Life in the diaspora, he writes, remained in many ways oriented to the politics of the old center. Although the immigrant press was a force for Americanization, equally striking, says Jacobson, "is the tenacity with which many of these journals positioned their readers within the envisaged 'nation' and its worldwide diaspora. . . . In its front-page devotion to Old World news, in its focus upon the ethnic enclave as the locus of U.S. news, in its regular features on the groups' history and literature, in its ethnocentric frame on American affairs, the immigrant journal located the reader in an ideological universe whose very center was Poland, Ireland, or Zion."[32] According to Michael Topp, the ideas, activities, and strategies of Italian American radicals in the years just before and after World War I were shaped, at least in part, by communications with unionists and other activists in Italy, their reactions to events in Italy, and their physical movement back and forth between countries.[33]

Lobbying the American government about home-country issues has a long history. Eastern European Jews, with help from longer-established and better-connected German Jews, conducted massive protest demonstrations against the bloody pogrom of the Kishinev Jews in Russia in 1903 and successfully lobbied the American government to issue an official protest.[34] American immigrants have also long been tapped by homeland politicians and political parties as a source of financial support. Today, Caribbean politicians regularly come to New York to campaign and raise funds; earlier in the twentieth century, Irish nationalist politicians made similar pilgrimages to the city. Irish immigrants, who arrived in large numbers in the mid-1800s, were deeply involved in the Irish nationalist cause in the early decades of the twentieth century. In 1918, the Friends of Irish Freedom sponsored a rally in Madison Square Garden attended by fifteen thousand people, and street orators for Irish freedom spoke "every night of the week" in Irish neighborhoods around the city. In 1920, Eamon de Valera traveled to New York seeking support for Sinn Fein and an independent Irish Republic, raising $10 million for his cause.[35]

Homeland governments were also involved with their citizens abroad. The enormous exodus to the United States and return wave brought a reaction from the Italian government, which, like many immigrant-sending states today, was concerned about the treatment of its dispersed populations—and also saw them as a global resource.[36] The Italian government gave subsidies to a number of organizations in America that offered social services to Italian immigrants and set up an emigration office on Ellis Island to provide the newly arrived with information on employment opportunities in the United States. The current of remigration, an Italian senator said in 1910, "represents an economic force of the first order for us. It will be an enormous benefit for us if we can increase this flow of force in and out of our country." In 1901, the Italian government passed a law empowering the Banco di Napoli to open branches or deputize intermediaries overseas to receive emigrant savings that could be used for Italian development. Beyond wanting to ensure the flow of remittances and savings homeward, Italy tried to retain the loyalty of emigrants overseas as part of its own nation-building project. A 1913 law addressed the citizenship issue: returnees who had taken foreign citizenship could regain Italian citizenship simply by living two years in Italy; their children were considered Italian citizens even if born elsewhere.[37] Although it never came to pass, there was even discussion of allowing the colonies abroad to have political representation in Italy.

## Transnationalism: What's New

Clearly, transnationalism was alive and well a hundred years ago. But if there are parallels with the past, there is also much that is new at the beginning of the twenty-first century. Advances in transportation and communication technologies have made it possible for immigrants to maintain more frequent, immediate, and closer contact with their home societies and, in a real sense, have changed the very nature of transnational connections. Today's global economy encourages international business operations; the large number of professional and prosperous immigrants in contemporary America are well positioned to operate in a transnational field. Dual nationality provisions, in conjunction with other changes in the national and international political context, have added new dimensions to and altered the scope and thrust of transnational political involvements. Moreover, greater tolerance for ethnic pluralism and diversity, and changed perspectives of immigrant scholars themselves, have put transnational connections in a new, more positive light.

Transformations in communication channels and transportation systems have increased the density, multiplicity, and importance of transnational connections and made it possible for the first time for immigrants to operate more or less simultaneously in a variety of places.[38] A century ago, the trip back to Italy took about two weeks, and more than a month elapsed between sending a letter home and receiving a reply. Today, immigrants can hop on a plane or make a telephone call to check out how things are going at home, thereby allowing them to be involved in everyday life in the home community in a fundamentally different way than in the past.[39] Or as Patricia Pessar observes for New York Dominicans: "It merely requires a walk to the corner newsstand, a flick of the radio or television dial to a Spanish-language station, or the placement of an overseas call" to learn about news in the Dominican Republic.[40]

In the jet age, inexpensive air fares mean that immigrants, especially from nearby places in the Caribbean and Central America, can fly home for emergencies, such as funerals, or celebrations, such as weddings; go back to visit friends and relatives; and sometimes move back and forth, in the manner of commuters, between New York and their home community. Among the immigrant workers I studied in a New York nursing home in the late 1980s, some routinely spent their annual vacation in their home community in the Caribbean; others visited every few years.[41] A study of New York's Asian Indians notes that despite the distance and cost, they usually take their families back to visit India every year or two.[42] Inexpensive air travel means that relatives from home also often come to New York to visit. In the warmer months, Johanna Lessinger reports, when relatives from India make return visits to the United States, "a family's young men are often assigned to what is laughingly called 'airport duty,' going repeatedly to greet the flights of arriving grandparents, aunts and uncles, cousins and family friends."[43] Thanks to modern communications and air travel, a group of Mexicans in New York involved in raising money to improve their home community's water supply was able to conduct meetings with the *municipio* via conference call and fly back to the community for the weekend to confer with contractors and authorities when they learned the new tubing had been delivered.[44] At Queens package centers—*paqueterias*—Mexican immigrants can pick up freshly baked bread or mole sauce that has been flown to New York—made by relatives in their home villages only forty-eight hours before.[45]

Now that telephones reach into the far corners of most sending societies, immigrants can hear about news and people from home right away and participate immediately in family discussions on major issues. It was not possible to make a transatlantic phone call until 1927, and it was prohibitively expensive—about $200 in present-day currency for a three-minute call to London.[46] Today, with various special long-distance plans, rates have become cheap—in 2003, on one plan, a three-minute call to the Dominican Republic cost 57 cents and to India, 99 cents. Phone parlors and prepaid phone cards are even cheaper. Cristina Szanton Blanc describes how a Filipino couple in New York maintained a key role in childrearing decisions although several of their children remained in Manila. On the telephone, they could give advice and orders and respond to day-to-day problems. When their only daughter in Manila had an unfortunate romance, they dispatched a friend visiting the Philippines to investigate the situation. Adela, the mother of the family, had herself been back to visit the Philippines three times in six years.[47] In the 1990s, Asian Indian New Yorkers typically phoned relatives in India weekly or biweekly, and Lessinger reports that one well-to-do young woman called her mother in Delhi every day.[48] Some Mexicans in New York have even purchased cellular phones for relatives in their home village so they can call easily.[49] Maxine Margolis offers an illustration of how readily Brazilian New Yorkers call home: "When I was in a home furnishing store in Manhattan and asked the Brazilian owner, a long time resident of New York City, how to say 'wine rack' in Portuguese, he was disturbed when he could not recall the phrase. As quickly as one might consult a dictionary, he dialed Brazil to ask a friend."[50]

Faxes and videotapes also allow immigrants to keep in close touch with those they left behind. Some Brazilians in New York, Margolis tell us, regularly record or videotape sixty-to-ninety minute messages to send family and friends back home.[51] Like other immigrant New Yorkers, they can participate, vicariously, through videotape, in important family events. Lessinger recounts how Indians in Queens gather to watch full-length videos of weddings of widely scattered relatives, able to admire the dress and jewelry of the bride and calculate the value of pictured wedding gifts.[52] The better-off and better-educated may use e-mail as well. An Irish journalist in New York explains: "My grandfather, who came here in the late 1800s . . . he was an immigrant. . . . We don't have the finality of the old days. I can send E-mail. I can phone. I can be in Bantry in twelve hours."[53] Immigrant cable-television channels, moreover, allow an immediate, and up-close, view of homeland news for many groups; Koreans in Queens can watch the news from Seoul on the twenty-four-hour Korean channel, while Russian émigrés can view live performances from a Moscow concert hall.[54] Peggy Levitt describes how migrants in Boston from the Dominican village of Miraflores can visit the website, Miraflores.com, to find out the weather back home and view photos of the funeral home, baseball stadium, and health clinic funded by the Miraflores Development Committee.[55] Even more recent is videoconferencing. In spring 2004, it became possible for Dominicans in Washington Heights to communicate with family back home through videoconferencing that cost between $1.00 and $3.00 per minute, depending on the size of the room, time of day, and length of the videoconference.[56]

Modern forms of transportation and communication, in combination with new international forms of economic activity in the new global marketplace, have meant that more immigrants today are involved in economic endeavors that span national borders. Admittedly, quantitative studies show that transnational entrepreneurship remains quite limited in scope. A recent study based on probability surveys of Colombian, Dominican, and Salvadoran immigrants in several areas of urban concentration in the United States (including New York) found that the percentage of self-employed persons regularly involved in transnational activities was in the single digits for all three groups. Still, Portes and his colleagues argue that the impact of transnational entrepreneurs goes beyond the entrepreneurs themselves, bringing customers of the firms into transnational circles on a repeated basis and helping to keep alive ties with the home countries.[57]

Certainly, it is much easier today than a hundred years ago for immigrants to manage businesses thousands of miles away, given, among other things, modern telecommunications, information technologies, and instantaneous money transfers. Entrepreneurs can also travel back and forth more easily to take advantage of economic opportunities both "here" and "there," as in the case of Dominican entrepreneurs in New York who build a base of property, bank accounts, and business contacts in New York and then make regular trips to the Dominican Republic to exploit opportunities in both places.[58] Many Asian Indian New Yorkers, encouraged by the Indian government's attempt to capture immigrant capital for development, invest in profit-making ventures in India, including buying urban real estate and constructing factories, for-profit hospitals, and medical centers. Often, relatives in India provide on-the-spot help in managing the business there.[59] After receiving a graduate degree in engineering in the United States, Dr. S. Vadivelu founded a factory in New Jersey that makes electrolytic capacitors. He later opened two factories in his home state of Andhra Pradesh, where he manufactures ceramic capacitors for sale to Indian electronics manufacturers. His father and brothers manage both plants on a daily basis; Dr. Vadivelu travels back and forth several times a year to check on the factories.[60]

The Indian example points to something else that is new about transnationalism today. Compared to the past, a much higher proportion of newcomers today come with advanced education, professional skills, and sometimes substantial amounts of financial capital that facilitate transnational connections—and allow some immigrants to participate, in the manner of modern-day cosmopolitans, in high-level institutions and enterprises here and in their home society. The affluence of Indian New Yorkers, Lessinger argues, makes them one of the most consistently transnational immigrants in behavior and outlook. Indeed, within the Asian Indian immigrant community, it is the wealthiest and most successful professionals and business people who maintain the closest links with India and for whom "extensive transnationalism is a way of life." They are the ones able to afford many phone calls, to invest in India, to frequently fly home where they mix business with pleasure, and who have a "certain influence and standing wherever they go."[61] The Chinese "astronauts" who shuttle back and forth by air between Taiwan or Hong Kong and the United States are typically well-educated and well-off professionals, executives, and entrepreneurs who move easily in financial, scientific, and business worlds around the globe.[62] Pyong

Gap Min describes international commuter marriages involving high-level Korean professionals and business executives who have returned to Korea for better jobs while their wives and children remain in New York for educational opportunities. The couples talk on the telephone several times a week; the husbands fly to New York two to five times a year while the wives visit Korea once or twice a year.[63]

Technological advances also play a role in transnational political involvements. The newest New Yorkers can hop on a plane to vote in national elections in their home country, as thousands did in a Dominican presidential election in the 1990s, before it was possible to vote in Dominican elections from polling sites in New York. Politicians from home, in turn, can make quick trips to New York to campaign and raise funds. On one weekend in the 1990s, for example, the opposition leader from St. Vincent, the mayor of Georgetown, Guyana, and the chiefs of state from Barbados and Antigua were all in New York visiting constituents.[64] Candidates for U.S. electoral positions have been known to return to their country of origin for the same reason. Guillermo Linares, for example, briefly visited the Dominican Republic during his 1991 campaign for New York's City Council, where rallies held in support of his candidacy generated campaign funds and afforded opportunities for photographs that were featured in New York newspapers.[65]

Apart from technological advances, there are other new aspects to transnational political practices today. A hundred years ago, Russian Jews brought with them a notion of belonging to a broader Jewish diaspora community, but they had no interest in being part of the oppressive Russian state they left behind. Italians, coming from a country in the midst of nation-state consolidation, did not arrive with a modern "national identity." Except for a tiny group of political exiles, migrants did not care much about building an Italian state that "would welcome them back, protect them from the need to migrate further, or represent the character and glories of the Italian people."[66] Among other groups in the past, like the Irish, migration became part of their continuing struggle for national liberation. What is different now is that immigrants are arriving from sovereign countries, with established nationalist ideologies and institutions, and are a potential basis of support for government projects, policies, and leaders in the homeland. Today, some homeland states are redefining their territories to include emigrants living outside them, owing, it has been argued, to the desire to guarantee the continuous flow of remittances, the development of competitive party politics in the home country, and the attempt to gather financial and political support among conationals abroad.[67] In the 1990s, then-president Jean-Bertrand Aristide of Haiti popularized the notion of overseas Haitians as the Tenth Department in a country that is divided into nine administrative departments and set up a Ministry of Haitians Living Abroad within the Haitian cabinet.[68] Campaigning among Mexicans in California in 2000, Vincente Fox "played upon the broader boundaries of an imagined nation and declared he would be the first President to 'govern for 118 million Mexicans,' including 100 million in Mexico and 18 million living outside the country."[69]

Today, when the United States plays such a dominant role in the global political system and development strategies depend heavily on U.S. economic and political support, many sending states view their migrant populations as potential lobbies to influence U.S. policy. It has been argued that one reason that some nations are encouraging their nationals to become U.S. citizens is their desire to nurture a group of advocates to serve the home country's interests in the American political arena.[70]

And this leads to the dual nationality provisions that now cover a growing number of New York's immigrants. Although the United States naturalization oath requires renunciation of other citizenships, increasingly U.S. law has "evolved in the direction of increased ambiguity or outright tolerance in favor of dual nationality"—what Jones-Correa calls a "don't ask, don't tell" policy.[71] What is striking is the growing number of states of origin that permit their citizens to retain nationality despite naturalization elsewhere.[72] By 2000, 17 of the top 20 sending countries to the United States between 1994 and 1998 allowed some form of dual nationality or citizenship.[73]

The details of dual nationality policies vary from country to country. In 2000, for example, ten Latin American countries recognized dual nationality, but only Colombia and Peru allowed voting through their consulates abroad; other Latin American countries were exploring the option of expatriate voting but had postponed making any commitment.[74] In 1994, the Dominican Republic recognized the right to dual nationality; three years later, as part of an electoral reform package, the government adopted a proposal to give Dominicans, including naturalized Americans of Dominican descent, the right to vote in Dominican elections while living in New York, which had been implemented by the 2004 Dominican presidential election.[75]

A powerful economic incentive is involved in the recognition of dual nationality by so many sending countries. For one thing, there is the desire to ensure the flow of money and business investment homeward. The record-breaking naturalization rates in recent years may have increased concern about losing the allegiance—and dollars—of emigrants. According to the Inter-American Development Bank, migrants in the United States sent back a whopping $31 billion to Latin America and the Caribbean in 2003. In 2000, remittances from abroad comprised more than 10 percent of the gross domestic product of countries such as El Salvador, Jamaica, Haiti, and Nicaragua and more than half the value of exports in the Dominican Republic and Nicaragua. Remittances are so important to the economies of many nations that they are now used as a valuation instrument to upgrade the credit-worthiness of poor countries to secure large-scale international loans.[76] Beyond remittances, immigrants trade with their home countries and bring in large quantities of tourist dollars.[77]

Political calculations also come into play in the policies of sending states toward dual nationality. Extending dual nationality or citizenship provisions may be a way of trying to secure the role of overseas nationals as "advocates of *la patria's* interests in the United States, the new global hegemon"[78] as well as giving these nationals the political power as American citizens to defend their own rights in the United States. And though migrants' economic clout often has been an important reason for the effectiveness of their lobbying efforts for dual nationality, as in the Dominican case, political developments and conflicts in the home country have also been involved.[79]

Although some scholars and public figures worry about the trend toward dual nationality—it makes citizenship akin to bigamy, the newspaper columnist Georgie Anne Geyer complains in her book on the "death of American citizenship"—by and large transnational connections are viewed in a more favorable light today than they were in the past.[80] Early in the twentieth century, return migration inflamed popular opinion. "Immigrants were expected to stay once they arrived," writes Walter Nugent. "To leave again implied that the migrant came only for money; was too crass to appreciate America as a noble experiment in democracy; and spurned American good will and helping hands."[81] Another historian notes: "After 1907, there was tremendous hostility . . . toward temporary or return migrants. . . . The inference frequently drawn was that [they] considered the United States good enough to plunder but not to adopt. The result was a high degree of antipathy."[82] Indeed, Randolph Bourne's classic essay, "Trans-national America," published in 1916, responded to rising anti-immigrant sentiment, arguing that the nation should "accept . . . free and mobile passage of the immigrant between America and his native land. . . . To stigmatize the alien who works in America for a few years and returns to his own land, only perhaps to seek American fortune again, is to think in narrow nationalistic terms."[83]

At the time, a common concern was that the new arrivals were not making serious efforts to become citizens and real Americans. Schools, settlement houses, and progressive reformers put pressure on immigrants to abandon their old-fashioned customs and languages. A popular guide on becoming American advised immigrant Jews to "forget your past, your customs, and your ideals." The Americanization movement's "melting pot" pageants, inspired by Israel Zangwill's play, depicted strangely attired foreigners stepping into a huge pot and emerging as immaculate, well-dressed, accent-free "American-looking" Americans.[84] Expressions of ethnicity were suffocated in the schools where, in the words of New York City's Superintendent William Maxwell, the goal was "to train the immigrant child . . . to become a good American citizen."[85]

If, in Ewa Morawska's phrase, earlier-wave immigrants were "closet transnationalists," today they have come out into the open.[86] Now, when there is an official commitment to cultural pluralism and cultural diversity, transnational ties are more visible and acceptable—and sometimes even celebrated in public settings. Anti-immigrant sentiment is still with us, and immigrant loyalties are still often questioned—as the heightened suspicions about Muslims after the September 11th attack on the World Trade Center make plain—but rates of return are not, as in the past, a key part of immigration debates. In an era of significant money flows, and huge U.S. corporate operations abroad, there is also less concern that immigrants are looting the United States by sending remittances home. Indeed, transnationalism is good for American businesses. U.S. corporations unintentionally reinforce transnationalism by developing marketing incentives to promote migrants' monetary transfers, long-distance communications, and frequent visits to their countries of origin.[87]

Increasingly today, the message is that there is nothing un-American about expressing one's ethnicity. In New York, officials and social service agencies actively promote festivals and events to foster ethnic pride and glorify the city's multiethnic character. Practically every group has its own festival or parade, the largest being the West Indian American Day parade on Brooklyn's Eastern Parkway, which attracts between one to two million people every Labor Day. Exhibits in local museums and libraries highlight the cultural background of diverse immigrant groups; special school events feature the foods, music, and costumes of various homelands; and school curricula include material on different ethnic heritages. In the quest for votes, New York politicians of all stripes recognize the value of visits to immigrant homelands. The Dominican Republic—the ancestral home for nearly 600,000 New Yorkers—has become a required stop for aspiring (or sitting) city mayors. In the summer of 2003, Mayor Bloomberg had already visited the Dominican Republic three times since being elected two years before. This kind of campaigning across borders by U.S. politicians adds further legitimacy to transnational connections and plays a role in constructing what Guarnizo calls a transnational political field of action between New York and Dominican politics.[88]

Scholars are more interested in transnational ties and see them in a more positive way than in the past. In a transnational perspective, the maintenance of multiple identities and loyalties is seen as a normal feature of immigrant life; ties to the home society complement—rather than necessarily detract from—commitments in this country. Indeed, a number of scholars now emphasize that assimilation and transnationalism are not mutually exclusive but are often combined.[89] At the same time as immigrants buy property, build houses, start businesses, enter into marriages, and influence political developments in their home societies, they are also deeply involved in building lives in New York, where they buy homes, work on block associations and community boards, join unions, and set up businesses.[90] Generally, the literature stresses the way transnational relationships and connections benefit immigrants, enhancing the possibility of survival in places full of uncertainty. In an era when globalization is a major subject of scholarly study—and when international travel is easy and international communications instantaneous and inexpensive—it is perhaps not surprising that migrants' contacts with, and visits to, their home societies have, on the whole, excited little negative comment. "Today," writes journalist Roger Rosenblatt, "when every major business enterprise is international, when money is international, when instant international experiences are pictured on T.V., more people think of themselves as world citizens. Why should immigrants not do likewise?"[91]


## Second-Generation Transnationalism

And so we come to what some regard as *the* critical question: Is transnationalism a one-generation phenomenon or will it continue to play an important role in the lives of the second generation? In thinking about this question it is useful to look back to the past to see if the experiences of the descendants of earlier immigrants offer any hints about the social, economic, and political conditions that may promote and sustain —or alternatively, undermine—transnational relations and attachments among today's second generation.

Among earlier Italian and eastern European Jewish immigrants, ongoing, day-to-day involvement in and connections to the communal life of sending societies fell off sharply after the first generation. To be sure, some members of the second generation continued to play a role in sending-society politics or international political movements such as Zionism or, in the case of Italians, raising funds for ancestral communities in times of crisis or disaster.[92] To mention another important New York group, the children of Irish immigrants, a good number remained concerned about and involved in political struggles in Ireland. Many second- and third-generation Jews have identified with and given support to Israel, although most do not have close relatives in Israel or regular contact with people there.

On the whole, connections with their parents' homelands became extremely attenuated among the children of Jewish and Italian immigrants. Consider the Jewish *landsmanshaftn* which, as I mentioned earlier, sent large sums of money to their home communities after World War I. They were, as Daniel Soyer observes, a one-generation phenomenon and had "little attraction for most of their members' American children, who had developed their own sense of Jewish-American identity and to whom their parents' parochial loyalties seemed irrelevant at best. The fact that the aging societies continued to utilize Yiddish and Yiddish-accented English as their official languages made them seem all the more old-worldly."[93]

Jews, of course, were exceptional in their low rates of return migration—and in having most of their number wiped out in eastern Europe by the Holocaust. But transnational ties appear to have largely atrophied among second-generation Italians too. A recent study that discusses the transnational links maintained by Philadelphia's Italian Americans speaks of the "American born second generation of individuals with loose ties to the land of their parents."[94] Among Irvin Child's second-generation Italian informants in New Haven in the late 1930s, only one mentioned even wanting to return to Italy. "I don't care for the country and I don't care what they do there," said one informant. "My father may care, but I don't. I was born in this country, and I'm only interested in it."[95] How widespread such attitudes were is unclear, but, as Robert Smith comments: "Given the series of questions Child asks about the informants' opinions about Italy and things Italian, and a chapter devoted entirely to 'in group' Italian Americans, it seems likely that if return to Italy was an important part of the second generation's experience it would have been mentioned."[96] In East Harlem in the 1920s and 1930s, according to Robert Orsi, Italian immigrant parents created an idealized version of southern Italy "into which they demanded their children gaze while making it clear that their children could never enter it. . . . They were 'Americani.'"[97]

What happened to undercut transnationalism among second-generation Italians and Jews in the past? For one thing, there were the processes of assimilation that went on in schools and other institutions as those born and bred in the United States learned English and American ways and became engaged with life in this country. Many members of the earlier second generation also managed to climb the socioeconomic ladder, if only in small steps. Another critical factor was that Italian and Jewish communities received hardly any fresh recruits after the 1920s, in the wake of legislated immigration restrictions and the back-to-back cataclysms of the Great Depression and World War II. Without replenishment, the numbers of Italians and Jews with fresh memories of and connections to the homeland became steadily smaller. The economies of Italy and eastern Europe, moreover, had little to offer the children of immigrant parents. And political events—World War II and the Holocaust—cut off connections there and heightened their patriotic embrace of the United States.

What about today? Some of the same factors still operate to undermine second-generation transnationalism. Most of the current second generation do not engage in regular transnational practices and sustain continuing relations that link them with their parents' home societies. As members of the second generation enter the labor force, a good number will do well and carve out successful careers in the United States. The forces of assimilation are still strong. English, as Rubén Rumbaut has observed, is triumphing with "breathtaking rapidity."[98] He reports that by the time the children of immigrants in an ongoing longitudinal San Diego survey were in their mid-twenties, the vast majority preferred English over their parents' native language, fewer than one-third said they could speak a foreign language very well, and fewer than one quarter could read it very well. English may have become the global language of money, but the loss of the parental language surely has implications for the second generation's ability to maintain ongoing ties with their parents' homelands.[99]

But if members of the present second generation, like their predecessors, are becoming more and more American, history is not simply repeating itself. Different circumstances today and in the years ahead are likely to support ongoing transnational connections for at least some of the current second generation so that transnationalism will have a longer, and more vibrant, life than it did in the past. Indeed, a study of over 2,000 young adult New Yorkers born to immigrant parents found that transnational ties—as measured by frequency of visits to parents' home country and remittances—continued to play a regular, sustained, and integral role in the lives of a minority in every group (Anglophone West Indians, Dominicans, South Americans, Chinese, and Russian Jews), with especially significant minorities of Dominicans, West Indians, and South Americans "highly embedded in transnational social structures" into the second generation.[100]

Barring cataclysmic events such as World War III or a Holocaust wiping out relatives of any one immigrant group, and even if there is some move toward restrictionism, it is likely that the United States will continue to allow substantial numbers of new immigrants to enter for a good time to come. Continued inflows will bring new recruits who will enrich and replenish ethnic communities—and include substantial numbers of people, of all ages, with close ties to their homelands. Some scholars, in fact, argue that even if the second generation do not maintain social relations across borders, they may be enmeshed in transnational social fields because they are raised in networks and settings permeated by people who *do* maintain connections to the home country or community.[101] Moreover, as I have already noted, transnational ties are more visible and acceptable in today's multicultural America, so that the second generation often feel pride—not shame—in connections to their parents' homelands.

Where dual nationality provisions extend to the second generation—as is now the case for Dominican New Yorkers—this may foster continued political involvement in the home country among the second generation. And there is the fact that some members of the second generation will have spent significant periods of their childhood and teenage years in the parents' homeland, thereby creating and reinforcing ties to relatives and friends there. Some immigrants send their children home to grandparents because they need child care. Others ship teenagers home for high school to protect them from the drugs, gangs, and sexual precociousness in inner-city neighborhoods and to expose them to cultural values and institutions in the home society. In the late 1990s, Dominican educators and government officials estimated that as many as ten thousand students from schools in the United States, mainly from the New York area, were enrolled in schools in the Dominican Republic.[102] In the study of over 2,000 young adult New Yorkers born to immigrant parents, Philip Kasinitz and his colleagues found that a surprising number of West Indians and Latinos were sent back home to live with relatives at some point in their teen years by parents terrified of the dangers of the New York City streets.[103] Even if extended homeland visits are less frequent—or end—in the adult years, they may form the basis for ties that persist into adulthood, especially if there is at least some visiting back and forth.

At the other end of the life course, parental retirement patterns may also strengthen transnational ties. Some of the first generation will end up retiring to their birthplace, ensuring that their children will make trips to see them and keeping children and grandchildren connected, however tenuously, to the sending country. Indeed, some second-generation Mexican New Yorkers send their third-generation youngsters to Mexico during winter and summer vacations from school to live with grandmothers who, after many years in the United States, have retired in the home community.[104] Language may also play a role, particularly among Latinos who, studies show, are more likely than Asian-origin groups to be bilingual in the second generation.[105] In the context of the huge Spanish-speaking community in New York and other American cities, with their Spanish-language newspapers, radio, and television programs, many children of Latino immigrants will speak and understand Spanish, thereby facilitating the maintenance of ties to the homeland. There is another intriguing possibility: some children will assume the responsibility of maintaining ties to relatives in the country of origin, including remittance assistance, at the death of their parents.[106]

If, as some predict, economic restructuring of the American economy and the declining demand for less-educated labor threaten the ability of many members of the second generation to advance, then some may try their hand at ventures (including illegal ones) that involve transnational connections. In today's global economy this is a tack the more successful may take up as well. Robust and growing economics in some countries of origin may attract a number of educated and well-trained descendants of current immigrants, who will find it profitable to invest in their parents' homeland, return there for a time to work, or end up commuting back and forth. These paths may be especially attractive to those who experience professional barriers to mobility in the United States.[107]

Cheap air travel and widespread global tourism in the modern era will also increase the firsthand contact that members of the second generation have with their homelands. Evidence already shows that visits to the parents' home country are especially common in some groups. In the New York and San Diego surveys I have mentioned, Dominicans in New York and Mexicans in San Diego stood out, with around one-fifth having visited their parents' home country more than ten times. Overall, however, the vast majority in the two surveys had visited much less often—only once or twice, maybe three times, if at all.[108] In any case, caution is needed in evaluating whether short vacations or special "roots tours" to the homeland are evidence of, or lead to, significant transnationalism. Trips "back home" may, paradoxically, end up reinforcing notions of how American the second generation are—and bring out the fact that the United States is indisputably home.[109]

The verdict is not yet in on how important transnational ties really are—or will be—in the lives of today's second generation, particularly as they grow up, move into the work force, and establish their own families. We are only starting to get studies of the second generation, and those we have are of schoolchildren, teenagers, and college students, or young people at the beginning of their working lives. In addition, many of the people in the studies are not really second generation at all but were born abroad and in some cases spent their early childhood there.

It is possible, of course, that some members of the second generation who had little involvement in their parents' homelands in their youth and young adulthood will develop stronger ties when they get older and become more interested in their roots; growing older may also bring the time, money, and resources to cultivate transnational ties.[110] And there are the effects of political developments in the years ahead. On one side, Alba and Nee speculate that political attachments to the homeland could be weakened by the desire to demonstrate patriotism to the United States if, on account of war, overt enmity, or other conflicts, the country of origin becomes an enemy of the United States and suspicions grow about those with loyalties to the enemy nation.[111] Another possibility is that political events in the home country—war, revolution, or ethnic persecution, for example—could revitalize or intensify intermittent and weak transnational involvements among second-generation adults, particularly when a small minority have continued to sustain strong transnational connections to political organizations in the homeland.[112]

On the whole, however, it is when they are young and still living with their parents that children of immigrants are more likely to be influenced by their parents' transnational connections—and sometimes they have even been sent back to the homeland to stay with relatives. Whether these youths will maintain the same kind of transnational links when they marry and form their own families and have children of their own is, at the moment, an open question.

## Conclusion

Obviously, much is new about transnationalism. Modern technology, the new global economy and culture, and new laws and political arrangements have all combined to produce transnational connections that differ in fundamental ways from those maintained by immigrants a century ago. Once ignored or reviled, transnational ties are now a favorite topic at conferences and sometimes even celebrated in today's multicultural age. Also, transnationalism now seems headed for a longer life. The evidence suggests that connections to their parents' homelands will be more important for the present second generation than they were for immigrants' children of an earlier era.

This said, the novelty of contemporary conditions should not be exaggerated. Immigrants who move from one country to another seldom cut off ties and allegiances to those left behind, and immigrant New Yorkers a century ago were no exception. It may have been harder to maintain contacts across the ocean than it is today, but many immigrants in the last great wave maintained extensive, and intensive, transnational ties.

A comparison of transnationalism then and now raises some additional issues that need to be addressed. If many academic observers who studied earlier immigrants were guilty of overlooking transnational ties in the quest to document assimilation, there is now a risk of overemphasizing the centrality of transnationalism and minimizing the extent to which immigrants "become American" and undergo changes in behavior and outlook in response to circumstances in this country. Indeed, as David Hollinger observes, today's immigrants "are more prepared for a measure of assimilation by the worldwide influence of American popular culture; most are more culturally attuned to the United States before they arrive here than were their counterparts a century ago."[113]

A transnational perspective bids us to explore the transnational engagements and attachments of the second generation, yet, here too, there is a danger of seeing transnationalism everywhere and exaggerating its importance. Although some members of the second generation will maintain ongoing and close connections to their parents' country of origin, they are bound to be a minority. The vast majority, having been born and raised in the United States, will be primarily oriented to people, institutions, and places in this country—and it is the implications of growing up in the United States, not ties to their parents' homelands, that should be our primary object of study. As Peggy Levitt has observed: "Their primary socialization occurs in the US. Even if they travel frequently to their parents' countries of origin or host relatives during numerous visits, the air they breathe, the food they eat, and their primary social contacts are with North Americans."[114]

Perhaps because studies using a transnational approach are in their infancy, we still know little about how extensive various transnational ties actually are among the first or the second generation today—or in earlier eras. Portes and his colleagues have made important steps forward in their study of transnational political and economic activities of Colombian, Dominican, and Salvadoran immigrants, yet there is a need for additional, and more inclusive, studies that measure the incidence and range of transnational activities among immigrants in a broader range of groups.[115] In the past, Italians were more transnational in behavior and outlook than Russian Jews, mainly because Jews came to stay, whereas large numbers of Italians were labor migrants, who aimed to—and often did—go back home after a spell of work in New York. Today, as well, rates of participation in transnational activities (or certain types of transnational activities) are also likely to vary by group— and we need research that explores and explains the differences. Among the many factors apt to be involved are geographic proximity of the homeland to the United States; the degree to which homeland leaders and organizations actively recruit support abroad; and the size of the group and extent of residential concentration.[116]

A comparison of Mexican and West Indians in New York indicates that social organization and cultural patterns in the home community influence the types of transnational linkages that develop. The Mexican New Yorkers from the small *municipio* of Ticuani described by Robert Smith belong to what have been called transnational villages or localities; migrants from Ticuani organized a New York committee to help build schools and support other projects in the home community, while young Ticuanis in the city formed a Ticuani youth group that sponsored sports tournaments to raise funds for public works projects in the *municipio*. In Mexico, communities such as Ticuani have been historically important units for the organization of politics and society; they have a set of indigenous corporate institutions, including communal landholding and religious cargo systems with offices linked to communal rituals. This is not the case in the West Indies, where, as my study of a Jamaican community demonstrates, the social organization of rural life is very different.[117] There are few parallel structures of the Mexican type found in West Indian communities. And, as far as I know, there are no village-based West Indian associations in New York. By and large, West Indian migrants' connections to the home society are mediated by informal personal networks; the formal associations that link New York and the West Indies are mostly island-based and cross-cut local community ties.[118]

There is also variation in the frequency, depth, and range of transnational ties *within* national origin groups. Just as well-off Asian Indian immigrants have more resources to maintain transnational connections than do their poorer counterparts, so, too, this may be true in other immigrant groups. Legal status is likely to affect the types and extent of transnational connections maintained; undocumented immigrants cannot easily go back and forth, for example. Whether migrants came on their own or with their families must be considered. There are also bound to be differences in the nature and impact of transnational ties between men and women and among the old, young, and middle-aged. Transnational activities, it has been shown, ebb and flow at different stages of individuals' life course, varying with, among other things, the demands of work, school, and family.[119] And transnational connections may well lose force with length of stay in the United States, as suggested by research showing that remittances tend to taper off with time.

Finally, there are the consequences of transnational connections for migrants' lives here. If scholars of the last great wave of immigration once tended to blame home country ties for a host of problems, from poor English skills to lack of interest in naturalizing, today's transnational perspectives often have a celebratory tone. Transnational ties are seen as providing a protective layer against discrimination and prejudice in this country as well as access to a wide range of resources, including business and investment opportunities, political and organizational leadership positions, and assistance with child care. In an insecure world, they allow migrants to keep their options open. As Glick Schiller and her colleagues write: "By stretching, reconfiguring, and activating . . . networks across national boundaries, families are able to maximize the utilization of labor and resources and survive within situations of economic uncertainty and subordination."[120] Even involvement in home country-based organizations has been said to strengthen migrants' ability to mobilize a base of support for political issues and elections in New York.[121] At the least, allegiances to the home country need not detract from involvements in the United States, as Patricia Pessar and Pamela Graham show for Dominican immigrants, who may be simultaneously incorporated into the political systems of New York and their country of origin.[122] A recent study of Latin American immigrants reveals, in fact, that immigrants from countries recognizing dual nationality are more likely to seek American citizenship than those from countries that do not recognize it.[123]

For the second generation, too, transnational ties are portrayed as facilitating successful adaptation by providing access to resources, skills, and connections in two societies—operating as a safety net for those having trouble making it in the U.S. economy or, for the more successful, an avenue for economic and social mobility through business, investment, and other occupational opportunities. Peggy Levitt notes that some of her highly educated respondents saw their transnational connections as a "Plan B" that could be put into action to circumvent blocked mobility or as a way to diversify risk and produce additional income.[124] Ties to the home community can also bolster a sense of ethnic pride among adolescents and provide second-generation youths with cultural anchors that counter the negative influences experienced in New York schools and neighborhoods.[125] For some West Indians and Latinos in New York, going to school "back home" has even given them a leg up in getting into U.S. colleges and jobs, as compared to their cousins who remained in New York City public schools.[126]

But modern-day transnationalism may have costs, as well. Financial obligations to relatives left behind can be a drain on resources needed for projects in New York. The family separation involved in transnationalism often brings great personal strain. Transnational mothers worry about the children left behind in the home country—about the care they are receiving, whether they will get in trouble in adolescence, and whether they will transfer their allegiance and affection to the "other mother."[127] When children move back and forth between New York and their parents' country of origin, they may feel that they do not completely belong to either place, and such movement can add to children's educational difficulties. In the realm of politics, involvement in political and organizational affairs of the home country may draw energies and interests away from political engagement and activism on behalf of the immigrant community in the United States.[128]

That scholars are debating the contradictory pressures of transnational ties is a sign of their importance for today's immigrants. What is clear is that transnational practices are very much a part of the contemporary scene and have far-reaching effects for the lives of immigrants as well as for their children. It is also clear, to return to the historical comparison, that they are not just a modern-day phenomenon. This chapter shows that in trying to understand transnationalism among the latest arrivals it is useful to revisit the past to sort out the parallels as well as the contrasts between then and now. Transnationalism has been with us for a long time, although in its modern guise it appears to be more far-reaching and more intense—and may also turn out to be more durable and long-lasting.

# 4

# Immigrant Women and Work, Then and Now

Today's immigrant women enter a society that has undergone remarkable changes since the last great immigrant influx at the turn of the twentieth century. Perhaps most dramatic, is the virtual revolution in women's involvement in the labor force. Whereas in 1900, only 20 percent of women in the nation were in the paid labor force, by 2000, the figure was just over 60 percent. There is a difference in who works, too. A hundred years ago, the vast majority of women workers were young and single. It was generally assumed that work outside the home was temporary for a young girl; when she married, she would move back into the domestic domain. Indeed, in 1900, only 6 percent of the nation's married women were in the labor force.

Today, working daughters have given way to working mothers.[1] Women now enter the labor force later—and they stay. Whether they work for economic need, to maintain or raise their family's living standards, or for personal satisfaction, the fact is that by 2000, seven out of ten women in the United States with children under eighteen worked in the paid labor force, many doing so full-time and year-round.

How have these broad changes in women's participation in the American labor force affected the experiences of immigrant women today as compared to the past? An analysis of immigrant women and work that compares past and present is useful for a number of reasons. We have come a long way from the days when scholars lamented that women were ignored in migration studies, yet the growing literature on contemporary immigrant women in the United States often proceeds without much awareness of the experiences of, or the literature, on migrant women of earlier eras. Historian Donna Gabaccia's important and wide-ranging book, *From the Other Side,* provides an overview of immigrant women's experiences past and present, but she emphasizes the continuities that characterize women of both the nineteenth century and present-day migrations.[2] In this chapter the stress is on the differences, particularly those shaped by the contrasting structure of work opportunities—and cultural norms and attitudes to women's work—that greeted immigrant women on arrival. Comparing a time when few married immigrant women worked for wages to a period when most do highlights the relationship between migrant women's work and their overall status—and helps us to understand the conditions that lead women to experience gains as well as losses when they come to the United States.

As in the preceding chapters, the analysis of earlier immigrants focuses on eastern European Jews and Italians, who were the vast bulk of the new immigrants in New York City at the turn of the twentieth century. Because no two groups predominate this way today, the discussion of the contemporary period draws on material on a larger number of groups, from Asia, the Caribbean, Latin America, and Europe.

A comparison of migrant women in the two eras reveals some striking differences. Wage work has empowered immigrant wives and mothers in today's New York in ways that were not possible for Jewish and Italian married women of an earlier era, who rarely worked outside the home. Yet, despite this contrast, gender inequalities are still very much with us, and, despite improvements when many women move to New York from abroad, migration has not emancipated the latest arrivals. As feminist scholars have emphasized, simple models that portray migration as leading to female emancipation will not do: migration often leads to losses, as well as gains, for women.[3] Among other things, "traditional" patriarchal codes and practices may continue to have an impact, and women—immigrants as well as the native-born—still experience special burdens and disabilities as members of the "second sex." Indeed, immigrant mothers' continued responsibilities for child care and domestic tasks add new complications for them today when they are more likely to work outside, as well as inside, the home.

## Jewish and Italian Women Then

From the beginning, in the move itself, Jewish and Italian women typically followed men—husbands, fiancés, and fathers—who led the way. Women were a minority, too. The Italian migration was, more than anything else, a movement of single men coming to make money and go home. In most years of the peak migration between 1880 and 1910, about 80 percent of Italian immigrants to the United States were male.[4] The Jewish movement was mainly a family affair, but even then men predominated; women made up 43 percent of the migration stream to the United States between 1899 and 1910.[5]

What work did women do in the Old World? In eastern Europe, Jewish women had a central role in economic life. Patriarchy ran deep in Jewish communities—women were excluded from seats of power and positions in the religious sphere—but they were expected to, and did, make important economic contributions to their households. Indeed, the hardworking scholar's wife, who supported a highly-respected man who devoted himself to full-time religious study, "acted as a legitimating symbol of the female breadwinner for the masses of east European Jews. If the scholar's wife worked, then why not the merchant's, the trader's, the watchmaker's, or the tailor's? And that was the pattern."[6] Women's work, throughout the world of eastern European Jews, was considered necessary and respectable: "The frequency of married women's work was high enough and had sufficient cultural support to make it something of a norm."[7]

Large numbers of Jewish wives worked in business or trade, sometimes helping in a store formally run by their husbands or keeping a store or stall on their own, where they sold food, staples, or household wares. Some women were peddlers who stood in the marketplace or went from house to house selling food they had prepared at home or manufactured goods that were bought in small lots in cities.[8] Jewish wives became tough bargainers who developed a knowledge of the marketplace and a certain worldliness about the society outside their own communities. In the market, women had a better command of local languages spoken by the peasants than did the more learned men, and many developed a reputation for being outspoken and aggressive.[9]

The Jewish community itself provided some jobs for women, for example, rolling and baking matzos at Passover. By the end of the nineteenth century, with the development of factory production in Russia and the movement of many Jews to cities, increasing numbers of unmarried Jewish women were drawn to artisans' shops and small factories, where they made matches, cigarettes, and other goods. When they married, Jewish women rarely took factory jobs that demanded long hours away from home, but many were involved in various kinds of home-based artisanal or outwork production. The sewing machine created new opportunities for doing outwork, and thousands of Jewish married and single female homeworkers made dresses or did other kinds of needlework for contractors who then distributed the garments to stores.

In the Sicilian and southern Italian villages that most Italian immigrant women left behind, married women supervised household chores, organized the making of clothes and food preparation, and managed the family budget. Often, they tended animals and tilled the garden, producing food for family consumption and for sale at the local market. While artisans' wives, who helped out in the shop, worked in the privacy of their homes, peasant women's work took them outside the house as they hauled water, sat together at open streams laundering clothes, or did their chores in the street or courtyard alongside neighbors. Wives in poor families often had no choice but to help as day laborers during harvest periods, picking fruits and nuts, husking almonds, and threshing wheat.[10]

These patterns of work underwent significant change in New York. Although it may be too strong to say, along with one historian, that immigration disempowered women who came as wives and mothers, and intensified their subordination,[11] for many Jewish and Italian women, the journey to New York imposed new constraints, and they were forced to lead more sheltered lives than they had in the Old World.

Hardly any Jewish or Italian wives went out to work for wages. The 1905 census recorded only 1 percent of immigrant Russian Jewish households in New York City with wives working outside the home; for Italians the figure, at 6 percent, was not much higher.[12] Marriage, typically around the age of twenty to twenty-two, spelled the end of wage work for the vast majority of Italian and Jewish immigrant women. (This was the general pattern for married white women in American society at the time, with fewer than 5 percent of them in the labor force in 1890 and 1900.)[13] Eventually, some returned to the paid work force in the 1930s and 1940s when their children were grown, but immigrant women who came to New York as married adults often never worked outside the home at all.

Most Italian and Russian Jewish wives and mothers earned money by working at home. In the early years of the immigration, in the 1880s and 1890s, many Jewish women did piecework at home in the needle trades, but by the early twentieth century, the numbers had fallen sharply. By this time, taking care of boarders, virtually indistinguishable from other domestic duties, had become a more attractive alternative —and the main way Jewish wives contributed to the family income. According to the Immigration Commission's 1911 report, as many as 56 percent of New York Russian Jewish families had boarders living with them.[14] Many immigrant wives helped their husbands in "mom-and-pop" stores and some ran the shops on their own. Minding the store was considered an extension of a woman's proper role as her husband's helpmate; often the family lived above or in back of the store so that wives could run back and forth between the shop counter and the kitchen.

Although many Italian wives added to the family income by taking in boarders, this was a less-frequent practice than among Jews. Homework was more common. By the first decade of the twentieth century, most industrial homeworkers in New York City were Italian. Working in the kitchen or a bedroom, Italian women finished garments or made artificial flowers while raising their children and caring for the house. Women were aware that factory jobs paid better, but the demands of caring for young children and household duties, as well as the widely accepted notion that women should leave the workplace after marriage, usually kept them at home.[15]

In one view, immigrant women's "retirement" to the domestic arena was a blessing.[16] By taking in boarders and doing piecework at home, they contributed much-needed money to the family income at the same time as they reared children and performed time-consuming domestic duties. Cleaning, cooking, and doing the laundry were labor-intensive chores for poor immigrant women who could not afford mechanical conveniences or hired help. The weekly laundry, for example, meant a laborious process of soaking, scrubbing, wringing, rinsing, and drying and ironing clothes. Although women did a tremendous amount of daily housework, they defined their own rhythms.

Unlike the factory, where bosses were in control, women exercised real authority and set the pace in their own households. Apart from nurturing and disciplining children, women managed the family budget. Husbands and unmarried sons usually gave them the larger part of their wages each week; most unmarried daughters handed over their entire paycheck. The role of housewife and mother, moreover, if done well, carried with it respectability and the approval of family and neighbors.

Yet women's housebound existence had a downside as well. By and large, married women's lives were more circumscribed in New York than in the Old World. Immigrant mothers did, of course, socialize with friends and neighbors and go out to shop. The Jewish housewife, as the family member most responsible for decisions about household purchases, presided over a process of acquisition of consumption items.[17] But whereas in eastern Europe, Jewish wives were often the worldly ones, in America their housebound existence made it more difficult to learn the new language and customs. Their husbands picked up English in the workplace; their daughters learned American ways in factory work groups. Many Jewish mothers, however, remained fluent only in Yiddish and felt uncomfortable in new situations outside the Jewish community.[18] They had to depend on their children to learn American customs or, as a few managed to do, attend night school to learn English.[19] Italian women working at home were also more insulated than other family members from the world outside. While Andrea Bocci's father frequented a Prince Street saloon every night, her mother never went out: "If one of her friends would be sick, she would go and help them out, but otherwise she would stay at home."[20]

Most household chores, as well as industrial homework, were done within the four walls of their tenement apartments. Those from small towns and villages, used to doing chores like laundry in the company of other women, now faced the more lonely and difficult task of washing clothing by themselves inside cramped tenement apartments.[21] Because they now lived a more "inside" life, the move from Sicily to Elizabeth Street, Gabaccia concludes, "limited immigrant women's opportunities to interact with others," and these limitations were a source of dissatisfaction with their new environment.[22]

Even as modern plumbing freed women from some of the more rigorous chores they had known in the Old World, the more rigorous standards of cleanliness and new household acquisitions complicated housework. In small eastern European towns and villages, women went to the nearest stream or lake once a month to wash clothes; now the laundry was a weekly task. Another example: mattresses in eastern Europe were generally made of straw, and in cold weather feather bedding was common. In America, beds came with mattresses that required sheets and blankets; these needed washing and airing on a regular basis.[23]

For the Jewish women who had been charged with providing a major portion of the family livelihood in eastern Europe, migration reduced their economic role. In New York, immigrant wives' income-earning activities rarely represented the major contribution to the family economy.

Industrial homework or taking in boarders was not as lucrative as work outside the home, and wives were seen as helping out their husbands in family businesses. Married women's earnings in America were now eclipsed by the wages of working daughters in the industrial labor force, who emerged as the main female breadwinners in the Jewish family.[24]

## Immigrant Women Now

Much has changed for the latest arrivals. Women immigrants now outnumber men in virtually all the major groups in New York, and more women come on their own rather than follow in the footsteps of men.[25] Today's immigrant women also include a much higher proportion with professional and middle-class backgrounds.[26] Above all, the world they live in gives women opportunities and benefits unheard of a century ago —and this is particularly evident in the sphere of work.

Today, adult immigrant women are the main female contributors to the family income, while their teenage daughters are generally in school. With the expansion of high schools and colleges over the course of the twentieth century and the raising of the school-leaving age, women (and men) start working later than they used to.[27] Today's immigrant daughters are often eighteen or older when they enter the labor market full-time compared to fourteen or fifteen a century ago. Marriage no longer spells a retreat from paid employment outside the home. Industrial homework, while not entirely a thing of the past, is much rarer than in the era of Italian and Jewish immigrants. Now it is socially accepted, even expected, throughout American society that wives and mothers will go out to work.

At the time of the 1990 census, 60 percent of New York City's working-age foreign-born women (compared to 66 percent of the city's working-age women generally) were in the labor force. At one end, Filipino women, who often came specifically to work in health-care jobs, had a labor force participation rate of more than 85 percent; West Indian women were not far behind, with labor force participation rates in the range of 70 to 80 percent. Dominican women were near the bottom, with 52 percent in the work force. Given the wide variety of groups today, and the diversity of immigrant backgrounds, immigrant women occupy an equally wide range of jobs, from nurses, secretaries, and health technicians to domestics and factory workers.[28]

These new patterns have important consequences. Now that most immigrant women work outside the home, they are able to obtain a kind of independence and power that was beyond the reach of Jewish and Italian wives and mothers a century ago, and that was often beyond their own reach before migration. How much improvement women experience when they migrate depends to a large degree on their role in production and their social status in the home country—and gender roles, norms, and ideologies there—as well as their economic role in New York.[29] What is important here is that for the majority of migrant women, the move to New York has led to gains because they earn a regular wage for the first time, earn a higher wage than in the country of origin, or make a larger contribution to the family economy than previously.[30]

In cases where women did not earn an income or earned only a small supplementary income prior to migration, the gains that come with regular wage work in New York are especially striking. The much-cited case of Dominican women fits this pattern. They left a society where, in 2001, 41 percent of women were in the labor force.[31] Now that so many Dominican immigrant women work for wages—often for the first time—and contribute a larger share of the family income, they have more authority in the household and greater self-esteem. They use their wages, observes Patricia Pessar, "to assert their right to greater autonomy and equality within the household."[32]

In New York, Dominican women begin to expect to be copartners in "heading" the household, a change from more patriarchal arrangements in the Dominican Republic. "We are both heads," said one woman, echoing the sentiments of many other Dominican women in New York. "If both the husband and wife are earning salaries then they should equally rule the household. In the Dominican Republic it is always the husband who gives the orders in the household. But here when the two are working, the woman feels herself the equal of the man in ruling the home." In a telling comment, a Dominican migrant visiting her home village told her cousin about New York: "Wait till you get there. You'll have your own paycheck, and I tell you, he [your husband] won't be pushing you around there the way he is here."[33]

In the Dominican Republic, men generally controlled the household budget, even when wives and daughters put in income on a regular or semiregular basis; in New York, Pessar found that husbands, wives, and working children usually pooled their income in a common fund for shared household expenses.[34] Indeed, she reports that Dominican women are eager to postpone or avoid returning to the Dominican Republic, where social pressures and an unfavorable job market would probably mean their retirement from regular employment and a loss of new-found gains.

Of course, many immigrant women, including some Dominicans, had regular salaries before emigration. Even these women often feel a new kind of independence in New York, because jobs in this country pay more than most could ever earn at home and increase women's contribution to the family economy. This is the experience for many Jamaican women, who come from a society where, at the beginning of the twenty-first century, two out of three women were in the labor force.[35] Many Jamaican women I interviewed who had held white-collar jobs before emigration said they had more financial control and more say in family affairs in New York where their incomes are so much larger.[36]

The sense of empowerment that comes from earning a wage—or a higher wage—and having greater control over what they earn comes out in studies of many different groups. Paid work for Chinese garment workers, according to one report, not only contributes to their families' economic well-being, but also has "created a sense of confidence and self-fulfillment which they may never have experienced in traditional Chinese society." "I do not have to ask my husband for money," one woman said, "I make my own."[37] For many Salvadoran women, the ability to earn wages and decide how they should be used is something new. As one woman explained: "Here [in the U.S.] women work just like the men. I like it a lot because managing my own money I feel independent. I don't have to ask my husband for money but in El Salvador, yes, I would have to. Over there women live dependent on their husbands. You have to walk behind him."[38] Or listen to a Trinidadian woman of East Indian descent: "Now that I have a job I am independent. I stand up here as a man."[39]

The female-first migration pattern involving adult married women that is common in some groups reinforces the effects of wage-earning on women's independence. Many women who have lived and worked in New York without their husbands become more assertive; one Dominican woman noted that she had changed "after so many years of being on my own, being my own boss."[40] One study suggests that Asian men who move to the United States as their wives' dependents often have to subordinate their careers, at least initially, to those of their wives since the women have already established themselves in this country.[41]

Work outside the home in New York brings about another change that women appreciate. Many men now help out more *inside* the home than before they moved to New York. Of course, this is not inevitable. Cultural values in different groups as well as the availability of female relatives to lend a hand influence the kind of household help men provide. A study of the division of labor in Taiwanese immigrant households in Queens found that, as in Taiwan, men who held working-class jobs or owned small businesses did little around the house.[42] Korean men, staunch supporters of patriarchal family values and norms, generally still expect their wives to serve them and resist performing household chores like cooking, dishwashing, and doing the laundry. Such resistance is more effective when the wife's mother or mother-in-law lives in the household, a not infrequent occurrence in Korean immigrant families. Yet much to their consternation, Korean men in New York with working wives often find themselves helping out with household work more than they did in Korea—and wives often make more demands on them to increase their share.[43]

Research on Latin American and Caribbean groups shows that when wives are involved in productive work outside the home, the organization of labor within it changes. We are not talking about a drastic change in the household division of labor or the emergence of truly egalitarian arrangements. Indeed, Latin American and Caribbean women strongly identify as wives and mothers and like being in charge of the domestic domain. What they want—and what they often get—is more help from men than they were accustomed to back home. Mainly, men oblige because they have little choice.

West Indian men, for example, recognize that there is no alternative to pitching in when their wives work and children (particularly daughters) are not old enough to lend a hand. Working women simply cannot shoulder all the domestic responsibilities expected of them, and they do not have relatives available to help as they did back home. Even if close kin live nearby, they are usually busy with work and their own household chores. Wives' wages are a necessary addition to the family income, and West Indians cannot afford to hire household help in New York.[44] "In order to have a family life here," said a middle-class Trinidadian woman, "he [her husband] realizes he has to participate not only in the housework but in the childrearing too. It's no longer the type of thing where he comes home and the maid is there, having prepared the dinner . . . Here . . . [he] has to pick up the children, or take them to the babysitter, or come home and begin the dinner."[45] Indeed, West Indian couples with young children often arrange their shifts so that the husband can look after the children while the wife works.

More than behavior changes. As men become accustomed to doing more around the house, their notions of what tasks are appropriate—or expected—often also shift. Research shows that Dominican and Jamaican men and women believe that when both partners have jobs, and daughters are too young to help, husbands should pitch in with such tasks as shopping, dishwashing, and child care. Women tend to view their husband's help as a moral victory;[46] men accept their new duties, however reluctantly.

Although the exigencies of immigrant life—women working outside the home, a lack of available relatives to assist, and an inability to hire help—are mainly responsible for men's greater participation in household tasks, American cultural beliefs and values have an influence, too.[47] As Jennifer Hirsch puts it, "what changes with migration may be not only the resources and style with which men and women bargain, but also what couples bargain for—that is, their marital goals."[48] Many of the Dominicans whom Sherri Grasmuck and Patricia Pessar spoke to claimed that they self-consciously patterned their more egalitarian relations on what they believed to be the dominant American model. They saw this change as both modern and a sign of progress.[49] Among recently arrived Central Americans, Cecilia Menjivar notes that women in private domestic work bring home new ideals of husbands and wives sharing cooking and childrearing, although their husbands, who work with other Latino men in construction, gardening, or restaurants, find support for maintaining their old ways of life.[50] Whatever men think, immigrant women may feel they can make more demands on their husbands in this country, where the dominant norms and values back up their claims for men to help out.

In addition to the independence, power, and autonomy that wages bring, there are the intrinsic satisfactions from work itself. Women in professional and managerial positions gain prestige from their positions and often have authority over others on the job.[51] Those in lower-level occupations often get a sense of satisfaction from doing their job well and from the new skills they have learned in New York.[52] And there is the sociability involved. In factories, hospitals, and offices, women make friends and build up a storehouse of experiences that enrich their lives and conversations. Indeed, when women are out of work, they often complain of boredom and isolation. "Sometimes," said a Chinese garment worker, "I get frustrated if I am confined at home and don't see my coworkers." Dominican women who are laid off say that they miss not only the income but also the socializing with workmates and the bustle of the streets and subways.[53] Friendships formed on the job may extend outside the bounds of the workplace as women visit and phone each other, attend parties, and go on shopping jaunts with coworkers.[54]

But it is important not to romanticize or idealize immigrant women's work outside the home as a path to self-fulfillment or economic autonomy. If wage work enables many immigrant women to expand their influence and independence, these gains often come at a price. Wage work brings burdens as well as benefits to immigrant women and may create new sets of demands and pressures both on the job and at home. Moreover, despite changes in women's status in New York, premigration gender role patterns and ideologies do not fade away; they continue to affect the lives of migrant women, often in ways that constrain and limit them. Cultural ideals about gender and spousal relations held at the point of origin, observes Pierrette Hondagneu-Sotelo in another context, influence the outcome of the changing balance of economic resources in the United States.[55]

Wage work, as immigrant women commonly explain, is not an option but a necessity for their family's welfare. And it typically brings a host of difficulties. On the job, women's wages are still generally lower than men's—and, for many, perhaps most, immigrant women, too meager to sustain their economic independence from men.[56] In addition, women are limited in their choice of work due to gender divisions in the labor market—often confined to menial, low prestige, and poorly paying jobs. Working in the ethnic economy does not help most women, either. Studies of Chinese, Dominican, and Colombian women in New York who work in businesses owned by their compatriots show that they earn low wages and have minimal benefits and few opportunities for advancement.[57] Sociologist Greta Gilbertson argues that some of the success of immigrant small-business owners and workers in the ethnic enclave is due to the marginal position of immigrant women. The many Korean women who work in family businesses are, essentially, unpaid family workers without an independent source of income. Although

many are working outside the home for the first time, they are typically thought of as "helpers" to their husbands; the husband not only
legally owns the enterprise but also usually controls the money, hires
and fires employees, and represents the business in Korean business
associations.[58]

For many immigrant women, working conditions are extremely difficult. Apart from the low wages and long hours, most garment workers
have to keep up a furious pace in cramped conditions in noisy, often
unsafe, sweatshops; domestic workers often have to deal with humiliat-
ing and demeaning treatment from employers. Some women with full-
time jobs have more than one position to make ends meet. I know many
West Indian women, for example, who care for an elderly person on the
weekend to supplement what they earn from a five-day child-care job.

Added to this, of course, are the demands of child-care and burdens
of household work. Going outside to earn means that childrearing is
more complicated than at the turn of the twentieth century, when married women typically worked at home. Only very affluent immigrants
can afford to hire maids or housekeepers, and female relatives, if present in New York, are often busy at work themselves. Occasionally,
women can juggle shifts with their husbands so one parent is always
around, and sometimes an elderly mother or mother-in-law is on hand
to help out. Many working women pay to leave their children with
babysitters or, less often, in day-care centers. Child-care constraints are
clearly a factor limiting women to low-paid jobs with flexible schedules;
they may prevent women from working full-time—or, in some cases, at
all. Some women leave their young children behind with relatives in the
home country so as to manage work more easily, a common pattern
among West Indian live-in household workers (see chapter 7).[59]

Immigrant women of all social classes have the major responsibilities
for household chores as well as childrearing, so that a grueling day at
work is often followed or preceded by hours of cooking, cleaning, and
washing. "I'm always working," is how Mrs. Darius, a Haitian nursing
home aide with eight children put it. Although her husband, a me-
chanic, did not help much around the house, Mrs. Darius got assistance
from her mother who lived with her. Still, there was a lot to do. "I have
to work 24 hours. When I go home, I take a nap, then get up again;
sometimes I get up at two in the morning, iron for the children, and go
back to sleep."[60]

Korean working wives, according to Pyong Gap Min, suffer from overwork and stress owing to the heavy demands on their time. After doing their work outside the home, they put in, on average, an additional twenty-five hours a week on housework, compared to seven hours contributed by their husbands. Altogether, working wives spend seventy-six hours a week on the job and doing housework—twelve more hours than men do. Although professional husbands help out more around the house than other Korean men, their wives still do the lion's share.[61]

Or take the case of Antonia Duarte, a Dominican mother of three, who put in a seventeen-hour day. At 5:00 A.M., she was up making breakfast and lunch for the family. She woke her three children at 6:00, got them dressed, fed, and ready for school, and then took them to the house of a friend, who cared for the four-year-old and oversaw the older children's departure to and return from school. By 7:15, Antonia was on the subway heading for the lamp factory where she worked from 8:00 A.M. to 4:30 P.M. five days a week. She collected her children a little after 5:00 and began preparing the evening meal when she got home. She did not ask her two oldest children to help—the oldest was a twelve-year-old girl—because, "I'd rather they begin their homework right away, before they get too tired." Her husband demanded a traditional meal of rice, beans, plantains, and meat, which could take as long as two hours to prepare. She and the children ate together at 7:00, but her husband often did not get back from socializing with his friends until later. He expected Antonia to reheat the food and serve it on his arrival. By the time she finished her child-care and other domestic responsibilities, it was 11:30 or 12:00. Like other Dominican women, she explained that if she did not manage the children and household with a high level of competence, her husband would threaten to prohibit her from working.[62]

Women in groups where strong traditional patriarchal codes continue to exert an influence may experience other difficulties. In some better-off Dominican families, wives are pressured by husbands to stay out of the work force altogether as a way to symbolize their household's respectability and elevated economic status.[63] It is still a point of pride for a Latin American man to say that his wife doesn't work; part of making it into the middle class is seeing to it that the women in the household remain at home.[64] In many groups, working women who are now the family's main wage earners may feel a special need to tread carefully in relations with their husbands so as to preserve the appearance of male dominance and to avoid making the men feel inadequate. Indeed, one study shows professional Korean women making conscious attempts to keep their traditional lower status and to raise the position of their husbands by reducing their incomes. A nurse explained: "My basic salary exceeds his. If I do overtime, my income will be too much —compared to his—and so, when overtime work falls on me, I just try so hard to find other nurses to cover my overtime assignments. . . . By reducing my income, I think, my husband can keep his ego and male superiority."[65]

Finally, there is the fact that women's increased financial authority and independence—or being more economically successful in New York than their husbands—can lead to greater discord with their spouses. Conflicts often develop when men resent and try to resist women's new demands on them; in some cases, the stresses ultimately lead to marital break-ups. Special problems may develop when men are unemployed or unsuccessful at work and become dependent on women's wage-earning abilities, yet still insist on maintaining the perquisites of male privilege in the household.[66] In extreme cases, the reversal of gender roles can lead to serious physical abuse for women at the hands of their spouses. Indeed, in some instances, increased isolation from relatives in the immigrant situation creates conditions for greater abuse by husbands, who are freer of the informal controls that operated in their home communities, where friends and family would have been more likely to intervene and play a mediatory role.[67]

## Conclusion: Immigrant Women in the Two Eras

Comparing immigrant women today and at the turn of the twentieth century makes clear that women's involvement in the world of work is critical to understanding why moving to New York has been liberating in many ways for so many contemporary immigrants—and why, at least for immigrant mothers and wives, it was more limiting in the past. Jewish and Italian women came to New York at a time when there was a social stigma attached to the wife who worked for wages outside the home; the mother's wage was considered a "final defense against destitution," to be undertaken only on account of severe economic or family emergency.[68] Often, Jewish and Italian immigrant wives found themselves more cloistered in their homes than in the Old World. The work they did to earn money—taking in boarders and industrial homework —did not lead to reallocating household tasks among other household members. Because virtually all of their income-producing activities were done in the home, these activities ended up preserving and intensifying the gender division of housework and child care.[69] The main female wage earners in the family, immigrant daughters, handed over their pay to their mothers, who, as managers of daily financial affairs, used it for running the household.

Now that female wage earners are typically wives and mothers, they have more leverage in the household than working younger daughters once had. Indeed, adult women's employment has begun to transform their family relationships more so than in the earlier generation. Because an immigrant working mother today is often absent from the home for forty or forty-five hours a week, or sometimes longer, someone must fill her place—or at least help out. Often, it is her husband. Women's labor force participation, in other words, frequently increases husbands' participation in household work and leads to changes in the balance of power in immigrant families. Daughters in modern-day families, growing up in an era when female labor participation is the norm and the working mother is commonplace, may go even further in redefining family roles as they enter the labor force for an extended period of their lives.[70]

As the main female wage earners in the family, today's immigrant mothers contribute a larger share of the household income than they did a hundred years ago. Their regular access to wages—and to higher wages—in the United States often gives them greater autonomy and power than they had before migration. Working outside the home also broadens their social horizons and enhances their sense of independence. "A woman needs to work," said one Cuban sales worker. "She feels better and more in control of herself. She doesn't have to ask her husband for money. It seems to me that if a woman has a job, she is given more respect by her husband and her children."[71] Many contemporary immigrant women would heartily agree. For a good number, the opportunities to work—and earn more money—represent a major gain that has come with the move to New York.

If immigrant wives and mothers have come a long way in the past hundred years, it is clear that they are not fully emancipated. Not only do they suffer from gender inequalities that are a feature of American society generally, but important vestiges of premigration gender ideologies and role patterns may place additional constraints on them. Wage labor, as one scholarly observer puts it, both oppresses and liberates immigrant women.[72] Many work in low-status, dead-end positions that pay less than men's jobs. Immigrant working wives in all social classes experience a heavy double burden since the household division of labor remains far from equal. If husbands help out with domestic burdens, they may do so only grudgingly, if at all, and it is women, more than men, who make work choices to accommodate and reflect family and child-care needs. While many, perhaps most, immigrant women feel that the benefits of wage work outweigh the drawbacks, others would, if they could afford it, prefer to remain at home. As a Korean woman who worked as a manicurist in a nail salon fifty-four hours a week said: "If my husband makes enough money for the family, why should I take this burden?"[73]

A comparison of women in the two eras should not, in short, blind us to the barriers and difficulties immigrant women still face. Improvements in women's status today go hand in hand with the persistence of male privilege. At the same time, the comparison is a powerful reminder that "the New York we have lost," to paraphrase Peter Laslett, was hardly a utopia for women, and that working outside the home, for all its problems, has brought significant benefits to migrant women today.[74]

# PART II

# Comparisons Across Space

*West Indians in New York and London*

# 5

# Being Black in London and New York

## *The Caribbean Experience*

When West Indians move to New York and London, one of
the most jarring changes is being labeled "black." They have found
themselves living in societies where blackness is more devalued than it
was in the Caribbean and facing significant barriers on account of their
African ancestry and skin color. Being black and being West Indian have
taken on new meanings in the immigrant situation and form the basis
for new alliances as well as new divisions with people of other racial
and ethnic groups they have come into contact with away from home.

Because being black is, in effect, the master status which pervades
migrants' lives in both London and New York, it is a fitting theme with
which to start the comparative analysis of West Indians in the two
cities. Through cross-national comparisons we can better understand
the complex, often subtle, and sometimes surprising ways in which the
racial context in different receiving societies leads to specific responses
among West Indian migrants. It is a commonplace in the social sciences
to say that race is a social and cultural construction, but as Fredrickson
has noted, this statement is the beginning of an inquiry rather than the
end of it.[1] A comparative perspective highlights just how this process of
construction takes place. While West Indian migrants have brought with
them a racial sensibility that is nurtured in their home societies, they
have developed new images of themselves, as blacks and as West Indians, in response to the particular nature of racial and ethnic relations
and hierarchies in the new setting.

If being black penetrates and pervades West Indians' lives in both
London and New York, there are critical differences in the way the racial context shapes identity construction as well as the structure of opportunities. Above all, there is the presence of a large African American

community in New York—and the place of African Americans in the city's ethnoracial hierarchy. These have had complex and contradictory implications for West Indian migrants in New York as well as for their children. On the one hand, they have played a key role in insulating— or perhaps more accurately, segregating—West Indian New Yorkers from whites in neighborhoods, schools, and informal contexts in a way that has not happened in London. On the other hand, they have created opportunities for political and other alliances with African Americans. The presence of African Americans has also shaped West Indian attempts to maintain ethnic distinctiveness in a way that their cousins in Britain have not experienced.

The encounter with racism in New York and London has implications for large numbers of Caribbean migrants. At the beginning of the twenty-first century, close to 350,000 Afro-Caribbeans (including the British born) lived in London, the product of a mass immigration that brought hundreds of thousands to Britain from the early 1950s to the mid-1960s. The Afro-Caribbean population in Britain, which was estimated to be about 28,000 in 1951, had, by 1991 increased to 500,000, with 265,000 born in the Caribbean.[2] In New York City, large-scale West Indian migration in the post–World War II period was made possible by the 1965 amendments to the Immigration and Nationality Act and has continued apace since then. When counted altogether, West Indians from the English-speaking Caribbean are now the largest immigrant group in the city; in the late 1990s, foreign-born West Indians numbered about a half million.[3] Jamaicans are the largest West Indian nationality group in New York and London, and I have done research among them in both cities, in London in the 1970s and in New York in the 1980s. What follows draws on this research; continued informal contacts, and several dozen interviews conducted by students, with West Indian New Yorkers since the 1980s; and what is, by now, a large secondary literature on West Indian migrants and their children on both sides of the Atlantic.[4]

A few preliminary words about terminology. In New York, the term West Indian is commonly used and acceptable; in Britain, it is out of favor, where African Caribbean or Afro-Caribbean is preferred. Because the main focus of this book is New York, I generally adopt the common American usage, using "West Indian" to refer to people from the Anglophone Caribbean, including the mainland nations of Guyana and Belize.

The spotlight is on West Indians of African ancestry, not those of East Indian descent, who confront a different set of identity issues.[5]

## Moving Abroad: The Parallels

Whether they moved to London or New York, West Indian migrants have had to cope with living in a radically different racial order: blacks are not just a minority, but a disparaged minority group. This does not mean that they left racial paradises back home. There is no denying that the long history of West Indian plantation slavery and colonial social arrangements have left, in their wake, the assumption that African ancestry is inferior; dark skin, moreover, continues to be correlated with poverty.[6] But blackness does not have the same stigma that it does in the United States and Britain, and blackness is not, in itself, a barrier to social acceptance or upward mobility. In most West Indian societies, people of African ancestry are the overwhelming majority (the exceptions are Trinidad and Guyana where East Indians are, respectively, 40 and 50 percent of the population), and there are hardly any whites or Europeans. That people with dark skin occupy high status roles, including dominant political, government, and business positions, is a fact of life—and unremarkable. "Blackness," as Milton Vickerman has put it, is normal in the West Indies the way "whiteness" is normal in the United States and, I would add, in Britain, as well.[7]

The very notion of who is considered black also differs in the Caribbean. Whereas in the United States and Britain, the category black includes people who range from very dark skinned to very light skinned, in the West Indies blackness is a matter of ancestry, skin color, hair type, facial features, and socioeconomic status. Or to put it another way, many people labeled "black" in London and New York would not be seen this way in West Indian societies. West Indians defined as black in the United States and Britain belong to different groups in the Caribbean, where there is a keen consciousness of shade—the lighter, the better. Thus, in Jamaica, "blacks" are generally thought of as impoverished individuals with African ancestry, dark skin, and certain facial features and hair type. People who combine features from several types (African and European, Asian, or Middle Eastern) are traditionally considered "brown" or "colored."[8] Moreover, money "whitens." As individuals improve their income, education, life style, and wealth, they seem progressively "whiter"; two individuals with the same skin coloring can be seen as different degrees of white or black if one is middle class and the other poor.[9] What matters, above all, is having education, wealth, manners, and well-placed associates, not race.

The situation in New York and London is very different. There, education, income, and culture do not partly "erase" one's blackness. Nor are whites sensitive to shade differences among West Indians. Whatever their achievements or their shade, West Indians of African ancestry are considered "black," and have been subject to prejudice and discrimination of a sort they had not encountered back home. They have come up against racial barriers in housing and employment, and confronted hostility from sections of the white population. And for the first time, they have become acutely and painfully aware that black skin is a significant status marker. In a real sense, West Indians learn to "become black" in America and Britain. "I wasn't aware of my color till I got here," one New York man told me. In nearly identical words, a London migrant said that he had never known he was black until he came to England.

## Different Expectations and Experiences

Although being black is more of a stigma in London and New York than in the Caribbean, the meaning and effects of blackness are not the same for migrants in the two places. Partly it is a matter of expectations. When West Indians left for London in the 1950s and 1960s, they had little idea of the prejudice and discrimination that awaited them. West Indian societies were then British colonies, and they thought of themselves not just as Jamaican, for example, or Trinidadian, but also as British citizens. Brought up with a respect for British culture and people and "a lingering faith in British fairmindedness," most expected to have the right to live and work in Britain and to be treated, as they had been taught, on the basis of merit rather than color.[10] They were in for a rude awakening. They soon realized that to most English people they were, as blacks, considered lower class and inferior to whites. "We had been taught all about British history, the Queen, and that we belonged," one Jamaican man told me. "When I got here I discovered we weren't part of things. My loyalty at age fifteen was to England. I felt that Jamaica was part of England. The shock was to find I was a stranger."

West Indians who came to New York were not so shocked by the racial situation. They knew about American racism before they came; most migrants had learned about it through the mass media as well as from friends and relatives. In quite a few cases, they had seen it first-hand on previous visits. But it is one thing to hear about racial prejudice or even experience it on a short visit and quite another to live with it as a fixed part of one's daily existence. As Mary Waters notes, West Indian immigrants in New York arrived expecting to encounter structural racism—blocked mobility for blacks in the society and a hierarchy in which whites have political and economic power. When they encountered this kind of racism, the people she interviewed were able to handle these situations well, mainly by challenging them. What they were not prepared for was the degree of interpersonal racism they experienced in the United States: "the overarching concern with race in every encounter, the constant role race plays in everyday life, and the subtle experiences that are tinged with racial suspicions and overtones."[11] Indeed, whatever the migrants' expectations of life abroad, the reality of the structure of race relations ultimately determined their experiences as blacks in their new home.

The crucial factor explaining the different meaning and impact of blackness among West Indians in New York and London is that in New York, in contrast to London, there is a large residentially segregated native African American population. Being submerged in a wider African American community has affected West Indian New Yorkers in ways that their London counterparts simply do not encounter. For one thing, West Indians in New York are less visible to the white population than their counterparts in London. When they moved to Britain in the 1950s and 1960s, West Indians, along with immigrants from India and Pakistan, entered a society that, in racial terms, was homogeneous and white. In the course of political debate, in media treatment of topics connected with them, and in statements by public officials, black immigrants were stigmatized as inferior. Immigrant, in fact, became a code word among the English for the large number of nonwhites living in their midst.

Whereas West Indians in London have a history of being seen in the public eye as a problem or threat to the British way of life, in New York they are often seen as part of a sea of anonymous black faces, undifferentiated from the wider African American population. (In 2000, non-Hispanic blacks represented a quarter of New York City's population;

about two-fifths of the city's blacks were foreign-born or children of the foreign-born.)[12] As West Indians have grown in numbers, and become a much larger proportion of black New York, they are increasingly visible to white New Yorkers;[13] yet West Indians still often find themselves lumped with black Americans. Even when other New Yorkers recognize them as West Indian, as foreign, or, as many whites say, "from the islands," West Indians are seen as an ethnic group within the larger black population. And this means being identified with African Americans.

It does not, it should be noted, mean being identified with the large number of Hispanic Caribbeans in the city—a point that requires emphasis and that has bearing on the issue of nomenclature that I raised at the beginning of the chapter. In England, it will be recalled, the term West Indian sounds antiquated, indeed, politically incorrect, and African Caribbean or Afro-Caribbean are preferred. (The British Sociological Association's guide to anti-racist language lists Afro-Caribbean as a term associated with a commitment to anti-racism.)[14] In New York, the category West Indian is commonly used by others and by people from the Commonwealth Caribbean themselves.[15] Although the terms Afro-Caribbean or African Caribbean have the virtue of emphasizing shared race among people of African descent, in New York—unlike in Britain— they encompass people of African ancestry from the Spanish-speaking islands who form separate communities in the city; language as well as differences in historical and political background distinguish the large number of Haitians (as well as Dominicans, Puerto Ricans, and Cubans) from their English-speaking counterparts.[16] In some areas of public life, as Kasinitz notes, the boundaries between English-speaking West Indians and Haitians are blurring, and both groups are considered "black" in New York, whereas immigrants from the Spanish-speaking Caribbean, whatever their phenotype, are generally categorized as "Hispanic."[17]

And there is yet another difference in terminology on the two sides of the Atlantic that requires comment. In the 1970s and 1980s, "black" was widely used in Britain to include people of African, Caribbean, and South Asian origin, a period when it was reserved in the United States for people of African ancestry. The British usage reflected "field experiments which showed [that] white employers treated members of different non-white groups quite similarly, and political exigencies, which implied that a united minority community would be more effective than a divided one."[18] In recent years, British usage has moved in the American direction. As one sociologist notes, there has been "increased attention to the diversity of experiences of ethnicity and 'race' among ethnic minority groups in Britain" and questions about the legitimacy of calling Indian or Bangladeshi Britons "black." Some British scholars continue to use the term black to encompass both South Asians and African Caribbeans; the media also sometimes follow this practice.[19] Yet, increasingly—and commonly—black refers to people of African ancestry, with Asians viewed as not black, as "ambiguous blacks," or as occupying a space between black and white.[20] The sociologist Claire Alexander notes that while she had once felt called upon to explain to an American academic audience that black in the British context included peoples of African and Asian descent, in 2002, "this British peculiarity (to paraphrase Gilroy) would now seem anomalous even within Britain . . . it has come increasingly to refer . . . only to (selected) peoples of African descent."[21] Indeed, research reveals that most Asians in Britain do not think of themselves as black, whereas the use of black among African Caribbeans is prevalent.[22]

If there has been a terminological coming-together, so to speak, between Britain and the United States in defining "black," there is still a profound difference related to demographics in the two countries. In Britain, black may now be "primarily evocative of people of African origin,"[23] but they are immigrants or descendants of immigrants from the Caribbean and Africa who arrived in the second half of the twentieth century. (In 2001, about 10 percent of London's population was black; 4.8 percent were of Caribbean origin, 5.3 percent of African origin, and .8 percent Other.) In the United States, black mainly means African Americans—whose ancestors were brought to this country as slaves many years ago and who represent the bulk of the black population in the nation as a whole as well as in New York.

## Ethnic Identity and Racial Segregation

What are the consequences of being identified with, and suffering the same kind of racial discrimination, as African Americans in New York? And how does this differentiate West Indians' experiences in New York and London? An important difference is that in New York, West Indians' sense of identity is intimately bound up with their relations with African Americans—in a way that obviously is not relevant, and does not happen, in London.

One response to coming to a city with a large native black population is to emphasize their ethnicity to distinguish themselves from, and avoid the stigma associated with, African Americans, especially poor African Americans. Many West Indian New Yorkers assert an ethnic identity—in terms of their country of origin or as West Indian—in order to make a case that they are culturally different from and superior to black Americans, emphasizing their strong work ethic, their valuing of education, and their lack of antisocial behaviors. (The decision to identify as West Indian or Jamaican is situation-specific, and the terms are often interchangeable.)[24] In my research among Jamaican immigrants in New York, I was often told that Jamaicans are more likely to buy homes than American blacks and that they place more value on education and discipline. Many felt that when whites found out they were Jamaican and not African American, they viewed and treated them more favorably. "Once you say something," one man explained, "and they recognize you're not from this country, they treat you a little different."[25] To what extent this is actually the case is hard to say.[26] What is clear, however, is that many West Indian New Yorkers believe it to be true—and the belief itself further bolsters their sense of ethnic pride and distinctiveness and their feeling of superiority to African Americans.

This is in contrast to London where "black" is generally synonymous with West Indians (or Africans), and stressing West Indianness, as David Lowenthal has remarked, is "seldom affirmative."[27] When an Afro-Caribbean television producer in London complains that "here we behave like black Americans in northern cities. Our experience is just the same as that of the blacks who migrated from the South to Chicago," he is getting, I think, at the notion that in Britain, West Indians are the structural equivalents of American blacks; in New York, by contrast, West Indians commonly feel (and are sometimes viewed by others as) superior to African Americans.[28]

Then there is the residential segregation, and general social separation, from whites in New York that have profound implications for the lives of West Indians (and African Americans) there. West Indians, like African Americans, tend to be confined to areas of New York City with large black concentrations, where they are residentially isolated from non-Hispanic whites and most other groups as well. Sociologists have developed a statistical measure of residential segregation, called the index of dissimilarity, that gives the percentage of people in a group who would have to move in order to achieve an even or completely integrated pattern: 100 represents total segregation between two groups, and 0 represents minimum segregation. In 1990, the index of dissimilarity between West Indians and non-Hispanic whites in New York City was 83, almost the same as for African Americans (84). West Indians have carved out distinct enclaves within the larger black sections of the city (in Brooklyn, Queens, and the Bronx), yet, overall, they are not very segregated from African Americans—in 1990, the dissimilarity index comparing West Indians and African Americans (42) was in the mid-moderate range. In fact, West Indians were less segregated from African Americans than from any other group.[29] In analyzing black residential patterns in the city between 1970 and 1990, Arun Peter Lobo and Joseph Salvo describe a process whereby West Indians pioneered the movement into formerly white neighborhoods, to be joined by native blacks looking for housing.[30]

Paradoxically, the extraordinary residential segregation from whites that West Indian New Yorkers experience has had some benefits. For one thing, living out much of their lives apart from the presence of whites has reduced the opportunities for racial tensions and conflicts to develop. When West Indians in New York walk in the street, go to the shops, talk to neighbors, worship, and send their children to school, it is, on the whole, other blacks whom they see and deal with. Said one black Briton: "I love going to New York because I can walk down the street and the place is full of black people."[31]

Although many West Indians distance themselves from African Americans, at the same time strong affinities draw the two groups together, so that West Indians are caught in a welter of contradictory pressures, or cross-pressures, of ethnic separatism and racial identification.[32] That West Indians have a sense of racial, as well as ethnic, identity is not an either/or situation. West Indian immigrants may embrace both their racial and ethnic identities without contradiction, although one identity may be more salient than another depending on the particular context and circumstances. Reuel Rogers notes how most of the West Indian immigrants he interviewed in New York expressed a shared racial group identification, in terms of a sense of awareness and attachment to a racial group, with African Americans.[33] West Indians and African Americans tend to live in the same neighborhoods and sometimes work together, experience similar episodes of racial discrimination in public, and often perceive important social institutions as biased against blacks. Cultural affinities also exist between the two groups—black American popular and religious music, for example, and admiration for American heroes of the civil rights struggle such as Martin Luther King, Jr. West Indians find, as Vickerman observes, that race usually trumps ethnicity. He notes that the longer they live in the United States, and thus the longer they are exposed to racial discrimination, the more they identify with African Americans—even as they still maintain a distinctiveness as West Indians.[34]

As much as London West Indians move in West Indian social circles, they are less insulated from contact with whites. In spite of the fairly dense concentration of West Indians in particular areas and particular streets, there is not the same pattern of residential segregation found in New York. Ceri Peach's analysis of the 1991 census found that the index of dissimilarity for London's black Caribbean population at the enumeration district level (the smallest census unit of about 700 people) was 49 percent; only 3 percent of the black Caribbean population of London lived in enumeration districts in which they formed 30 percent or more of the population.[35] According to another analysis of 1991 census data, over three-quarters of London Afro-Caribbeans lived in areas where whites were the majority population.[36]

In black sections of New York, as one West Indian activist in London pointed out, you can walk through and not see a white face, except passing in a car. "But that's not the case in Britain. We see them every day. We move with them every day."[37] Or as well-known Afro-Caribbean television producer and broadcaster Trevor Phillips said: "When I go to New York to visit my sisters, I can, if I so choose, never speak to someone who is not black. Here [in London] that is not possible."[38] Brixton may be a heavily West Indian neighborhood (in south London), but as Henry Louis Gates notes, "Americans who imagine Brixton to be analogous to Harlem are always surprised to see how large its white population is."[39] In the 1970s, many incidents that London migrants told me to illustrate their experience with racial prejudice involved contacts with whites in the neighborhood—queuing for buses, for example, buying groceries at the corner, speaking to neighbors, or observing fights between local white and black children.[40]

The presence of the large native African American population in New York has affected the way West Indians there participate in the political process. Even though most West Indian immigrants in New York cannot vote because they are not citizens, unlike their English counterparts, they have tended to live, from the very start, in districts where black voters predominated and where they were represented in city, state, and federal legislative bodies by black politicians who spoke for black interests. Gaining political office has taken longer in London, and blacks do not have as much political clout as in New York. Non-Hispanic blacks are the most reliably Democratic of any voting group and a significant component of the electorate in New York City—in 2000, they comprised about a quarter of the city's eligible voters and one-third of Democratic primary voters.[41] As a result, in recent years many high-ranking elected and appointed officials in New York City have been black, and, of course, the city had an African American mayor, David Dinkins, in the early 1990s.

The shared experience of being black in America, and West Indians' identification with African Americans around a "linked racial outlook," provide a basis for solidarity on many issues and coalition building. West Indians often unite with African Americans in a black bloc, especially when black and white interests are seen as being in conflict.[42] By the same token, as Rogers argues, a politically unified black community does not exist on all issues and in all political contexts, partly because West Indians have a different frame of reference than African Americans for making sense of the political world.[43] Increasingly, West Indian politicians in New York City play the ethnic card to appeal to the growing number of West Indian voters, and some local elections have been fought, quite explicitly, between native-born and Caribbean blacks. A recent example was the fight in 2000 between Major Owens (African American) and Una Clarke (Jamaican) in a Brooklyn Democratic primary for Congress (which Owens, the incumbent, won).[44]

Part of the romance with America among black Britons, Henry Louis Gates notes, has to do with a sense that America "has, racially speaking, a critical mass."[45] In fact, West Indian New Yorkers have benefited from political initiatives put in place as a result of the gains African Americans won in the civil rights movement. This is a point that needs to be underscored. Indeed, Una Clarke owed her seat in the City Council to redistricting in Brooklyn in the early 1990s in the wake of the Voting Rights Act. West Indians have also reaped rewards from affirmative action programs and policies designed to assist African Americans in gaining access to government employment as well as entry and scholarships to colleges and universities. In addition to programs promoting black educational achievement, the African American community has provided West Indian New Yorkers, of the first and second generation, with a market for goods and services.[46] There is now a considerable African American middle class. For aspiring West Indian Americans, incorporation into the growing African American middle-class "minority culture of mobility" has also offered strategies for economic mobility, including black professional and fraternal associations and organizations of black students at racially integrated high schools and universities.[47]

There is, however, another side to the story. Being submerged in black America—and living in such highly residentially segregated neighborhoods—brings many disadvantages (see chapter 1). Residential segregation in New York may reduce opportunities for day-to-day conflicts with whites to develop at the neighborhood level, but it also reduces opportunities for friendships with whites in informal settings and for West Indians and whites to become comfortable with each other in noninstitutional and nonwork locations. Listen, again, to Henry Louis Gates, an African American observer of the British scene:

> I'm always struck by the social ease between most blacks and whites on London streets. I was recently near the Brixton market . . . and two men—tall, coal-black, muscle-bound—came loping toward a small young white woman who was walking by herself in the opposite direction. What happened then was—well nothing. The needle on the anxiety meter didn't so much as quiver. Throughout the area, blacks and whites seemed comfortable with one another in a way that most American urbanites simply aren't and never have been.[48]

One might argue that Gates is idealizing the London situation. Many of the young black men of Caribbean origin in Les Back's study of youth clubs in South London referred to instances where white adults with whom they came into contact there held "onto their bags tightly" or "put their heads down and walk[ed] away."[49] Nonetheless, I think Gates is capturing the less tense, and less rigidly segregated, nature of Caribbean neighborhoods in London. Indeed, the kind of friendships, mingling, and intimate dialogues found among black and white London young people—and the development of what Back calls a syncretic working-class youth culture that is neither black nor white—are not a part of New York City's youth scene.[50] Most West Indians in New York live on streets where virtually everybody is black and attend virtually all-black schools in ghetto neighborhoods, whereas in London, their classmates—and their streetmates—are often white.

Britain also offers a more hospitable environment for black-white interracial unions. An analysis of 1990 U.S. and 1991 U.K. census data shows that black Caribbeans in Britain are significantly more likely than their U.S. counterparts to have a white partner: in the United States only 3 percent of foreign-born West Indian men and 2 percent of foreign-born West Indian women had a native white partner; the comparable figures for foreign-born West Indian men and women in Britain were 18 percent and 8 percent, respectively. Among the native born, 12 percent of West Indian men and 9 percent of West Indian women in the United States had a native white partner; in Britain, the figures were 40 percent for native-born West Indian men and 24 percent for native-born West Indian women.[51]

The American racial situation has also shaped scholarship on West Indians so that in the United States, unlike in Britain, their achievements are viewed by the dominant white majority and come to be viewed by West Indians themselves in the context of African Americans. To be sure, this comparison often puts them in a relatively favorable light. In Britain, by contrast, West Indians are measured against the white majority or Asian minorities, which often puts West Indians at a disadvantage.[52] Academic debates about whether U.S. West Indians are an economic success story typically focus on whether they do better than African Americans and, if so, why.[53] In New York City, West Indians' median household income is higher and the percentage of households in poverty is lower than for African Americans. A consistent finding is that West Indian immigrants have higher labor force participation rates than native-born blacks. West Indians' dense social networks connect them to jobs, and they have what Waters calls a "different metric" for judging the worthiness of jobs than African Americans; even low wages in New York look good compared to what is available back home, and West Indians' sense of self is still tied to their status in the home country. Waters also argues that white employers generally prefer foreign over native blacks; they view the latter as less reliable, less productive, and less tractable than immigrants.[54]

That West Indian New Yorkers are constantly compared with African Americans rather than with other groups has a downside, however. It has led to a situation, Kasinitz argues, where scholarship on West

Indians has ignored or minimized the significance of certain features of their economic incorporation. Although researchers have paid much attention to the fact that West Indians are slightly more entrepreneurial than African Americans, they have largely missed the significance of the lack of an autonomous West Indian economic enclave in New York and of West Indians' low self-employment rates compared with those of other immigrant groups in the city. (Low self-employment rates, it should be noted, are something that West Indian New Yorkers share with their London counterparts.)[55] Without an economic enclave—characterized by multilevel structures of coethnic workers, bosses, service providers, and customers—less educated West Indians in both the first and second generations may be at a disadvantage compared with other immigrants who have access to a safety-net for the less fortunate. Also, because African Americans in New York are well represented in public-sector employment, it is not considered particularly noteworthy that West Indians' rates in this sector are also relatively high.[56] Often overlooked is that they have high rates of public-sector employment compared with other immigrant New Yorkers, and Kasinitz suggests that this may partly explain why so many West Indians are involved in electoral politics.[57]

## The Second Generation

So far the analysis has focused on the first or immigrant generation. I have shown how the racial context shapes their experiences in London and New York—particularly the important role of the presence (or absence) of a large, disadvantaged native-born black community. Part of the adjustment to life in America involves coming to terms with America's culture of race, and learning that identification with African Americans is something that, at least on some occasions, they may wish to avoid. This dynamic, of course, is absent in Britain, where post–World War II immigrants of African ancestry and their descendants are generally thought of as *the* nation's blacks. Afro-Caribbeans in London cannot profit from alliances with a large native black community or "piggyback" on gains won by African Americans. At the same time, the racial system in London is less rigid than in New York, where West Indians find themselves more segregated residentially and less likely to intermarry and socialize with whites.

What about the experiences of the second generation? A crucial question is how the structure of race relations in Britain and the United States affects those who were born and raised there. Once again, the presence of the large African American population in New York, and the dynamics of race in America, have led to different identities and interethnic/racial relations and shaped the kinds of questions posed and explored by scholars on the two sides of the Atlantic.

On the American side, a key question—some would say *the* key question—is whether the children of West Indian immigrants will become African American. How they identify themselves therefore takes on special significance. Waters has pointed to three possible paths: the assertion of a strong ethnic identity that involves a considerable amount of distancing from American blacks, an immigrant identity stressing national origins and their own or their parents' experiences in the home country, and an American—that is, an African American—identity, in which they choose to be viewed as black American and do not see their ethnic origins as important to their self-image. As Waters notes, these three categories are ideal types that simplify a more complicated reality. Ethnic and racial identities, as is often noted, are situational, fluid, and contextual—and the categories Waters puts forward are not mutually exclusive and frequently overlap.[58]

Several studies of the West Indian second generation underline these complexities. The second-generation New Yorkers in Sherri-Ann Butterfield's ethnographic study saw themselves as both black and as West Indian; whether they emphasized a racial or ethnic identity depended on the circumstances or the audience. Many engaged in code-switching, using West Indian accents with their parents and American English with their peers. One respondent said that during her high school years, when she (like many other second-generation West Indians) felt a strong pressure to conform to being "black American in school," she was "black by day and . . . West Indian by night."[59] Vickerman describes second-generation individuals who shifted back and forth between "American," "black," and "West Indian" in discussing their identity. Nearly all of the second-generation individuals he interviewed saw themselves as partially West Indian—specifically as West Indian blacks. Indeed, they were more conscious of race as a life-shaping issue than their parents because they had grown up in the American, rather than Caribbean, racial system and had only a second-hand understanding of West Indian culture. At the same time as they became incorporated into the African American community, they saw their West Indian identity and cultural values as setting them apart from generalized negative views of blacks.[60]

How members of the second generation in New York identify themselves is rooted in structural circumstances. Waters found that those from middle-class backgrounds and families involved in ethnic organizations and churches were most likely to be strongly ethnic-identified.[61] Middle-class second-generation West Indians, according to Butterfield, seek to avoid identification with poor and working-class African Americans—but also with poor and working-class West Indians—as they struggle to maintain a middle-class identity in the face of persistent negative stereotyping of blacks by other New Yorkers. Gender makes a difference in identity formation, too. Second-generation West Indian men feel racial exclusion more strongly than women and thus tend to identify more strongly with African Americans.[62] Residential patterns are also involved. A West Indian identity, as Butterfield suggests, may be nurtured and reinforced among second-generation New Yorkers when they grow up and, as many do, continue to live in neighborhoods with a critical mass of West Indians.[63]

Identities can influence economic outcomes, and this leads to the segmented assimilation perspective, which has been so dominant in second-generation studies in the United States; it predicts divergent outcomes for today's second generation, depending on the human and social capital of immigrant parents, location in urban space, skin color, and the protective capacities of the ethnic community.[64] In the segmented assimilation view, children of immigrants growing up in inner cities in the midst of poor native minorities are at risk of being influenced by the oppositional stances said to prevail among inner-city youth. In the case of second-generation West Indians who strongly assert an ethnic identity, the argument is that this identity, as well as involvement in the ethnic community, can reinforce attitudes and behavior that contribute to success in school and shield them from the negative features of American—and black American—youth culture.[65] In Waters's study, the young people she labels the "American identified" mostly came from poorer families and attended dangerous, substandard, and virtually all-black schools. Their experiences with racial discrimination and their perceptions of blocked social mobility led many to reject their parents' immigrant dream—and to be receptive to the black American peer culture of their neighborhoods and schools that emphasizes racial solidarity and opposition to school rules and authorities, and sees doing well academically as "acting white." Such an adversarial stance is often a recipe for failure.

Recent critiques of the segmented assimilation perspective have challenged these gloomy predictions, pointing out, among other things, that identification with African Americans need not—indeed often does not —lead to downward assimilation for the second generation and can actually provide avenues and resources for upward mobility (see chapter 2). What is important here is not whether the predictions of the segmented assimilation model are right or wrong. It is that the perspective reflects, once more, the view that the fate of the West Indian second generation is closely tied to becoming incorporated into black America. On this point virtually all scholarly observers agree: given the nature of racial divisions in America, assimilation into black America (including the growing black middle class) is, at least at the current moment, an inevitability for most second-generation West Indians in New York. This is so even if, at the same time, they embrace cultural elements from their West Indian heritage.[66] (Following Richard Alba and Victor Nee, assimilation, as I use the term, does not require the disappearance of ethnicity or ethnic markers—it is not a zero-sum game; it refers to the decline of an ethnic distinction, in that the ethnic distinction attenuates in salience and the occurrences for which it is relevant diminish in number and contract to fewer domains of social life.)[67] What is at issue is the consequences of this incorporation—not that it takes place.

Whatever the second generation's economic outcomes and self-identities, the question remains as to how others will view them. Will they be recognized as West Indian? As black ethnics? Or as black American? At present, as Vilna Bashi Bobb and Averil Clarke note, second-generation West Indians have difficulty marshaling their West Indianness in a society that racializes black people with little regard to ethnicity. Or as Vickerman puts it, American society has a powerful tendency to homogenize blacks.[68] Whether these trends will continue largely depends on the future of the color line in America. It may be, as some suggest, that New Yorkers will become more sensitive to ethnic distinctions within the black community, particularly if continued mass Caribbean immigration sustains, and probably increases, the proportion of Caribbeans in the city's black population. Ongoing replenishment of the West Indian immigrant community may not only enhance its visibility and chip away at notions of a monolithic "blackness," but also keep alive an ethnic awareness among the second and third generations in a way that did not happen in the past. From the 1930s to the 1960s, migration from the Caribbean dwindled to a trickle; in contrast, many of today's second and third generations will grow up alongside immigrants of the same age and in communities where sizable numbers retain ties to the home country.

Yet if, as some predict, the United States is moving toward a black/nonblack racial order, then the West Indian second—and third—generation will have fewer options. "Because being black," Waters writes, "involves a racial identity, people with certain somatic features—dark skin, kinky hair, and so on—are defined as blacks by others regardless of their own preferences for identification. . . . For most nonblack Americans the image of blacks as poor, unworthy, and dangerous is still very potent, despite the success of many black Americans and the growth of a sizeable black middle class."[69] Without an accent or other clues to immediately telegraph their ethnic status to others, second-generation West Indians, in the words of Kasinitz and his colleagues, are likely to fade to black.[70] Those who continue to identify with their ethnic backgrounds are aware that unless they are active in conveying their ethnic identities, they are seen as African Americans and that their status as "blacks" is all that matters in encounters with whites. The crux of the problem is that being seen as black American, they are subject to the same kind of racial prejudice and exclusion as black Americans.[71]

In London, there is, of course, no question of the second generation assimilating into a large native black population. Nor are blacks as segregated from whites as they are in New York (and the United States as a whole). Partly for these reasons, the experiences and dilemmas of British-born African Caribbeans are different from those of their cousins in New York, and the scholarly literature on them has a different emphasis as well. No concept akin to segmented assimilation has arisen in England, where scholars instead write of hybridity, creolization, and the emergence of syncretic cultures bringing together white and black.[72] African Caribbean communities, in the words of one social scientist, have been defined as outward looking, moving into mainstream culture, and redefining notions of Britishness.[73] There is no notion of West Indian ethnic communities and networks acting as a source of protection from a potentially corrupting native minority culture. Indeed, when reasons are sought by social workers and others for social problems among African Caribbean youth in Britain—underachieving children, delinquency, or "dysfunctionality"—West Indian homeland culture and institutions, particularly lone parent families, are often among the factors blamed.[74]

As for identities, it is often pointed out that African Caribbeans born in London, like those in New York, are less likely than their parents to identify themselves, or see their primary identity, in terms of their island origins. Yet encounters with discrimination lead many to express doubts about or feel uncomfortable describing themselves as "British." To the extent that the West Indian New York second generation understand "American" (or "real" American) to mean native white American, something similar is going on across the Atlantic.[75] At the same time, many second-generation West Indian New Yorkers have trouble or resist thinking of themselves as American because in New York, non-Hispanic Americans with visible African ancestry are African Americans. For the London second generation, the difficulty with identifying as British has to do with what one sociologist calls the "racist identity riddle"—that blackness and Englishness are mutually exclusive identities. The second generation in London form their identities, in other words, in a context in which many whites do not accept them as British —or, as one youth said, they think that "'black English' people do not exist."[76]

The response of many young people in London has been to focus on their blackness as a basis for identification, with language and music playing a particularly important role. Some resist notions that they are British or English and emphasize their Caribbean origins and being black: "I don't want to be classified on the British sides" is how one young man in Back's study put it.[77] Others see themselves as British, yet also stress their black identity. The London youth in Alexander's study felt they could only describe themselves as "British" if they made further qualifications; they saw themselves as black first, with views of nationhood secondary. "I do see myself as British," said one young woman, whose parents were from the Caribbean. "But I see myself as Black British. There is a difference. You see I've got my identity and culture about being black. It's very important to me; it's foremost than being British."[78] It is not, as Back argues, that black youth are suffering from a crisis of identity; rather, they are seeking to actively "define what their identities are and what their culture means."[79] Or as Alexander notes, being black "is at once a demand for inclusion within the bounds of 'British' identity and a celebration of 'hybridity.'"[80] "Well, I am British, I was born in London," said a young woman, "but I am not the same as the English people, it's like I am a different kind of English —a different way. I mean we have different ways of—a different culture. But I am still British."[81] For most of the second generation, and as Stuart Hall argues for the third generation, it is a question of multiple identities—knowing, as Hall states, that "they come from the Caribbean, . . . that they are Black, . . . that they are British. They want to speak from all three identities. They are not prepared to give up on any of them."[82]

The process of working out their identities in London takes place in communities where there is much more mixing with whites than in New York City neighborhoods. Even in London neighborhoods where black young people are a significant, even dominant, presence, there are usually many whites. Young people of Afro-Caribbean origin often socialize with white youth in school playgrounds, youth clubs, and street corners, where they come to know each other and may develop close friendships. Ethnographies of working-class areas in South London indicate that black-white friendships are common and unremarkable, and they report cultural borrowing, exchange, and creolization between black and white working-class youth—in speech, modes of dress, and music.[83] Back argues that the young people living in a South London council estate he studied were creating syncretic cultures that were neither black nor white—what he calls new ethnicities. As one black youth he knew said: "It's like if you are white living in a black area you'll have a little black in you, and if you are black living in a white area you will have a little white in you."[84]

In New York City neighborhoods, the West Indian second generation has little, if any, contact with whites in public schools or other local arenas, where they interact mainly with other West Indians and African Americans. To the extent that friendships develop between second-generation West Indian and white young people, they are most likely to occur among the middle or upper-middle class who live in more integrated suburban areas or attend magnet schools, or, later on, when they enter college or university. Even in these settings, friendship groups and social circles tend to be highly segregated by race. The syncretic or hybrid cultures in the process of creation in New York City that involve West Indian young people are developing in the context of interactions with other first- and second-generation immigrant groups and native minorities. American scholars are becoming more sensitive to the dynamic possibilities of these hybrid youth cultures—and the limits of an exclusive focus on assimilation or a view of assimilation that fails to appreciate how the second generation are remaking not only the mainstream but native minority communities as well. Vickerman speaks of cross-fertilization occurring between second-generation West Indians and African Americans on the level of popular culture, particularly music.[85] Kasinitz and his colleagues write of how the "city abounds in clubs where African American hip hop has been fused with East Indian and West Indian influences into new musical forms. . . . African American young people dance to Jamaican dance hall and imitate Jamaican patois, even as West Indian youngsters learn African American slang. . . . Whether one looks at the music in dance clubs, the eclectic menus in restaurants, or the inventive use of slang on the streets, one cannot help but be impressed by the creative potential that second generation and minority young people are contributing to New York today."[86]

Finally, there is the role of intermarriage. The ease and frequency of relations with whites in working-class communities in London is reflected in the high rates of intermarriage—rates, as I noted, that are far higher than in the United States. In Britain as a whole, the Fourth National Survey of Ethnic Minorities (conducted in 1994) found that half of British-born Caribbean men (and a third of women) who were married or cohabiting had a white partner. For two out of five children with a Caribbean mother or father (who were living with both parents), their other parent was white.[87] Thus, in that most intimate arena, the family, many of the second (and third) generation in Britain have grown up with a white parent, and, in adulthood, have a white partner. Whether the high rates of black-white unions are contributing to the erosion of the color line is a key question. Much depends on the range of options available to the children—and whether the dominant society automatically assigns them the heritage of the parent who belongs to the more stigmatized group or, alternatively, allows them to take on the identity of either parent or a separate biracial identity.[88] The jury is still out on this question. Some argue that young people of mixed-parentage in Britain are, invariably, viewed as black or nonwhite, whatever their own preferences. Others point out that these young people may assert an identity as mixed-race, which is recognized, or at least not challenged, by their peers.[89] Since black-white unions are steadily on the rise in Britain, where they constitute a growing sector of British society —and are increasing in the United States as well—this is obviously an important topic for research. In the United States another crucial question is on the table: the extent of intermarriage between the children of West Indian immigrants and African Americans, and the impact for identities and social relations.[90]

Although London, as an African American journalist living there notes, may be more at ease with integration than New York, and mixed race friendships and couples more common, it is well to remember that London is not yet a postracial city (or Britain a postracial society).[91] Racial prejudice and racial inequalities, unfortunately, persist in London, and young people of Caribbean origin continue to encounter racism in numerous contexts.[92] Nevertheless, the lives of the West Indian second generation in London, like those of their parents, are much more intimately involved with whites than in New York—where interactions with African Americans remain of paramount importance.[93] And to come back to the statement with which the chapter began, it is clear that, whether we look at first- or second-generation West Indians, the meaning and effects of blackness vary considerably in the two cities and countries. Because race is so central to the lives of West Indians in both London and New York, it also inevitably comes into the analysis in the next chapter, where I begin to sketch out a more general framework for analyzing the West Indian migrant experience in comparative perspective.

# 6

# Place Matters

## Comparative Perspectives on the West Indian Migrant Experience

The responses of West Indians to life abroad, it is already clear, are neither inevitable nor "natural." Much depends on where they move—something that a comparative perspective brings out in a powerful way. I have discussed the impact of the racial context in London and New York, but many other differences in the two places also affect the experiences of West Indians there.

In a recent article on cities as contexts for immigrant incorporation, Caroline Brettell lays out a broad range of features in what, broadly speaking, can be called structures of incorporation. In addition to the character of racial and ethnic relations, these include the city's history as a receiving area for immigrants (or particular groups of immigrants) and the extent to which it is dominated by a single immigrant population; the spatial distribution of immigrants and housing stock; and the structure of the political system and the urban labor market.[1] When cities are located in different nation-states—as in the case of London and New York—there are national policies and institutions to consider as well as the nature of the welfare state.

Important as these contextual features are, additional factors need to be considered in comparing immigrant groups in different urban and national destinations. The characteristics of the migration stream—its size as well class, gender, and age composition—are obviously critical. There is the timing of the migration—the historical period of mass migration—which helps to shape reactions and adaptations in the new setting. For international migration, there is the legal context in which it takes place in terms of the freedom of, or alternatively barriers to, movement. Also relevant is distance from the home society which, even in the era of jet planes and electronic communications, can make a difference.

Just how these various factors operate and interact in the case of West Indian migrants in various destinations is the concern of this chapter, where I begin to elaborate a framework for understanding the West Indian migration experience in comparative perspective. The focus is on West Indians in New York and London—in particular, on Jamaicans, the group I know best from my research in both cities as well as in Jamaica itself. This, of course, is a cross-national comparison, yet within the *same* nation, there are also important regional/urban differences that have not received sufficient attention. [2] To get at these dynamics, I also briefly sketch out some of the ways that different cities in the United States provide particular contexts for the reception and incorporation of West Indian immigrants.

## The Legal Context and Historical Period of Migration to London and New York

The Jamaican migration to London and New York has taken place in different legal contexts; the two movements have different histories as well. The migration to London in the postwar years was the only mass inflow of Jamaicans (or West Indians) there (or anywhere else in Britain) in the twentieth century; it was of rather short duration; and it was characterized by the right of free entry. On each point, the exact opposite obtains in New York.

The seeds for the mass Jamaican migration to Britain were sown during the Second World War, when some 8,000 West Indians (mainly Jamaican) were recruited as ground crew in the Royal Air Force and a few hundred for munitions factories in northwest England.[3] The beginning of the West Indian postwar migration is usually reckoned from the 1948 arrival of the S.S. *Empire Windrush,* which brought the first large group of migrants to Britain from the West Indies—492 in all—after the Second World War.[4] However, it was not until the early 1950s that the migration truly gained momentum and became, in effect, a mass movement. In 1951, the Caribbean-born population in Britain was tiny, only a little over 17,000; by 1966, it had grown to 269,000, more than half of them Jamaican and over half living in London.[5] The period of most rapid growth was from 1955 to 1962; by the late 1960s, the movement had slowed to a trickle, and by 1974, the whole cycle of primary immigration from the Caribbean was over.[6] Since then the African

Caribbean population has grown through increases in the British-born population.

Until 1962, there was basically an open admissions policy for people from the British Caribbean. The British Nationality Act of 1948 had granted all citizens of the colonies and the Commonwealth unrestricted entry and the right to live and work in Britain. For Jamaicans wishing to move to England, it was only necessary to obtain a birth certificate in order to get a passport which described them as "British subjects and citizens of the United Kingdom and Colonies."[7] After the passage of the Commonwealth Immigrants Act in 1962, the right of free entry ended. Only Jamaicans (and other West Indians) qualifying as dependents of migrants living in Britain or who obtained one of a quota of work vouchers issued by the Ministry of Labour could move there. Not surprisingly, the number of West Indian migrants soon plummeted.

Unlike in Britain, the recent mass movement to the United States from Jamaica, and the rest of the West Indies, was not the first large wave in the twentieth century; the first wave began a few years after 1900 and peaked in the late 1910s and early 1920s. In 1930, the census counted close to 100,000 foreign-born blacks in the United States, the vast majority West Indian; more than half of all black immigrants lived in New York City.[8] Only small numbers trickled into the United States during the 1930s and 1940s. In 1952, the McCarran-Walter Act cut off legal immigration for all but a handful of West Indians by restricting the use of "home country" quotas by colonial subjects and reducing the colonies to quotas of 100 a year. Indeed, the 1952 restrictions were a factor behind the redirection of West Indian migration to Britain at the time.

Shortly after Britain shut down as a migrant destination, the United States reopened its doors. The Hart-Celler immigration reforms of 1965 made it possible for West Indians to come in large numbers once again. Whereas only 8,335 Jamaicans officially migrated to the United States between 1961 and 1965, between 1966 and 1970, 62,676 did so; in the period 1981 to 1985, the number increased to 100,560.[9] After several decades of heavy migration, the Jamaican foreign-born population in the United States stood at 513,228 in 2000; together with the foreign-born from Trinidad and Tobago, Guyana, Barbados, the Bahamas, Dominica, St. Vincent, and Antigua-Barbuda, the figure was about 1.1 million. Half of these West Indian immigrants resided in New York State, the overwhelming majority in New York City.[10] According to the

2000 census, 179,000 foreign-born Jamaicans lived in the city, about double the number present in 1980.[11]

That New York had already experienced a large West Indian migration earlier in the century meant that many long-time immigrants and their children were established in the city when the recent influx began in the late 1960s and early 1970s—although how important this was for the new arrivals is hard to say. For some, family members from the first-wave were on hand to offer assistance at the outset. Also, there were a number of island-based voluntary organizations that had formed early in the twentieth century and had persisted and even grown in the 1940s and 1950s.[12] Yet by the late 1960s, most of the children (and grandchildren) of the early-twentieth-century immigrants had become incorporated into the African American community, which overwhelmingly dominated black New York. In 1960, New York's estimated 67,000 foreign-blacks (presumably most from the West Indies) were only 6 percent of the city's black population, down from 24 percent in 1920, at the time of the first wave (see Table 2.1). Moreover, as Kasinitz argues, because the first-wave West Indian immigrants played down their ethnicity, and emphasized their identification with African Americans, in public activities, and because their numbers were relatively small, the earlier West Indian community was much less visible than it is today.[13]

Then there is the duration of the post–World War II movements. The recent mass West Indian migration to the United States has lasted much longer than the influx to Britain—already more than thirty-five years, and it shows no signs of stopping.[14] Not surprisingly, the U.S. (and New York) West Indian population is much larger than Britain's (and London's)—whether one includes immigrants alone or adds the second generation.

The continued migration affects more than sheer numbers. That new recruits keep coming to New York, while the movement to Britain basically stopped about thirty years ago, has implications for processes of incorporation. Recent immigrants bring a continual infusion of people steeped in West Indian ways and culture and who maintain close ties to their communities of origin. Compared to Britain, perpetual immigration in the United States may well expand the relative influence of the first generation in creating an "ethnic culture" and in keeping alive transnational ties to home communities. In New York, today's second and third generation are growing up alongside recent immigrants of the same age, something that does not occur in London—and that generally did not occur in New York either from the 1930s to the 1960s.[15]

There is yet another way that the particular historical period of the migrations to Britain and the United States makes a difference. How migrants evaluate their new home depends on their basis of comparison: Jamaica was a different place in the 1950s than in the 1970s, 1980s, and 1990s. Among other things, Jamaican independence in 1962, and subsequent political changes, have brought new leaders, new social programs, expanded mobility opportunities, and new expectations. There is less stigma attached to being dark-skinned and more pride in "things Jamaican." "When I left Jamaica in the 1950s," Stuart Hall has written:

> it was a society which did not and could not have acknowledged itself to be largely black. When I went back to Jamaica at the end of the sixties and in the early seventies . . . it had passed through the most profound cultural revolution. . . . It was not any longer trying to be something else, trying to match up to some other image, trying to be something which it could not. . . . You know the biggest shock for me was listening to Jamaican radio. I couldn't believe my ears that anybody would be quite so bold as to speak patois, to read the news in that accent. My entire education, my mother's whole career, had been specifically designed to prevent anybody at all, and me in particular, from reading anything of importance in that language.[16]

Since the 1950s, Jamaica has also experienced devastating economic downturns and crises and, in recent years, a rising crime wave. The society has been inundated with cultural influences from the United States—owing to the increasing availability of television, the expansion of the tourist industry, and the growing number of migrants from abroad on visits or return trips. "The interpenetration of the cultures and economies of the Caribbean and the United States," Waters writes in relation to exports of American ideas about race, "means that media images of the beating of Rodney King are shown constantly on Jamaican television. Whites from suburban New York make comments about black laziness as they wait for their bags at the Kingston airport, and little children called niggers on playgrounds in Queens tell their grannies in Trinidad about it on the phone that night."[17]

Technology and transportation have been revolutionized since the

1950s in ways that not only make it easier for people in the Caribbean to learn about life abroad before they leave—but also for migrants to maintain transnational ties afterward. In the 1950s, before chartered air flights assumed a dominant role in the early 1960s, most migrants traveled to England by boat. The time of the journey—sometimes as long as eighteen days—varied depending on whether the ship went directly to England or, like many of the Italian liners, landed at Genoa, after which migrants had to take a train to Calais and then cross the Channel to Dover.[18]

The post-1965 movement to the United States has taken place in the jet age, when New York is only a few hours away by plane. Over time, airline travel has become relatively less expensive, as well. In my New York study in the early 1980s, all but one of the forty Jamaican migrants interviewed had visited Jamaica since emigrating, the vast majority having been back in the last three years. A few visited every year; some went back every other year; and most had returned several times since they had come to New York.[19] Unfortunately, I did not ask the people I interviewed in London in the 1970s about visits to Jamaica, but a study of over a hundred West Indians in a Midlands city conducted at around the same time found that only 36 percent had visited the Caribbean since coming to England.[20] Now that flights from London to Jamaica have gotten cheaper, the frequency of visits has probably increased. Indeed, the Fourth National Survey of Ethnic Minorities, conducted in 1994, found that 44 percent of the Caribbean respondents in Britain, including many born there, had visited their family's country of origin in the last five years.[21]

Not only has the migration to New York occurred in the jet age, but also in an era of electronic communications. Faxes, videotapes, and e-mail—these methods of staying in touch across borders were, of course, unknown in the 1950s and early 1960s during the migration to Britain, and in the earlier years of the recent influx to the United States as well. Migrants in London I met in the 1970s usually had their own phones; the problem was that their relatives in Jamaica often did not. In the late 1960s, when I was doing fieldwork in a rural Jamaican village, telephone lines had not yet reached the community—and the only kind of "instantaneous communication" was by telegram, filtered through the not so discrete eyes of the village postmistress. Migrants in England—and many people in the community had relatives in England—communicated by letter. Today, many villagers have phones. With various kinds of international plans, and prepaid phone cards, it has become inexpensive to call Jamaica, whether from New York or London.

Of course, not all Jamaican New Yorkers can readily visit home. Despite cheap fares, it is still costly for people with modest salaries. Moreover, for those without proper documents, a visit home is risky—since it might turn out to be a one-way trip. And so we come back to the issue of the legal context for immigration. Following Ramón Grosfoguel's analysis, Jamaican migration to the United States is from a nation-state rather than a colonial territory, as in the British case prior to 1962, and is subject to a host of regulations that restrict who is eligible for legal entry.[22] The immigration reforms enacted in the United States in 1965 allowed many more people from the former British Caribbean territories to move there, but they set up strict limits. Initially, there was a 120,000 annual quota for the Western Hemisphere, with no per country limit, but in 1976, quotas of 20,000 immigrants per country were put in place for the Western Hemisphere, as was a preference system with family reunification and occupational categories. (Spouses, parents, and minor children of U.S. citizens were, and still are, not subject to this numerical restriction.) The entire process of getting an immigrant visa has been difficult, complex, and costly—and can take a long time. Those unable to get an immigrant visa often try another route: they travel to the United States on temporary visas and become illegal immigrants, or in immigrant parlance "visa overstayers," by failing to leave when their visas expire.

In London in the 1950s, there was no such thing as an illegal West Indian immigrant; in New York, several decades later, thousands of Jamaicans and other West Indians were in this status, without the proper documents. Undocumented immigrants, as an extensive literature shows, experience a host of difficulties on account of their illegal status, among them vulnerability in the labor market and inability to gain access to certain government benefits. As mentioned, they may be afraid to visit home in case they cannot return. The one man in my New York study who had not visited Jamaica since arrival had only received a green card the week before the interview; previously, he had been afraid to chance a trip to Jamaica, in case he was unable to return.

Undocumented immigrants obviously are not U.S. citizens, but neither are many of those who obtained immigrant visas and have permanent resident status. Again, this is a difference from Britain in the 1950s, when Jamaicans were British citizens on arrival, with all the rights and privileges that this entailed, including the ability to vote in elections. According to U.S. law, permanent resident aliens can obtain citizenship through the process of naturalization, usually after approximately five years of residence in the United States. (Applicants must show they can read and write simple words and phrases in English, have knowledge of U.S. government and history, and good moral character, and pay a fee that, in 2004, was $320.) Immigrant New Yorkers without citizenship cannot vote in city, state, and national elections, are ineligible for some federal government positions, do not qualify for certain social welfare provisions, and can, under certain circumstances, be deported. Substantial numbers of Jamaican New Yorkers are not citizens, either because they are undocumented, have not been permanent residents for five years, or for various reasons, choose not to naturalize. In 2002, 45 percent of the foreign-born Jamaicans in the United States as a whole had naturalized, the rates, not surprisingly, much higher for those who had been in the country for fifteen years or more.[23]

## Characteristics of the Migrant Flows to London and New York

Who moves—the composition of immigrant flows—is obviously a critical factor in any comparison of migrants in different locations. So is sheer size of the flows. In the heyday of the migration to Britain, before restrictions were enacted, the annual net inflow of Jamaicans was huge —soaring to nearly 30,000 in 1960 and 39,000 in 1961 in the rush to beat the ban.[24] By comparison, even in the peak years of Jamaican immigration to the United States in the 1980s, the average annual legal inflow was about 20,000.[25] Yet these yearly flows need to be placed in the context of the total movement, which ended in Britain after the introduction of immigration controls and is still going strong in the United States. The number of Caribbean-born people in Britain peaked in 1971, at 304,000, and has been in decline since.[26] In 2000, after three decades of heavy immigration, almost twice as many West Indian immigrants lived in New York City alone, and more than three times as many in the United States as a whole.

The difference in admissions regulations in Britain and the United States also helps account for the class composition of the two streams. Because moving to the United States was harder than moving to Britain prior to 1962, it has been argued that the Jamaican immigration to

Britain then may have been less skilled than the stream to the United States.[27] Although there has been a tendency for Jamaican immigration to the United States to become less skilled over time, overall the flow to the United States has included a higher percentage of professionals and nonmanual workers than the immigrant stream to Britain in the 1950s and early 1960s.

The class composition of the migrant stream has implications for, among other things, immigrants' occupational placement and success. It is, I would argue, an important factor accounting for the relatively high percentage of Jamaican immigrants in New York in managerial and professional occupations. According to the 1990 census, 21 percent of Jamaican women and 13 percent of Jamaican men in New York City in the labor force who had arrived in the 1980s were in managerial and professional occupations. Figures available for Jamaicans (in 1966), who had been in Greater London about the same amount of time, show a much smaller proportion in professional and managerial jobs—14 percent of Jamaican women and 2 percent of Jamaican men.[28]

Another difference in the two inflows is the pattern of male-female migration, a topic I take up in the next chapter, where the focus is on gender. However, available figures indicate that the age composition of the Jamaican flows to Britain and the United States was fairly similar; both were primarily movements of younger working-age adults and their children, with relatively small proportions over the age of forty-five and even fewer over sixty-five.[29]

## *The Context of Reception: London and New York*

It is not just who moves—and how—but where migrants settle that makes a difference in how they experience and react to life abroad. The context of the urban destination encompasses a broad range of features —from various social and political institutions to the structure of economic opportunities and the character of racial and ethnic relations. A full analysis of all these features is beyond the scope of this chapter or indeed this book; rather, I consider a few of the features as a way to begin to see how the context of the receiving area matters. In the next chapter, I discuss the structure of occupational opportunities, particularly as they influence women's jobs, and although issues pertaining to the racial context come up here, these of course were discussed at length in chapter 5.

One important difference in the context of reception and incorporation relates to the level of development of the welfare state.[30] Britain
may be a relatively anemic welfare society in contrast to other western
European countries, but compared to the United States, its provisions
are more generous.[31] This was even more so at the time West Indian
migrants arrived in Britain, before the dismantling of many welfare programs by the Thatcher administration. Bear in mind, too, that as colonial migrants West Indians had access to the benefits available to British
citizens. Consider two important benefits: health care and housing. The
National Health Service in Britain may not be ideal, but it provides a
cushion that New York West Indians do not have. Indeed, in 2001, 28
percent of Jamaican immigrants in the United States (149,000 people)
did not have health insurance, a figure that doubtless includes many living in New York City.[32] Unlike their cousins in London, Jamaican New
Yorkers have to worry about finding jobs that provide health insurance
or, if unsuccessful, negotiate the complex bureaucratic requirements
involved in obtaining even minimal government health care. In certain
periods, many legal immigrants have even faced the possibility of losing
access to publicly funded health-care programs, like Medicaid.[33]

Housing is another area where London Jamaicans have benefited
more from government assistance. To be sure, intense housing shortages
in postwar London added to the difficulties of finding decent housing
when Jamaicans arrived in the 1950s; many white landlords were unwilling to take black tenants or imposed higher rents on black migrants;
and council housing not only was in short supply but newly arrived
migrants also did not qualify (in the borough of Lambeth, for example,
there was a three-year residency requirement). Those who did obtain
council housing in the 1960s and 1970s often ended up in inferior
accommodation, partly due to the systems for allocation.[34] Still, the fact
is that many Jamaicans did obtain council housing, and the subsequent
improvement in West Indians' housing conditions, Cross and Entzinger
argue, was largely because of a major move into publicly owned dwell-
ings.[35] In 1974, 26 percent of the West Indians in a national survey of
ethnic minorities rented council housing; twenty years later, in a similar
survey, one-third of the Caribbean households (including British-born)
were council tenants and 15 percent of the Caribbean home owners
lived in properties that they had previously rented from the local
authority. (The 1980 Housing Act offered local authority tenants the
right to buy their accommodations at subsidized rates.)[36] In New York,

Jamaicans had no choice but to go on the open market in looking for accommodation, which has become steadily more expensive in a city that has one of the tightest housing markets (and among the highest rents and house prices) in the nation. Hardly any Jamaican immigrants live in public housing, which, in 2002, had a waiting list of over 100,000 families and an average wait of eight years for an apartment; according to the 1996 Housing and Vacancy Survey, only 3 percent of foreign-born non-Hispanic blacks in New York City lived in public housing compared to 26 percent of native-born blacks.[37]

Another difference concerns the structure of educational opportunities in New York and London. In my earlier writings, I argued that New York offered a wider array of college and university options in the vast network of colleges in the City University of New York (CUNY) and State University of New York (SUNY) systems as well as affirmative action programs—that have not been used in Britain—designed to assist the native black population. Large numbers of West Indians have gone to one of CUNY's eleven senior or six community colleges; some have gained entry and scholarships to elite colleges and universities in the nation, many helped by admissions procedures designed to increase diversity in their student bodies.[38] Nationwide, at the time of my research in New York and London, there were pronounced differences in rates of enrollment in higher education. In 1980, about half of high school graduates in the United States went directly to college; in 1979 in Britain, the percentage of school leavers going directly on to higher education was just 12 percent.

In general, American education has a less rigid hierarchical structure than Britain's, and the higher educational system is more open and flexible. One of the best things about America to many of the West Indian immigrant teachers in Waters's study was the availability of college for anyone graduating from high school. "In the British system," said one Grenadian teacher who had moved to New York as an adult, "there are not enough slots at the high school level, and then to go on to college. . . . if you haven't studied from day one and put in your hours of homework and what have you in study, then by the time you take the exam you won't be ready. . . . Whereas here in America you can basically slide through almost twelve years and then get into a college [a two-year community college], do fantastically well, and then transfer to another college [a four-year institution]."[39] In New York, it is possible, and not uncommon, to start out at a two-year CUNY community college (open to any high school graduate), earn some credits, and then move on to a four-year institution. Reflecting the city's ethnic and racial diversity, CUNY is now a majority-minority institution; the student body is almost three-quarters nonwhite (and about a third black).[40]

With regard to less diverse U.S. colleges and universities, although affirmative action programs have been under attack, the institutions are still under pressure (and are legally allowed) to consider race in admissions procedures to achieve diversity in their student bodies. Widened access of black students to elite institutions in recent years has clearly benefited West Indians. A 1999 survey of freshmen at thirty-five selective colleges and universities in the United States found that blacks with immigrant origins were substantially overrepresented among black freshmen.[41] (These selective institutions, it should be noted, included four historically black colleges—which do not exist in Britain.) In New York City, the path to elite higher education has been helped by Prep for Prep, a privately funded program, that since the early 1980s has provided an avenue of mobility for more than 2,500 selected young people from minority backgrounds; they receive intensive academic training in preparation for admissions to leading boarding schools and independent schools in New York City.[42] Many of the black students in the program are first- or second-generation West Indians.

Although New York continues to offer more opportunities for higher education than London, the difference has become less pronounced than it was several decades ago. The proportion going directly to higher education in Britain is still under 50 percent, but the gap with the United States (where the rate is over 60 percent) has narrowed as opportunities for higher education have expanded in Britain. It needs to be remembered, too, that higher education in Britain has been less expensive than in the United States, where costs of public higher education have risen in recent years, and fees in the private sector have skyrocketed. The City University of New York, tuition-free before 1976, cost $4,000 a year in 2003 for a full-time student at a four-year college, and tuition was more than six times that amount at elite private institutions. British universities, by comparison, have been, at least until recently, a bargain—with a flat-rate tuition fee of about $2,000 in 2003, although recent legislation will allow universities to charge up to about $5,500 beginning in 2006.

Below the college level, the picture in New York is bleaker, in large part owing to racial inequalities. To be sure, the inner-city schools that

Jamaican immigrants' children attended in London when they arrived were far from problem-free—in the 1970s, various reports noted the high rates of pupil turnover, absenteeism, and other features associated with less than satisfactory educational progress.[43] In New York City, however, the neighborhood public schools that Jamaicans' children are slated to attend are more racially segregated and plagued by more serious drug and crime problems than was (or is) the case in London. On the one hand, as Waters notes, the New York City public schools offer a wide variety of subjects and activities as well as special programs for students of low abilities and poor academic preparation; on the other hand, many of the schools Jamaicans attend are marked by lack of control and discipline, the presence of weapons and fear, racial segregation and prejudice, and large size and the resulting bureaucracy.[44]

These problems mean that Jamaicans in New York City who can afford it look for alternatives to the public school system, typically to the extensive parochial system that developed in New York to service the city's white Catholic immigrants of an earlier era. This is not an option restricted to Catholics; a large proportion of the students at New York's Catholic schools are minorities from a Protestant background who want a better education for their children. Many of the nursing aides I met during my study of a New York nursing home made enormous financial sacrifices to send their children to Catholic schools.[45] There are also a number of church-sponsored and church-subsidized West Indian–run schools; like the Roman Catholic schools, their fees, compared to those for most private (independent) schools in the city, are quite low. In London, virtually all Jamaican migrants have sent their children to state-funded primary and secondary schools.

Broadly speaking, the distance of the receiving society from the home community can be conceived of as another feature of the new context that needs to be considered. Modern transportation and technology have made the world a smaller place and facilitate the maintenance of transnational ties for Jamaicans (and their children) in both London and New York, but it still makes a difference that New York is a lot closer to the Caribbean. National surveys in Britain, as I noted above, indicate that many, including those born in Britain, have visited the Caribbean; there is also considerable contact with parents living in the Caribbean through phone calls and letters, and money is still flowing from Britain to the Caribbean.[46] No comparable surveys have been conducted in the United States, and, of course, the Jamaican population there continues to receive recent arrivals from the Caribbean who are most likely to retain close ties to home. Still, I think it matters that, despite reduced airfares, the trip from Kingston to New York is cheaper than to London.[47] It is also a lot shorter—by some five hours. What this means is that it is easier for Jamaicans in New York to visit home with greater frequency and to go back in times of family emergency or for special celebrations.

The greater ease of flying home from New York also colors immigrants' view of return. At least this was so when I did my research in the 1970s and 1980s, when the trip from London was more costly and difficult. One reason the Jamaicans I interviewed in New York were less likely to think of returning home on a permanent basis than those I spoke to in London was because it was feasible to visit home from New York with fair regularity. Better yet, some planned to move even closer to home, to Florida, which also has warm "Jamaica-like" weather and has attracted substantial numbers of Jamaican and other West Indian immigrants. (It goes without saying that no comparable retirement location exists in Britain.) There is another possibility for Jamaicans in the United States. Given the relatively close distance to home, many Jamaicans plan to "commute back and forth," spending part of the year in Jamaica and part in the United States when they retire. Not one of the people I interviewed in London mentioned this option.

This discussion of transnational relations raises another issue concerning the emphasis on the place where migrants move. Some social scientists would argue that it is misleading to speak of one context in which migrants live, since many maintain ongoing ties to their home community as they reside abroad and are embedded in relations that cross-cut nation-states (see chapter 3). Even if this is the case for some migrants—and data are not available to document how common or extensive such ties have been for Jamaican migrants in London or New York—the relevant question here is what difference it makes that transnational relations or practices encompass London and Jamaica rather than New York and Jamaica. Not only is it easier to maintain active and ongoing ties to Jamaica from New York, given the shorter distance, but also to relatives in Canada (in 1996, Toronto was home to over 70,000 Jamaicans). In Karen Fog Olwig's research on a Jamaican family network, she found that New York had become the family place where relatives who lived elsewhere could meet and get to know each other.[48] This may well be true for other families, given New York's strategic location—closer to the Caribbean than London and also not far from (and easily accessible to) the large Jamaican communities in Toronto and Florida. That New York is home to a flourishing and growing Jamaican population may also play a role in making it a meeting place for some families.

Olwig's analysis also reminds us that New York and London may be temporary places of residence for many migrants, where they live for a number of years before heading back home, elsewhere in the Caribbean, or to another destination.[49] Still, the question remains: What are the implications for their lives of having spent a long period of time in New York rather than London (or vice-versa) before moving elsewhere. In this regard, an intriguing and unexplored research topic is the experiences of West Indians who have lived in Britain for many years before moving to New York—a not uncommon pattern. Undoubtedly, the cultural patterns and social practices that develop among these "twice migrants" in New York—including racial and ethnic identities and understandings—are influenced and complicated by their earlier experiences in London.

How transnational ties and connections interact with the receiving context is only one of the many questions that await further study. A host of additional contextual features that distinguish London and New York require research. One is mainstream cultural conceptions and practices in the two cities, which are often taken for granted in social science studies but have a decided impact on daily life. Take something as basic as food. In both London and New York, Jamaican immigrants continue to cook Jamaican dishes, like curried goat and rice and peas, yet in London in the 1970s, they ate fish and chips and drank bitter in pubs, while in New York in the 1980s, pizza and bagels (a legacy from the Italian and Jewish immigration a century ago) became part of their diet. Of critical importance is the structure of the political system, which affects West Indians' ability to gain office and have influence in the political arena. How has the class-based nature of British politics affected African Caribbeans' ability to "buy" their way into the political system? Across the Atlantic, how have the dynamics of New York City ethnic politics helped or hindered them?[50]

In chapter 5, I showed what difference the presence of the large, residentially segregated African American community makes for West Indians in New York as compared to London, but what about the impact of other groups in the two cities? Of particular interest is the African population, which has grown rapidly through immigration in the last decade. London's black African population (many from Nigeria, Somalia, and Zimbabwe) more than doubled between 1991 and 2001 to about 379,000, overtaking the number of black Caribbeans by about 30,000, and constituting about half of London's black population.[51] New York City's African-born population, mostly from West Africa, is also expanding, but it is still relatively small; in 2000, the census counted 69,000 Africans born in sub-Saharan Africa, only about 3 percent of New York City's black population, as compared to more than seven times as many Afro-Caribbeans, who constituted a quarter of the city's non-Hispanic blacks.[52] Whereas in London Africans often live in the same neighborhoods as Caribbean blacks, in New York they have been more likely to settle in different parts of the city, often in the Bronx.[53] How does the presence of a growing number of Africans affect what it means to be black in London and New York? What is the nature of relations between Africans and African Caribbeans? How do cultural and other divisions among Africans themselves complicate the picture? These are just some of the questions that require investigation.

## The City as Context: Beyond London and New York

So far, the analysis has focused on West Indians in London and New York—where I have done my own research and where, in fact, most of the research on West Indians in Britain and the United States has been conducted.[54] The two cities are home to the largest West Indian populations in their respective countries. And they are the symbolic centers for West Indians in both nations. It is no accident that the largest West Indian street festivals in Britain and the United States, Notting Hill Carnival and the West Indian American Day Parade, are held in London and New York—the London event drawing crowds of over a million on August Bank Holiday weekend and the New York street festival on Brooklyn's Eastern Parkway attracting an estimated two million on Labor Day. With its huge numbers of Caribbean people, New York has become, in the words of Bryce-Laporte, the special object of their "dream[s], curiosity, sense of achievement, and desire for adventure."[55] To Caribbean immigrants, New York is often synonymous with America. The city is salient in Caribbean immigrants' mental map as a center

TABLE 6.1
*Top Seven States of Settlement for Jamaican Immigrants in the U.S., 2000*

| Total in U.S. | N.Y. | Fla. | N.J. | Conn. | Md. | Mass. | Ga. |
|---|---|---|---|---|---|---|---|
| 513,220 | 214,993 | 127,591 | 30,010 | 28,757 | 20,804 | 13,749 | 11,845 |

Source: Camarota and McArdle 2003.

of North American influence and power and as a logical entry point into the country.

Important as New York and London are as destination points for West Indian migrants, other cities have also received large numbers. In Britain, Birmingham, with about 48,000 black Caribbeans in 2001, is the second most popular city; in the United States, this status goes to the Miami–Fort Lauderdale urban area. How does it matter for West Indians that they moved to Birmingham rather than London or to Miami–Fort Lauderdale rather than New York? How important, in other words, is the urban context *within* one nation for understanding the impact of migration? In what follows, I begin to explore this question for the United States, where the inflow from the West Indies continues to bring new arrivals and where there has been some attempt, however minimal, to tackle comparative questions, perhaps because the urban destinations—and the migrant flows to them—are so distinctive.[56] (See Table 6.1 on the major U.S. states of settlement for Jamaican immigrants.) Indeed, for some migrants New York is a first stop, where they live for a number of years, but then move on to greener—often warmer—pastures within the United States.

What emerges from even a brief comparison of West Indians in different American cities is that findings and analyses based on New York studies do not necessarily hold true for West Indians elsewhere in the country. To be sure, given the realities of race in urban America, wherever West Indians go in any number their relations with African Americans are a complex tangle of conflict and cooperation. Yet how these relations unfold on the ground varies from one location to another. In general, each urban destination is distinct in important ways, reflecting, among other things, the types of West Indian migrants who move there and the particular social and political context that greets them on arrival.

The only full-length account of West Indians outside of New York is, surprisingly, about the San Francisco Bay Area. I say surprisingly because so few West Indians live there—only about 9,000 in 1990.[57] As Percy Hintzen details in *West Indian in the West,* the West Indian immigrant community in the San Francisco Bay Area not only is tiny compared to New York's, but also geographically dispersed throughout the region, with no neighborhood center. Nor is the Bay Area the first stop for West Indian immigrants—for most this was New York. They moved westward to join family or friends or because they were transferred by employers or offered jobs, came to attend one of the area's colleges or universities, or, in a few cases, were military personnel assigned to California bases who decided to remain after discharge. Also unlike New York's West Indians, the Bay Area's are disproportionately middle and upper-middle class.[58] In fact, Hintzen argues that the overwhelming presence of Mexican, Latino, and Pacific Rim migrants in labor intensive and service sector jobs has shut out unskilled and low-skilled West Indians. Were low-skilled West Indians to move to California, he writes, they "would have enormous difficulty penetrating the networks that provide access to these jobs."[59] By the same token, middle and upper-middle class West Indians are well positioned to exploit opportunities for the skilled and educated in northern California's economy by using "their racial identity to gain access to the 'affirmative action' positions available to the African American population."[60]

Because of the West Indian population's small size and dispersion, the Bay Area's West Indians do not have the same opportunities for political mobilization that New York's large concentrations afford. They must also make an effort to get together—which many do, in social and sports clubs, associations, and the annual San Francisco Carnaval held on Memorial Day weekend. Unlike New York's West Indian American Day Parade, Carnaval is not an exclusive West Indian event, but what Hintzen calls a "collective performance by exoticized immigrant communities with African influences and African roots," in which Brazilians as well as Caribbeans "occupy pride of place."[61] The San Francisco Carnaval is targeted at a predominantly white audience, and many floats and costume bands are even mainly, sometimes completely, white. In New York, the participants are virtually all West Indian, the audience primarily black, and the parade is partly a statement of a claim to ethnopolitical turf. Attendance at the West Indian American Day Parade on Eastern Parkway has become a requirement for politicians seeking city and state office and those representing districts with large concentrations of West Indians. This is not the case for San Francisco's Carnaval which, Hintzen claims, "signifies a festive, exotic ac-commodation of white America."[62]

The small number, geographical dispersion, and class composition of San Francisco's West Indians have given a particular twist to relations with African Americans. In New York City, West Indians live in neighborhoods with, or near, African Americans, including poor African Americans, and many West Indian immigrants in the five boroughs have low-level jobs, with relatively few in professional positions.[63] West Indian New Yorkers seek to distinguish themselves from African Americans, but there is also frequent interaction and familiarity between them. In northern California, residential dispersion of West Indians and their small numbers have, by Hintzen's account, prevented the development of such familiarity.[64] Or at least it appears that relations with African Americans have been strictly channeled along class lines. The Bay Area's many middle- and upper-middle-class West Indians distance themselves from less successful African Americans and emphasize their foreignness and their achievements. To the extent that they socialize with African Americans—and they prefer to socialize with their compatriots—it is with middle-class and professional African Americans. Another element is also involved in relations with the African American community. Black political clout in northern California has, in recent years, opened up opportunities for African Americans in the public and private sector; associations with African Americans "ensure West Indians of access to the social, political, and occupational networks of the African American middle and professional classes"—a development that has parallels in New York as well.[65]

Another city with a relatively small West Indian population and a significant share of professionals is Washington, D.C. According to the 2000 census count, the Washington metropolitan area was home to 18,310 immigrants from Jamaica and 9,648 from Trinidad and Tobago, or 3.4 percent of the foreign-born in the region.[66]

A major draw has long been Howard University, which, according to Ransford Palmer, is the private institution with the single largest concentration of West Indian professionals in Washington, D.C.; over the years, Howard has maintained links with the Caribbean and trained many West Indian professionals.[67] Many graduates of Howard and other universities have remained in the region, working as doctors, lawyers, and accountants. Other West Indians in the Washington area have come to work in international organizations like the World Bank or the

Organization of American States. Still others hold government positions. Although Washington's West Indians are not just professionals—many work in lower-level jobs as limousine drivers, for example, or in hotels—the substantial number of professionals and students has given the West Indian community an upscale reputation.[68]

In moving to Washington, West Indians come to a city with a majority black population (and black political leaders) and nearby suburbs that are home to a flourishing African American middle class. West Indians are scattered residentially throughout the area, and tend to live in mostly African American neighborhoods, many in the District of Columbia itself or the Maryland suburbs.[69] Just how West Indians and African Americans get along in their neighborhoods and at work is unclear since, as far as I know, there is no research on West Indians in the area. Journalistic accounts suggest that African Caribbean and African American professionals mingle easily in social settings. Studies are required to see how class and race interact to shape relations with African Americans in Washington as well as with the large number of African immigrants who are a growing presence in the area.[70]

Hartford's West Indian community offers yet other variations. It dates back to the 1940s when West Indians came to the Hartford area to work on tobacco farms in the Connecticut River Valley, and following the 1965 U.S. immigration reforms, their numbers mushroomed with a continuing stream of new arrivals.[71]

In 2000, the city of Hartford was home to 10,114 people of West Indian ancestry. By New York standards, these numbers are tiny, but Hartford, of course, is a much smaller city—only about 122,000 in 2000—and West Indians are a significant proportion, almost 10 percent, of the population. In 2000, they were also a quarter of the city's non-Hispanic blacks. (Hartford, like New York, is a majority-minority city, although whites are an even smaller fraction—only 18 percent in 2000, with 41 percent Hispanic, 36 percent non-Hispanic black, and 2 percent Asian.) A distinct West Indian residential community developed in Hartford where, by Palmer's account, in the 1990s, "a plethora of small businesses [along Albany Avenue] evokes Spanish Town Road in Jamaica, a main commercial thoroughfare leading into . . . Kingston."[72] Hartford's West Indians, who are overwhelmingly Jamaican, have been described by Palmer as "for the most part solidly middle class," and many have moved outside the city limits, often northward to towns like Windsor and Bloomfield.[73]

West Indians in Hartford are a well-organized ethnic community. The Caribbean-American Society and the West Indian Social Club each have their own buildings; the West Indian Social Club building can accommodate 800 people at the group's functions.[74] This club featured prominently in the Connecticut Historical Society's 2003 exhibition on the Hartford area's West Indians, which drew heavily on the club's archives.[75] In Hartford itself, as well as several nearby towns, a number of churches have a West Indian cast. Hartford, moreover, has become one of the hubs of the nation's reggae market, replete with clubs and concerts that draw people from a wide area.[76]

Given their relative numbers, residential concentration, community organizations, and many middle-class members, it is not surprising that West Indians have gained political office in the city. What is surprising is that they have done so as Republicans, since in New York City, West Indians are solidly, and reliably, Democratic. In Hartford, two West Indians who have served on the City Council ran as Republicans—including Veronica Airey-Wilson, who after several terms on the council became Deputy Mayor in 2001–03. In the 1990s, moreover, the president of the Hartford chapter of the Jamaica Progressive League, which is affiliated with the People's National Party (the more left-leaning of Jamaica's two main political parties), was also a Republican. Whether this represents what Palmer calls a right-of-center drift in the politics of Hartford's West Indians—or a pragmatic jockeying for power in the context of Hartford's political landscape—is unclear.[77] Do Hartford West Indians also vote Republican in state and national elections? How do ethnic politics play out in the context of Hartford's wider black community? And, to come back to a comparative perspective, what are the differences from—and resemblances to—West Indian politics in New York?

Finally, there is the growing West Indian population in south Florida, centered in Miami-Dade and Broward counties, what might be called the Miami–Fort Lauderdale urban region. Black immigrants have been a presence in south Florida since the nineteenth century, when a Bahamian community developed there, yet until immigration reforms and the civil rights movement, their numbers were very small. Segregation made the region unattractive to black immigrants, and even after the civil rights movement, as one study notes,

> middle-class black economic gains were slower in coming to Miami than to other parts of the South. However, by the late 1970s middle-class black

progress and a growing economy, plus other attractions—including, not incidentally, the climate—made Dade and Broward counties more attractive to West Indians, both those coming directly from the Caribbean and those coming from other parts of the United States.[78]

Miami may be a low-wage region compared to New York City, but housing costs are also lower, and there are other allures. When I was doing fieldwork among New York Jamaicans in the 1980s, many had plans to retire to Florida, and several had bought land there, with an eye to building retirement homes. A story in *The Jamaican Weekly Gleaner* in those years extolled the virtues of preplanned communities in Florida which were already attracting large numbers. "I grow vegetables and fruits in my backyard. . . . Everything here is just like Jamaica," said one man. Another man who had moved from New York spoke of how his wife's arthritis was improved in the warm climate and of the easier pace of Florida life.[79] The year-round tropical climate, combined with good health care and other benefits—and close proximity to Jamaica—continue to hold their appeal to retiring West Indian New Yorkers. "I had always planned to go back home," said one seventy-five-year-old transplanted New Yorker, "but never made it except for vacation. This is the next best thing to home, being in this tropical environment. . . . You . . . participate in a health program and a retirement program, and your children and grandchildren are here [in the United States]."[80]

How many West Indians have moved to South Florida from the New York area is not known, yet the retirees and "twice migrants" are part of the mix, alongside others who have come directly from the Caribbean. In 1990, Dade County was home to 53,676 Anglophone West Indian immigrants, who constituted 11.5 percent of the adult black population; 32,208 Anglophone West Indians had settled in Broward County, where they constituted 8.7 percent of black adults. The Jamaican predominance is striking: in 1990, almost two-thirds of Miami-Dade County's foreign-born Anglophone West Indians were Jamaican, nearly three-quarters of Broward's.[81] (This is a far higher proportion than in New York City, with its very large Guyanese and Trinidadian populations.)[82] Ten years later, the West Indian population in South Florida had mushroomed, with an estimated 68,000 people of Jamaican ancestry alone living in Broward County.[83] As in New York, South Florida's West Indians are highly represented in professional services (including nursing and other health-related services), and the proportion of college-educated and professionals among the foreign-born is roughly similar.[84] Miami's and Broward's West Indians are more likely to live in black neighborhoods than not—although analyses of 1990 census data indicate that they were less segregated from non-Hispanic whites than New York West Indians.[85]

There is no one dominant West Indian ethnic neighborhood in Broward or Dade County like Central Brooklyn in New York City, although residential clusters have developed in several areas. As Kasinitz and his colleagues observe, there are "large concentrations in the traditional black ghettos north of downtown Miami (Overtown and Liberty City) and the western part of Fort Lauderdale and the adjacent unincorporated areas."[86] Lauderhill in Broward County, often called "Jamaica Hill," may be the most distinct Jamaican community in the South Florida area, with a heavily middle-class population. "It's like being in Kingston, but more upscale," is how one academic described it.[87] A six-block business corridor on U.S. 441 features Jamaican grocers, beauty salons, and restaurants, one journalist writes, "alongside the cornerstones of American capitalism: McDonald's, Wendy's, Shell and a slew of shiny-new car dealerships."[88]

South Florida's growing West Indian community supports West Indian newspapers, magazines, radio shows, and cable television shows as well as Caribbean festivals and numerous organizations, including alumni associations representing graduates of several elite Jamaican secondary schools and associations of Jamaican professionals. Jamaican residential clusters in several small cities outside of Fort Lauderdale, with populations under 100,000, have translated into numbers at the ballot box and chances for elected office. By 2003, six Jamaican Americans had been elected to municipal office in three Broward cities, including mayor of Lauderdale Lakes; in 2003, Miramar elected a Jamaican-American majority city commission.[89]

Once again, there is the question of relations with African Americans. In South Florida, these relations are played out against a different ethnoracial background than in New York. Miami's African Americans feel beleaguered in a Latino-dominated city and county—overtaken demographically, politically, and economically by the Hispanic majority, who have transformed the cultural and linguistic character of the region.[90] In the Miami context, African Americans might see West Indians as much-needed allies who share a racial bond as "blacks." No doubt this is part of the story. Given the overwhelming impact of race in southern Florida, a study of second-generation West Indians there predicts a growing, if ambivalent, identification with the broader African American community, and that successful children of Anglophone Caribbean immigrants will merge into the African American middle class.[91] This sounds much like the forecasts for New York. Yet in Florida, as in New York, there is distancing and tension, as well as accommodation and identification, with African Americans, and future studies need to explore whether—and how—there is a particular South Florida cast to these dynamics.

Relations with Haitians further complicate the picture in South Florida. Haitians are not only a sizable population there, but, unlike in New York, a highly visible and stigmatized group. Reports in the 1980s referred to the "pariah status of Haitian boat people" in Florida and Miami's Haitians being looked down on by all segments of the local community, including native blacks.[92] Moreover, unlike in New York City—where Haitians generally live in Queens and Brooklyn neighborhoods among English-speaking West Indians—in Miami, Haitians have their own distinctive neighborhood, Little Haiti; as Haitians have spread north into the Miami suburbs, North Miami has become a new community base, electing a Haitian-American mayor and a Haitian-American majority council.[93] Despite these Haitian residential clusters, there is intermingling with Jamaicans in other neighborhoods as well as in schools and other arenas. Does the shared experience as black immigrants in South Florida bring the two groups together? And in what situations and settings does it become relevant or significant? Is there economic and political competition between them, particularly since South Florida Jamaicans, as a group, have a considerably better socioeconomic profile than Haitians? How do relations between Haitians and Jamaicans vary depending on which group is numerically dominant in a particular area?

This analysis of the West Indian experience in different U.S. contexts, in the end, raises more questions than it answers, which is inevitable given the paucity of research outside of New York. What it makes clear, however, are some of the ways that "place matters"—and the need for research on West Indian migrants that goes beyond the boundaries of the New York area and indeed beyond the United States. I have focused on West Indians in New York and London, but cross-national comparisons should include Toronto, as well—the West Indian capital in Canada that, at the time of the 1996 census, was home to more than 120,000 West Indians. There is also a benefit to branching out to bring West Indians from the Dutch and French Caribbean into the comparisons—Martinicans/Guadeloupeans in Paris, for example, and Surinamese/Dutch Antilleans in Amsterdam.[94] It would be useful, too, to consider the West Indian communities in Costa Rica and Panama, which consist of the descendants of migrants who arrived at the beginning of the twentieth century from Jamaica and other then-British islands to work on the canal and plantations. In short, I see the analysis of West Indians in different locations in this chapter as a beginning step in a comparative project that can more fully document, and contrast, the experiences of Caribbean migrants in the continuing diaspora that has spread across continents and cities.

# 7

## Gendered Transitions
*Jamaican Women in New York and London*

Gender relations, it has been observed, shape immigration patterns just as migration experiences reshape gender relations.[1] By now, after several decades of feminist scholarship on immigration, this is almost a sociological truism. Yet despite a growing body of research on gender and immigration, we still have much to learn about how the two are connected. This chapter adds a new twist by introducing a comparative lens—in this instance across space rather than, as in chapter 4, across time.

The focus is on Jamaican women in New York and London: how gender has structured the pattern of their movement abroad as well as their work and family lives. This comparative analysis raises some intriguing questions: Why, for example, were Jamaican women in New York more often the pioneers in the move abroad and more likely to work in caregiving jobs in private homes than their counterparts in London? Why has the need, and desire, to work led to similar satisfactions and dissatisfactions for Jamaican women on both sides of the Atlantic? As it brings out the similarities and contrasts in New York and London, the comparison sheds additional light on the role of the context of reception in shaping the way Jamaican migrants reconstruct their lives in their new homes. It also makes clear that gender cannot be viewed in isolation, thereby contributing to an understanding of what Patricia Pessar has called the simultaneity of the impact of gender and other statuses—including race, class, generation, and legal position.[2]

This analysis comes at a particular juncture in the study of gender and immigration as it has developed over the last few decades. In her introduction to a recent volume on gender and U.S. immigration, Pierrette Hondagneu-Sotelo has sketched out three stages of feminist scholarship in immigration research.[3] The first stage, which she labels "women and migration," sought, in the 1970s and early 1980s, to remedy the exclusion of women subjects from immigration research: the goal was a modest one of taking women immigrants into account. In the second stage, in the late 1980s and early 1990s, the focus was on gender, not just women—more specifically, on the gendering of migration patterns and how gender reconfigured systems of gender inequality for women and men, particularly in the family and household. Now, in an emerging third stage, the emphasis is on gender as a key constitutive element of immigration—in going beyond families and communities to analyze how gender is incorporated into a wide variety of daily operations and institutional political and economic structures.

What follows incorporates insights from all three stages. As recent critiques of earlier research point out, immigrant women cannot be considered apart from men—their lives are intertwined in innumerable ways—yet putting the spotlight on Jamaican immigrant women, as I do here, is not an atavistic or backward-looking enterprise. Far from it. Just as studies of aging often focus on one stage of the life course, or studies of class relations on one social class, so, too, studies of gender that focus on men *or* women can enrich our understanding of the migration experience. Nor have we exhausted the need for research on the way migration changes gender roles in families and households—a "second-stage" topic explored in this chapter. The chapter also considers some third-stage concerns, including how gender influences patterns of labor market incorporation and the dynamics of gender and transnational practices.

As in the previous two chapters, this analysis of Jamaican migrant women draws on research conducted among Jamaican immigrants in London in the 1970s and in New York in the 1980s; unless otherwise noted, these are the time periods I refer to in the pages that follow. This is especially important to bear in mind in the London case. Given that mass migration ended around 1970, virtually no new recruits now come from the Caribbean, and London's Jamaican immigrant population is an aging one, outnumbered by the second and third generation. Because the experiences of Jamaican and other West Indian immigrants of African ancestry from the Anglophone Caribbean have often been similar—and because so many researchers focus on this larger group, rather than on Jamaicans—I often use the more inclusive term West Indian instead of Jamaican.

## Gender Patterns of Migration

In the beginning, in the very move itself, the pattern of male-female migration differed in the two great Jamaican migrations of the mid- and late twentieth century. This does not mean that the underlying causes for leaving Jamaica were much different for men and women in either case. They were not. Scarce resources, overpopulation, high unemployment and underemployment, limited opportunities for advancement—these have long spurred Jamaican men and women to look abroad for economic security and better job prospects, improved living standards, and ways to get ahead.

In this regard, it should be emphasized that limited employment opportunities in Jamaica have had a deep impact on women as well as men. Women in the Anglophone Caribbean have always worked, going back to the days of slavery when women toiled on the plantations.[4] Since emancipation in the 1830s, Jamaican women have been actively involved in occupations outside the home.[5] In the late 1970s, women constituted about 40 percent of the Jamaican labor force, although they suffered more than twice the rate of male unemployment, a situation that had not improved by the late 1990s, when women were 46 percent of the labor force.[6] Whether they went to Britain or the United States, Jamaican women intended to work for wages. This was a basic part of their plan.

Given these intentions, one might expect that male-female migratory patterns would be similar in both the British and American cases. This is, in fact, not the case. In Britain, the man in the family typically emigrated first, later followed by his wife (or common-law wife or female partner) and children. Although Jamaican migration to Britain was characterized from the start by a high percentage of women, the proportion of men in the migration was higher than for women—and it was especially high in the early years. Figures for all West Indian migrants show that between 1952 and 1962, the peak years of the migration, male migrants outnumbered female migrants in all but one year; about 70 percent of West Indian migrants in 1952–1954 were men and about 55 percent in 1960. After the imposition of immigration controls in Britain in 1962 and throughout the rest of the 1960s, the migration consisted mainly of those classified as dependents, overwhelmingly children but also a good many women.[7]

At first glance, this migration pattern might suggest that Jamaican men are more adventurous, independent, and ambitious than Jamaican women, setting out for foreign parts while their womenfolk trail behind. Hardly. Jamaican women have tremendous ambition and desire to work and be financially independent. As a number of scholars have noted, the desire for economic independence is a strong characteristic of Jamaican and other West Indian women and a vital component of their self-image.[8] Just as wage work is normal and accepted for women in Jamaica, so, too, there is no social barrier preventing women from migrating without and prior to a man. Nor do wage-earning opportunities in Britain seem a significant factor in explaining why men were often the migrant pioneers, since these opportunities were available for both men and women. In most cases, there was simply not enough money for the whole family to emigrate together, and men, as the expected family providers, probably received preference in raising the rather considerable funds to pay for the passage. Perhaps, too, knowledge of job opportunities for men in Britain was more readily available than for women.

If anything explodes the myth of the dependent female Jamaican migrant, it is the recent movement to the United States. There, Jamaican women, not men, have dominated the migration, and women frequently came on their own, before their spouses or children. The nature of U.S. immigration law—indeed, the very fact that legal rules defined who could enter the United States in contrast to the open immigration from Jamaica to Britain prior to 1962—in combination with job opportunities were largely responsible for this pattern.

In virtually every year since 1967, Jamaican women in the legal stream to the United States have outnumbered men. The proportion of women was particularly high in the first few years of the "new" (post-1965) immigration, as high as 76 and 73 percent for 1967 and 1968—and leveling off in the 1970s and throughout the 1980s and 1990s to between 52 and 54 percent.[9] The 1965 immigration legislation, and subsequent revisions, favored persons in particular occupations as well as close relatives of U.S. citizens and permanent residents. In the early years of the new immigration, it was easier for women than men to qualify for labor certification largely due to the demand for domestic labor in American cities. It is not surprising that the percentage of total Jamaican workers immigrating who were classified as private household workers peaked in the very same years that the percentage of women migrants was so high: in 1968, 50 percent of total Jamaican workers were listed as private household workers; in 1967, 48 percent.[10] Women could also easily obtain visas as nurses, and in fact about one-third of legal Jamaican immigrants classified as professionals between 1962 and 1972 were nurses.[11] Several decades later, between 1990 and 1992, according to Immigration and Naturalization Service data, 28 percent of the professional and technical immigrants from Jamaica were nurses.[12]

As the migration progressed, and a larger proportion qualified for immigrant status on the basis of family ties rather than occupation, women were probably as likely as men to have relatives in the United States to sponsor them—a major reason why the sex ratios began to even out after the first three years of the new immigration. Between 1983 and 1991, of the over 90,000 Jamaican immigrants legally admitted to the United States, 90 percent entered the country through family reunification provisions of U.S. immigration law. Of the 10 percent who came through occupational categories, the large majority were in the "6th preference," the nonprofessional category frequently used by "live-in" domestics, which was cut back by U.S. immigration legislation in 1990.[13] My guess is that women have made up a high proportion of the large undocumented stream as well, partly because they have been able to readily find jobs in private households as domestics, child-care workers, and companions to the elderly.

Unlike in Britain, it was common for women to migrate to New York first, often followed by their husbands. Many women in the Jamaican village I studied in the late 1960s left their families to take jobs in New York.[14] Mrs. R., for example, a middle-aged higgler (market woman), lived on a hill behind the house where I stayed. Soon after I left Jamaica, I learned that she had moved to New York as a live-in domestic worker. Like Mrs. R., once Jamaican women established themselves in New York, they frequently sent money and plane tickets for children and sometimes husbands as well. In a recent book of stories of successful graduates of the Prep for Prep program—a New York program placing gifted minority students in independent day and boarding schools— one of the Jamaicans in the group (a Harvard graduate and soon-to-be Yale M.D.) recalled how he, his father, and brother moved to New York in the mid-1980s to join their mother who had been recruited as a nurse at a Brooklyn hospital.[15] As it turns out, Johnson was born, and spent his first nine years, in the town of St. Ann's Bay, several miles from the community where I did my fieldwork. A few Jamaican women I spoke with in New York in the 1980s told me they had been reluctant to emigrate but were pushed to pave the way for men. They came first because they, rather than their husbands, could get an immigrant visa.

Some Jamaican migrants never sent for their husbands at all, and a number of women I interviewed had actually moved to New York to bring about or formalize a separation. The New York migration stream has included many women without spouses—single, divorced, separated, or widowed—who, once in New York (at least at the beginning), often took up live-in employment as private household workers. The easy availability of this type of work may well have encouraged or enabled such women to come to New York in the first place.

## *Where Jamaican Immigrant Women Work*

And this leads to the question of jobs. Jamaican women left the island to work—and wherever they went, they entered the workforce in exceedingly high proportions. In 1990, 75 percent of foreign-born Jamaican women of working age were in the U.S. labor force; in Britain, according to the 1991 census, Caribbean women of working age (including the native as well as foreign-born) had an economic activity rate of 73 percent.[16] In both New York and London, Jamaican immigrant men and women tended to cluster in different occupational spheres, in quite a number of cases the same concentrations in both cities. Much of the employment for Jamaican immigrant women in New York, as in London, has been in "women's work," in positions that often involve performing domestic activities in the workplace. When I did my research in London and New York, for example, Jamaican immigrant women were often found in the health-care field as nurses and nurse's aides in hospitals or in various kinds of clerical and sales jobs.[17] Jamaican men in London often worked in transport—on the railroads, buses, and underground—just as many in New York City became truck, bus, or jitney van drivers. A combination of skills Jamaicans brought with them—nurses being especially noteworthy in this regard—and available opportunities in the two cities mostly explain these similarities. Once established, occupational niches became self-reproducing, as new arrivals learned about and got help finding jobs through personal networks in the immigrant community.[18]

This is one part of the job story. Another is the differences in Jamaican women's (and men's) job patterns in London and New York. The structure of demand, together with ethnic/racial patterns in the labor market, help account for the contrasts. In London during the 1970s, for example, many Jamaican women were office cleaners—a field they did not enter in New York City, where Jamaicans' English language ability made other options more attractive and which, instead, drew on the large number of newly arrived Latino and other non-English speaking immigrants. Largely for the same reason, Jamaican immigrant women in New York City did not go into the garment industry—an ethnic niche for Chinese and Latina immigrant women—whereas quite a number of their counterparts in London worked in clothing factories and other manufacturing jobs when they arrived.[19] In general, for women, as well as men, in New York, job choices have been influenced by the availability of health benefits, so that Jamaican women—the unmarried or those whose spouses lacked health benefits—often sought out (and stayed) in particular jobs, despite unpleasant conditions and poor pay, in order to provide health coverage for their families.[20] National health insurance, and other government benefits available to all British citizens (including Jamaicans), led to a different job calculus in London.

And then there is the Jamaican—indeed, the West Indian—domestic caregiver. West Indian women make up a sizable proportion—more than one out of ten—of New York City's domestic workers. One might almost say that domestic work is part of the New York West Indian female experience. Whatever job West Indian immigrant women now have, large numbers, at some point in their work careers in New York—almost always at the start—had a spell as a domestic worker.[21] In sidewalks and in parks and apartment lobbies throughout New York City, the nanny caring for a young child, or the woman helping an elderly, usually white, person is often West Indian. One New York–based journalist writes that as our parents and grandparents live longer, a caring woman from the Caribbean will very likely be the last human contact many of them will have.[22] No such image exists in London, where far fewer Jamaicans and other West Indians have been engaged in private household work.

In New York, a number of factors explain the development of this occupational niche—which, incidentally, has a long history. In the early twentieth century, West Indian migrant women were mainly employed as household workers or in other personal service jobs—in 1925, this description fit three-quarters of foreign-born West Indian women in Manhattan's labor force as well as two-thirds of African American working women.[23] Whereas European immigrant women during and after the First World War were able to find better-paid work in New York City's factories and as clerks, southern and Caribbean black migrant women were largely excluded from these occupations. In New York's racialized landscape, it was difficult or impossible for most to find alternatives to household work.[24]

By the end of the twentieth century, racial exclusion from other jobs was no longer this kind of barrier as employment options for black women widely expanded. (It should also be noted that race generally has not been an obstacle to domestic employment; although employment agencies report that some parents refuse to hire black child-care workers—and if they do, expect to pay them less than whites—New Yorkers have a long familiarity with hiring black domestics.)[25] Demand has been critical—for live-in and live-out nanny/housekeepers, housecleaners, and home-care attendants to the elderly. In the past few decades, domestic caregiving jobs have grown in number as more middle-class women with young children entered the labor force. Alternative child-care arrangements are often unavailable: grandmothers are often working or do not live nearby, and high-quality child-care centers are in scarce supply. In any case, many middle-class New Yorkers view day-care centers as offering institutional, second-class child-care and prefer the convenience and flexibility of having someone look after their children at home. At the other end of the life course, demand for home-care attendants has expanded with the growing number of elderly, the increased likelihood that adult daughters will be working outside the home or living far away, and changing state regulations which facilitate or encourage home (rather than nursing home) care.

While demand has been growing, African American women have largely withdrawn from the field; in the post–civil rights era, they have been unwilling to take jobs imbued with racial subordination and servitude, and many of the better educated have taken advantage of opportunities in public sector employment. The very supply of immigrant workers has fueled demand for domestic workers. The top-ranked U.S. cities in paid domestic work (measured by the proportion of employed women in this field) have large concentrations of Caribbean or Latina women.[26] The increasing number of immigrants searching for work in New York has made modestly priced domestic services more widely available by keeping them affordable and relatively inexpensive.

English facility has given Jamaican and other West Indian immigrants an advantage over non-English speaking immigrants in competing for jobs caring for children and the elderly. Although poorly paid, many domestic positions (especially live-out jobs) are more lucrative than low-skilled manufacturing jobs that have employed large numbers of Latina and Chinese immigrant women.

For undocumented West Indian women, whose employment options are severely constrained by their immigration status, domestic work has provided the chance to work where papers are not checked carefully or not checked at all. (Many West Indian women arrive on, and "overstay" their, tourist visas, thereby becoming undocumented.) In the United States, especially in the late 1960s, 1970s, and 1980s, domestic employment offered a way that many West Indian women could qualify —through sponsorship on the job—for immigrant visas, thereby legalizing their status. Generally, it has been the newly arrived, typically undocumented, West Indian women who have been willing to take live-in domestic jobs.[27] Often, they moved to the United States on their own —no doubt in many, or perhaps, most cases, because they knew of the availability of private household jobs. In general, women on their own have been less averse to live-in domestic service than those arriving with spouses, partly because such jobs assure them a place to live when they first arrive.[28]

Once West Indian women got a toehold in domestic service, friends and relatives followed as social networks passed along valuable information about how to find jobs (for instance, advertisements in the *Irish Echo*) and contact with agencies.[29] As Hondagneu-Sotelo shows in her study of Los Angeles domestics, employers prefer informal referrals from coworkers, neighbors, friends, and relatives. Not only is it cheaper —avoiding an agency fee—but also network hires inspire automatic trust; employers feel they can find someone reliable and trustworthy to look after their children or an elderly parent through referrals from employers they know.[30] The very development of an ethnic niche can help reinforce it in yet another way: as groups cluster in occupations, this tends to foster prejudice among employers about desirable and undesirable ethnic traits—with preference for those who have established themselves in a field.[31] To many New Yorkers, nanny and West Indian ("from the islands") have become synonymous, increasing their comfort with hiring someone from the West Indies for a caregiving job.

Why did this not happen in London? Lack of demand in the years of the mass migration, racial preferences, male-female migration patterns, and the legal context of colonial migration, I would argue, go a long way in providing the answer. Given the male-female migration pattern among West Indians in the 1950s and early 1960s, newly arrived West Indian women were often joining their spouses—and therefore not open to live-in jobs, like many of their counterparts in New York who arrived after 1965. Nor, of course, was there a concern about legal status in London: when most Jamaicans (and other West Indians) moved to England, they came freely, without quotas or visas, as citizens of the British colonial empire.[32] Women leaving for Britain, in short, had no need to think about getting a job that would lead to an immigrant visa—an important reason why many came to work in domestic jobs in New York and were the family pioneers in the first place.

The fact is, too, that others—*white* others—already dominated the domestic work field in London. In the days of colonial rule, English settlers in the West Indies may have hired black women there to mind their children—a legacy of course from the days of slavery—but in England itself there is no tradition of black nannies. In the 1950s and 1960s, Londoners seeking caregivers for their children or women to clean their houses preferred to hire domestic servants from groups they had long depended on for such work—Irish women, working-class Londoners, young women from northern England, or au pairs from the continent —rather than unfamiliar Caribbean immigrants, with their black skin and strange accents. The upshot is that London West Indians did not become associated with domestic work. When I did research in London in the 1970s, not one Jamaican woman in the 110 households I surveyed then worked in a private household or told me she had done so since coming to England; not one English person I knew hired a West Indian domestic worker. (Many Jamaican women I interviewed had cleaning jobs, but they worked in offices.)[33] By the late 1990s and early twenty-first century, when West Indian immigration had long stopped, second-generation West Indian women, born and educated in England, had other job opportunities and no motivation to take on the low-paid servant role in white houses.[34]

## Work and Its Impact: Constraints and Difficulties

In one view, Jamaican migrant women's lives in both London and New York have been plagued with difficulties—and often the same ones.

Not only have most suffered the disadvantages of lower-class (or lower middle-class) status and the problems that come with being black in white-dominated societies, but also various constraints because they are women—what some have called triple oppression.

The wages of Jamaican migrant women are generally lower than those of men. They have been limited in the choice of work due to gender divisions in the labor market—often confined to menial, low prestige, and poorly paying jobs that involve performing domestic activities in the workplace. In New York, the problems of live-in domestic work have received special attention in the media and scholarly literature, including the arbitrary working conditions, low pay, social isolation, and lack of autonomy. Owing to child-care constraints, women with young children in both New York and London have had to manage a complicated juggling act in combining work with family responsibilities, sometimes leaving children behind in Jamaica for years as one of their strategies.[35]

Child-care responsibilities create a complex tangle of demands for Jamaican women that are often more difficult abroad. No matter how helpful husbands or older children are around the house, the immigrant household in London and New York, as in Jamaica, has been primarily women's domain. Migrant women, as mothers and wives, have had the major responsibility for household chores and childrearing so that an exhausting workday is often preceded or followed by hours of cooking, cleaning, and washing. In London, I met a number of women who awoke at three or four in the morning to get to an early morning cleaning job. After several hours at work, they returned home to make breakfast for their children and sometimes for their husbands as well. They usually could not sleep much during the day because they then cared for their babies and preschool-aged children. In the afternoon, they sometimes picked up their older children at school. In a few cases, the women returned to work in the early evening, after making dinner for the family and cleaning house, to do office or school cleaning for another few hours.

When I asked Jamaican women in New York and London if there were any ways that migration had made their lives as women more difficult, many spoke of childrearing. Women with young children often explained that, unlike in Jamaica, they were not able to rely on relatives or neighbors to look after their children while they worked, shopped, or engaged in other activities outside the home. As a result, many complained that childrearing limited their independence and ability to get the kinds of jobs they wanted.[36] In the rural Caribbean, as one Barbadian commentator put it, "If your child is out in the street and your neighbour down the road sees your child in some mess, that woman is going to take the responsibility of dealing with that child. But in Brooklyn, or in London, you're stuck in that apartment. You're there with that kid, you can't expect that child to be out on the street and be taken care of. You know the day care situation is lousy, you're not in that extended family, so you have a big problem on your hands."[37]

Another set of stresses and strains comes from "transnational motherhood"—a term that had not yet come into use when I was writing about Jamaican migrant women in the 1970s and 1980s and which, regrettably, I (and many other scholars at the time) did not pay much attention to then.[38] Many Jamaican immigrant women, at some point in New York and London, have had children on the island whom they left with relatives. Davison's early 1960s study of Jamaicans who had been living in England for two years found that 89 percent of the children of the migrants (male and female) were still in Jamaica.[39] Studies of West Indian New Yorkers indicate that leaving children behind is a common pattern as well. In one sense, this pattern can be viewed as the "internationalization" of a long-standing West Indian tradition of childminding or child-fostering by female kin.[40] Indeed, leaving children with a grandmother (nearly always the mother's mother) in rural areas while the mother goes to work in Kingston has long been an accepted practice. Nonetheless, many migrant women in London and New York left children behind because they felt they had no choice. In Britain, according to Davison's study, financial reasons—including lack of money to pay the children's fare—were major considerations in leaving children in Jamaica; housing difficulties were also cited and, in some cases, inability to find an adult escort for the child on the journey.[41]

In New York, legal issues complicate matters. Because many women arrived with tourist visas—and overstayed them to become undocumented—they were unable to bring their children with them. Others who arrived with green cards, often had to wait to sponsor their children under family reunification provisions of U.S. immigration law. As in Britain, financial considerations played a role in that many women preferred to leave children (or some children) in the Caribbean, at least at first, because they worked long and often irregular hours or because they wanted to save on the expense of child care or housing when they were getting settled in New York. In New York, women without dependent children were free to accept live-in domestic jobs; even in live-out jobs, employers prefer child-care workers who do not have their own children and can maintain constant availability.[42] Another factor entered into some women's calculations: fears that their children would be affected by violent crime in New York City and have to attend inferior, and dangerous, schools in the poor neighborhoods in which they live.[43]

Whatever the motivations—and despite the cultural roots of child-fostering—transnational mothering has often created strains for the women involved. In Davison's British study, there were many reports of "great distress felt by the parents concerning their children and yet they felt unable to surmount the formidable obstacles in the way of a family reunion."[44] In London in the 1960s and 1970s—and New York in later decades—mothers missed children left behind and often worried about the care they were receiving back home or whether they would get in trouble in adolescence.[45] Shellee Colen notes that West Indian nannies' attachments to their charges in New York often assumed more importance when they were separated from their own children. " I give them more," said one worker, "because I just think of them as my own. Just because I was lonely I gave them all I have."[46] And while working mothers who leave children behind are free of child-care worries in New York—as they were in London—and save on expenses abroad, the women are obliged to send money to relatives in the West Indies for their child's (or children's) support. Indeed, studies in the Caribbean note that although grandmothers and aunts are usually emotionally attached to the children in their care, they worry that when the children join relatives in New York or London, the flow of funds will be reduced or dry up altogether. In some cases, this has led relatives to try to delay the children's migration.

How many of the children left behind have ended up joining their mothers (or fathers) abroad is an open question. In Davison's British study, only about a quarter of the female migrants with children in Jamaica intended to bring them to England; a quarter were still undecided; and half had no intention of bringing them. Many may well have changed their mind, since the interview took place only two years into their stay abroad and since plans to return to Jamaica—a major reason why many intended to leave children there—may not have panned out. Still, as Davison observes, some of the children were happily settled in Jamaica with a grandmother or other relative, and in a few cases the parent so disliked living in England that he or she did not want to bring them over.[47]

When children did finally join their mothers, the reunions often led to different problems, as has been described for London in the 1960s and New York in subsequent decades. For the children, as discussed in the British case, the separation from relatives who cared for them in Jamaica—many called the grandmother they grew up with "mother"— was often wrenching. Added to this grief was the shock of finding themselves in an unfamiliar country with people they hardly knew or remembered.[48] These dynamics have been replayed in New York, where, as also happened many times in London, the children may find their mother with a new partner so that they not only have to become reacquainted with her but have to adjust to a stepparent—and sometimes new siblings—as well.[49] While they are coping with racial hostility, an unpleasant climate, and new schools, teaching methods, and life styles, their mothers (and fathers) are working long hours and often unable to give the children much attention or supervision. One woman I knew brought her two sons to New York in the early 1980s, and while the oldest one did well, the youngest, who had been robbed at school on his second day, was so terrified that he vomited before leaving for school every morning. Although the mother was able to take him to school every day, the demands of her full-time child-care job and her own schooling—she was attending community college to upgrade her skills and get a better job—meant that she was unable to spend much time with him. For their part, mothers (and fathers) have often been bitterly disappointed if their children were confused, resentful, or withdrawn instead of grateful for the reunion, which usually entailed great financial sacrifices to bring about.[50] Trying to establish discipline over children they had spent little time with or often had not seen for over five or six years posed another, often frustrating, challenge.

If this were not enough, the women I interviewed often worried about their spouses' wandering eye. Not unlike in Jamaica, men in London and New York typically spent much of their nonworking time outside of the household—and this seemed to be more pronounced in London, given the culture of pubgoing that is absent in New York. Meanwhile, women were often tied to the home, minding the children and frequently fretting that their husbands were "fooling around" with and spending needed money on other women.

## Satisfactions and Improvements

So far, the picture I have painted is rather bleak, but it is only a partial view of Jamaican migrant women's world. On both sides of the Atlantic, Jamaican migrant women themselves felt that, in many ways, they were better off as women than they had been back home. Nor was this simply their perception of the situation. In fact, women's position as women had, in objective terms, improved in a number of ways in the move abroad.

In the eyes of the women I interviewed, the move to the United States and England increased women's independence—a strong desire for economic independence being something that women brought with them from the Caribbean. Eighty percent of the New York women (79 percent of the working women and the one nonworking woman) and 64 percent in London (73 percent of the working and 47 percent of the nonworking women) said that women were more independent than in Jamaica. The overwhelming majority who gave this answer also agreed on the reason: women had greater employment opportunities abroad. Jamaican immigrant women, of course, work out of economic necessity, but it is much more than that for them.

In the London case, the chance to earn a regular and, by Jamaican standards, high wage in England represented a real improvement in the women's eyes. They had been eager to work for wages back home, but too often economic activities available on the island were limited and did not permit them to achieve the much-desired goal of financial independence. Hardly any women interviewed in London held jobs with regular and assured incomes prior to emigration or, for that matter, at any time in Jamaica. Many, for example, had been part-time dressmakers. Quite a number had been domestics in their teens, before settling into coresidential unions, but such work was poorly regarded and poorly paid, to be avoided if at all possible as one grew older, especially if it meant subordination to someone not much higher up on the social scale. In England, by contrast, women rarely had trouble finding steady jobs with regular wages when they wanted them. All but two women in the London sample had held a job in England, and most of the twenty nonworking women were unemployed when interviewed because they chose to stay home to care for preschool-aged children. Jamaican women thus felt that they could earn more money and have more financial autonomy than they did in Jamaica, a theme that was echoed in many interviews. As one woman said: "Here you work for yourself. In this country we do as we like. I have my own pay packet and don't wait on my husband for money."

The New York women interviewed also spoke of the independence and financial control that migration brought for women. This was so even though many had enjoyed relatively high occupational status on the island. The recent Jamaican migration to the United States is marked by a higher percentage of professionals and other nonmanual workers than the emigration to Britain in the 1950s and early 1960s, and this was reflected in my samples. Virtually all the New York women had worked before leaving Jamaica, and most had white-collar jobs there—such as secretary, teacher, and stenographer—with steady and, by Jamaican criteria, quite high incomes. Even though many still occupied similar jobs in New York, they, along with service workers and downwardly mobile women, felt that women were more independent than in Jamaica. Like the London women, they stressed the greater opportunities abroad. Jobs, several women said, give women in New York more financial independence because they pay higher wages than in Jamaica. Many told me that in Jamaica, women usually have to depend on their husbands, whereas in New York they can "work their own money." Also a number pointed out that a wider range of good jobs is available in New York for those with training. As in London, many said that women had more say in family affairs now that they had larger incomes. "We were brought up to think we have to depend on a man, do this for a man, listen to a man," said a New York secretary, "but here you can be on your own, more independent."

To most women in low-level manual and service occupations in New York and London, the benefit of earning higher incomes than would have been possible in Jamaica outweighed the low prestige of their jobs and such unpleasant working conditions as shift work or, in the New York case, live-in employment. They viewed their present jobs as offering not only more financial control, but also the means to achieve a higher standard of living and a better future for their children and to accumulate savings to invest or send to relatives back home.

Especially interesting in this regard is the way private household workers in New York feel about their jobs. After all, as I have noted, this work is held in low esteem in the wider society; conditions are sometimes abysmal; and many of the women have experienced pronounced downward occupational mobility. Such was the case for Mrs.

S., a woman in her early sixties who had been a teacher and one of the most respected people in her community back home. When I met her in New York, she had been working for more than two years in a particularly bad situation while she waited for her green card to be processed. She cared for a sick, cantankerous old woman in a tiny apartment where she slept in the same room as, and had to constantly tend to, the old woman. The pay, she knew, was low compared to what other household workers earned in New York; the food was meager; and Mrs. S. was not even allowed out of the apartment on most days. Despite these drawbacks, Mrs. S. saw the job as offering the means to finance her daughter's university education in Jamaica, since her pension from the Jamaican government was insufficient. Like many others in private domestic work in New York, Mrs. S. insisted she would not have done this type of work in Jamaica. "I'm no scrubber," is how she put it. Indeed, what bothered her most about the job was that she could not, given her worries about her undocumented status, tell her employer her "real" status.

Mrs. S., moreover, viewed her present position as only temporary. When she got her green card and her daughter graduated, she intended to "commute" between New York and Jamaica, coming to the United States to do household work when she needed the extra money. (In fact, after legalizing her status, she ended up moving to, and eventually buying a house, in South Florida where she continued to look after the elderly, although on a live-out basis.) In general, once migrant women obtain a green card and/or have been in the United States awhile and their families join them, those who remain in domestic work shift to live-out positions with better pay and working conditions and more personal rewards; others leave domestic work altogether, usually for a move up the career ladder.

Many younger women have viewed domestic employment as a way station on the move up to a better job, and while they are doing domestic work enroll in classes or training programs or study, on their own, for their GED (high school equivalency diploma test) to qualify for other jobs. Mrs. A., a notable success story, attended college part time during the eight years when she was a live-in child-care worker ("governess," she termed it). After graduating with honors, she became an assistant editor at a publishing company. Many turn to occupations in health care; quite a number of the West Indian nursing aides I studied in the late 1980s in a New York nursing home had begun their work lives in New York as domestic workers.[51]

Those who remain in domestic work—and a substantial number do —usually manage to negotiate better working arrangements once they become legal residents or simply more knowledgeable about New York ways. Mrs. B., who started out her working life in New York in the late 1960s as a live-in companion to various elderly people, had learned to "handle" her employers. When I interviewed her in the early 1980s, she was caring for an elderly woman, initially on a live-out basis. When the woman asked her to live in, Mrs. B. demanded and received a hefty raise, and insisted on starting her chores later in the morning than her employer requested. The work, Mrs. B. said, was not too strenuous or unpleasant—she got along well with her employer and went out every day to shop—and she actually preferred to live in. Commuting on the subway was "getting her down," and, besides, she saved money on car-fare and food.

To Mrs. B. and most other Jamaican domestic workers, the money earned is, of course, the key. And by Jamaican standards, even low wages in New York are good. Mrs. S., to mention just one example, earned considerably more as a live-in companion in New York than she did teaching primary school in rural Jamaica. While the women soon became aware of wage scales in New York, they also continued to view their earnings in terms of standards in the "old country"—a perspective that was reinforced and renewed by trips home and visits from relatives, by Jamaican social networks in New York (which, given continued im-migration, often include new arrivals), and, in the case of many domes-tic workers, by their definition of their stay in New York as temporary. Private household workers usually evaluated their social standing, at least in part, in terms of their position on the island, and this evaluation tended to be acknowledged by their former associates. In their Jamaican social world in New York, their former, rather than present, occupa-tional or class status was usually the primary basis of their rank. Mrs. S., for instance, was thought of by her friends and relatives in New York as a teacher—not as a domestic.

Whatever the job, work abroad has meant more than the chance to earn money. For Jamaican immigrant women in London whom I met in the 1970s and in New York in the 1980s, work provided contact with people and relief from the isolation of domestic labor and child care.[52]

A number of women boasted of skills they had acquired abroad, and many, including some domestic workers in New York, were proud of the useful services they performed. In London, for instance, many nurse's auxiliaries talked with enthusiasm and pride about their dealings with hospital patients and the care they provided for the old and sick. Nurse's aides, and even many live-in companions to the elderly, echoed the same sentiments in New York. "I like to help people," said one New York woman, the former mistress of a successful sewing school in Jamaica who cared for a frail elderly couple on a live-out basis. "People don't realize how hard it is to work in the home and deal with sick people. Have to please them, make them comfortable, keep them happy. I like to work and I love my job . . . I may not be an R.N. but I help people." Many child-care workers get enormous pleasure from taking care of children, and some keep up contact with, and continue to visit, their previous charges long after they have moved on to other jobs.

And then there are the changes that have taken place within the home. In both London and New York, working women were often gratified by their husbands' increased participation in household chores. In Jamaica, men hardly ever did housework, even when their wives had cash-earning activities. There, as one recent study notes, women are supposed to cook, keep the house clean, wash the clothes, and take care of their partners and their children.[53] In the case of many women interviewed in London, work back home—dressmaking, for instance—did not ordinarily take them out of the house for long periods of time. Moreover, in Jamaica, neighbors and kin (especially mothers and sisters) frequently helped with childminding. Those with salaried jobs, like many who came to New York, usually employed domestics and nannies to cook, clean, and mind their children.

The situation is different abroad. Although the women interviewed still did most of the cooking, cleaning, shopping, and washing, men often helped out with this "women's work," particularly when their wives' worked and children were not old enough to help out. In New York and London, relatives were seldom available to lend a hand; even in those cases where they lived nearby, they were usually busy with work and their own household responsibilities. Wives' wages were a necessary part of the family income, and Jamaicans in New York and London could not afford to hire household help. As a result, as one Brooklyn woman said: "Men come here and will help wash, cook, and clean." Several men I met in New York—exceptions, to be sure—even served as the main family cooks. "In Jamaica, oh please, that was slavery," a New York nurse told me. "Bring the man his dinner and his slippers, do the laundry, you're kidding. Not anymore." In New York, her husband did the laundry, made the children's breakfast, and, when the children were babies, got up at night to feed and change them.

In both cities, couples with young children often arranged their shifts so that the husband looked after the children while the wife worked. I interviewed several men in London and New York who worked night shifts and were at home during the day, minding their children, a pattern also noted in a recent discussion of black mothering in Britain that complains that Afro-Caribbean men's role in caring for children has been ignored and undocumented. One first-generation retired nurse in London, whom the sociologist Tracey Reynolds interviewed in the late 1990s, recalled that when she first arrived, she worked nights and her husband worked during the day. After she left for work in the late afternoon, her husband would care for the children until the next morning when she arrived home.[54] Elsewhere, Reynolds, who describes herself as "a typical second-generation, black working-class woman" from South London, speaks of her father performing a variety of domestic functions "so as to support my mother who was in full-time employment and had to commute daily to Central London. Indeed, some of my earliest memories are of my dad bathing and dressing my sisters and myself for school and later beginning preparations for dinner."[55]

It is, of course, possible that many Jamaican men withdrew their help when their children got older. Margaret Byron found this to be the case among the Nevisians she studied in Leicester in the mid-1990s. By then, she writes, "the situation had reverted to that which existed in the Caribbean where the woman undertook full responsibility for housework" and men only helped with gardening and household repairs. As one woman said, "He did more when the kids were young. Now I do everything."[56]

Whatever help men provided, and however long it lasted, it should be emphasized that Jamaican migrant women never intended to cede control of the home to their partners. Although the women I interviewed in London and New York wanted their husbands to share in domestic chores, most felt that women should organize and run the household. Most also believed that women should assume the major responsibility for bringing up children. Jamaican women's sense of identity, both in Jamaica and abroad, is connected in important ways to their role as mothers, and motherhood brings deep and lasting rewards. To be childless is a terrible tragedy for a Jamaican woman. A woman receives great prestige in the family in the valued role of mother, and her children are among her greatest joys. She can count on them, especially daughters, for close companionship and support throughout her life.

If Jamaican women abroad were more likely to demand that men help out around the house, at least when the children were young, my sense is that they were also more demanding in other ways. The London and New York interviews suggest that women were less tolerant of men's outside sexual exploits than they were in Jamaica. To be sure, as in Jamaica, women said that men had a propensity to wander, and they feared—and many knew from bitter experience—that such wanderings would deprive the home of the man's money, time, and affection.[57] Again and again, women spoke with bitterness about how men "play around." "It's always the woman who is suffering," one London woman said, "men leave their wives and have other women." Jamaican women, on the island and abroad, viewed themselves as the ones holding the household together, their spouses as likely to divert resources and attention away from it.

Yet in London and New York, women appeared more willing to openly complain about men's outside sexual exploits and to demand that men spend time at home. Although many London women said that their husbands spent too much time and money at pubs and at parties, couples tended to engage in more joint activities than in Jamaica.[58] One reason migrant women in London and New York were more intolerant and demanding of men was that they were influenced by English and American values that extol the ideal of "family togetherness." Also, migrant women were more likely to look to spouses for comfort, companionship, and assistance because mothers and other close female kin —ballasts of support in the West Indies—were not around. Perhaps, too, women were more willing to make demands on and complain to their husbands, and even risk breaking up their marriages altogether, because wage-earning opportunities and government assistance offered them greater possibilities for financial independence than were available in Jamaica. "If you're not working, the man take liberty," one London woman said. "When the wife is independent, she doesn't have to put up with it. Man more quiet when you work, behave themselves more; when them go out, them take you out."[59]

## Conclusion

In comparing Jamaican immigrant women's experiences in London and New York, the parallels stand out. Because they are black, because so many are in the lower rungs of the class system, and because they are women, in both cities they have suffered from what some would call triple oppression. As I have shown, the stresses of combining work and child care and of transnational motherhood have been problems for migrant women on both sides of the Atlantic. Happily, there have been gains, too, in moving to countries with greater economic opportunities for women and where mainstream norms support the increased participation of men in household affairs and family activities. While women missed close kin who remained behind in Jamaica, paradoxically, their absence in London and New York was one factor behind male partners' greater involvement in household tasks.

These similarities should not lull us into thinking that the changes Jamaican women experience abroad are an inevitable product of migration to North America or Europe. They are not. The particular social and legal context in the place where they move has shaped, among other things, patterns of female migration and occupational niches abroad. As chapter 5 made clear, for immigrant women, as well as men, being black has different meanings and implications in London and New York, so that race and gender interact in distinct ways in the two places—West Indian intermarriage with whites being one example, with the rates being substantially higher for both men and women in Britain.[60] The gender-class connection also takes on different overtones in London and New York, partly because a larger proportion of female Jamaican immigrants in New York had middle-class backgrounds on the island. Also, the Britain that greeted Jamaicans on arrival was (and still is) a more class-conscious society than the United States, where class is a less significant basis of self-identification.

As I have indicated previously, this chapter is based on research done a while ago and since then, of course, much has changed. By now, the African Caribbean population in Britain is largely second and third generation, the immigrants an aging group. Across the ocean, Jamaican migration to New York continues apace, and while the second generation is growing, so, too, many new immigrants are coming every day. Studies are required to understand the experiences of the latest female arrivals in light of social, political, and economic changes that have taken place in the Caribbean, as well as New York, in the last decade or so.

And we have much to learn about the role of gender among second-generation African Caribbeans in Britain and the United States. Various studies point to some striking similarities. These include a gender gap in educational attainment, with daughters of West Indian immigrants on both sides of the Atlantic doing better in school than sons, and a gender difference in overt hostility from and exclusion by native whites, with young men in both places experiencing more racial harassment from whites and the police than young women and generally being perceived as more dangerous and threatening. The less pervasive negative stereotypes surrounding black women (as compared to men) and "the image of the independent, well-educated, successful black woman," Alexander argues in her London study, have become something of a self-fulfilling prophecy: one reason African Caribbean women have more opportunities than their male counterparts is that they are more easily accepted into mainstream white working environments.[61] In New York, Mary Waters suggests another dynamic is at work: because second-generation girls experience less virulent, direct, and all-encompassing racial hostility than boys, they may feel less desire to develop oppositional or adversarial components of racial identities, which can hinder academic and occupational success.[62]

There is also the fact that second-generation young women, in both London and New York, spend more time at home than young men and less time in what Alexander calls "public leisure activities"—a gender difference which American researchers argue helps to explain why girls do better in school than boys.[63] Paradoxically, U.S.-based research suggests that gender inequalities that tie girls to the home and reward female compliance and passivity end up helping them succeed academically. Being responsible for domestic chores and helping to look after younger siblings take time away from studies, yet these activities also keep girls away from the temptations of the street. Boys have fewer family responsibilities and are encouraged to be independent, which is often counterproductive for school work. West Indian parents tend to be stricter with their daughters than sons, feeling a need to protect the girls from early sexual activity and pregnancy. Also, teachers in overcrowded inner-city schools may reward what are seen as traditional feminine traits such as cooperativeness, compliance, and passivity and see girls as less menacing than the boys.[64]

Of course, it is important not to downplay the achievements of second-generation African Caribbean men or glorify those of the women.[65] Many second-generation African Caribbean men, in both London and New York, have done well in school and in the labor market. By the same token, second-generation women have their own problems. If young men are more likely to have negative encounters with police and other authorities, young women, like their mothers, face the challenge of having primary responsibility for bearing and rearing children, which sometimes interrupts their education and their careers.[66] Clearly, we need more studies of second-, and by now third-, generation women in London and New York that chart their school, work, and family careers. To date, studies of second-generation African Caribbeans have proceeded separately in Britain and the United States, with scholars on one side of the Atlantic often unaware of what has been written about the second generation on the other side. Given the timing of the migrations, researchers in the United States have come later to the subject than those in Britain. As interest grows, as it is sure to do, in understanding the pathways of the children of West Indian immigrants in the United States, researchers there have much to gain from the literature on the British experience, and from a comparative perspective that seeks to identify—and explain—both the parallels and the divergences in the different national contexts.

PART III

# Comparisons Across Space
*Urban and National Perspectives*

# 8

# How Exceptional Is New York?
*Immigration in Contemporary*
*Urban America*

There may be only one New York, but how exceptional really is New York as an immigrant city in the United States? To what extent is the story I have told in earlier chapters about newcomers to New York peculiar to the Empire City? How much relevance does it have for other major U.S. immigrant receiving cities, with their own unique social, economic, and political contexts and immigrant flows with particular skills and nationality backgrounds?

As the field of immigration studies advances—and immigrants continue to spread out to new destinations in the United States—the issue of urban or regional variation increasingly has come to the fore. Not surprisingly, most of the comparisons of U.S. immigrant cities today have focused on New York and Los Angeles, the premier destinations for contemporary newcomers, together home to about one in five of the nation's foreign-born.[1] Whether the comparisons are restricted to these two urban areas, or go beyond them to include other cities, they have, to date, mostly been concerned with a limited number of questions: the labor market experiences of immigrants in different U.S. urban locations and the attitudes toward, and political incorporation of, immigrants in Los Angeles and New York City.

This chapter has a different emphasis. In looking at contemporary immigration to New York compared with other U.S. cities and urban regions, it puts the spotlight on race and ethnicity. Chapter 6 touched on this theme as it briefly explored some of the ways that the West Indian migrant experience differs in urban centers around the United States. In this chapter I am concerned with a broader range of groups and with a specific set of questions. As the massive immigration of the past few decades has dramatically transformed the social construction of race and ethnicity and the nature of intergroup relations, how—and in what ways—is New York distinctive in the U.S. context? Inevitably, I devote attention to comparing New York with Los Angeles, but I also view New York in light of other gateway cities, as well as smaller cities and suburban regions where new immigrants have been heading in recent years.

New York's remarkable ethnic and racial diversity, its immigration history, and its institutions have combined to make it a receiving city, in many ways, like no other in the United States. At the same time, national developments have led to certain changes in conceptions of race that New York shares with other parts of the country. There is also another dynamic. As a major cultural capital of America, what happens in New York has the potential to affect the shape of change elsewhere in the nation. This may be a good thing. It could be argued that as America's quintessential immigrant city, with a long history of ethnic succession and immigrant inclusion, New York, in many ways, offers an optimistic scenario about the future of intergroup relations for the nation.

## What Makes New York Unique?

A host of features make New York special as an immigrant city. New York, in truth, is America's classic immigrant town. It served as the historic port of entry for European immigrants in the late nineteenth and early twentieth centuries and still attracts a significant share of the nation's new arrivals. Since 1900, about 10 percent or more of the nation's foreign-born population has lived in New York City. For much of the twentieth century, a fifth or more of New York City's residents were foreign-born; the figure reached 41 percent in 1910 and, by 2000, it was as high at 36 percent. The immigrant buildup in the last four decades, in other words, started from a fairly high level (see Table 8.1).[2]

Given the continued influx of new arrivals in the twentieth century, the vast majority of New Yorkers have a close immigrant connection. If they are not an immigrant, they have a parent, grandparent, or great grandparent who is. This includes substantial numbers of non-Hispanic blacks and whites, myself, I should add, among them. Like many New Yorkers, my grandparents arrived at the turn of the twentieth century from eastern Europe; thousands of others have roots in Italy; and many of the city's blacks are descended from immigrants who arrived a hundred years ago from what was then the British Caribbean.

TABLE 8.1

*Foreign-Born Population of New York City, 1900–2000*

| Year | Total Population | Foreign-Born Population (in Thousands) | Percentage of Foreign-Born in New York City | Percentage of All U.S. Foreign-Born in New York City |
|------|------------------|----------------------------------------|---------------------------------------------|-------------------------------------------------------|
| 1900 | 3,437.2 | 1,270.1 | 37.0 | 12.2 |
| 1910 | 4,766.9 | 1,944.4 | 40.8 | 14.3 |
| 1920 | 5,620.0 | 2,028.2 | 36.1 | 14.5 |
| 1930 | 6,930.4 | 2,358.7 | 34.0 | 16.5 |
| 1940 | 7,455.0 | 2,138.7 | 28.7 | 18.3 |
| 1950 | 7,892.0 | 1,860.9 | 23.6 | 17.8 |
| 1960 | 7,783.3 | 1,558.7 | 20.0 | 16.0 |
| 1970 | 7,894.9 | 1,437.1 | 18.2 | 14.9 |
| 1980 | 7,071.6 | 1,670.2 | 23.6 | 11.9 |
| 1990 | 7,322.6 | 2,082.9 | 28.4 | 10.5 |
| 2000 | 8,008.3 | 2,871.0 | 35.9 | 9.2 |

*Source*: Foner 2000: 5; Singer 2004: 6.

Nor is immigration of Europeans or West Indians of African ancestry a thing of the past. At the time of the last census, more than a quarter of the city's black population was foreign-born, most of them West Indians. And a substantial proportion of the newest arrivals hail from Europe. In 2000, the former Soviet Union ranked fourth among the top sending countries to New York City, Poland was fifteenth, and altogether, about one out of four of the city's non-Hispanic whites was foreign-born.[3] Put another way, only about half of New York City's non-Hispanic whites were native-born people with two native-born parents. New York City's white population, as Mollenkopf has written, is dominated by first-, second-, and third-generation Catholics (Irish and Italian) and Jews, and white Protestants are practically invisible, if still economically and socially powerful.[4]

A striking feature of New York City's immigration population is its extraordinary diversity. It is often said that virtually every country in the world is represented in New York. What is remarkable is the large number from so many different countries: no one or two—or even three or four—nations dominate. Between 1990 and 1996 alone, as many as twenty countries each sent more than 5,000 immigrants to the city.[5] In 2000, the top three groups—Dominicans, Chinese, and Jamaicans—were just under 30 percent of all the foreign-born. No other foreign country accounted for more than 5 percent, and there were substantial numbers of many West Indian, Latin American, and European nationalities.

Immigrants from the largest source area, the Caribbean, are themselves "extraordinarily variegated culturally, linguistically, and ethnically."[6] There is, moreover, a huge native minority population of African Americans and Puerto Ricans. The product of a massive migration from the South between World War I and the 1960s and from Puerto Rico after World War II, blacks and Hispanics of native stock (native-born to native parents) made up about a quarter of the city's population in the late 1990s.

The remarkable diversity of New York City's immigrants is matched by the heterogeneity of their skills. Origins are not destinies, but, as Waldinger points out, they are influential because of their strong association with class; nationwide, rates of college completion among Indians, Koreans, Taiwanese, Chinese, and Iranians, for example, considerably surpass the native norm, while Mexicans are the least educated and also the overwhelmingly largest group among today's immigrants. New York's mixture of nationalities has ensured a mix of class and occupational origins. Indeed, high-skilled and low-skilled immigrants are roughly equal in numbers in the New York urban region.[7]

Then there is the long list of "place-specific conditions" that mark off New York City as an immigrant destination. These include the structure of economic opportunities, as they have evolved from the 1970s through the early twenty-first century, the nature of the immigrant employment sector consisting of enterprises organized and controlled by immigrants, the expanding service economy, and the relatively large public sector. New York is a high-wage city, at least for the native-born. This, as Mark Ellis has pointed out, is why comparisons of wages of the native-born and immigrants look so bleak there (and in Los Angeles); in the New York (and Los Angeles) urban regions, natives have access to jobs above the national average wage, but immigrants work at wage rates which are comparable to those of immigrants nationally.[8] At the same time, New York immigrants find a large share of their wages going for housing: the city has an extremely tight housing market with high median rents.[9]

On the positive side, New York is a city with strong labor unions, and local government provides a wide range of services, among them an extensive municipal health care system that focuses on serving the city's poor. At the beginning of the twenty-first century, the City University of New York (CUNY), the largest urban public university system in the nation, had more than 208,000 full-time students; 45 percent of

CUNY's first-time freshmen were born outside the U.S. mainland. Partly a legacy from earlier immigrant waves, the city is home to many non-governmental institutions, like settlement houses and Jewish and Catholic voluntary hospitals, that have helped immigrants. Recent arrivals from the former Soviet Union, in particular, have benefited from the wide array of organizations, such as the New York Association for New Americans, founded to help Jewish immigrants in earlier waves.

New York City's political culture also bears the stamp of earlier European immigration and is used to accommodating newcomers from abroad. Ethnic politics are the lifeblood of New York City politics. The city's political system, as Waldinger has observed "presents newcomers with a segmented political system, organized for mobilization along ethnic group lines, and a political culture that sanctions, indeed encourages, newcomers to engage in ethnic politics."[10] A large number of political prizes are up for grabs—many within reach of the newest groups. The New York City Council has fifty-one members; the city sends sixty-five representatives to New York's State Assembly and twenty-five to the State Senate. New York City also has fifty-nine community boards (with up to fifty members each), and until they were recently eliminated, thirty-five community school boards (with fifteen members each) whose elections were open to noncitizens.[11] Despite the importance of party support in sustaining native white or minority incumbents in immigrant districts, Logan and Mollenkopf argue that New York City's primaries have proven to be an effective path for immigrant political mobility when one group becomes predominant in a district—as happened in the 1990s among West Indians and Dominicans, and, more recently, the Chinese in city council elections.[12]

## The Construction of Race and Ethnicity

Given this background, how have the special features of New York City and its immigrant population affected the way race and ethnicity are constructed? And is this different—and in what ways—from what has happened in other major immigrant destinations? At the time of the last census, as Table 8.2 shows, the ten metropolitan regions with the largest immigrant concentrations were New York, Los Angeles, San Francisco, Miami, Chicago, Washington, D.C., Houston, Dallas, Boston, and San Diego, and I refer to many of them in the analysis that follows.[13]

TABLE 8.2
*Top Ten Metropolitan Regions of Immigrant Concentration, 2000*

| Metropolitan Area | Number of Foreign-Born (in thousands) | Percentage of Population |
|---|---|---|
| New York – northern New Jersey – Long Island | 5,182 | 24.4 |
| Los Angeles – Anaheim – Riverdale, Calif. | 5,068 | 30.9 |
| San Francisco – Oakland – San Jose, Calif. | 1,902 | 27.0 |
| Miami – Fort Lauderdale, Fla. | 1,558 | 40.2 |
| Chicago – Gary, Ind. – Lake County, Ill. | 1,467 | 16.0 |
| Washington, D.C. – Baltimore, Md. | 981 | 12.9 |
| Houston – Galveston – Brazoria, Tex. | 896 | 19.2 |
| Dallas – Fort Worth, Tex. | 785 | 15.0 |
| Boston – Worcester – Lawrence, Mass. | 721 | 12.4 |
| San Diego, Calif. | 606 | 21.5 |

*Source*: Alba and Denton 2004.

New Yorkers may sometimes think they live in their own country—and some Americans may wish they did!—but, of course, the city is very much part of the larger United States. Inevitably, perceptions of race and ethnicity in New York have been shaped by national trends and developments. The growing number, and significance, of Hispanics and Asians in the past few decades in New York, as elsewhere in the nation, have led to a move away from thinking about race as a matter of black and white—the black-white binary as some scholars call it—and to the common usage of the terms "Hispanic" or "Latino" and "Asian." Furthermore, New Yorkers' views of ethnoracial differences have been influenced by, among other things, national political debates, the use of ethnoracial categories by the U.S. census and federal and local government agencies, and television and other national media.

Yet the construction of race and ethnicity in New York City has taken its own direction in some ways, and this is largely a result of basic demographics, both past and present. Consider first the way that "whiteness" is constructed. On the one hand, virtually everywhere in the United States "white" is shorthand for, and generally synonymous with, "non-Hispanic white." (As some scholars complain, this practice ignores the fact that a significant number of Hispanics/Latinos classify themselves as white when asked their race by the census.)[14] In the urban capitals of immigrant America, moreover, Euro-Americans—read "white" to most Americans—are increasingly absent from the lower and even middle ranks, so that, as Waldinger points out, class and ethnicity tend to overlap in ways that cumulate advantages for Euro-Americans, who set the standard to which others aspire.[15]

On the other hand, "whiteness" has particular associations depending on the region. There are even different terms to describe it.[16] In Texas and southern California, "Anglo" is commonly used to describe a white person who is not of Hispanic origin, whereas in New York it is rarely heard. The use of "Anglo" derives from the long-term Mexican presence in the U.S.-Mexico border region—a region that was once part of Mexico and now has an enormous Mexican-origin population. "Anglo" has not caught on in New York (or other northeastern and midwestern cities), where, given the history of immigration, ethnic differences among the non-Hispanic white population still have a strong resonance, and "Anglo" conjures up images of white Anglo-Saxon Protestants or WASPs, a category that excludes white ethnics.

In New York City, in addition, the immigrant strains in the white population have been kept alive by the ongoing influx of European newcomers from areas that were important sending countries in the past, Poland and Russia, in particular. Indeed, the large proportion of immigrants in the non-Hispanic white population distinguishes New York from most other major American immigrant cities. In contemporary New York, to put it another way, the term "immigrant" encompasses a substantial number of whites from Europe.

"Blackness" also has a different meaning in New York than in many major immigrant cities because of the large West Indian community and growing number of Africans. New York is not alone in this regard. More than a third of the non-Hispanic blacks in the Miami and Fort Lauderdale metropolitan areas are Afro-Caribbean; over a third of the Boston metropolitan area's non-Hispanic blacks and 10 percent of Washington, D.C.'s are Afro-Caribbean and African.[17] However, in the main gateway cities in California, Texas, and the Midwest with substantial African American populations, there are few foreign-born blacks: black there unambiguously means African American. This is not so in New York and other urban centers which have experienced a large influx of black immigrants and where notions of blackness are changing as a result.

Admittedly, given the history of racism in America, and the legacy of the one-drop rule, whites in New York City, as in South Florida, Washington, D.C., and Boston, often lump blacks together and are insensitive to ethnic differences among them. But there is evidence for a growing awareness of such distinctions. In Vickerman's phrase, monolithic conceptions of blackness are being "tweaked" rather than dispelled. According to Vickerman, the increasing number of black immigrants in cities like New York (along with the expansion of the African American middle class and rising number of mixed race individuals) is challenging notions of a monolithic blackness there and pushing negative stereotypes of blacks to change. He contends that there is a growing scope for immigrants to lay claim to a West Indian or African identity instead of undergoing submersion into a larger black identity, and even the possibility that the conceptions of race that black immigrants bring with them from their countries of origin will have an influence.[18]

A further complication in New York is that many Hispanics in the city identify as black when asked their race by the census, which is unusual in the U.S. urban context. (Of the New York metropolitan area's Hispanics, 9 percent identified as black on the 2000 census, compared to 1 percent in the Los Angeles–Long Beach metropolitan area, 2 percent in Chicago, 3 percent in Miami, and 1 percent in Houston.)[19] This no doubt has to do with the large numbers of Dominicans and Puerto Ricans in New York, many of whom are dark-skinned and have some African heritage.

Another distinguishing feature of New York's Hispanic population is its heterogeneity. New York has no one dominant Latino nationality like southern Californian and Texas cities, where Mexicans predominate, and Miami, where Cubans outnumber other Latino groups. In 2000, in Los Angeles and Houston, for example, around two-thirds or more of the Hispanic population was of Mexican origin; in New York City, 38 percent was of Puerto Rican ancestry, 27 percent Dominican, 9 percent Mexican, 16 percent South American, and 7 percent Central American.[20]

The ethnic strands in each city's Hispanic population affect how Hispanics are viewed—and how they see themselves. There may well be, as Itzigsohn contends, a national trend toward understanding Latino or Hispanic as a racialized category that is neither black nor white—often equated with "brown" as an intermediate race—yet this categorization does not always jibe with self-identity. On the 2000 census, almost half of all Latinos in the nation chose "white" as their race, and, as many studies show, immigrants from Latin America and the Hispanic Caribbean prefer to be known in terms of their country of origin. Moreover, the combination of nationalities, generations, and class backgrounds of

Latinos in particular cities influences the way the panethnic category "Latino" or "Hispanic" is constructed.[21] Even the preference for "Latino" or "Hispanic" varies by region. A 2002 survey conducted by the Pew Hispanic Center and the Kaiser Family Foundation of almost 3,000 adults who identified themselves as Latinos or Hispanics found that they tended to refer to themselves first by the country where they or their parents were born. Fifty-three percent had no preference when it came to Hispanic or Latino; of those with a preference, preferences varied by where they lived. Texans and people in the South tended to favor "Hispanic," while "Latino" was the term of choice for Californians and people in the Northeast.[22]

In Texas, as the historian Neil Foley notes, the word "Mexican" historically denoted a race as well as a nationality from the mid-nineteenth to the mid-twentieth century. In that period, "a fifth-generation Mexican American was still a 'Mexican' rather than an American in the eyes of most Anglos." Anglos, he writes, do not call Mexican Americans "Mexicans" anymore; they have become "Hispanic . . . a post-1960s, post–civil rights term that unites Mexican Americans to other groups who trace their heritage to Spanish-speaking countries."[23] Still, the overwhelming dominance of people of Mexican origin among Hispanics in cities like Houston and Los Angeles has had an impact on how panethnic categories are constructed there, and, indeed, the extent to which these categories are meaningful at all. To Houston and Los Angeles residents, Hispanic or Latino usually means "Mexican" or "Mexican American," which is not the case in New York.

People from the Hispanic Caribbean may have a very different understanding of the Hispanic or Latino label than those from Mexico and Central America—which has important implications for New York City where, in 2000, two out of three Latinos were of Caribbean origin. Caribbean Latinos, Itzigsohn argues, construct their racial identity vis-à-vis blackness: "First-generation Dominicans, for example, reject being associated with blackness because in the Dominican Republic blackness is associated with Haiti and Dominicans construct their national identity in opposition to Haitians. Mexican Americans, on the other hand, particularly those who adopt a Chicano and Chicana identity, build their racial identity around notions of "mestizaje" and Native American origin."[24] An added complexity in New York City is the large number of Puerto Ricans, around 830,000 in 2000. In the mid-twentieth century, New Yorkers thought of minorities in the city as "black" and

"Puerto Rican." Now, Hispanic is often used in public discourse to refer to all Spanish-speaking Caribbean and Latin American groups, although the continued plurality of Puerto Ricans in the city's Hispanic population still gives Puerto Ricans a central role. Another dynamic is involved in the self-identity process. Given the stigma attached to Puerto Ricans in the city, people with origins in other Caribbean or Latin American countries generally want to avoid being identified as Puerto Rican—and make efforts to distinguish themselves in various ways.[25] Something similar has been reported for the city of Chicago, where there is a substantial—but, by New York City standards, much smaller—Puerto Rican population and a huge Mexican community. (In 2000, Chicago's 113,000 Puerto Ricans constituted 15 percent of the city's Latino population compared to over 530,000 Mexicans who accounted for 70 percent.) As in New York, Chicago Mexicans tend to stigmatize Puerto Ricans as lazy and lacking a good work ethic; for their part, many Puerto Ricans construct Mexicans as "illegal" and unsophisticated newcomers from the Third World.[26]

The dominance of Cubans in Miami is an altogether different story. Not only are Cubans the main Hispanic group in terms of numbers, but also persons born in Cuba or of Cuban descent are Miami's largest ethnic group. Cubans are politically dominant in Miami, economically powerful, and largely set the cultural tone for the city.[27] The dominance of Cubans, many of whom are phenotypically white or light-skinned, no doubt helps explain why 86 percent of the Hispanics in the Miami metropolitan area identified themselves as white on the 2000 census— compared to, for example, 45 percent in Los Angeles, 42 percent in New York, 50 percent in Chicago, and 54 percent in Houston.[28] One journalist writes that "Cubans are probably the only people who really do feel comfortable in Dade County these days . . . Miami is their town."[29] Having acquired unprecedented economic and political power that they do not share with other Hispanic groups reinforces a focus among Cubans on national identity, a tendency to repudiate the stigmatizing tag "Hispanic," and a resistance to making linkages to other less successful Hispanic newcomers—although the recent growth of new Hispanic populations in Miami (Nicaraguans, Colombians, and others) may lead Cubans to reach out, at least in some situations, to these other groups.[30]

Miami stands out not just for the Cuban presence but for the Asian absence. Miami has attracted immigrants almost exclusively from the nearby Caribbean and circum-Caribbean—and hardly any Asians. In 2000, only 1.4 percent of Miami-Dade County's residents were Asian, a far smaller proportion than in any other major immigrant gateway city. Clearly, New York's four-part ethnoracial hierarchy—white/black/Hispanic/Asian—is not relevant in Miami. Even in many gateway cities with large numbers of Asian immigrants, the category "Asian" is constructed differently than in New York, depending on which Asian groups are present and predominate.

New York City's Asian newcomers are a varied lot. Chinese are still the dominant Asian group—prior to 1965, they were the only Asian population of note in the city—but significant numbers of South Asians, Koreans, and Filipinos have moved there in recent years. What the city lacks in any number, however, are Southeast Asians, who are much more numerous in California, including Los Angeles.[31] Given the extremely low levels of education and high poverty rates among foreign-born Cambodians and Laotians (including Hmong), these groups do not fit the "model minority" stereotype of Asians which flourishes in cities like New York. Where these Southeast Asian groups are a significant presence, for example, in Fresno, Long Beach, and Stockton, California and St. Paul, Minnesota, a less positive image of "Asians" may well emerge. There is another difference between New York's and California's Asians that may affect how they are perceived—and how they see themselves (including whether they develop a panethnic Asian identity). Several cities in the Los Angeles and San Francisco Bay regions have an Asian majority or near-Asian majority, with many well-to-do Asian residents. By 2000, there were five cities in the Los Angeles and San Francisco regions with an Asian majority; another nine were more than 40 percent Asian. Not a single city in the New York region came close to having an Asian majority.[32]

New York, in short, cannot stand for the nation as a whole. Regional and urban differences in immigrant flows, and in the ethnoracial makeup of the native-born population, have led, not surprisingly, to variation in the way that racial and ethnic categories are constructed and perceived.

I have argued that it is important to be sensitive to these variations, yet I do not support going to the other extreme—that is, a regional or urban relativism that sees only ways that each city or region is unique. No city (or urban region) is an island, and as I noted at the outset, various forces lead to commonalities in the way race and ethnicity are constructed across the country. Indeed, the views that develop in New York may have an undue influence, and diffuse across the United States, precisely because the city is such an important media center in the nation—hub of the advertising and publishing industries, headquarters of major television broadcasting companies, and location for the production of dozens of magazines.[33] Modern technology and communications have accelerated this cultural diffusion process, but it is not a new development. Earlier in the twentieth century, Guterl argues that although economic, cultural, and demographic differences in the Far West, Southwest, and Deep South affected popular sensibilities about race, the status of Manhattan

> as the cultural capital of America in the 1920s meant that the dominant national discourse on race did owe far more to the Northeast than to the New South or the Far West. In the simplest of terms, the centrality of Manhattan in modern American culture was assured by its role as the largest city in the United States, by its status as media capital, and by the hubris of the city itself. Hollywood films and national radio programs took their shape from the cultural patterns of the city of New York.[34]

Today, of course, Los Angeles plays a much greater role as a media capital than it did in the 1920s, yet New York's influence is still strong. And because Los Angeles and New York are the major immigrant centers in the nation, the production of popular culture is taking place in cities where notions of race and ethnicity have been deeply affected— though often in different ways—by the recent and massive immigrant influx.

## Intergroup Relations

The study of the relationship between immigration, race, and ethnicity is not just a matter of perceptions and attitudes; it is also about actual on-the-ground interactions. The incredible ethnic and racial diversity in New York City and its history of immigration have also created a mixing and mingling of ethnoracial groups. In the 1990s, when he was in office, former Mayor David Dinkins often referred to the city as a gorgeous mosaic. More recently, sociologists studying second-generation

New Yorkers argue that New York may serve as a "positive model of creative multiculturalism and inclusion" for the rest of the country.[35]

The city is not, of course, a racial paradise, as previous chapters have made clear. People of color continue to experience prejudice and discrimination, and tension and conflict between racial and ethnic groups are far from eliminated. Residential segregation between whites and blacks persists at extraordinarily high levels; black and Latino immigrants often engage in distancing strategies to set themselves apart from African Americans and Puerto Ricans; native minorities often resent what they see as numerical, residential, economic, or political encroachment by immigrants; and there is a general tendency, out of preference but also on account of prejudice, for members of racial and ethnic groups to stick to their own kind in day-to-day interactions. In the 1990s, the city witnessed several black boycotts of Korean-owned stores as well as two major riots.[36] One, in Crown Heights in 1991, which involved African Americans and Afro-Caribbean immigrants, began after a car driven by Hasidic Jews jumped the curb and killed a seven-year-old black (Guyanese) boy; the other, in the Dominican neighborhood of Washington Heights in 1992, was sparked by the fatal shooting of a suspected Dominican drug dealer by the police.

The fact is, however, that by and large, peaceful coexistence between members of different racial and ethnic groups is the rule in New York, just as it is in other gateway cities. Nor is it just a case of tolerance and accommodation; genuine cooperation and coalition building also often occur. Among other things, friendships develop in schools, colleges, playgrounds, and workplaces, and political alliances are formed on certain issues and electoral campaigns. A growing number of multi-hued neighborhoods have emerged in New York and elsewhere, providing the basis for the creation of ties, particularly among Asians, whites, and Latinos. Significant numbers of American-born Hispanics and Asians have non-Hispanic white spouses or partners, and though still relatively rare, black-white intermarriages are rising in frequency.[37]

These are national trends and dynamics. Of relevance here is whether the forces for accommodation are stronger in New York than in other immigrant gateway cities because of its history, its institutions, and what one journalist calls its polyglot cosmopolitanism.[38] Is New York City, to put it another way, really a model of multicultural tolerance and creativity for the rest of the country in terms of the way it incorporates immigrants?

## New York and Los Angeles

When it comes to comparisons of New York City and Los Angeles, the answer on both counts is a cautious "yes." A general assumption, in the scholarly as well as popular literature, is that New York City is a more immigrant-friendly place than Los Angeles, where the reception of immigrants has been much cooler—indeed, often hostile. In the mid-1990s, Angelenos provided the votes needed to pass Proposition 187, which, had it been implemented, would have made undocumented immigrants ineligible for government-funded social and health services. (Most of the provisions were later invalidated by California court decisions.) In the same period, proimmigrant New York City mayors supported an executive order barring city employees from disclosing a person's immigration status to federal authorities. When, in 2003, Mayor Bloomberg revised this policy in order to bring New York City in line with federal regulations, he backtracked after a few months in response to intense public pressure.

A number of reasons have been advanced to explain the warmer welcome extended to newcomers in New York City.[39] New York has always been an immigrant mecca, and the non-Hispanic native white population is closer to its immigrant roots. Large-scale immigration from abroad, by contrast, is something new in Los Angeles. Until recently, Los Angeles was a heavily Anglo city filled with transplanted white Midwesterners, many from rural areas and small towns. Los Angeles's native whites are less likely than Jewish-, Italian-, and Irish-American New Yorkers to identify with their immigrant ancestors, who tended to settle in America longer ago and in the midwestern or eastern homes the Angelenos left behind. That Europeans continue to constitute a significant proportion of first-generation immigrant New Yorkers has also, as Kevin Keogan puts it, "facilitated the reproduction of an inclusive immigrant identity."[40] In 2000, first- and second-generation immigrants accounted for less than a third of Los Angeles County's non-Hispanic whites compared to about half in New York City.[41]

The speed of the recent immigrant buildup plays a role. As against the more gradual increase in New York City in the past few decades, Los Angeles has experienced a growth spurt. The foreign-born population of Los Angeles County went from 9.5 percent in 1960 to 36 percent in 2000; in New York City, the increase was more modest, from 20 percent in 1960 to 36 percent in 2000. Moreover, the overwhelming dominance of Mexicans and Central Americans in Los Angeles—about three-fifths of the region's foreign-born—has tilted the immigrant profile there toward those with low skills, who are more likely than the better-educated and highly skilled to be perceived as putting extra pressure on social services. In New York, the proportion of high-skilled and low-skilled immigrants is fairly evenly balanced, and the region's least-skilled newcomers tend to arrive with higher levels of education than the Mexicans who predominate in Los Angeles.[42]

The large Mexican and Central American presence in Los Angeles has also led to a relatively high proportion of undocumented compared to New York City. Opposition to immigrants and high levels of immigration is generally greater when newcomers are seen as being largely undocumented. It has also been argued that New York City's political institutions and culture, with a strongly partisan political system and a long history of balancing ethnic interests and managing ethnic competition, have been more effective in recognizing and incorporating claims from immigrants.[43] Ethnic competition, moreover, is a fact of life in New York. As Mollenkopf has observed, far from finding intergroup competition threatening, the city's white population, largely made up of first-, second-, and third-generation Catholics and Jews, "are masters of the art."[44]

As a number of observers note, changes are in the air in Los Angeles. The pressure of demographics and, perhaps more important, the increasing political clout of Latinos have lessened anti-immigrant sentiment in the past few years. Indeed, as immigration continues and as more native-born Angelenos leave the region, a growing number of Los Angeles area residents are immigrants or descendants of recent immigrants. One scholarly observer even speculates that Los Angeles may emerge as "an engine of pro-immigrant sentiment comparable to, and even in some respects outdoing, New York City."[45] Whether this will come to pass is an open question. It has not happened yet, and New York City continues to be more tolerant of immigrants than Los Angeles.[46]

It should be noted that the reaction to immigrants has been less friendly in many suburban and outer-rim areas of New York City, where formerly all- or nearly all-white communities have been receiving large numbers of nonwhite, often Latino, immigrants in the last decade. This phenomenon is being duplicated in suburbs and small cities all around the country, and, not surprisingly, the reaction to immigrants and the resulting strains are often similar. As Sabagh and Bozorgmehr write, nativist sentiments generally are strongest in regions that have only recently received "floods of immigrants."[47] Not only (as in Los Angeles) is the immigrant influx a radical change in many small cities and suburbs, but, in the case of predominantly native white suburbs, residents have often moved there precisely to flee the problems and ethnoracial diversity of the inner city. Tensions are frequently rife between established residents and newcomers, particularly when the new arrivals are low-skilled, poorly educated, often undocumented Latinos who have entered the community in search of low-level work. In the New York area, conflicts have arisen over day-laborer sites in towns in Westchester County and on Long Island. Two hate crimes on Long Island in Farmingville, a community about fifty miles from New York City, attracted national attention; the first occurred in 2000, when two Mexican day laborers living there were beaten nearly to death by two men from nearby towns, and the second happened in 2003, when four Farmingville teenagers burned down the house of a Mexican family, who barely escaped.[48] While these two crimes are extreme, they are indicative of a deep anti-immigrant and anti-Latino sentiment and reaction that have not occurred, or at least been sharply curtailed and contained, in New York City.

## Hispanics and African Americans

If New York City has been more welcoming to immigrants generally than Los Angeles, many other American cities, and even many of its own suburbs, there is another way that New York has adjusted more easily to the influx of new arrivals. This concerns relations between Latino immigrants (and their children) and native blacks, which have become deeply strained, some would say even potentially explosive, in many cities around the country.[49] Nationally, Hispanics now surpass blacks as the largest minority, and in a number of cities Hispanics have numerically overtaken African Americans and begun to challenge their newly won accession to positions of power and control. Whether this demographic shift leads to open conflict depends on a host of factors, including the existence of interethnic political institutions and the actions of particular political leaders. There is, however, no denying the existence of competition between the groups for political influence, jobs, housing, and educational resources—competition which is often exacerbated by negative stereotypes and other factors such as language divisions.[50]

In cities in Texas and elsewhere in the Southwest, where Hispanics have recently outnumbered African Americans, the two groups are in direct competition for representation on school boards and city councils and in other local arenas of power.[51] South Central Los Angeles is another area where black-to-brown residential succession has been taking place in many neighborhoods. In the lower-income city of Compton, a community located at the southern end of South Central Los Angeles, African Americans finally achieved power after a long struggle, only to see their position contested by a growing Latino population that is almost exclusively of Mexican origin. (Blacks went from 73 percent of Compton's population in 1980 to 40 percent in 2000, while the Hispanic share went from 21 to 57 percent.)[52] Some black leaders have rejected the legitimacy of Latinos' calls for affirmative action, arguing that it was created to redress the wrongs of slavery, not to benefit immigrants, and that Latinos are latecomers who did not engage in civil rights struggles. For their part, Latinos complain of lack of access to municipal jobs and leadership positions in local government, as well as African American school officials' and teachers' biases against Latinos and insensitivity to Latino students' special language needs.[53]

In Compton and other places where once black-dominated schools are now increasingly Hispanic, the public schools have become a setting for conflict, as blacks feel their core educational institutions are threatened and Hispanics resent that a heavily non-Hispanic black teaching and counseling staff is not meeting their children's needs.[54] There is a different twist to African-American–Latino strains in Miami, where a large and established black minority now find themselves living in a city dominated demographically, politically, and economically by Latinos. Tensions between Miami's African Americans and Cubans, in the words of Guillermo Grenier and Max Castro, "are seething constantly and fuming periodically"—with the two communities divided by space, class, political party, ideology, and language. African Americans regard Cubans as their "new masters," who, among other things, give preferential governmental treatment to Hispanics and are indifferent to African American concerns.[55] Blacks, as one observer puts it, have felt engulfed "in a Latino maelstrom. Not only did Latinos end up controlling most of Miami's major political, economic, and educational institutions, but their leaders appeared to have little regard for the history of suffering that Blacks had been subjected to or appreciation for their pioneering role in the civil rights movement."[56]

New York City is not without tensions between African Americans and Hispanics, but several factors have reduced their salience and seriousness. Sheer numbers are critical. In New York City, Hispanics and blacks are almost equal in number—and this has been true for the past thirty-five years (see Table 1.1). In Los Angeles, Houston, Miami, and other cities, Hispanics far outnumber blacks, and this is a radical change that has taken place over the past few decades. (Between 1970 and 2000, for example, the proportion of Hispanics in metropolitan Miami more than doubled, from 24 to 57 percent, while blacks only slightly increased their share, from 15 to 19 percent. The city of Los Angeles was 17 percent black and 18 percent Hispanic in 1970; by 2000, blacks had declined to 11 percent while Hispanics were up to 47 percent. One-fifth of Houston's residents were black and only 5 percent Hispanic in 1960; by 2000, the proportion of blacks had grown only a little, to 25 percent, but the Hispanic share had mushroomed to 37 percent.) The demographic balance between Hispanics and blacks in New York City is partly owing to large-scale black as well as Hispanic immigration. It may be one reason why blacks there have been less likely to support white candidates, and more likely to ally with Latinos, in citywide elections and on political issues than in Los Angeles, where, it has been suggested, the fear of losing political power to Latinos (and Asians) has made African Americans more ready allies of white candidates.[57]

Moreover, in New York City, unlike the Southwest and California, where the Hispanic population is overwhelmingly Mexican, or Miami, where it is overwhelmingly Cuban, no one Hispanic group dominates—and there are large numbers from several nationalities. As a result, the different groups are sometimes at odds with each other rather than in conflict with native blacks. Robert Smith has suggested a potential division in the New York City's Latino community between those from the Caribbean (Puerto Ricans and Dominicans) and those from Mesoamerica and Andean countries (Mexico, Ecuador, Colombia, Peru, and others), based on cultural and racial differences as well as Dominicans' and Puerto Ricans' earlier access to elected office and political clout. Furthermore, Dominicans and Puerto Ricans are often competitors—not allies—in political contests, and Latino immigrants of all stripes often seek to distinguish themselves from Puerto Ricans.[58] And, as will be

recalled, an unusually high proportion of Hispanic New Yorkers identify themselves as blacks; "black Hispanics" may be especially likely to
develop amicable ties and alliances with native and Caribbean blacks,
and in some cases to intermarry. Indeed, oral histories collected for the
Bronx African-American history project reveal that in the 1950s and
1960s, the term "Bootarican" was used in that borough to refer to
those who had one Puerto Rican and one black parent, and thus were
both Puerto Rican and black.[59]

## Intermixing and the Second Generation

This brings us to the issue of "creative multiculturalism" in New York
City with which this section began, and the interactions between the
second generation, native minorities, and native whites. As the children
of immigrants come of age, new cultural patterns, often referred to as
cultural hybrids, are emerging as members of the second generation
grow up, go to school, work beside, and sometimes intermarry with
the long-established native-born. This is true throughout the United
States. Yet because of New York City's extraordinary ethnic heterogeneity, the creation of cultural hybrids involves a remarkable number of
groups—Asians, Latin Americans, and Caribbeans from many countries
as well as native-born African Americans, Puerto Ricans, and non-
Hispanic whites, the latter mostly Jewish-, Italian-, and Irish-American.
Moreover, because minority and second-generation immigrant young
people in New York dominate their age cohort, they have a great deal
of contact with each other in their neighborhoods and a variety of city
institutions.[60]

In the boroughs of New York City, young people in the first and second generation interact with each other as well as native minorities (less
often with native whites) in a range of contexts. It is in these interactions that new popular cultural forms are born—and that members of
the second generation come to see themselves as "New Yorkers," rather
than American. Discussing the second-generation respondents whom
they interviewed in their study, Kasinitz, Mollenkopf, and Waters write
that a "New York identity embraced the dynamic cultural activities
familiar to them, but not necessarily the larger white society. 'New
Yorkers,' for our respondents, could come from immigrant groups,
native minority groups, or be Italians, Irish, Jews, or the like."[61]

Anyone (like myself) who has taught at the City University of New York can see this identity-creation process in action, as students from places all over the world interact in class, become more comfortable with those from different national backgrounds, and come to take for granted the incredible ethnic mix in their classes, on the subway, in stores, and on the streets as a basic part of life in the city. Although many second-generation youth live in ethnic enclaves where one or two groups dominate, many also grow up in places like Jackson Heights, with its incredible ethnic stew, including Indians, Pakistanis, Mexicans, Colombians, Dominicans, Chinese, and Irish, or "a Puerto Rican, Mexican, Chinese, Arabic neighborhood like Sunset Park (where the aged population of 'real Americans' are Norwegians)."[62] Ethnic diversity, as I have noted elsewhere, is the expectation in New York—a fact of life, as it were.[63] Indeed, this can sometimes be confusing to the newest arrivals. Soviet teenagers whom Annelise Orleck studied were confounded when they entered high school in Brooklyn, wanting to know where the Americans were: "It is . . . hard to know what we are supposed to be becoming. Everybody here is from someplace else."[64]

In describing the vibrant inner-city youth culture that is emerging in New York, Kasinitz speaks of a "melting pot of urban youths, all 'of color' but from a variety of cultures." He writes of young people creating new forms of music (for example, Filipino and Indian hip-hop) that fuse Asian and African-American forms and of fluid exchanges between African Americans and Jamaicans and other West Indians: "The New York youth sporting dreadlocks . . . is as likely to be African American as Jamaican, and the street slang of central Brooklyn youth owes as much to Kingston and Port of Spain as to the American South. . . . African-American young people dance to Jamaican dance hall music and imitate Jamaican patois, even as West Indian youngsters learn African American street slang. Puerto Ricans can meringue and Dominicans can play salsa and rap in two languages."[65]

Does this mean that there is no interethnic/racial conflict among second-generation youth from different countries or among second-generation youth and native minorities and whites? Of course not.[66] Does it mean that the children of immigrants, in many contexts, do not "hang out" with peers from their own ethnic and racial group? Again, the answer is no. Nor does it mean that members of some groups—in particular those of African ancestry—do not experience subtle (and often not so subtle) barriers to inclusion into new kinds of ethnoracial mixes.

As I write this chapter, I am teaching a freshman seminar at CUNY that includes students from Colombia, the Philippines, Pakistan, India, Russia, the republic of Georgia, Uzbekistan, as well as an African American, Puerto Rican, and native white. It is clear that friendships have developed among students from different groups, although an Indian student complained that when Russians gather in the student lounge they speak Russian with each other, thereby excluding the others, and the lone African American student appears to have developed few ties to the other students in the class. There is a danger of reading too much into this one example, yet observations in my own and others' classes suggest that the kind of mixing among students of Asian, Latino, and European background that I have described in the seminar is nothing out of the ordinary in the context of CUNY. It is a normal feature of college life, which will, I suspect, continue for many students as they carve out careers in New York City workplaces after graduation. If students of African ancestry appear to be less integrated into informal social groups with those from other backgrounds, they, too, are developing multiethnic ties that include age peers of African American, Afro-Caribbean, and African background. In some cases, these ties include Latinos and Asians as well. A fascinating example comes from recent research in New York City high schools that indicates that some academically successful Mexican young people identify and hang out with their black counterparts as a way to become incorporated into the black middle-class culture of mobility and facilitate their own upward path.[67]

Thus, to return to the question with which I began this discussion, New York may not be a perfect model of inclusion for the rest of the country, but it does offer many optimistic signs—and the emergence of what Kasinitz and his colleagues call a "new kind of multiculturalism . . . of hybrids and fluid exchanges across group boundaries."[68]

## Conclusion

New York is clearly exceptional in many ways as an American immigrant city. The composition, and extraordinary diversity, of immigrant streams to New York City have created a racial and ethnic order that is unlike the Latinization of Los Angeles, Miami, or Houston. Nor is it just the immigrant flows that make a difference as they affect the basic demographic contours of the city. The particular shape of New York

City's political structure and culture—and the very history of immigration there—have implications for the dynamics of ethnoracial identities and relations.

At the same time, as I have also noted, New York is not a world—or, I should say, city—apart, and its ethnoracial structure is deeply affected by national laws, policies, and institutions. To give just three examples: notions of "blackness" have been shaped by the historical legacy of slavery and segregation in the nation as a whole; the category Hispanic emerged as a result of classifications developed by the U.S. Census Bureau; and views of Asians have been influenced by U.S. political relations with (and economic developments in) Asian countries. The fact is, too, that the national media, particularly television, and political discourse by national-level politicians and elected officials have had a role in the construction of race and ethnicity in New York. With regard to the media, however, another dynamic comes into play. New York has been, and may well continue to be, a trendsetter for the rest of the country. To the extent that much of the media in the country is based in New York City, the ethnoracial hierarchies, categories, and attitudes that hold sway there may have an impact elsewhere. Indeed, Gans even suggests that because New York, and Los Angeles, are the country's "prime creators of popular culture," their "distinctive racial and ethnic characteristics will probably be diffused in subtle ways through the country as a whole."[69]

The analysis in this chapter is a beginning attempt to compare the construction of race and ethnicity and intergroup relations across cities and regions in the United States in the wake of the enormous immigration of recent decades. Inevitably, it is limited by the availability of in-depth studies on these topics; future comparisons will benefit as more research is conducted. A host of questions await further study, including how racial and ethnic identities are changing and developing among various groups in different places, the impact of intermarriage for identities and social relations, the degree and effects of intermixing in schools, organizations, and neighborhoods, and the kinds of conflicts, as well as accommodations, that emerge in the political arena.

In looking ahead, there is also the question of "the future of race" in America or the way that racial hierarchies will be constructed in the years to come. Several years ago, the sociologist Orlando Patterson wrote a short piece in *The New Republic* in which he sketched out several major social patterns that he predicted would develop in different regions of the country. In the "California system," to mention one pattern, a hybrid population, mainly Eurasian but with a growing Latin element, will, he argued, come to dominate the middle and upper classes, while "lower-class Caucasians, middle-class racial purists, and most African Americans, under pressure from an endless stream of unskilled Mexican workers, will move away." A "Caribbean-American system" will have Florida as its metropolitan center, with people marrying lighter and "white" as they move up the social ladder; the "Atlanta pattern" is what he predicts for the Southeast, where African Americans and European Americans will remain highly segregated from each other.[70]

At around the same time, in a discussion of the possibility of a new black-nonblack racial hierarchy in the twenty-first century United States, another sociologist, Herbert Gans, put forward his own suggestions for regional variations. The racial hierarchy of the Deep South, he argues, will probably continue to bear many direct marks of slavery; in the Southwest, Mexicans and other Hispanics remain at the socioeconomic bottom and in California they may be joined by the Hmong, Laotians, and other poor Asians; and in the handful of mostly rural parts of the country where they now live, Native Americans still occupy the lowest socioeconomic stratum.[71]

One can, of course, challenge Patterson's patterns or quarrel with Gans's predictions. The details are not what matter here. The key point is that both highlight the need to consider regional variation in understanding the future of race in America—and, by extension, regional variation in perceptions of race and ethnicity, and relations among racial and ethnic groups, in the present as well. At the moment, there is no single U.S. pattern when it comes to the way race and ethnicity are constructed, and this is also bound to be true in the years ahead. Thus, the challenge is to more fully understand how constructions of race and ethnicity and intergroup relations develop in different urban centers in the United States in the context of immigration—and, at the same time, to place these social constructions and relations in comparative perspective as a way to appreciate, and explain, both the parallels and contrasts across cities and regions. My own eye has been on New York as the constant in the comparisons, yet future studies of immigration, race, and ethnicity will no doubt seek to place other cities on center stage in the quest to understand what makes them unique as well as what they share with other American cities.

# 9

# Immigration Past and Present
## *Some U.S.-European Comparisons*

Immigration is changing the face of Europe—just as it is
altering America—and a comparison of the immigrant experience in the
United States and Europe can illuminate processes of integration in both
places. Much of what has been written comparing immigration in the
United States and Europe focuses on political matters—state policies on
immigration control and regulation, for example, and citizenship and
political incorporation. Scholars are beginning to grapple with other
comparative U.S.-Europe questions, as European societies struggle with
ethnic and religious diversity in the context of large-scale immigration
and as issues, such as the banning of head scarves from French public
schools, become subject of heated public debate.[1]

In this final chapter, I offer some reflections on immigration on both
sides of the Atlantic that grow out of my comparative-historical research on New York immigrants today and a century ago.[2] It is a fitting
way to conclude for it considers comparisons across space *and* across
time. The taking off point is the United States, and in this sense the
chapter is an admittedly "American-centric" analysis. One theme focuses on popular myths or memories about immigrants in the past that
color views of immigrants today in Europe and the United States. The
second theme concerns the implications of past processes of racialization among immigrants in the United States for understanding race and
ethnic relations in western Europe. Finally, there is the question of the
emphasis on and discourse about race on the two sides of the Atlantic
in the context of contemporary immigration.

In comparing the United States and western Europe, there is, of
course, a risk of homogenizing both places. In Europe, there are, among
other things, critical national differences, as a growing literature makes
clear.[3] In the United States, views of immigrants and notions of race and
ethnicity, as well as the dynamics of racial and ethnic relations, vary by

city and region, as I discussed in the last chapter. By pointing to some broad general patterns that can be said to characterize much of Europe, on the one hand, and the United States, on the other, this chapter aims to contribute to a cross-national (or perhaps, more accurately, cross-continental) discussion in ways that can highlight aspects of, and suggest areas for further research about, immigration and views of immigrants in both places.

## Memories of the Past

A comparison of immigration today with the past invariably brings up the question of how the past is remembered. The concern here is less with individual memories or recollections, but with what have been called "collective memories" or representations of the past which are conveyed, maintained, and celebrated by speeches, monuments, scholarship, textbooks, and official ceremonies.[4] One reason, in fact, that I wrote *From Ellis Island to JFK*—and offered a systematic comparison of immigrants in New York's two great waves of the twentieth century —was to set the record straight.[5]

Many of the popular memories about the massive southern and eastern European immigration to the United States a hundred years ago are, in fact, myths—what I have called the invention of immigration. These myths or memories matter, as I have argued in the New York context, because they deeply color how the newest arrivals are seen.[6] A century ago, many native-born Americans viewed newly arrived eastern European and southern European immigrants with fear and loathing, as "repulsive creatures" who menaced the very foundations of American civilization.[7] These negative attitudes have long been forgotten in a haze of history, replaced by images that glorify the past. In New York, indeed in much of the United States, yesterday's European immigrants are often remembered as folk heroes who worked hard, strove to become assimilated, pulled themselves up by their own Herculean efforts, and had strong family values and colorful roots. They were, in short, what made America great. Against this image of immigrant giants of the past, present-day arrivals often seem like a pale imitation.

If long-established Americans today have an image of European immigrant heroes and heroines of the past who made America great, in western Europe there is a very different kind of notion about immigration and the past: that the presence of immigrants is new and unprecedented. In his analysis of immigration and national memory in France, Gerard Noiriel calls this a denial of memory or "collective amnesia with respect to the extraordinary role played by immigration in the renewal of the French population during the 20th century."[8]

Why did these different mythical constructions develop? After all, in western Europe, as Leo Lucassen observes, there was significant immigration in the earlier decades of the twentieth century—much of it from eastern and southern Europe.[9] Perhaps the most startling case, as Aristide Zolberg and Long Litt Woon point out, is France, where the foreign-born population reached 7 percent in 1930—about the same level as in the 1990s, when, by their account, nearly one out of every four nationals had at least one immigrant grandparent from Italy, Belgium, Spain, or Poland.[10] A substantial number of Germans, as Zolberg and Long state, trace their origins to French Huguenot refugees of the seventeenth century or Polish workers of the late nineteenth; a considerable number of Swiss are the children or grandchildren of early twentieth-century guest workers, mostly Italian; and in the 2001 census, more than half a million people in England and Wales described their ethnic group as Irish.[11]

Still, as Zolberg and Long also note, although the leading industrial nations of Europe around the turn of the twentieth century had substantial numbers of foreign residents, many were temporary workers. Then, too, there was the Holocaust. Hundreds of thousands of people in Germany, France, Belgium, the Netherlands, Norway, Denmark, Italy, and Greece would today trace their ancestry to immigrants from eastern Europe had it not been for the mass murder of Jews by the Nazis, which also prompted many of the survivors to emigrate to Israel or overseas.[12] And while in some countries, such as the French case that I just mentioned, the foreign-born were sizable in the early twentieth century, in most western European countries and major cities, the number and proportion of immigrants then were relatively small compared to today. In some countries, this is especially dramatic. Thus, in the Netherlands, 9 percent of the population was foreign-born in 2001, compared to less than 2 percent in 1920—23 percent in Amsterdam in 2001, compared to 2 percent in 1920.[13] Writing of foreign laborers and their families arriving in northwestern Europe in the 1960s and 1970s, in the context of a broad historical study of "moving Europeans," Leslie Page Moch calls the numbers in the contemporary period unprecedented.[14] Moreover, until recently several western European countries—Italy and Portugal, to name two prominent examples—were classic countries of emigration, where memories of exit, not entry, were prominent.

This is quite different in the United States. Across the Atlantic a hundred years ago, a massive wave of immigration—which came on top of a large influx in the mid-nineteenth century—dramatically transformed the United States. In 1920, after four decades of heavy immigration, 13 percent of the population of the United States was foreign-born. (Recently, the percentage has been about 12 percent.) In that year, more than one out of five residents in 35 of the nation's 68 cities with a population of at least 100,000 was foreign-born—in New York, Boston, Cleveland, Chicago, San Francisco, and Detroit, it was closer to one in three.[15] Indeed, in New York, in 1910, the foreign-born represented 41 percent of the city's population—a figure that still has not been reached today.

The result is that an enormous proportion of Americans have ancestors who came in the last great wave of immigration at the turn of the twentieth century. According to one estimate, over one hundred million Americans can trace their ancestry in the United States to a man, woman, or child whose name appears in the record book in the great Registry Room at Ellis Island. Perhaps not surprisingly, the descendants of the earlier immigrants—now fully established as Americans and having come a long way from the huddled masses who got off the boat at Ellis Island—look back to their immigrant ancestors with nostalgia. As Hasia Diner puts it in the context of Jewish memories of Manhattan's Lower East Side, many look to their immigrant roots to "explain who they are, where they came from, and the places they have been." In general, as Noiriel observes, there is a notion in the "American collective memory" of the United States as a "melting pot" and a place of refuge for all peoples.[16]

In his analysis of what he calls the "opposing uses of memory" in France and the United States, Noiriel advances two other explanations that may have some relevance as well. One reason, he suggests, why immigration has a prominent place in national memory in the United States is that it played a decisive role in the initial peopling of the new and largely unoccupied country; in France, mass immigration did not occur until the nineteenth century and immigrants were viewed as transient workers destined to return to their home countries. Also, Noiriel argues, there is the relation between the timing of immigration and the construction of the nation-state: "Contrary to the U.S., where the construction of the nation-state and mass immigration appeared at the same time, in France, mass immigration did not begin before the second half of the 19th century, at a time when socio-political structures and the nation-state had already been in place for quite some time."[17]

Whatever the reasons for the origins of the myths or memories about immigration, the fact is that many Europeans have been reluctant to see themselves as belonging to immigration societies. In Germany, where postwar immigrants and their children make up nearly 10 percent of the population, a familiar refrain has been "We are not a country of immigration," although Christian Joppke notes that by the late 1990s this "ritual formula" had receded from political discourse.[18] In the United States, by contrast, Americans have, for many decades, seen themselves as belonging to a "nation of immigrants"—or as one recent account puts it, as an immigration society through and through.[19] The incorporation of European immigrants has been one of twentieth-century America's most celebrated achievements. The Statue of Liberty and Ellis Island have become shrines to what makes America unique and, more and more in the decades since World War II, they have eclipsed images of the American Revolution in the nation's patriotic iconography.[20] The history of these two shrines, and their elevation to iconic status, is particularly interesting since the Statue of Liberty was originally conceived by its creator and backers as a symbol of French-American friendship and political liberty—not of immigration. Ellis Island, which ceased to be a mass processing station for immigrants during the 1920s, was actually closed in 1954 and abandoned, and left to fall into ruin, for some twenty years.

As John Higham writes in his essay "The Transformation of the Statue of Liberty," it was the termination of mass immigration that eventually led, in the 1940s and 1950s, to the special association of the statue with immigration:

> So long as millions of immigrants entered "the golden door," the Statue of Liberty was unresponsive to them; it served other purposes. After the immigrant ships no longer passed under the New Colossus in significant numbers, it enshrined the immigrant experience as a transcendental national memory. Because few Americans now were immigrants, all could think of themselves as having been immigrants. The Statue of

Liberty helped them to do so. Since it belonged to all the people and on the broadest level symbolized the nation as a whole, the statue connected the special heritage of newer Americans with the civic principles of all Americans. Fundamentally, the new meaning engrafted on the Statue of Liberty in the second quarter of the twentieth century worked to close the rift that mass immigration had opened in American society.[21]

As for Ellis Island, in 1990, after a six-year $170 million renovation—by which time, the descendants of the Ellis Island immigrants were part of the American mainstream—the Ellis Island Immigration Museum was opened in the restored Main Building. It now receives more than a million visitors a year. In April 2001, when the Statue of Liberty–Ellis Island Foundation digitized its immigration records and debuted its new website, the response was astounding, with the site recording 1.5 billion hits in its first six months. No similar kind of museum exists in western Europe, and Noiriel comments that "comparable symbols of immigration in France (such as the selection center in the city of Toul, in the East of the country, which recruited the bulk of Central European immigrants between the wars) were razed to the ground, as if a history which fits in so poorly with the mythology of the soil could be magically erased." Although a new Museum of Immigration and Diversity in Britain, which aims to recount the story of newcomers to Britain over time, opened in the East End of London in June 2003, it was struggling to raise $4.8 million so that it could be open year-round.[22]

Quite apart from Ellis Island and the Statue of Liberty, immigrant imagery is part of contemporary political discourse in the United States—with leading political figures (many with parents, grandparents, or great-grandparents who came from abroad) making much of their immigrant roots. This is especially pronounced in New York. The grandparents of the previous mayor, Rudolph Giuliani, came from Italy; former mayor Ed Koch's parents' entered Ellis Island fleeing anti-Semitism in eastern Europe. In a not atypical reference, the present Governor of New York State (George Pataki)—who has immigrant grandparents—spoke in his recent campaign of today's immigrants "living the American dream." On a national stage, in 2003, Governor Gary Locke of the state of Washington, began his televised rebuttal, on behalf of the Democratic Party, to President Bush's State of the Union address, this way: "My grandfather came to this country from China nearly a century ago and worked as a servant. Now, I serve as governor just one mile from where my grandfather worked. It took our family 100 years to travel that mile. It was a voyage we could only make in America."[23]

So the memories of immigration are perpetuated. In this context, it is not surprising that they have affected popular conceptions and the popular literature. They have also had an impact on the scholarship about the recent newcomers. To a great extent, the social science literature on new immigrants in the United States is comparative, in the sense that it often counterposes today's arrivals against their predecessors who arrived a century ago, even if it is only a passing nod to the earlier wave or brief assumptions about the "newness" of today's influx.[24] Clearly, this has enriched the American scholarly literature on immigration—especially when the comparisons are more systematic and fully developed.[25] But to the extent that the mythic constructions have seeped into the scholarship, they create problems. This is a concern raised by Zolberg and Long in their comparative analysis of immigration's impact in Europe and the United States. They argue that debates about incorporation on both sides of the Atlantic are imprisoned within divergent mythic constructions—endogenous nations of Europe, on the one hand, and, to add my own twist to their analysis, the United States as a nation that has always celebrated immigrants, on the other.[26] An uncritical acceptance of "the essentialized distinction between endogenous nations and nations of immigration fosters ignorance of Europe's historical encounters with immigrant populations . . . and clouds the . . . parallel objective experiences of Europe and the United States in the second half of the twentieth century."[27]

## The Dynamics of Racialization: How Exceptional Is the United States?

Then there is the question of race and processes of racialization. Is the American experience when it comes to racial divisions so exceptional that it is irrelevant for understanding issues of immigration, race, and ethnicity in Europe? Certainly, there have been distinctive features in the U.S. context, but these should not blind us to the possibility of certain similar developments and underlying processes shaping the social construction of race and ethnoracial relations on both sides of the Atlantic.

One reason for the central role of immigrants in the American imagination and dream has to do with the common, and invidious, comparison between immigrants and native blacks. Immigrants are often praised for their grit, determination, and work ethic in contrast to native minorities, who are often viewed as members of the "underclass" —as less reliable, less productive, less pliable, and less tractable than new arrivals. Indeed, as I noted in chapter 2, a number of studies document American employers' preferences for hiring immigrants over native blacks and Hispanics.

In general, it is impossible to understand the dynamics of racialization, past and present, in the United States without a consideration of the African American presence and America's history of slavery and segregation. Unquestionably, this makes the American experience with immigration strikingly different from Europe's. European countries oversaw slavery regimes in their colonies, but this was far from home. Slavery was on America's soil: since its formation the United States has had a large, subordinated black population inside its territorial boundaries. The special position of blacks has been an essential element in how ethnic or racial groups of immigrant origin have defined themselves and their position in American society.[28]

In the past, it will be recalled, one factor involved in the transformation of eastern and southern Europeans from disparaged racial outsiders to part of the racial majority was their attempts to distance themselves from African Americans (see chapter 1). The novelist Ralph Ellison wrote that "one of the first epithets that many European immigrants learned when they got off the boat was the term 'nigger'—it made them feel instantly American."[29] Although Ellison's periodization is wrong—when European immigrants got off the boat at the turn of the twentieth century, blacks did not figure much in their lives because so few blacks lived in northern cities like New York—his comment captures an important racial dynamic that operated later on, after the mass migration of African Americans to northern cities.

In Europe, distancing from African Americans obviously was not involved in changed attitudes to immigrants and their children in earlier periods—nor is it relevant today. It is important, however, not to go overboard in putting too much stress on the role of distancing from African Americans in the U.S. case. Indeed, an appreciation of other factors that played a role in making eastern and southern Europeans racial insiders in the United States may shed light on parallel developments among immigrants in the past in Europe. Moreover, precisely because of the different history of racial divisions in the United States, a cross-Atlantic comparison may sharpen the analysis of the way racialization has operated in Europe.

Among the factors that played a role in altering views of immigrants and their descendants in Europe in the past, as they did in the United States in the mid-twentieth century, were immigrant economic assimilation and upward mobility as well as intermarriage and intermixing—to say nothing of the reaction to the Holocaust in the years after World War II, which made anti-Semitism and racism generally less respectable and acceptable (see chapter 1). Just which combination of factors operated in particular national contexts will become clarified as historians of European societies do their own analyses to trace the changes in stereotypes of and discriminatory practices against earlier immigrants. An important step forward is Lucassen's study of the processes of integration among the Irish in Britain, Poles in Germany, and Italians in France in the nineteenth and twentieth centuries.[30]

## Discourse about Race: Color and Culture

So we come to the final topic concerning the discourse about race in contemporary Europe and the United States. And, once again, it is necessary to consider the impact of the American racial structure—in particular, the position of blacks and their history of special disadvantage—in shaping responses to immigration, the experiences of immigrants, and the way scholars themselves analyze the new arrivals.

In the United States today, as in the past, immigrants are often seen through the prism of race. In fact, many Americans who want to restrict immigration are worried that otherwise it will lead to "the end of the white race"—or as conservative critic Peter Brimelow has written in *Alien Nation*, that immigrants will end up swamping white America.[31] In the scholarly literature, this is obviously not an issue. What is a central concern in that literature is how the newest arrivals are changing conceptions and constructions of race and affecting relations between groups that are defined as ethnically and/or racially distinct.[32] In this regard, a major topic is the effect of the new immigration on relations with established racial minorities, especially African Americans. Mention almost any issue in the immigration literature and the question of immigrant relations with established minorities comes up—in political science, in terms of how the growing Hispanic population will affect relations with African Americans in communities where Hispanics have numerically overtaken and begun to challenge African Americans' newly won accession to positions of power; in economics, as to whether immigrants are hurting native minorities in the job market; and in sociology, whether some immigrant groups will experience segmented assimilation, as they are exposed to the life styles and outlooks found in inner-city minority schools and neighborhoods.

This is not surprising. Race, especially the black-white divide, has long been a significant (some might say *the* significant) social division in the United States—the classic American dilemma, given the history of slavery, Jim Crow, and ghettoization. The nation continues to deal with the impact of the civil rights revolution, which sought to redress the wrongs of the segregation era. Non-Hispanic blacks are a very substantial proportion of the nation's population—12 percent in 2000—and the proportion is much higher in many major cities.

In Cornel West's much-quoted phrase, in the United States "race matters."[33] Newspaper stories refer to race all the time; so do politicians and activists; and so do scholars. No African American public intellectuals, as far as I know, have embraced "ethnicity" as a model for their group self-consciousness; the reason for this reluctance to abandon race in favor of ethnicity perhaps has to do with the desire to emphasize that America's black population has confronted, and continues to confront, obstacles to equality and opportunity, and persistent racism, of a kind that European immigrants and their children did not experience.[34]

Hundreds of courses on college campuses—and dozens of textbooks—focus on "race and ethnicity" in the United States. In a landmark decision, the U.S. Supreme Court recently upheld the use of race in university admissions. And race is used to officially categorize people—the census being a case in point, with people now allowed to report themselves as belonging to two or more races, the races being White, Black, American Indian, Native Hawaiian or Other Pacific Islander, Asian, and "Some other race." Indeed, it is argued that attempts by anti-affirmative activists like Ward Connerly, and his ballot initiative to eliminate questions on race on California government forms, threaten social programs designed to ameliorate existing racial inequalities. While some American scholars have sought to substitute other terms—ethnoracial, communities of descent, or racialized groups—for race, the Census Bureau and much of the American public, as Hollinger observes, remain "in the thrall of the concept of race."[35]

In the American scholarly literature, there is agreement that race is a socially and culturally constructed category that usually has a close connection to "racism" as an ideology or attitude. However scholars define race in their studies, in everyday discourse in the United States, race tends to be a color-coded concept—Black, Red (Native Indian), Yellow (Asian), White, and Brown (Hispanic).

In much of western Europe, scholars often feel less comfortable talking about race. There is a concern that using the term gives legitimacy to discriminatory tendencies and inequalities by reifying races as biologically distinguishable groups and that the term is associated with rigid divisions, of a U.S. black-white variety, based on color and physical identification that are less relevant—and need to be avoided—in western Europe.[36] (In French public life, this unease extends to using ethnicity as a statistical category. To classify people, as is done in the United States, as non-Hispanic whites, Hispanics, blacks, and Asians, Noiriel writes, "would be considered racist in France, evidence of discrimination among French citizens; to Americans it seems natural.")[37] Miri Song notes that in Britain, there has been a tendency in much scholarship to use scare quotes around the word "race," whereas in the United States, "there is still widespread acceptance of 'race' (a term rarely placed in scare quotes), as a system of power, in both ideological and material terms."[38] In Germany, France, and elsewhere, there are other concerns, that go back to the particular historical circumstances in World War II. In the immediate postwar period, the word "race" was almost eliminated from French public discourse, given its identification with extremist Nazi positions.[39] In a recent paper for a conference on transnationalism, Dietrich Thranhardt argues that terms like "blood" and "race" are taboo in political discourse in Germany because they are associated with the Nazis. Thranhardt contends that using the term "race" (and ethnicity) as classification categories, even for such purposes as policing and preventing discrimination, legitimizes and gives priority to these categories. In his view, no racial discourse is the best racial discourse of all.[40]

In continental western Europe, immigrants are more likely to be stigmatized on the basis of culture than of color-coded race. (Here, I deliberately exclude England which is more like the United States in this regard, particularly when it comes to African Caribbeans and Africans.)

In the United States, it is the other way around: immigrants are more likely to be stigmatized on the basis of race-as-color than culture, although of course, claims of cultural inferiority are also involved just as skin color plays a role in continental western Europe. As an aside: Americans, even well-educated Americans and scholars outside of the immigration field, continue to be astonished that Turks and Moroccans in the Netherlands are seen, as Lucassen puts it, as more "black" in public opinion than Surinamese of African ancestry, who differ less from the native population in culture and language than Turks and Moroccans and do better in socioeconomic terms. The term "black schools" in the Netherlands is generally used to refer to schools where a large proportion of the pupils are first- and second-generation Moroccans and Turks.[41]

A key question is whether the use of allegedly deep-seated cultural differences as justification for hostility and discrimination against newcomers in Europe is, in fact, a kind of "cultural racism." (Also at issue, in the context of a past-present comparison, is whether cultural racism is something new or has a long history in particular countries.) Those who use the term "cultural racism" to describe the reaction to new immigrants in Europe argue that race is, in effect, "coded as culture"; the "central feature of these processes is that the qualities of social groups are fixed, made natural, confined within a pseudo-biologically defined culturalism."[42] In Fredrickson's conceptualization of racism, culture and even religion can become essentialized to the point that they can serve as a functional equivalent of biological racism—culture, put another way, can do the work of race, when peoples or ways of life are seen as unchangeable as pigmentation. Or as Orlando Patterson has recently argued, in so far as cultural determinism entails the conception of others as immutably different and inferior, it is racism.[43]

If cultural differences play such a large role in disparaging and stigmatizing immigrants in western Europe, what implications does this have for integration? Will integration be less problematic, or follow a different path, there because the stigma attached to immigrants is more closely associated with culture and religion than, as in the United States, with skin color and biological race?

One view, put forward by Fredrickson, suggests that cultural, especially religious, forms of racist bigotry may be more durable (although less rigid) than those tied to ideas about biology or genetics. He raises the possibility, to use his words, that because the foundations to racist

claims (based on blood or the genes) are "subject to empirical falsifica-
tion . . . [ they are] more fragile than the incontrovertible and unques-
tioning faith demanded by sectarian or fundamentalist religion."[44]

Yet there is an alternative view. After all, conversion, in the case of
religion, or change in cultural patterns, in the case of culture more generally, are always a theoretical possibility. (In fact, in his conceptualization of racism, Fredrickson argues that he would withhold the "R"
word if assimilation is genuinely on offer, and he writes that it might
be preferable to speak of "culturalism" rather than racism to describe
an inability or unwillingness to tolerate cultural differences.)[45] To the
extent that assimilation and acculturation take place, in other words,
cultural racism is undermined. However, when differences are believed
to be rooted in genes or biology, they are seen to be innate and impervi-
ous to change.

Or at least to change by acculturation. Perhaps this is why discussions about the future direction and shape of race and racial boundaries
in the United States put so much stress on the role of intermarriage—
which will, literally, change people's skin color and facial characteristics. The rising rates of intermarriage, in particular, between Hispanics
and whites and Asians and whites are creating large numbers of "multiracial" or blended offspring. As discussed earlier, one often-mentioned
scenario foresees multiracial individuals becoming part of an expanded
white group; another predicts that they will merge into a new "nonblack" or "beige" category that will be opposed to "blacks" (see chapter 1). Whatever happens, it is interesting how much the different
forecasts for the "future of race" in the United States are seen as being
tied to changing physical characteristics. Recall the quote from journalist Stanley Crouch in chapter 1, who predicts an America a hundred
years from now where "the sweep of body types, combinations of facial
features, hair textures, eye colors, and what are now unexpected skin
tones will be far more common."[46] There is the notion, in other words,
that it will take a change in pigmentation and physiology to alter notions of racial difference—cultural assimilation will not be enough.

## Conclusion: Other Comparative Questions

These comments about the future—and about the durability and change-
ability of different forms of racism—are, of course, highly speculative.

They suggest, however, differences in paths of integration for immigrants and their children in the United States and western Europe—differences that, at least in part, are rooted in historical experiences. This chapter has offered some reflections on U.S.-European comparisons. It has suggested some ways that comparisons of immigrants past and present in the United States can shed light on similar efforts in Europe, and pointed to contrasts in the way that immigrants of the past are remembered and immigrants today are analyzed on the two sides of the Atlantic.

Obviously, there are a great many themes and topics that call for further cross-national study. Social scientists in Europe and the United States have been seeking to document and understand the experiences of the contemporary second generation, yet as the introduction to a recent special issue of *International Migration Review* on the second generation in Europe notes, international comparative research on the second generation is still scant.[47] One question is whether, and to what extent, the segmented assimilation perspective developed to explain different patterns among the second generation in the United States pertains to Europe. The segmented assimilation model predicts that one outcome for the United States could be a downward trajectory among members of the second generation whose parents have few resources and who are exposed to the norms and oppositional ethos of disaffected inner-city native minority youth.[48] Others have raised doubts about whether this pessimistic prognosis is, in fact, accurate for the United States; new studies point to better outcomes for many of the offspring of working-class immigrants and stress the need to avoid confusing "ghetto" cultural styles with self-defeating behavior that impedes educational success (see chapter 2).

As for Europe, a key issue is what happens among the second generation in the absence of U.S. structural features, namely, an indigenous minority "underclass." Recent research on the Turkish and Moroccan second generation in Europe suggests that "the existence of large-scale ghettos and greater barriers to education in the United States may make the downward assimilation path more probable there."[49] Attempts to apply the segmented assimilation perspective to European countries, some would argue, may be a case of trying to apply American ideas and conceptualizations that do not necessarily fit the issues most salient in the European situation.[50]

Other studies point to alternative roots for oppositional outlooks in Europe.[51] Several Dutch studies suggest that an oppositional subculture can emerge because it is a legacy from the sending region or because "a subculture that the media packages as 'black' or 'Latino' emphasizes an adversarial stance."[52] Or it may just be a matter of class disadvantage and, as Roger Waldinger and Cynthia Feliciano argue, that an oppositional culture is generic to "'negatively privileged' groups pure and simple."[53] Along these lines, Joppke and Morawska contend that downward or segmented assimilation into "the lower cultural and economic segments of the host society"—and adoption of an adversarial culture that rejects mainstream norms, values, and role models—may apply in Europe as well as the United States "to lower-class immigrants' children who are racially or religiously 'othered' by the host society and whose upward mobility is blocked by structural disadvantage and racial or religious discrimination by host-country people and institutions." This could include Mexican Americans in Los Angeles, North African "beurs" in France, or what they call "opt out" groups of young Turkish "denizens" in Germany.[54] At present, much of this is speculation. How extensive such adversarial or oppositional outlooks—and, more important, downward mobility—actually are among various disadvantaged second-generation groups in both Europe and the United States are clearly topics that require careful empirical examination.[55]

Much has been written about different citizenship policies in the United States and Europe, including the acquisition of citizenship, naturalization policy, dual nationality, and the political and social rights of immigrants. The United States, of course, stands out in its unqualified— and long-term—attribution of citizenship to those born on American soil (jus soli) in contrast to the tradition of citizenship by descent from one or both parents who are nationals (jus sanguinis) in continental Europe.[56] By now, most western European countries provide the right of citizenship to the second generation, although in a more qualified form than in the United States; in many European nations, for example, a person born in the country to foreign parents can acquire citizenship at the age of majority after fulfilling certain residency requirements.[57] In the wake of recent legislation, Germany now provides provisional birthright citizenship for second-generation children, although the effects will not be fully felt among adult members of the second generation for two decades.[58] There is a need for studies that not only compare how different citizenship laws influence (and are influenced by) immigration and integration policies in Europe and the United States but also, at the micro-level, how they affect the lives of immigrants and their children (and grandchildren), including their identities, political involvements and sense of membership, and willingness and ability to make claims asserting rights.

Another important topic is how the nature of the welfare state in continental European countries shapes a range of policies, from admissions to integration, and influences immigrants' economic trajectories and attitudes to immigrants in ways that differ from the more laissez-faire United States. Given the stronger welfare state in European countries, it is not surprising that scholars of European immigration have paid more attention to the role of state welfare policy and regulatory mechanisms than their counterparts studying the United States, who often relegate government policy to a background variable and do not consider it central to their analyses. The study of immigrant entrepreneurship is one example where European scholars have put government policies on center stage while Americans often take them for granted —or as one European observer puts it, as an unproblematic given.[59] Indeed, the Dutch scholars Jan Rath and Robert Kloosterman argue that comparative international research on immigrant entrepreneurship requires a theoretical framework that takes into account "the institutional framework of the welfare state within which entrepreneurs operate."[60] Rath's comparison of immigrant garment entrepreneurs in European and American cities brings out the role of government policies, laws, rules, and regulations—as well as their enforcement (or lack of enforcement)—in encouraging or restricting business opportunities.[61]

More generally, an issue in the European literature is the unintended consequences of the welfare state for immigrants. While continental European welfare regimes have tended to provide generous social services and a high level of legal protection and rights for workers, a number of scholars argue that this has led to a deep insider-outsider cleavage, with immigrants displaying high rates of unemployment and low rates of labor force participation and being resented for taking advantage of liberal welfare-state provisions, thereby offering opponents of immigration a further push for closed borders. Immigrants in the United States, by contrast, come to a society with highly flexible labor markets where they find entry-level jobs fairly easily, although large numbers are stuck earning low pay without the kinds of government social supports, including health care and housing assistance, that are more widely available in Europe.[62] Welfare regimes in European countries, and in the United States, are, of course, constantly in the process of adaptation

222 | Immigration Past and Present

and change—the Netherlands, for example, moving to a more market-oriented welfare state in the 1990s, and welfare reform law in the United States reducing benefits.[63] These changes need to be taken into account in comparative studies that explore how state-level institutional arrangements and structures, on both sides of the Atlantic, affect the opportunities available to immigrants and their children.

Also on the agenda are analyses of the contrasting way that ethnic distinctions are institutionalized and reinforced in the domains of religion, language, and citizenship in the European and American contexts.[64] One approach that can help to illuminate differences in the social construction and impact of ethnic and racial distinctions in Europe and the United States is comparisons of the same ethnic group in different national settings. In previous chapters, I have offered a comparison of this type, focusing on Afro-Caribbeans in Britain and the United States. Comparative studies of other groups on the two sides of the Atlantic —South Asians in the United States and Britain, for example, or sub-Saharan Africans in the United States and France—can reveal the complex way that various social, cultural, political, and economic factors in different national contexts shape the experiences of the first and second generation.

If I have stressed trans-Atlantic differences in this chapter, I do not mean to suggest that they should be our only focus. Obviously, the differences stand out, but a sole focus on differences runs the risk of seeing only the unique features of the United States and ignoring parallels with contemporary Europe. Indeed, a number of scholars note a growing trend toward convergence among advanced liberal democratic states in certain policies in the context of mass immigration—citizenship policies a prime example, as most western European nations have reformed their citizenship rules to make it easier for long-settled migrants and their children to acquire citizenship.[65]

When it comes to ethnoracial distinctions, an exclusive focus on the unique position of African Americans should not blind us to commonalities in the experiences of racialized minority groups in Europe and the United States. Blacks may be the quintessentially racialized Americans —and the African American presence a vital component in understanding the U.S. immigrant experience—but racial inequality in America is not, and has not been, just a matter of black and white. When European scholars look at racism across the Atlantic, there is a tendency to focus on black-white issues, and in some cases, to see immigrants in their own societies as the structural equivalents of American blacks. This can be misleading. It may be useful to compare the experiences of many recent immigrant groups in Europe with those of Asian and Latino immigrants in the United States—Turks in Europe with Mexicans in the United States, for example; these comparisons are likely to bring out additional contrasts and perhaps parallels as well.

And finally, I come back to the broad use of western Europe and the United States in this chapter. In my own studies, I am constantly reminded that New York—where I do my research—stands out in many ways from other immigrant destinations in the United States, with their own special histories of immigration, distinctive social, economic, and political contexts, and immigrant streams with particular skills and nationality backgrounds. The previous chapter made this clear. Future trans-Atlantic comparisons of the immigrant experience should take into account differences among U.S. regions and cities as well, of course, as variations among nations—and cities—in western Europe.

As immigration continues to transform both the United States and Europe, there is, in short, much work to do in bringing a comparative lens to the analysis—a lens which allows us to rethink and reevaluate both past and present patterns in both places. In line with the strengths of a comparative perspective that I have emphasized throughout this book, comparisons across space and time not only underscore what is distinctive about immigrant flows to Europe and the United States and the national and urban contexts into which the immigrants have moved but also how European and American cities have changed as sites for receiving and incorporating immigrants over time. In the introduction to a special issue of *The Netherlands Journal of Social Sciences* comparing immigrants in New York and Amsterdam, Rath suggests that international comparative research can broaden our intellectual horizons in another way. In each country, he observes, there is a distinctive way of framing problems when it comes to immigration, and social science research is inevitably informed by these national representations. Comparative research that looks at both sides of the Atlantic, as he notes, can offer a way of "problematizing popular concepts and their theoretical and ideological foundations."[66]

Comparisons of more than one place, one group, and one time period are, inevitably, an ambitious undertaking, yet, as I have shown in this book, they have much to offer to studies of immigration. These chapters have given a taste of the kind of insights that can be gained from comparisons across time and space, as they have explored the dynamics of immigration to New York past and present, the experiences of West Indians in different settings, and migration to Europe and the United States. They raise a challenge for the future, and, it is hoped, will stimulate additional comparative studies that will bring new insights to our understanding of the consequences of migration for both the people who move and the places where they settle.

# Notes

NOTES TO THE INTRODUCTION

1. In addition to comparisons of Jamaicans in London and New York (Foner 1983, 1985, 1986, 1998a, 1998b), and immigrants in New York today and a hundred years ago (Foner 1997, 1999b, 2000, 2001b, 2002a), I have also been involved in comparisons outside of the migration field. In an earlier volume and series of articles, I analyzed relations and inequalities between old and young in cross-cultural perspective (see Foner 1984).

2. Some would even say that virtually all social science research is comparative. As Eugene Hammel has written about social science scholarship generally: "No analytic statement about empirical observation can be made without at least one comparison providing the contrast that permits either inductive generalization or deductive proof" (Hammel 1980: 145).

3. Green 1994: 15.

4. Fox and Gingrich 2002: 8.

5. Green 1994.

6. My own book, *From Ellis Island to JFK: New York's Two Great Waves of Immigration* (2000), is the only single-authored volume to provide a comprehensive comparison of the U.S. immigrant experience then and now, but it looks only at New York, offering no comparisons with other cities or countries. Since the book appeared, several edited collections have been published that were designed to compare today's immigration with earlier immigration in the United States: Gary Gerstle and John Mollenkopf, *E Pluribus Unum?* (2001), Pyong Gap Min, *Mass Migration to the United States* (2001), and a volume I edited with George Fredrickson, *Not Just Black and White* (2004). The few volumes explicitly organized to compare U.S. immigrants in different urban locations or with immigrants in other national societies have focused on economic or political issues—for example, Jeffrey Reitz, *The Warmth of the Welcome* (1998), a quantitative analysis of immigrants' economic performance in the United States, Canada, and Australia; Roger Waldinger's edited volume, *Strangers at the Gates* (2001), that compares immigrant economic incorporation in the five major U.S. immigrant urban destinations; and Michael Jones-Correa's edited book, *Governing American Cities* (2001), which brings together chapters on new immigrants and American political life to lay the foundation for a comparative,

cross-city approach to understanding changing interethnic relations. Several edited volumes have offered comparisons of immigrant entrepreneurship or particular industries in the United States and Europe (e.g., Waldinger, Aldrich, Ward and Associates 1990; Rath 2002) or citizenship and immigration policy (e.g. Aleinikoff and Klusmeyer 2000, 2001). One recent volume was organized to assess the impact of different host societies on the immigrant experience (with an emphasis on the American and Canadian cases), but as the editor notes, only about half of the eighteen chapters could be considered to include cross-national or interregional comparative analysis (Reitz 2003). As for the several books comparing the same immigrant group in different places, these are historical studies that do not include the contemporary period (see Baily 1999 on Italians in Buenos Aires and New York; Berrol 1994 and Godley 2001 on Jews in early twentieth century New York and London; and Green 1997 on immigrants in the Paris and New York garment industry).

7. One might say that my own earlier works are sources, as well. Most of the chapters in Part I, on New York's two great waves of immigration, have their origins in previously published work, although it has been significantly revised for this book (see Foner 1999b, 2000, 2001d, 2002a, 2002b, and 2003a). The chapters in Part II, on West Indians in New York and London, incorporate material from earlier articles, but, in truth, they bear little resemblance to them. I have reworked the analyses and reframed arguments, updated and expanded discussions in light of new research and material, and considered new topics and raised new questions. The chapters in Part III are, in every sense, altogether new and appear here for the first time.

8. Bendix 1964: 17.

9. Fredrickson 1997: 65.

10. Green 2002.

11. Gerstle and Mollenkopf 2001:3.

12. Fredrickson 1997: 23.

13. See Green 1994: 3.

14. Portes 1997: 803.

15. Foner 2003b discusses, and compares, a then-and-now approach as contrasted with what I call a "becoming approach," that analyzes how, in a dialectical process, migrant inflows in one period change the social, economic, political, and cultural context that greets the next wave.

16. As I have pointed out elsewhere, a then-and-now approach that only focuses on the two great immigration waves at both ends of the twentieth century runs the risk of paying insufficient attention to the impact of the huge influx of southern blacks that occurred in between (Foner 2003b).

17. Green 1994. Green cites my own comparisons of West Indians in London and New York as an example of the divergent model. Other comparisons of this sort on immigrants in the contemporary period include Brettell 1981 on

Portuguese immigrants in Toronto and Paris, Waldinger and Tseng 1992 and Zhou and Kim 2003 on Chinese in New York City and Los Angeles, and Guarnizo, Sanchez, and Roach 1999 on Colombians in New York City and Los Angeles.

18. Brettell and Hollifield 2000: 15.

NOTES TO CHAPTER 1

1. Foner and Fredrickson 2004: 2.

2. Kasinitz 1992: 4.

3. Foner and Fredrickson 2004: 3. The term "ethnicity" can be distinguished from race, and this is often done by defining ethnicity as based on ancestry and descent as opposed to biology or genes, but such distinctions are not as easy or unambiguous as scholars sometimes maintain. Fredrickson argues that race can be described as what happens when ethnicity is deemed essential or indelible and made hierarchical. He also notes that there are cases—and African American ethnicity is a prime example—in which ethnic identity is created by the racialization of people who would not otherwise have shared an identity (Fredrickson 2002: 154–155; see also Cornell and Hartmann 1998, 2004).

4. Okihiro 2001: 54.

5. Cornell and Hartmann 2004.

6. Hattam 2001: 63.

7. See the special issue of *International Labor and Working-Class History*, 60 (Fall 2001), which centers around Eric Arnesen's dismissive critique of the scholarship on whiteness, "Whiteness and the Historians' Imagination" (2001: 3–32).

8. Brodkin 1998; Barrett and Roediger 1997; Jacobson 1998; Topp 2003.

9. Guglielmo 2003; Gratton 2002.

10. Kolchin 2002: 165.

11. Arnesen 2001; Brody 2001; E. Foner 2001.

12. Guglielmo 2003: 93; Jacobson 1998: 6.

13. Lopez 1996.

14. Guglielmo 2003: 174.

15. E. Foner 2001.

16. On the development of a national Italian identity among Italians in the United States, see Guglielmo 2003 and Luconi 2001.

17. Grant 1916. *The Passing of the Great Race* appeared in 1916, but achieved peak popularity in the 1920s.

18. Quoted in Lind 1995: 108.

19. Ross 1914: 113, 114, 95.

20. Guglielmo 2003: 22–23.

21. *New York: A Collection from Harper's Magazine* 1991: 304.

22. Quoted in Jacobson 1998: 178.

23. See Jacobson 1998: 171–199.

24. Ibid.: 79.

25. Lieberson 1980: 32. Lieberson draws on a 1911 book, *The Jews,* by Fishberg.

26. Guglielmo 2003: 86.

27. Ibid.: 27.

28. Barker, Dodd, and Commager, cited in Fitzgerald 1979: 79–80.

29. DeSalvo 2003: 28.

30. Dinnerstein 1994: 93; see also Daniels 1997: 104–105.

31. Gambino 1974: 71.

32. Dinnerstein 1994: 75, 88.

33. Ibid.: 86, 159.

34. Berger 2002, 2003. In 1957, New York City was home to about two million Jews; in 1980, there were more than one million New Yorkers of Italian descent. Suburbanization is largely responsible for the declining numbers of Jews and Italians in the city. At the same time, immigration, especially the influx of Jews from the former Soviet Union, has boosted the number of Jews.

35. Alba 1999: 19; Alba 1990: 312–333.

36. Waters 1996: 445. See Waters 1990.

37. In 2000, according to the Current Population Survey, 26.1 percent of non-Hispanic white New Yorkers were foreign-born (Mollenkopf, Olson, and Ross 2001: 32). In that year, 162,000 foreign-born former Soviets and 66,000 foreign-born Poles lived in New York City (Beveridge 2002a).

38. Rodriguez 2000: 155; see also Naber 2000. The number of New Yorkers claiming Arab ancestry on the census is rising, and increased from 52,000 to 71,000 between 1990 and 2000 (Beveridge 2002b).

39. Logan and Mollenkopf 2003. In these figures, Afro-Caribbeans refer to those with ancestry in predominantly black, non-Spanish-speaking nations such as Jamaica and Haiti.

40. See, for example, the full-length studies by Kasinitz (1992), Vickerman (1999), and Waters (1999a), as well as the chapters in Foner 2001e.

41. Bashi Bobb and Clarke 2001: 226.

42. Waters 2001.

43. Quoted in Waldman 1998.

44. Logan and Deane 2003; see also Crowder and Tedrow 2001.

45. Harrison and Bennett 1995; Bean and Stevens 2003.

46. Vickerman 2001a: 207, 210. See also the chapters in Foner 2001e.

47. Gonzales and Rodriguez 2003.

48. Dominicans are the second-largest Hispanic group, representing 27 per-

cent of the city's Hispanic population, followed by South Americans (16 percent) and Mexicans (9 percent) (Logan and Mollenkopf 2003).

49. Cf. Fox 1996: 33.

50. Samantha Lyman interview with Cuban immigrant, Urban Anthropology class, Purchase College, SUNY, December 1997.

51. Smith 1996, 2001. See also Grosfoguel and Georas, who argue that "to be identified as Puerto Rican in the ethnic/racial hierarchy of New York City is a racist marker for a new Latino immigrant" because Puerto Ricans are associated in the "Euroamerican imaginary with traits such as laziness, criminality, stupidity, and a tendency toward uncivilized behavior" (2001: 97–98).

52. Massey 1993.

53. Itzigsohn 2004; Foner and Fredrickson 2004. On the role of New York's Hispanic marketing industry in the creation of panethnic categories and images of and for Latinos see Davila 2001. There are varying definitions of panethnicity. George Fredrickson defines panethnicity as what happens when previously discrete ethnic groups seek to join together in reaction to the dominant group's tendency to homogenize them for the purpose of discriminating against them (Foner and Fredrickson 2004). David Lopez and Yen Le Espiritu define panethnicity as "the development of bridging organizations and solidarities among subgroups of ethnic collectivities that are often seen as homogeneous by outsiders" (1997: 195).

54. Ricourt and Danta 2003.

55. Itzigsohn 2004.

56. Logan 2003.

57. Grasmuck and Pessar 1996: 284.

58. Logan 2003.

59. Quoted in Rodriguez 1994: 136.

60. Rodriguez 2000: 20.

61. Pessar 1995a: 42–43; Grasmuck and Pessar 1996.

62. Logan 2003.

63. Harrison and Bennett 1995: 165.

64. In the nation as a whole, 3 percent of Hispanics counted in the 2000 census identified themselves as black. Of the Hispanics in the United States who identified as black, almost a quarter lived in the New York metropolitan area (Logan 2003). In 1990, one out of four Dominicans in New York City identified themselves as black in the census (Grasmuck and Pessar 1996: 285).

65. Logan 2003.

66. Rodriguez 1994: 141.

67. Pessar 1995b: 43.

68. Grasmuck and Pessar 1996: 289–290; Pessar 1995b: 43.

69. Fox 1996: 24; Rodriguez 1996. See also Rodriguez 2000, ch. 6.

70. Andrew Hacker (2003) has recently made the same point.

71. Smith 2003.

72. Logan and Mollenkopf 2003. These figures refer to ancestry or origin.

73. Tuan 1998: 9.

74. For a detailed account of the history of legal restrictions on the Chinese, see Lee 2003.

75. Quoted in Lopez 1996: 55–56.

76. Wollenberg 1995.

77. Espiritu 1997: 109.

78. Alba et al. 1995.

79. In the late 1990s, more than a quarter of married Asians, including the native- and foreign-born, had a non-Asian spouse, typically someone white (Bean and Stevens 2003: 238–239).

80. Scott 1997; see also Sanjek 1994.

81. Harrison and Bennett 1995: 174. The odds of interracial marriage with whites sharply increases for Asian Americans with college and postgraduate educational attainment (Alba and Nee 2003: 265).

82. Tuan 1998: 164.

83. Tuan 1998.

84. Harold Isaacs, quoted in Mazumdar 1989: 34. In terms of color prejudice, "'brown,' even a non-American born as in Indonesians and Filipinos—is a good deal less mild; but it is 'black'—wherever it comes from—that sets the racial-color counters clicking the most violently. The Indian, shading along a wide spectrum from fair to brown to black, arouses these reactions in varying measures."

85. See Lessinger 1995.

86. Other damaging consequences that have been mentioned are that it leads people to ignore the pressing needs of the significant number of poorer, less successful Asian immigrants; it may result in undue pressure on young Asians to do well in school and their careers; and it may be used to discredit blacks and Hispanics by implying that if only they worked and studied hard, they, too, would be as successful as Asians (see Kwong 1987; Takaki 1993; and U.S. Commission on Civil Rights 1992).

87. Dublin 1996: 146.

88. U.S. Commission on Civil Rights 1992; Holloway 1995.

89. Lessinger 1995: 139–142.

90. Das Gupta 2003.

91. Healy 2003.

92. Espiritu 2004.

93. Kibria 2002: 72.

94. Espiritu 2004.

95. Foner and Fredrickson 2004.

96. Khandelwal 2003: 4. See Lopez and Espiritu 1997 for a comparative

analysis of the factors affecting panethnicity among Hispanics and Asians in the United States.

97. Kibria 2002: 199–200.

98. Ibid.: 199.

99. Alba and Nee 1997: 846.

100. Barrett and Roediger 1997: 11.

101. Lieberson 1980: 30.

102. Ibid.: 34–35.

103. Cf. ibid.: 31–32. Lieberson noted that because there was "sufficient overlap and variation" between northwestern and southern and eastern Europeans in physical features, these features did not operate very adequately to distinguish them. For some well-off Jewish women cosmetic surgery—the well-known "nose job"—helped in the process (Alba and Nee 2003: 63).

104. Child 1943: 81.

105. Lieberson 1980: 32–34.

106. See Gleason 1980; Higham 1984; Jacobson 1998.

107. See Brodkin 1998; Jacobson 1998, ch. 3.

108. Jacobson 1998: 104.

109. Guterl 2001.

110. Just when this distancing became prominent is unclear. Luconi argues that development of a white ethnic identity among Philadelphia Italian Americans was a post–World War II phenomenon, which owed much to antagonism to, and a desire to separate themselves from, African Americans (2001, ch. 6). In his study of Chicago's Italians, Guglielmo (2003) argues that it was not until World War II that many Italians identified openly and mobilized politically as whites; among other things, he emphasizes the role of struggles over housing in the late 1930s and early 1940s as some Italians fled old neighborhoods undergoing color succession and others stayed behind and fought battles with African Americans in many areas.

111. See Diner (1995). A posture of sympathy for blacks, Eric Goldstein (1997) argues, fulfilled Jews' emotional need to distinguish themselves as "whites of another kind."

112. Goldstein 1997.

113. Hattam 2004; also see Goldstein (1998).

114. Gerstle 2001: 231; Guglielmo 2003: 173.

115. Guglielmo 2003: 174.

116. Dinnerstein 1994, ch. 8.

117. Jacobson 1998: 246–273.

118. The very term nonwhite, as Roediger (2002: 17) points out, exemplifies the tendency in contemporary America "to place whites at the normative center of everything and to marginalize everyone else."

119. Perlmann and Waters 2004. Their analysis of the historical experience

of Italian immigrants shows that after the birth cohort of 1906–10 (women who turned twenty on the eve of the Depression), outmarriage for second-generation Italian women increased markedly, so that for the cohort of women who reached twenty during World War II, outmarriage stood at 41 percent.

120. Cited in Alba 1999: 18. See also Qian, Blair and Ruf (2001). According to an analysis of Current Population Survey data for 1995 to 2001, almost one-third of all married third-generation Asians and Latinos are married to a white (Bean and Stevens 2003: 236).

121. This is what Joel Perlmann and Mary Waters (2004) refer to as a "very strong hypothesis."

122. Prewitt 2004: 157. In 2000, almost half of the nation's Hispanics identified themselves as "white" on the census, a slight decline from 1990 when the percentage was 54 percent (Logan 2003).

123. For racial forecasts for the future see Alba 1999; Alba and Nee 2003; Bean and Stevens 2003; Gans 1999; Lind 1998; Perlmann and Waldinger 1997; Sanjek 1994.

124. Gans 1999: 375; Bean and Stevens 2003: 237.

125. Perlmann and Waldinger 1997: 905.

126. Lind 1998.

127. Yetman 1999: 253. Black-white marriages were still against the law in every state but one south of the Mason-Dixon line as late as 1967, when a Supreme Court decision ended legal restrictions on marriage against any and all color lines (Hollinger 2003: 1365).

128. See Alba and Denton (2004), who note the sharp distinction between the typical residential situation of Latinos and Asians and that of African Americans, who are more likely to reside in areas where their own group is in the majority and white neighbors are infrequent. Despite continued large-scale immigration in the 1980s and 1990s, Asians and Hispanics remain only moderately segregated from non-Hispanic whites. Black immigrants (including Latinos who self-describe as black) tend to be more segregated from whites, and channeled into or near black neighborhoods. An analysis of the segregation of black populations that looked at national metropolitan area averages found that the segregation of African Americans, Afro-Caribbeans, and the African-born from whites declined slightly between 1990 and 2000, but continued to be strikingly high (Logan and Deane 2003).

129. Wong 1995: 55.

130. Alba and Nee 2003: 63.

131. Cornell and Hartmann 1998: 244.

132. Crouch 1996: 170.

133. Alba 1999: 20.

134. Jaynes 2004: 115.

135. Prewitt 2004: 152, 157; see also Hattam 2004.

136. Alba and Nee 2003: 290–291.
137. Hollinger 2003: 1389.

1. Osofsky 1963: 32.
2. Kasinitz 1992: 41. For full-length studies of West Indians in early twentieth-century New York, see James 1998 and Watkins-Owens 1996.
3. Haslip-Viera 1996: 7.
4. Binder and Reimers 1995: 110; Lieberson 1980: 31, 34–35.
5. In Osofsky 1963: 48.
6. Osofsky 1963: 49; see Scheiner 1965: 124–127.
7. Binder and Reimers 1995: 113.
8. Dinnerstein 1994: 71–72.
9. Also a factor was that Irish Tammany bosses gave Jews a number of positions to prevent their defection to the Socialists and Republicans. Before 1920, Italians, the other large new immigrant group at the time, held fewer political positions and had less political influence than Jews. Italian political organization was slowed by the large number of returnees to Italy and the high illiteracy rate among Italian immigrants. Italians were slower than Jews to adopt citizenship or to register to vote. They were also less concentrated residentially than Jews: they neither dominated a district nor won a Tammany district leadership before World War I (Henderson 1976). Moreover, Tammany was less worried about wooing Italians, who were more likely than Jews to give the Democrats a majority of their vote.
10. McNickle 1993; Rischin 1962.
11. Gurock 1979: 73–85.
12. In 1900, the largest concentration of blacks in an assembly district in Manhattan was the 19th District, the area between 61st and 63rd Streets and between Amsterdam and 11th Avenues commonly called "San Juan Hill," where they were 13.8 percent of the total (Haynes 1968: 49).
13. Lieberson 1980: 57–65; Osofsky 1963: 171–177.
14. Diner 1995: 19; Diner 1997: 98.
15. White, Dymowski, and Wang 1994. In 1920, according to John Logan's (1997) analysis of census data, in which he calculated exposure indices for different groups, the average black, Russian Jew, and Italian in New York City lived in districts where their group constituted close to a majority of the population. The average Russian and Italian lived in a district that was only 1 percent black; an average black lived in a district that was 6 percent Russian and 7 percent Italian. The Lower East Side of Manhattan and Morrisania/Longwood in the Bronx—with some 300,000 Russian Jews—had no blacks; in Brooklyn's Williamsburg and Brownsville, blacks made up 1 percent of the population, in

the Jewish parts of Harlem, 2 percent. In the most popular Italian district, Greenwich Village, there were no blacks, and the highest proportion of blacks in an Italian neighborhood—4 percent—was in Italian sections of Brooklyn's Fort Greene, which housed only a small proportion of the city's Italians. Italian East Harlem, home to 74,000 Italians, was only 1 percent black.

16. Gurock 1979: 49–50.

17. Scheiner 1965: 19.

18. Gurock 1979: 50.

19. Gurock 1979: 148.

20. Diner 1997: 97.

21. Gurock 1979: 146.

22. Goldstein 1997.

23. Vecoli 1969: 23.

24. Cf. Roediger 1994. On relations between African Americans and Italian immigrants in Chicago, see Guglielmo (2003), who notes that in the pre–World War I era Italians fought most often among themselves or with other white groups rather than with African Americans. While there were instances of amicable relations between Italians and African Americans, Italians, he notes, "were largely an insular group, preferring to be around people as similar to themselves as possible, especially family members and *paesani*" (2003: 36).

25. See for example, Jacobson 1998; Roediger 1994.

26. Goldstein 1997; Diner 1995.

27. Suzanne Model's (2001) analysis of 1925 census data for Manhattan shows that black men, whether native or foreign-born, were (compared to all Manhattan men) overrepresented in transport and personal service jobs; black women mainly toiled in personal services.

28. Model 1993: 181–182; Waldinger 1996a: 141.

29. La Sorte 1985: 151; compare Kessner 1977: 57.

30. These figures refer to non-Hispanic black New Yorkers.

31. Nee 2003: 496.

32. Mollenkopf, Olson, and Ross 2001. These figures are from the March 2000 Current Population Survey.

33. Mollenkopf 1992: 224.

34. Mollenkopf, Olson, and Ross 2001: 35–36. Seventy-one percent of the black eligible electorate in 2000 were natives born to native parents. Latinos of native-stock were the third largest electoral bloc in 2000.

35. Waldinger and Lichter 2003: 19.

36. Foner 2000: 101–102. With the exception of island-born Puerto Ricans and Russians, the foreign-born advantage held for all post-1965 groups.

37. Wilson 1996: 141.

38. See Hammermesh and Bean 1998.

39. Smith and Edmonston 1997: 236; Howell and Mueller 1997.

40. See Kirschenman and Neckerman 1991; Kasinitz and Rosenberg 1996; Lee 1998; Newman 1999; Waldinger 1997; Wilson 1996.

41. Waldinger and Lichter 2003: 227, 180, 175, 215.

42. Foner 2000; Kasinitz and Rosenberg 1996; Waldinger 1997.

43. Lim 2001: 204.

44. Ibid.: 220.

45. Lim 2001: 221.

46. Wright and Ellis 2001.

47. See Foner 2000; Perlmann and Waters 2004.

48. See Foner 2001a; Kasinitz 1992; Watkins-Owens 1996.

49. See Kasinitz 1992.

50. Smith 2001.

51. Itzigsohn and Dore-Cabral 2001.

52. See Lessinger 1995, 2001.

53. Abraham 2000: 12.

54. Prashad 2000: 94.

55. Min 1996.

56. Lee 2002. Note that I am referring here to animosity rather than conflict. Although conflicts do occasionally break out, and anger and tensions often simmer beneath the surface, the vast majority of interactions involving immigrant (including Korean) entrepreneurs and their customers are free from conflict, and merchants work to maintain civility which, of course, is good for business (see Gold 2004; Lee 2002). Thus, Jennifer Lee notes that although relations between Korean and Jewish merchants in Harlem in the 1990s were an "odd mixture of prosaic routine and explosive tension, of expressions of affection and racial anger . . . the most striking feature of these relations is their sheer ordinariness" (2002: 84).

57. Osofsky 1963: 127; see Diner 1995: 79–81 on the 1930s period.

58. Unfortunately, Board of Education figures, on which this proportion is based, do not distinguish between native and foreign-born blacks.

59. See Portes and Rumbaut 2001a and b.

60. Perlmann and Waldinger 1997: 915.

61. See Foner 2000.

62. See, for example, Fordham 1996; Fordham and Ogbu 1986; Ogbu and Davis 2003; Olsen 1997; Stepick 1998.

63. Kasinitz, Mollenkopf, and Waters 2004: 396.

64. Kasinitz, Mollenkopf, and Waters 2002: 1031.

65. Hirschman 2001.

66. Farley and Alba 2002. As Farley and Alba admit, a problem with Current Population Survey data is that they contain no information about the socioeconomic characteristics of parents of those surveyed so cannot be used to measure socioeconomic mobility directly. Moreover, the U.S.-born children of

very recent immigrants are not represented in their study of second-generation adults. See also Zhou's (2001) analysis of second-generation mobility patterns for five urban regions, including New York.

67. Kasinitz, Mollenkopf, and Waters 2002: 1027.

68. Ibid.: 1032.

69. Neckerman, Carter, and Lee 1999; Foner 2001a; Kasinitz 2001.

70. Whether adopting African American cultural forms leads to racial tolerance or the blurring of racial boundaries is another matter. As David Roediger (2002: 233) writes in his analysis of "wiggers"—contemporary white youths who are said or claim to be imitating African Americans—"infatuation with African American and African American-influenced music is too often a separate matter from loving and respecting African Americans."

71. See Foner 2000.

72. See, for example, Abraham 2000 on Asian Indians; Min 1996 on Koreans; Levitt 2001 on Dominicans.

73. Waters 2001: 214.

NOTES TO CHAPTER 3

This chapter is a revised and expanded version of "Transnationalism Then and Now: New York Immigrants Today and at the Turn of the Twentieth Century," in Hector Cordero-Guzman, Robert C. Smith, and Ramon Grosfoguel, eds., *Migration, Transnationalization, and Race in a Changing New York* (Philadelphia: Temple University Press, 2001), and "Second-Generation Transnationalism, Then and Now," in Peggy Levitt and Mary C. Waters, *The Changing Face of Home: The Transnational Lives of the Second Generation* (New York: Russell Sage Foundation, 2002).

1. Speranza [1906] 1974: 310.

2. Basch, Glick Schiller, and Szanton Blanc 1994: 7. For a review of various definitions of transnationalism, see Levitt 2001; Levitt and Waters 2002.

3. Levitt and Waters 2002: 8.

4. Basch et al. 1994.

5. For a review of the literature see Levitt and Waters 2002; Vertovec 2003.

6. Foner 1997.

7. On this point, also see Portes, Haller, and Guarnizo 2002: 281, who note that the existence of precedents to contemporary transnationalism does not invalidate its potential theoretical importance.

8. Pessar 1995a: 76.

9. Glick Schiller (2003) has defined transmigrants as those persons who, having migrated from one nation-state to another, live their lives across borders, participating simultaneously in social relations that embed them in more than one nation-state.

10. Cahan [1896] 1970: 27. According to Ewa Morawska (2001a: 182), between 1900 and 1906 alone, immigrants in the United States sent five million letters to Russia and Austria-Hungary.

11. Wyman 1993: 61.

12. Morawska 2001a: 183.

13. Speranza [1906] 1974: 309. See also Watkins-Owens 2001 on the trans-national practices of early twentieth-century West Indian immigrant New Yorkers, who, in 1920, numbered about 35,000. Letters went back and forth between New York City and the Caribbean, and handmade clothing and shoes traveled the Brooklyn-Barbados network. West Indians at the time sent substantial amounts of money home, and many left children behind with relatives or sent them back home.

14. Soyer 1997: 172.

15. Ibid.: 177. Watkins-Owens (2001) describes New York–based West Indian associations in early twentieth-century New York that raised money for scholarships, school supplies, and other projects in the home societies.

16. Cinel 1982b: 71.

17. Wyman 1993: 130–131.

18. Jones-Correa 1998: 96.

19. Glick Schiller 1996.

20. Sarna 1981.

21. Ibid.: 264.

22. Wyman 1993.

23. Joseph 1967.

24. Wyman 1993: 79.

25. Ibid.: 131.

26. Speranza [1906] 1974.

27. On Italian "birds of passage" and return migration, see Archdeacon 1983; Cinel 1982a, b; Foerster 1924; Tomasi 1975; Wyman 1993. For a general discussion of return migration to Europe, also see Morawska 1991.

28. Wyman 1993: 79.

29. Sarna 1981: 266.

30. Kramer and Masur 1976: 2.

31. See, for example, Glick Schiller 1999; Portes 1999.

32. Jacobson 1995: 2, 62.

33. Topp 1997.

34. Morawska 2001a: 187.

35. Doyle 1996; McNickle 1996.

36. See Smith 1998a and 2003 for an interesting comparison of the involvement of the Italian and Mexican states in their emigrant populations.

37. Wyman 1993: 93–94, 199.

38. Glick Schiller, Basch, and Szanton Blanc 1995; Rouse 1995.

39. Levitt 2001: 22.

40. Pessar 1995a: 69.

41. Foner 1994. On the frequency of visits to the homeland among West Indian immigrants in New York, see Foner 2001a.

42. Lessinger 1992.

43. Lessinger 1995: 42.

44. Smith 1998b.

45. Elliott 2003.

46. Sontag and Dugger 1998.

47. Basch et al. 1994: 237. See Vertovec 2004 on "cheap calls" in the current era. As Vertovec notes, the 1990s witnessed plummeting prices and surging international telephone traffic, and the spread of prepaid phone cards in recent years has enabled migrants in the United States to make a two- or three-hour phone call to Latin America for only a few dollars.

48. Lessinger 1992.

49. Smith 1998b

50. Margolis 1998: 115.

51. Ibid.

52. Lessinger 1995. See Levitt 2001: 23 on the use of video cameras among Dominicans in Boston, who record events such as baptisms, weddings, and birthday parties so family members not present can also "attend."

53. Mathieu 1998: 140.

54. Sontag and Dugger 1998.

55. Levitt 2003: 177.

56. Sipprelle 2004.

57. Portes, Haller, and Guarnizo 2002.

58. Portes 1996.

59. Lessinger 1992, 1995.

60. Lessinger 1995: 91.

61. Ibid.: 89.

62. See Wong 1998.

63. Min 1998.

64. Basch 2001: 131.

65. Pessar 1995a.

66. Gabaccia 1998.

67. Itzigsohn 2000; Levitt and Glick Schiller 2003; see also Guarnizo 2001; Glick Schiller 1999; Kivisto 2001.

68. Glick Schiller and Fouron 1998. Under the government of Preval, who succeeded Aristide, migrants were no longer referred to as the Tenth Department, but the government was still committed to incorporating the Haitian diaspora into the political and economic life of Haiti (Itzigsohn 2000).

69. Vertovec 2003. It should be noted that about half of the 18 million are U.S.-born Mexicans.

70. DeSipio 1998; Guarnizo 1998; Itzigsohn 2000; Levitt and Glick Schiller 2003; Smith 1998a.

71. Jones-Correa 2001a: 1012.

72. Aleinikoff 2000: 139–140.

73. Renshon 2000.

74. Jones-Correa 2001a: 1010–1011.

75. More than 24,000 Dominicans were registered to vote in New York in the 2004 Dominican presidential elections (Elliott 2004). The reforms have the potential to make the Dominican community in New York the second largest concentration of voters in any Dominican election. In general, as Jones-Correa (2001a) argues, political parties in the home country walk a fine line. On the one hand, they seek support and funding from migrants, who, not surprisingly, then make demands for inclusion in home-country political affairs; on the other hand, parties in the sending state do not necessarily want to open up the political system to emigrants.

76. Batchelet 2004; Guarnizo 2003; Levitt and Glick Schiller 2003; Vertovec 2003.

77. Levitt and Glick Schiller 2003.

78. Guarnizo 1998: 79.

79. See Graham 2001; Guarnizo 2001; Jones-Correa 1998, 2001a.

80. Geyer 1996.

81. Nugent 1992: 159.

82. Shumsky quoted in Nugent 1992: 159; see Shumsky 1992.

83. Quoted in Goldberg 1992: 212.

84. Schwartz 1995.

85. Brumberg 1986.

86. Morawska 2001a: 193. Earlier-wave immigrants, according to Morawska, were subject to exclusionary demands regarding their national commitments from home and host nation-states, which showed little tolerance or protection for diversity; today's immigrants have many more legitimate options in terms of identities and participation (ibid.: 192).

87. See Guarnizo 2003, who notes, among other things, that the remittance market is a multibillion dollar industry in the United States, dominated by large corporate firms such as Western Union and MoneyGram, and that by 1998, Latin Americans in the United States made $2 billion (or 5 percent of the U.S. residential long-distance market) worth of international phone calls a year to friends and family in their countries of origin.

88. Guarnizo 2001: 232.

89. Morawska 2003; see also Levitt 2003.

90. Basch et al. 1994; see also Foner 2001b.

91. Rosenblatt 1993.

92. See Luconi 2001 on Italian Americans in Philadelphia.

93. Soyer 1997: 204.

94. Luconi 2001: 149. The transnational links documented by Luconi for Philadelphia's Italian Americans in the post–World War II era included: the mobilization of aid to Italy during World War II through the heavily Italian local of the Amalgamated Clothing Workers of America; anti-Communist letter-writing campaigns to friends and relatives in Italy in the late 1940s, organized by Italian newspapers and religious leaders; and fund-raising efforts, spear-headed by ethnic associations, to help earthquake victims in Friuli in the 1970s (ibid.: 110–111, 120, 147). Luconi does not specify whether these efforts in-volved only the first generation, but his observation that the American-born sec-ond generation had only loose ties to their parents' homeland suggests that those involved were mainly members of the immigrant generation.

95. Child 1943: 88–89.

96. Smith 1998a: 202; see also Smith 2003.

97. Orsi 1990:141.

98. Quoted in Dugger 1998.

99. Rumbaut 2002. In the past, the Jewish second generation was, by and large, an English-only group; members of the Italian second generation often spoke Italian dialects at home and on the streets. On the Italian second genera-tion and language, see Alba and Nee 2003: 73; Child 1943.

100. Kasinitz, Waters, Mollenkopf, and Anil 2002: 115.

101. See Glick Schiller 2003; Levitt and Glick Schiller 2003.

102. Rohter 1998.

103. Kasinitz, Waters, Mollenkopf, and Anil 2002: 115.

104. Smith 2002a.

105. Portes and Rumbaut 2001b; Rumbaut 2002.

106. Rumbaut 2002.

107. Levitt 2002.

108. Kasinitz, Waters, Mollenkopf, and Anil 2002; Rumbaut 2002.

109. Kasinitz, Waters, Mollenkopf, and Anil 2002.

110. Levitt 2002.

111. Alba and Nee 2003: 151–152.

112. See Kasinitz, Waters, Mollenkopf, and Anil 2002; Levitt 2002.

113. Hollinger 1995: 154.

114. Levitt 2003: 183.

115. Alba and Nee 2003: 150; Portes, Haller, and Guarnizo 2002.

116. Levitt 2000; Morawska 2003.

117. Foner 1973.

118. Foner 2001a: 9.

119. Levitt 2002: 139.

120. Glick Schiller et al. 1995: 54; see also Portes 1999 on the positive effects of transnationalism.

121. Basch 1987.

122. Pessar and Graham 2001.

123. Jones-Correa 2001a.

124. Levitt 2002.

125. Smith 2002a; Portes 1999.

126. Kasinitz, Waters, Mollenkopf, and Anil 2002.

127. Hondagneu-Sotelo and Avila 1997.

128. Jones-Correa 1998.

NOTES TO CHAPTER 4

This chapter is a revised version of "Immigrant Women and Work in New York City, Then and Now," *Journal of American Ethnic History* (spring 1999) 18: 95–113.

1. Among the factors that explain this shift are the growth of the clerical and sales sectors and the rising demand for white-collar office workers; declining fertility rates and the proliferation of labor-saving devices in the household that made mothers more available for work outside the home; and the expansion of high school education and the rise in school-leaving age which kept teenage girls out of the labor market. See Goldin (1994); Kessler-Harris (1982); Lamphere (1987); and Weiner (1985). On the contemporary period see Spain and Bianchi (1996).

2. Gabaccia 1994; see also Gabaccia 1992.

3. See, for example, Espiritu (1997); Morokvasic (1984); and Pessar (1999).

4. The percentage of women in the Italian immigration increased over time: from 21.1 percent in 1881–1890 to 22.9 percent between 1901–1910 and 30.6 percent between 1911–1920. See Tomasi (1975: 22).

5. Although Jewish men usually made the journey first, later sending for working-age children and then arranging for wives and younger family members to follow, occasionally Jewish daughters came first. Once a network of relatives was established in New York, according to Susan Glenn, many Jewish families were willing and found it practicable to send one or more children, including working-age daughters, in advance, ahead of the rest of the immediate family. See Glenn (1990: 48).

6. Glenn 1990: 12.

7. Ibid.: 14.

8. Baum, Hyman, and Michel 1976: 68.

9. Ewen 1985.

10. Cohen 1992: 15–36; Gabaccia 1984: ch. 3.

11. Friedman-Kasaba 1996: 184.

12. Kessner and Caroli 1978. The argument has been made that, for Italians in particular, these figures are probably too low. A 1913 study of Italian women in lower Manhattan found that in more than half (279) of the 515 families where the mother was living at home, she contributed to the family income; as many as a third of the income-earning mothers did factory work. See Odencrantz (1919: 20). More Italian than Jewish married women worked in factories outside the home or in formal employment because their husbands generally earned less. See Cohen (1992) and Friedman-Kasaba (1996).

13. By contrast, in 1900, 38 percent of single white women (15 to 24 years old) in the United States were in the labor force (see Goldin 1990: 17–18, 54, 119).

14. Glenn 1990: 74.

15. On patterns of industrial homework among Italian women, see Cohen (1992); Friedman-Kasaba (1996); and Van Kleeck (1913).

16. Tentler 1979: 176–179.

17. See Heinze 1990.

18. Baum et al. 1976: 214.

19. Most first-generation Jewish women attending evening school in New York City were single working women or women preparing for the job market. Married immigrant women may have been overwhelmed by the pressures of homework, household tasks, and family life. Many would have felt uncomfortable in alien surroundings or had to remain at home with their children since Jewish men were reluctant to stay home with the children (Baum et al. 1976: 128–129).

20. Peiss 1986: 25.

21. Glenn 1990: 71; Breckinridge 1994: 104–105.

22. Gabaccia 1984: 99.

23. Ewen 1985: 149.

24. Glenn 1990:89.

25. In the early 1990s, there were 92 male immigrants for every 100 female immigrants entering New York City, down from 98 males per 100 females in the 1980s (Lobo, Salvo, and Virgin 1996: 19–20). Among the reasons for the predominance of females: U.S. immigration law favors the admission of spouses and children to reunite families and has made it relatively easy for certain kinds of workers, like nurses, to get immigrant visas (see Donato 1992, and Houston, Kramer, and Barrett 1984).

26. In the 1980s, a fifth of the working-age immigrant women intending to live in New York City who reported an occupation to the Immigration and Naturalization Service were in professional/technical and administrative/managerial positions; in the early 1990s, the share in these categories went up to 36 percent (Lobo et al. 1996).

27. Goldin 1994.

28. See Foner 1998c.

29. While most migrants to New York come from countries that are more uniformly patriarchal than the United States, this is not always the case, and Steven Gold (2003) points to Israel as a country that offers women arrangements that women prize—and often miss—when they move to the United States.

30. The focus here is on gains that contemporary immigrant women reap from working outside the home, but migration has improved their status as women in other ways that are particular to the current era. See Foner (1998c) for a discussion of the impact of liberalized legislation about divorce, greatly expanded government social welfare programs, improvements in household technology, and increased freedom for wives and mothers outside the home.

31. United Nations Development Program 2003. This is a big change from 1960, when only 11 percent of women in the Dominican Republic were in the labor force. Among the reasons for the dramatic increase: urbanization, the growth of the service sector, and the growth of export processing industries as well as a rise in educational levels for women and a marked decline in fertility (Deere et al. 1990: 61).

32. Pessar 1995b: 44; see also Pessar 1987, 1995a.

33. Pessar 1987: 121; Grasmuck and Pessar 1991: 147.

34. Pessar 1995a: 50. In her study of Boston Dominicans, Levitt (2001: 101) found that the majority of the migrant women either put the money they earned into a jointly managed account or kept their own check and paid for household expenses by themselves; about 40 percent of the women still gave their paychecks to their husband.

35. This is the figure for 2001 (United Nations Development Program 2003).

36. See Foner 1986.

37. Zhou and Nordquist 1994: 201.

38. Mahler 1996.

39. Burgess and Gray 1981: 104.

40. Pessar 1995a: 60.

41. Espiritu 1997: 70.

42. Chen 1992: 77–78. Taiwanese professional men helped out slightly more around the house than men in the working and business-owner classes; Chen links this pattern to the work schedules of the different classes of men and the fact that professional men had the shortest working hours. See Espiritu 2003 for an analysis of the differential impact of women's wage work on gender relations in the families of Asian salaried professionals, self-employed entrepreneurs, and wage laborers.

43. Min 1998; Park 1997.

44. See Foner 1986.

45. Burgess and Gray 1981: 102. Among Indian professionals, the absence of servants in the United States may have the same effect. Kurien (2003: 162), for example, cites the case of an immigrant man who now takes out the garbage, washes the dishes, and helps with groceries; he explained that he would definitely not do this in India where "you will have servants to help out."

46. Pessar 1984.

47. See Foner 1999a.

48. Hirsch 2000: 370.

49. Grasmuck and Pessar 1991: 152.

50. Menjivar (2003) studied Salvadoran and Guatemalan immigrants in San Francisco and Los Angeles who had been in the United States no longer than five years.

51. See Foner 1994 on immigrant nurses and Kurien 2003 on Indian professional women.

52. See Foner (1994; 1986) on the satisfactions that immigrant nursing home aides and home-care attendants receive from caring for the elderly.

53. Zhou 1992: 178; Pessar 1995b: 45.

54. Foner 1994.

55. Hondagneu-Sotelo 1999: 569.

56. See Espiritu 2003.

57. Gilbertson 1995; Zhou and Logan 1989.

58. Gilbertson 1995; Min 1998: 45–46.

59. See Colen 1989; Soto 1987. For a discussion of the difficulties involved in this kind of transnational motherhood for Latina women, see Hondagneu-Sotelo and Avila 1997.

60. Foner 1994: 107.

61. Min 1998.

62. Pessar 1982.

63. Pessar 1995b: 41–44.

64. Jones-Correa 1998: 171.

65. Kim 1996: 170; see also Menjivar 2003 on cases where Central American women are the sole or main earners because of their husbands' inability to earn a regular wage, and also continue to cater to the men at home in a conscious effort to avoid making their husbands or partners feel inadequate.

66. See Margolis 1998; Min 1998; Pessar 1995a.

67. See Abraham 2000; Kurien 2003; and Lessinger 1995 on marital abuse in the South Asian community.

68. Weiner 1985: 84–85; Tentler 1979: 139–142.

69. See Lamphere 1987.

70. Lamphere 1987: 288.

71. Prieto 1992: 190.

72. Espiritu 1997: 117; see also Brettell and Simon 1986.
73. Min 1998: 38.
74. Laslett 1965.

NOTES TO CHAPTER 5

1. Fredrickson 1997: 78.
2. The number of Caribbean born Afro-Caribbeans has steadily declined. By the 1970s, the number of West Indians migrants moving to England had been reduced to a trickle, under 1,000 a year; in 1991, the number of Caribbean-born people in Britain was 265,000, down from 295,000 ten years earlier. See Hennessy 1988; Owen 2001: 66. In 2001, 344,000 Londoners described themselves as Black Caribbean in the census—about 60 percent of Black Caribbeans in England and Wales, who numbered about 564,000.
3. Foner 2001a. At the time of the 2000 census, about 550,000 New Yorkers claimed non-Hispanic West Indian ancestry (Beveridge 2002a).
4. My research among Jamaican migrants in London, conducted in 1973, included in-depth interviews with 110 respondents (55 men and 55 women) as well as follow-up interviews with 20 people from the original sample and participant observation (see Foner 1978). My research among Jamaican immigrants in New York in the early 1980s was based on in-depth interviews with 40 immigrants (20 men and 20 women) and participant observation (see Foner 1983, 1985, 1987). In both studies, respondents were chosen so that all had spent the first 18 years of their lives in Jamaica and had lived in New York or London for 7 to 20 years. In the late 1980s, I also conducted research among health care workers, many of them Jamaican immigrants, in a New York nursing home (Foner 1994). Since the 1980s, many students in my urban anthropology and immigration courses at the State University of New York at Purchase and at Baruch College, City University of New York—a good number West Indian migrants themselves—have conducted interviews with West Indian immigrants in New York.
5. On Indo-Caribbeans in Britain, see Vertovec 2000, chapter 5, "Category and Quandary: Indo-Caribbean Hindus in Britain." While regularly identified as "Asian" by most whites, Indo-Caribbeans are not fully accepted as belonging to that category by other South Asians. At the same time, they do not wish to be identified as "West Indian." British-born Indo-Caribbeans seem to be adopting a generalized British Asian youth culture which cuts across the cultural divide which faced their West Indian-born parents (Vertovec 2000: 109–110, 122–123). In New York, according to a recent study, second-generation Indo-Caribbeans identify as "Indians" but face questions of authenticity about their "Indian-ness" from Indian immigrants and others (Warikoo 2004). For a dis-

cussion of Indo-Caribbean identity in Toronto (Canada), see Premdas (2004), who argues that this identity is taking shape as Indo-Caribbeans seek to distinguish themselves from South Asians and Afro-Caribbeans.

6. Donald Robotham (1998: 320) notes that the negative associations with blackness continue in Jamaica. Informal Jamaican popular culture, he argues, accepts the "hegemony of brownness," identifying blackness as "slackness" or "X-rated." "The black DJ from the ghetto sings: '. . . Me love me money and thing. But most of all me love me browning [brown girl].'"

7. Vickerman 2001b; see also Vickerman 1999.

8. Vickerman 1999: 42.

9. Waters 1999a: 30.

10. Sutton and Makiesky 1975: 124.

11. Waters 1999a: 153; see also Vickerman 2001a.

12. Mollenkopf, Olson, and Ross 2001; Kasinitz, Mollenkopf, and Waters 2004: 281.

13. See Kasinitz 2001; Waters 1999a.

14. Harry Goulbourne (2002b: 1105) writes that the nomenclature West Indian sounds "rather antiquated" in the British context "because of the changing expression of identity" there (also see Goulbourne 2001: 239). The British Sociological Association's guidelines on anti-racist language are available at http://www.socreasonline.org.uk/info/antirac.html.

15. Witness, to give just one example, the title, the West Indian American Day Carnival event, held every Labor Day in Brooklyn, the city's largest ethnic celebration which draws crowds of one to two million people. It is also useful in social science analysis.

16. An analysis of residential segregation patterns among West Indians in New York City shows that English and Spanish-speaking Caribbeans are highly segregated from each other (Crowder and Tedrow 2001).

17. Kasinitz 1992: 14.

18. Model 1999: 966; see also Song 2003: 99–100.

19. Song 2003: 100–101, 103.

20. Sudbury 2001; Alexander 1996.

21. Alexander 2002: 552, 554.

22. See Baumann 1996: 161–172; Modood, Berthoud, et al. 1997: 290–338; Toulis 1997.

23. Modood cited in Song 2003: 102.

24. See Foner 1987; Sutton and Makiesky 1975; Vickerman 1999. In her study, Mary Waters (1999a) found that people tended to identify as West Indian when they were with large numbers of non-West Indians; they tended to identify in terms of national origin, when there was a critical mass of people of their own ethnic group, or when they were with West Indians from other places as a way to make distinctions and draw boundaries between different islands.

25. Foner 1987; see also Waters 1999a: 64–79.
26. For a discussion of this issue see Waters 1999a.
27. Lowenthal 1978.
28. Trevor Phillips quoted in Gates 1997: 200. Alexander (2002: 559) notes that scholarly analysis in Britain often conflates the African-Caribbean experience there with the African American experience.
29. Crowder and Tedrow 2001.
30. Lobo and Salvo 2000.
31. Quoted in Gates 1997: 201. Kasinitz et al. (2004: 11) report that the poorer and younger West Indian respondents in their second-generation New York study were less likely than the better-off to report having been the victims of discrimination, which the authors attribute to a greater isolation from whites. The better-off respondents shopped in more expensive stores, left their neighborhoods more frequently, and were more likely to meet, and compete with, native whites on the job and in public.
32. Vickerman 2001a.
33. Rogers 2001: 175–176.
34. Vickerman 2001a: 213.
35. Peach 1995; see also Glazer 1999.
36. Johnston, Forrest, and Poulsen 2002.
37. In Cockburn and Ridgeway 1982.
38. Worrall 2000: 14. In 2003, Phillips became chair of the Commission for Racial Equality.
39. Gates 1997.
40. Foner 1978.
41. Mollenkopf 1992, 2001.
42. Kasinitz 1992; Rogers 2001.
43. Rogers 2001; see also Vickerman 2001a.
44. Logan and Mollenkopf (2003) note that emerging West Indian political leaders often see African Americans as not terribly interested in accommodating their political advancement; Democratic Party county leaders often have favored native minority over immigrant minority candidates. By the same token, two Brooklyn districts, explicitly drawn in 1991 to give West Indians an effective voting plurality, have elected West Indian members of the City Council.
45. Gates 1997: 202.
46. Kasinitz 2001.
47. See Neckerman et al. 1999.
48. Gates 1997: 201.
49. Back 1996: 164.
50. Back 1996; see also Hewitt 1986.
51. Model and Fisher 2002.
52. See Model 1999; Modood, Berthoud, et al. 1997.

53. For a summary of this research see Waters 1999b.

54. Waters 2001.

55. According to the 1994 national ethnic survey, 4 percent of Caribbeans in inner London and 6 percent in outer London were self-employed. In New York City, according to 1990 census figures, under 6 percent of foreign-born Jamaicans, Trinidadians, and Guyanese were self-employed (Modood, Berthoud, et al. 1997: 125; Foner 2000: 97). Contrary to stereotypes about West Indians' "genius for business" in the early twentieth century—and my own earlier writings on the subject—a recent analysis of 1925 census data for Manhattan shows that West Indian men had extremely low self-employment rates then as well, under 2 percent (Model 2001: 57). A number of factors help explain the low self-employment rates in contemporary New York, including fluency in English which enables West Indian men and women with skills to find decent positions in the mainstream economy; West Indians' heavy concentration in large-scale bureaucratic organizations like hospitals that limits their exposure to the skills, information, and contacts needed to start their own businesses; a lack of an orientation to business in the home society, where self-employment has been associated with marginal enterprises among the lower class and large-scale entrepreneurial activities have long been dominated by white, Middle Eastern, and Asian minorities; and racial barriers that confine West Indians to inner-city residential areas with weak markets and make it hard to attract a white customer base (see Foner 2000: 98–99). Whether these (or other) factors are involved in Britain is a subject that needs to be explored (on African-Caribbean underrepresentation in business ownership in Britain, see Jones, Barrett, and McEvoy 2000 and Ward 1988).

56. Kasinitz 2001; see Model 2001 on West Indian employment patterns in New York.

57. Kasinitz 2001.

58. Waters 1999a, 2001.

59. Butterfield 2004: 298.

60. Vickerman 2001b.

61. Waters 1994, 2001. In this regard, it should be noted that both Vickerman's and Butterfield's samples were weighted toward the middle class. Of the 37 second-generation West Indians (mostly New Yorkers) whom Vickerman interviewed, about two-thirds were college-educated; the 65 second-generation West Indian New Yorkers in Butterfield's study were disproportionately middle class with college degrees.

62. Butterfield 2004; Kasinitz et al. 2004: 305. In Waters's (2001) study, boys discussed being black American in terms of racial solidarity in the face of societal exclusion and disapproval; girls discussed being American in terms of the freedom they desired from strict parental control, which was a much more salient issue in their lives.

63. Butterfield 2004.

64. See Portes and Rumbaut 2001a and b.

65. See Zhou and Bankston 1998.

66. Vickerman 2001b: 255.

67. Alba and Nee 2003: 11. See also Kasinitz (2004: 293) who makes the point that assimilation is not a zero-sum game.

68. Bashi Bobb and Clarke 2001: 233; Vickerman 2001b: 254.

69. Waters 2001: 213.

70. Kasinitz, Battle, and Miyares 2001.

71. See Waters 1994, 1999a.

72. See Foner 1977, where I argued for conceptualizing the experiences of first- and second-generation West Indians in England in terms of creolization models. See also Foner 1999a.

73. Alexander 2002: 563.

74. See Barn 2001: 215; Goulbourne and Chamberlain 2001: 7.

75. See Kasinitz et al. 2004.

76. Back 1996: 151. See Gilroy 1993: 27–28.

77. Back 1996: 149; see Goulbourne 2002a: 178. In the Fourth National Survey of Ethnic Minorities in Britain, just over a quarter of British-born Caribbeans did not think of themselves as British (Modood, Berthoud, et al. 1997: 329).

78. Alexander 1996: 40, 48–49.

79. Back 1996: 151–152.

80. Alexander 1996: 199.

81. Back 1996: 149.

82. Hall 2000: 152.

83. See Back 1996; Hewitt 1986.

84. Back 1996: 159.

85. Vickerman 2001a: 214.

86. Kasinitz, Mollenkopf, and Waters 2002: 1033–1034. See also Kasinitz 2004.

87. Modood, Berthoud, et al. 1997: 30–31.

88. Model and Fisher 2002: 747–748.

89. Back 1996: 156–157, 242; see also Tizard and Phoenix 1993; Song 2003: 77–79. In 2001, people were allowed to describe themselves as being of mixed ancestry on the census: of those in England and Wales who indicated that they were "not white," 5.2 percent said they were Caribbean and white, 12.6 percent that they were black Caribbean.

90. In his study of Jamaican immigrant men in the New York City area, Vickerman (1999: 146) found that the longer they were in the United States, the more likely they were to have favorable views of intermarriage with African Americans, although most still had unfavorable views even after more than ten years' residence.

91. Cited in Alibhai-Brown 2000.

92. Back notes that racist practices survive and to some degree militate against the cultural bridges being built by black and white young people. "The institutional production of racial inequality introduces divisions even as young people are struggling to repel the divisive nature of 'race.'" The young people in his study indicated that it was in the institutions of education and the police that racism was mostly encountered (Back 1996: 168–169).

93. African Americans, as Kasinitz et al. (2004: 397) put it, are the reference population for second-generation West Indians in New York.

NOTES TO CHAPTER 6

1. Brettell 2003.

2. To the extent that social scientists have compared Caribbean migrants in different settings, the comparisons have been cross-national. See Cross and Entzinger 1988 on Caribbean migrants in Britain and the Netherlands; Grosfoguel 2003 on colonial Caribbean migrants in the United States, Britain, the Netherlands, and France; Model 1997, Model and Fisher 2002, and Model and Ladipo 1996 on Caribbean migrants in Britain and the United States; and Model, Fisher, and Silberman 1999 on Caribbean immigrants in the United States, Britain, Canada, and France.

3. Lucassen forthcoming.

4. It was not the first passenger ship to bring West Indian migrants after the war. The *Ormonde* arrived in early 1947 with 110 Jamaican workers, including ten stowaways, on board (Chessum 2000: 27).

5. Peach 1998. Between 1955 and 1961, nearly two-thirds (143,000) of the 222,000 Commonwealth Caribbean immigrants moving to Britain were Jamaican (Byron 1994: 79).

6. Peach 1998.

7. Dodgson 1984: 13; Byron 1994: 81. For an analysis of British immigration policy see Hansen 2000.

8. Kasinitz 1992. In 1930, New York City was home to 55,000 foreign-born blacks. On West Indians in New York in the early twentieth century, see Kasinitz 1992; Reid 1969; Watkins-Owens 2001.

9. Kasinitz and Vickerman 1999.

10. Camarota and McArdle 2003.

11. Beveridge 2002a; Kraly 1987.

12. Kasinitz 1992: 115. See Olwig 2001 on the migration of members of one Jamaican family to New York over time.

13. Kasinitz 1992.

14. Between 1990 and 2000, in the United States as a whole, the Jamaican

foreign-born grew by 54 percent, the Guyanese by 70 percent, and the Trinidadian and Tobagan by 68 percent (Camarota and McArdle 2003).

15. See Kasinitz 2001: 273.

16. Hall 1995: 12.

17. Waters 1999a: 38.

18. Dodgson 1984: 15.

19. In Reuel Rogers's study, four out of five of the fifty-nine first-generation Afro-Caribbean immigrants in New York he interviewed made regular trips back. Mary Waters, by contrast, found that only six of the thirty-four West Indian food service workers interviewed in her study had been back for a visit, and only nine of the twenty-five teachers had traveled home in the last ten years (Rogers 2001; Waters 2001).

20. Pearson 1981: 66.

21. Modood, Berthoud, et al. 1997: 313–314.

22. Grosfoguel 2003.

23. Camarota 2002; Bouvier 1996.

24. Peach 1968: 48. The net inflow was considerably lower in the preceding years, about 13,000 in 1959 and 10,000 in 1958, for example (ibid.: 42).

25. In 1981, the figure was almost 24,000, and then maintained at an annual rate of between 16,000 and 20,000 for the rest of the decade; between 1990 and 1994, the average annual inflow from Jamaica to the United States was about 17,000 (Lobo, Salvo, and Virgin 1996; Thomas-Hope 1992: 60).

26. Peach 1998: 204.

27. Model and Ladipo 1996: 490. See also Grosfoguel 2003.

28. Mollenkopf, Kasinitz, and Lindholm 1995; Rose et al. 1969: 160–161. Model and Ladipo's (1996) comparison of foreign-born West Indians in London and New York, which controls for years since migration (as well as age and educational credentials and schooling) in considering occupational attainment relative to foreign-born whites, shows foreign-born West Indian men and women in New York suffering less disadvantage than those in London. Also see Heron's analysis (2001) of census data for Britain (1991) and the United States (1990), which shows a much higher proportion of foreign-born blacks in the United States with postsecondary education than those in Britain.

29. In 1961 and 1966, according to the British census, about 9 percent of the West Indian population was 45 years and older. Of those Jamaicans officially entering New York City between 1982–1989 and 1990–1994, about 12 percent was 45 years and older (Rose et al. 1969; Salvo and Ortiz 1992; Lobo, Salvo, and Virgin 1996).

30. See Grosfoguel 2003, who develops this theme in his comparison of colonial Caribbean migrants in four European destinations and Puerto Ricans in the United States.

31. See Cross and Entzinger 1988.

32. Camarota 2002: 15. These figures are based on Current Population Survey data.

33. In 1996, the federal welfare reform law sharply restricted legal immigrants' access to Medicaid, but in 2001, New York State restored full Medicaid eligibility to New York's legal immigrants and extended health coverage to legal immigrants through a new insurance program for low-income adults (Bachrach and Lipson 2002). As Bachrach and Lipson note, undocumented adults are ineligible for any state health benefits other than prenatal, postpartum, and emergency care.

34. See Foner 1978; Dodgson 1984. On housing accommodations in this period see Rose et al. 1969; Smith 1976.

35. Cross and Entzinger 1988: 23.

36. Smith 1976; Modood, Berthoud, et al. 1997: 199–202.

37. Schill, Friedman, and Rosenbaum 1998.

38. In 2004, the City University of New York had more than 208,000 students enrolled in eleven senior colleges, six community colleges, a graduate school, law school, and school of biomedical education.

39. Waters 1999a: 280.

40. In 2001, 29 percent of the students at CUNY's senior and junior colleges were white, 32 percent black, 25 percent Hispanic, and 14 percent Asian.

41. Roughly a quarter of all black freshmen at these selective institutions had a foreign-born parent, and 9 percent were themselves born abroad, whereas in the population at large, the share of foreign origins among African Americans in the United States is around 5 percent. Among the selective colleges in the study were four historically black colleges: Howard University, Morehouse College, Spelman College, and Xavier University (Massey et al. 2003: 40, 199).

42. In 2003, about 215 children were admitted to one of the preparatory programs; over 800 Prep for Prep graduates were enrolled in independent day and boarding schools; and nearly 650 were enrolled as college undergraduates (Simons 2003).

43. Foner 1983.

44. Waters 1999a: 279.

45. In 1991, about a quarter of the Catholic school student body in New York City was non-Catholic; in 1995–96, 24,000 black students attended the city's Catholic elementary and high schools, presumably a significant chunk of them of Caribbean origin.

46. In the 1994 National Survey of Ethnic Minorities, three quarters of the Caribbean respondents who had come to Britain aged 16 or over (and who still had any parents) said that their mother and/or father was abroad; about a third of Caribbean respondents with parents who lived abroad had phoned them within the previous four weeks and about a third had been in contact by letter.

Of Caribbean households with any adult born abroad, 42 percent—and 14 percent with all adults born in Britain—were sending money abroad (Modood, Berthoud, et al. 1997: 48, 51, 168).

47. A ten-day trip to Kingston in July 2004 on a major airline—booked in January 2004—was about $400 less from New York than London.

48. Olwig 2001.

49. Ibid.

50. See Rex and Tomlinson 1979; Logan and Mollenkopf 2003.

51. In 2001, black Caribbeans represented 4.8 percent of London's population, black Africans, 5.3 percent, and other blacks, .8 percent. It should be noted that another 3.1 percent of Londoners said they were of mixed heritage, a great many of them Caribbean and white.

52. Logan and Mollenkopf 2003. The figure on Afro-Caribbeans is based on ancestry in a predominantly black, non-Spanish speaking Caribbean nation, including Haiti, for example, as well as Jamaica.

53. In 2001, to consider two London boroughs with large black populations, Lambeth's black population was evenly divided between Africans and Caribbeans; in Brent, 11 percent of the population was black Caribbean, 8 percent African. An analysis of residential patterns in the New York metropolitan area based on 2000 census data shows segregation between Africans and Afro-Caribbeans in the high range (Logan and Deane 2003).

54. More British than American writings on West Indians look beyond the "capital" city. See, for example, studies of West Indians in Bristol (Pryce 1979; Richmond 1973), Birmingham (Rex and Tomlinson 1979), Leicester (Byron 1994; Chessum 2000), Nottingham (Lawrence 1974), and the pseudonymous Midland city of "Easton" (Pearson 1981). In the United States, the only book on West Indians outside of New York focuses on San Francisco (Hintzen 2001); there are scholarly articles on West Indians in Florida (Kasinitz, Battle, and Miyares 2001) and Los Angeles (Ho 1993).

55. Bryce-Laporte 1979: 216.

56. Unlike the few American studies of West Indians outside of New York City, British studies of West Indians outside of London often try to make the case that they are representative of Britain generally—see, for example, Rex and Tomlinson on Birmingham (1979: 79) and Richmond on Bristol (1973: 41).

57. This number refers to persons who listed themselves on the census as West Indian (excluding Hispanics) in their first or second response to the ancestry question; the San Francisco Bay Area is a ten-county region which, in 1990, had a population of 6.25 million (Hintzen 2001).

58. Ibid.: 1, 9–10.

59. Ibid.: 89–90.

60. Ibid.: 17.

61. Ibid.: 45.

62. Ibid.: 47, 49.

63. In 1990, 13 percent of post-1965 foreign-born Jamaicans in New York City had a college degree or more and 18 percent were professionals or managers—about the same proportions as native-born non-Hispanic blacks (Foner 2000: 100).

64. Hintzen 2001: 92.

65. Ibid.: 190.

66. Singer 2003; see also Palmer 1995 and Singer et al. 2001.

67. Palmer 1995. In his book *Pilgrims from the Sun,* Palmer offers a brief profile of the Washington, D.C., and Hartford West Indian communities (ibid.: 27–30).

68. See, for example, Sheridan 2003.

69. Ibid. In Prince George's County, Maryland, for example, over one-half of the census tracts in this inner suburban zone were either 70 percent black or 70 percent white in 1990 (Manning 1998: 346).

70. The Washington area's more than 90,000 African immigrants, many from Ethiopia, Nigeria, Ghana, Sierra Leone, and Somalia, make up a greater share of the foreign-born population (11.2 percent) than in New York (Singer 2003; Singer et al. 2001).

71. The Hartford metropolitan area, with some 1.2 million people, received 5300 Jamaican legal immigrants between 1991 and 2000, the second largest nationality group in those years (Federation for American Immigration Reform Metro Area Factsheet: Hartford, Connecticut).

72. Palmer 1995: 29.

73. Ibid. Palmer's is the only scholarly attempt to document the experiences of West Indians in different U.S. destinations, but it takes up only a few pages of his book on West Indian migration.

74. Ibid.

75. Highlights of the exhibit, "Finding a Place, Maintaining Ties: Greater Hartford's West Indians," can be found on the historical society's website, www.chs.org.

76. Salzman 2003.

77. Palmer 1995: 29.

78. Kasinitz et al. 2001: 273–274. This account offers insights into the West Indian population in South Florida, although it is primarily concerned with an analysis of survey data on the second generation.

79. Quoted in Foner 1983.

80. James-Johnson 2003.

81. Kasinitz et al. 2001: 274–275.

82. In 2000, about 131,000 foreign-born from Guyana and 89,000 from Trinidad and Tobago lived in New York City (Beveridge 2002a).

83. Charles 2001.

84. In 1990, 11 percent of the West Indian–born population in Dade County and 10 percent in Broward were college educated; in New York City, 13 percent of post-1965 Jamaican immigrants, 10 percent of Trinidadians, and 8 percent of Guyanese had a college degree or more. Eighteen percent of Dade County's West Indian–born population and 15 percent of Broward's were professionals; in New York City, the comparable figures for post-1965 Jamaicans, Trinidadians, and Guyanese were, respectively, 18, 18, and 16 percent (Kasinitz et al. 2001: 276; Foner 2000: 100).

85. The index of dissimilarity between West Indians and non-Hispanic whites in the New York metropolitan area in 1990 was 82 compared to 66 in Miami-Dade County and 56 in Broward (Kasinitz et al. 2001: 275).

86. Kasinitz et al. 2001: 274.

87. Anthony Maingot quoted in Elliott 2001.

88. Elliott 2001.

89. Elliott 2001; McNeal 2003. In 2000, Miramar's population was about 73,000, Lauderdale Lakes' about 32,000, and Lauderhill's about 58,000.

90. In 1960, black Americans greatly outnumbered Hispanics in Miami-Dade; by 1990, there were more than twice as many Hispanics as non-Hispanic blacks in Dade County (Grenier and Castro 2001: 143).

91. Kasinitz et al. 2001: 294–295.

92. Portes and Stepick 1992.

93. Elliott 2001.

94. See Grosfoguel 2003; Cross and Entzinger 1988.

NOTES TO CHAPTER 7

1. Hondagneu-Sotelo 1994: 2.

2. Pessar 1999: 69.

3. Hondagneu-Sotelo 2003.

4. Massiah 1986.

5. See, for example, Massiah 1986; Senior 1991.

6. Austin 1979: 513; http://www.worldbank.org/date/wdi.2001.

7. Rose et al. 1969: 76, 89.

8. Senior 1991: 115; Anderson 1986: 315.

9. Donato 1992; Zhou 2002

10. After 1970, the percentage of total workers listed as private household workers was much lower, ranging from 26 percent in 1972 to 12 percent in 1978.

11. Palmer 1974: 576.

12. Palmer 1995: 33.

13. Kasinitz and Vickerman 2001: 195–196.

14. Foner 1973.

15. Johnson 2003.

16. This compared with a 63 percent rate for the white female population in Britain and 53 percent for all women in the United States (Byron 1998; see Zhou 2003). A national survey conducted by Political and Economic Planning in Britain in the 1970s found 74 percent of West Indian women working compared with 45 percent of women generally (cited in Stone 1983: 35).

17. In 1990, of the Jamaican women aged 16–65 in New York City who reported an occupation to the census, nearly a third were in the health care field as nurse's aides, orderlies, attendants or nurses. In Greater London, in 1966, 12.8 percent of Jamaican women in the labor force were nurses. Kasinitz and Vickerman 2001; Rose et al. 1969: 157.

18. Waldinger 1996a; also see Foner 2000: 91–92 for a discussion of the development of the West Indian niche in health care in New York City.

19. See Rose et al. 1969; Davison 1966.

20. This was the case for a number of Jamaican nursing aides whom I studied in a New York nursing home in the late 1980s, who told me that a major reason why they remained in the job was because of the health and other job benefits (see Foner 1994).

21. Census data on the number of Caribbean domestics must be interpreted with caution since domestic employment is undercounted in official statistics, yet they suggest some general trends and give a sense of Caribbean representation in the field. In 1970, according to census figures, 18 percent of foreign-born West Indian women in the New York metropolitan area labor force worked in private households; the percentage dropped to 10 percent in 1980 and to 6 percent in 1990. Although the proportion of West Indian women migrants in domestic work has declined since the 1960s and 1970s, West Indians are still overrepresented in this field (Model 2001). According to the 1990 census, more than one in ten New York City immigrant domestic workers was from the English-speaking Caribbean, with the largest percentages from Jamaica (5.4 percent) and Trinidad (3.2 percent) (Kaufman 2000). An analysis of 1990 census data for the wider New York urban region shows 13 percent of Jamaican immigrant women working in personal services, many in domestic child care. Kasinitz and Vickerman (2001) stress that the 13 percent figure is almost certainly an undercount: personal services is an area in which undocumented immigrants are often employed, and thus one where census data are particularly suspect.

22. Conover 1997.

23. Model 2001.

24. Watkins-Owens 2001: 35–36.

25. Wrigley 1995.

26. Hondagneu-Sotelo 2001:6.

27. On the particular problems of live-in domestic jobs, see Colen 1986, 1989; Hondagneu-Sotelo 2001; Wrigley 1995.

28. Marshall 1987.
29. Kasinitz and Vickerman 2001: 202.
30. Hondagneu-Sotelo 2001.
31. Marshall 1987.
32. See Grosfoguel 1998.
33. This is confirmed by a study of Jamaican immigrants in Britain in the early 1960s, based on follow-up interviews with a random sample of migrants first interviewed in the Kingston Passport Office in Jamaica in 1961. Of the 100 employed Jamaican immigrant women interviewed in Britain, none was working as a "domestic help" in a private home (Davison 1966: 76).
34. It may be that there is also less demand in London than New York for live-in companions to the elderly, since services provided by the government are more extensive.
35. In London, many women I interviewed in the early 1970s did not work at all for a while, or only part-time, in order to take care of young children; this was unusual among the women interviewed in New York. This difference may well be a product of the way I generated the samples; knocking on doors during the day in London probably led to a higher proportion of stay-at-home (or partially stay-at-home) mothers than in New York, where respondents were located through referrals and I did more interviewing in the evenings and on weekends. Statistics reported in Britain show very high rates of full-time employment for African Caribbean women (including those with young children) from the 1970s through the 1990s (see, for example, figures cited in Byron 1998; Reynolds 2001).
36. See also Stone 1983: 48–49.
37. Prescod-Roberts 1980: 28–29.
38. For a discussion of West Indian transnational families see, for example, Chamberlain 2001; Goulbourne 2002a; Ho 1993; Watkins-Owens 2001.
39. One hundred and eighty-nine Jamaican adults in Britain were included in the study (Davison 1966: 115–116). See also Gmelch (1992: 271–273), who discusses the separation between migrant couples and their Caribbean-based children in the context of his case studies of migrants who returned to Barbados from Britain and North America.
40. Ho (1993: 37) defines childminding as the informal and temporary transfer of parental rights and duties to kin other than biological parents or to trusted friends, and she discusses the creation of international families or an international version of West Indian customs.
41. Davison 1966: 117.
42. Kaufman 2000.
43. Soto 1987; Waters 1999a.
44. Davison 1966: 117.
45. See Hondagneu-Sotelo and Avila 1997 on Latina transnational mothers in California.

46. Colen 1990: 106.

47. Davison 1966: 117.

48. Cheetham 1972: 87–88. See also Fitzherbert 1967, ch. 9.

49. Waters 1999a: 203–208.

50. Cheetham 1972.

51. Decisions to remain in household work are based on a complex combination of factors, including life-cycle stage, migration career, and family responsibilities. Some women with "good" child-care jobs and "better" salaries may be reluctant to switch to clerical or health care jobs, especially if they are older and if their spouse is already supplying health coverage for the family. While held in higher regard, more contractually secure, and offering better long-term benefits and conditions, these jobs may pay lower starting salaries than some workers receive doing child care. Even if the salary is the same, what they take home will be lower since they will not (as in most domestic jobs) be paid off the books; in office jobs, there are additional expenditures for such things as clothes and lunches (see Colen 1990).

52. See Stone 1983: 39.

53. LaFont 2000: 244; see also Senior 1991, ch. 6.

54. Reynolds 2001: 1056–1057.

55. Reynolds 1997: 106.

56. Byron 1998: 228

57. See Smith 1988 for an account of the Jamaican system of sex-role differentiation and the cultural assumptions underlying Jamaican marriage patterns.

58. See Foner 1978.

59. In her study of Nevisians in England, Olwig (1993: 192) argues that "some of the women have asserted their newfound independence by refusing to tolerate their husbands' life style, seeing that divorce is a respectable solution to an unhappy marriage."

60. Model and Fisher 2002.

61. Alexander 1996: 99–100. Also see Back 1996: 164–165 on the different stereotypes of black men, as opposed to black women, in London, with black men seen as violent, dangerous, and aggressive whereas women are seen as being overly emotional and sexual.

62. Waters 1999a: 317–322.

63. Alexander 1996: 129.

64. See Smith 2002b on similar dynamics among Mexican New Yorkers and Lopez's (2001) study of second-generation Caribbean youth, especially on the influence of gender-based childrearing practices in the home and on the rewarding of femininity on school achievement; in the New York City high school she studied, second-generation Caribbean young women were not disciplined as harshly as their male counterparts, even when they engaged in the same type of infractions of school rules.

65. See Alexander 1996.
66. Mollenkopf et al. n.d.

NOTES TO CHAPTER 8

1. In 2000, when the census counted 31.1 million immigrants in the nation, New York City was home to 2.9 million immigrants and Los Angeles County, 3.4 million. If only the city of Los Angeles is considered—home to 1.5 million immigrants in 2000—then the figure is one in seven (Singer 2004). If the larger New York and Los Angeles metropolitan areas are considered, they were home to one out of three immigrants in the nation in 2000 (see Table 8.2).

2. Waldinger 1996a. The starting level is even higher if one considers island-born Puerto Ricans, who are not counted as immigrants because they are U.S. citizens by birth; adding this group, one out of four New Yorkers in 1970 was born outside the mainland United States.

3. Mollenkopf, Olson, and Ross 2001; Beveridge 2002a.

4. Mollenkopf 1999: 419. In 2000, 49 percent of New York City's non-Hispanic white population was foreign-born or had at least one foreign-born parent; this was also true for 42 percent of the city's non-Hispanic blacks (Mollenkopf et al. 2001: 32).

5. Kraly and Miyares 2001.

6. Waldinger and Lee 2001: 62.

7. Waldinger and Lee 2001: 50, 52, 63.

8. Ellis 2001: 151.

9. Schill, Friedman, and Rosenbaum 1998.

10. Waldinger 1996b: 1084.

11. Ibid.; Mollenkopf 1999.

12. Logan and Mollenkopf 2003.

13. Alba and Denton 2004.

14. See Halle, Gedeon, and Beveridge 2003.

15. Waldinger 2001b: 328

16. It is not a question, it should be noted, of the term Euro-American, which is sometimes adopted by academics but not used anywhere in the United States in everyday or popular discourse.

17. Logan and Deane 2003, based on 2000 census data.

18. Vickerman 2001b.

19. Logan 2003.

20. Logan and Mollenkopf 2003.

21. Itzigsohn 2004.

22. Rodriguez 2003.

23. Foley 2004: 341.

24. Itzigsohn 2004: 208.

25. On the stigmatization of Puerto Rican New Yorkers, see Grosfoguel 2003.

26. DeGenova and Ramos-Zayas 2003.

27. See Grenier and Perez 2003: 47–48.

28. These figures are from Logan's (2003) analysis in which "white Hispanics" refer to those who identified neither as "other race" nor as "black"—virtually all (more than 95 percent) identifying only as white.

29. David Reiff quoted in Grenier and Perez 2003: 48.

30. Itzigsohn 2004: 212.

31. As a refugee population, Southeast Asians have been spread out around the country and stand out in a number of states that have very small immigrant populations. In 2000, Vietnamese were the largest immigrant group in Louisiana, and Laotians the second largest in Minnesota and Wisconsin. A third of the nation's foreign-born Cambodians, 41 percent of the nation's foreign-born Vietnamese, and 32 percent of the nation's foreign-born Laotians lived in California (Camarota and McArdle 2003).

32. Zhou and Kim 2003: 129–133.

33. See Gans 1999: 379.

34. Guterl 2001: 11–12.

35. Kasinitz, Mollenkopf, and Waters 2002: 1034.

36. Halle and Rafter 2003 classify these two riots as "major" because one or two, but not more, of the components of the riots' intensity reached very high levels; these components are how long it lasts, how many people are killed or injured, number of arrests, amount of property damage, and the riot's geographic spread.

37. See Foner and Fredrickson 2004 for a fuller discussion of the forces leading to accommodation and cooperation among ethnoracial groups in the United States in the contemporary period.

38. Tilove 2004.

39. This comparison of New York and Los Angeles draws on Keogan 2002; Mollenkopf 1999; Sabagh and Bozorgmehr 2003; and Waldinger 1996b.

40. Keogan 2002.

41. Mollenkopf et al. 2001. In these calculations, the second generation includes those with one as well as two immigrant parents.

42. Waldinger and Lee 2001: 62–63.

43. Mollenkopf 1999; Logan and Mollenkopf 2003. Logan and Mollenkopf argue that New York City's partisan political system does better than the nonpartisan "reformed" system of Los Angeles in drawing voters, including minority and new immigrant voters, to the polls.

44. Mollenkopf 1999: 419.

45. Halle 2003b.

46. Sabagh and Bozorgmehr 2003: 123.

47. Ibid.: 119.

48. Gootman 2003; Smith 2004. See also Mahler 1995.

49. See Johnson, Farrell, and Guinn 1999; Vaca 2004.

50. In an analysis of relations between immigrants and African Americans in three U.S. cities (New York, Los Angeles, and Miami), Morawska (2001b) identifies a number of "basic hostility-generating factors" for native blacks, including shared perceptions of numerical, residential, economic, or political encroachment by immigrants and competition with them in one or more arenas, combined with the belief that other groups have made their gains undeservedly and at the cost of blacks' progress.

51. Foley 2004.

52. Camarillo 2004: 366.

53. Camarillo 2004; Johnson et al. 1999. See also McLain and Tauber 2001 and Mindiola, Niemann, and Rodriguez 2002.

54. Mindiola et al. 2002: 115; Camarillo 2004; Johnson et al. 1999.

55. Grenier and Castro 2001. See also Morawska 2001b: 78–81.

56. Vaca 2004: 110.

57. Logan and Mollenkopf 2003.

58. Smith 2001; Pessar and Graham 2001.

59. Naison 2004.

60. Kasinitz, Mollenkopf, and Waters 2002: 1027.

61. Ibid.: 1034.

62. Ibid.

63. Foner 2001c: 7.

64. Orleck 1987: 295.

65. Kasinitz 2000: 41.

66. The respondents in the New York second-generation study conducted by Kasinitz, Mollenkopf, and Waters (2004: 10) reported that the greatest hostility occurs between groups that are relatively close to each other in residential space and the labor market—English-speaking West Indians reporting conflicts with Haitians and African Americans, for example, and South Americans colliding with Puerto Ricans and Dominicans.

67. Smith 2004.

68. Kasinitz, Mollenkopf and Waters 2002: 1033. As they put it in another context, New York's second-generation groups "have achieved, if not perfect harmony, a widespread rough-and-tumble tolerance for each other" (Kasinitz et al. 2004: 397).

69. Gans 1999: 379.

70. Patterson 2000: 6.

71. Gans 1999: 378–379.

NOTES TO CHAPTER 9

1. See, for example, Alba (2005).

2. This chapter is a revised and expanded version of a paper presented at the workshop, Paths to Integration: Similarities and Differences in the Settlement Process of Immigrants in Europe, 1880–2000, Osnabrueck, Germany, June 2003.

3. See, for example, Brubaker 1992; Cross and Entzinger 1988; Favell 1998; Freeman 1979; Hollifield 1992; Kastoryano 2002—all full-length works that compare policies toward and integration of immigrants in different European countries.

4. Noiriel 1999: 42, 54.

5. Foner 2000.

6. Ibid.

7. Nadell 1981: 274–275.

8. Noiriel 1999: 42. See also Green 1994: 9.

9. Lucassen 2002a.

10. Zolberg and Long 1999: 11. According to Noiriel, in the late 1990s, about 20 percent of people born in France had at least one parent or grandparent of immigrant origin; adding great-grandparents and the foreign population living in France but born outside French territory, the figure was nearly one third of the overall population (1999: 41).

11. Zolberg and Long 1999: 11; see also Moch 1992. In 1910, some 80,000–100,000 Poles lived in Berlin alone, about four percent of the city's population. In 2001, 13 percent of Berlin's population was foreign-born; Poles were the third largest immigrant group, following Turks and immigrants from the former Yugoslavia (Praszalowicz 2003). In 1871, London was home to 91,000 Irish migrants, owing to the large influx in the mid-nineteenth century, and although the number of Irish migrants dwindled to a trickle by the beginning of the twentieth century, the inflow picked up again in the interwar years, especially in the 1930s, when the annual number of migrants to Britain climbed, in 1936, to 32,000 (Lucassen forthcoming). Lucassen also discusses Italian migrants in France in the late nineteenth and early twentieth centuries.

12. Zolberg and Long 1999: 11–12.

13. Lucassen 2003. According to Patrick Simon (2000: 100), a little over 9 percent of the population of Paris was of foreign origin in 1901 compared to over 25 percent in 1990.

14. Moch 1992: 174.

15. Alba and Denton 2004.

16. Diner 2000: 129; Noiriel 1999: 42.

17. Noiriel 1999: 43–44; see also Horowitz 1998.

18. Joppke 1999a: 261; Alba and Nee 2003: 167. In the Netherlands, Jan Rath (2000: 120) notes that even after the government acknowledged (in 1979)

that the country was dealing with people who had come to stay—rather than sojourners—the government and leading politicians have been reluctant to accept the fact that the Netherlands is a country of immigration.

19. Alba and Nee 2003: 167. Joppke (1999a: 24) speaks of the "recovery of the 'nation of immigrants' formula in the United States" as a post–World War II phenomenon. That Americans see themselves as belonging to a nation of immigrants does not mean, of course, that they necessarily embrace an open-borders policy. As Erika Lee (2002: 40) points out in her study of the Chinese exclusion laws, the United States has a long gatekeeping tradition which, she argues, provides "a powerful counter-narrative to the popular 'immigrant paradigm,' which celebrates the United States as a 'nation of immigrants' and views immigration as the fulfillment of the 'promise of American democracy.'" Moreover, as has been noted, while Americans continuously affirm their identity through a "nation of immigrants" narrative, anti-immigrant politics often contradict this collective identification (see Keogan 2002: 232).

20. See Bodnar 1995.

21. Higham 1984: 80.

22. Noiriel 1999: 47–48; Riding 2003.

23. Hulse and Stolberg 2003.

24. See Kasinitz 2004: 279

25. See for example, Foner (2000); Foner and Fredrickson (2004); Gerstle and Mollenkopf (2001); Min (2001); Perlmann and Waldinger (1997).

26. Zolberg and Long (1999: 10) indicate that the myth concerning the United States is the European assumption that immigration in the United States is not a new phenomenon, with inadequate appreciation of distinctive patterns today. This may be the European view, but in the United States it is quite the reverse; the tendency in popular discourse in the United States is to stress what is different about immigration today—not parallels with the past.

27. Zolberg and Long 1999: 13.

28. Foner and Fredrickson 2004: 8.

29. Ellison quoted in West 1994: 3.

30. Lucassen forthcoming.

31. Brimelow 1995.

32. See Foner and Fredrickson 2004.

33. West 1994.

34. I am indebted to George Fredrickson for this observation, which appears in Foner and Fredrickson 2004: 8.

35. Hollinger 2003: 1378.

36. See Lucassen and Penninx 1997: 201; Miles 2000.

37. Noiriel 1996: xxii. As Alba (2005) notes, since race and racism have no place in official thinking in France and Germany, no data comparable to those available in the U.S. census have been collected in either country.

38. Song 2003: 147. Some American social scientists do, of course, use race in what Song calls "scare quotes" in their analyses, one recent example being DeGenova and Ramos-Zayas (2003). American historians have also challenged the use of the term race—see, for example, Hollinger (2003: 1378), who argues that characterizing race as a "social construction" is not a solution since the term has maintained its currency in the English language "of denoting exactly those features of a human being that cannot be changed by social conditions" (also see Fields 2003).

39. Grosfoguel 2003: 201.

40. Thranhardt 2002.

41. Lucassen 2002b: 91–92.

42. Solomos and Back quoted in Fredrickson 2002: 8.

43. Fredrickson 2002: 8, 145, 141; Patterson 2003: 62.

44. Fredrickson 2002: 147.

45. Ibid.: 7.

46. Crouch 1996.

47. Crul and Vermeulen 2003a: 966.

48. See Portes and Rumbaut 2001a and b.

49. Crul and Vermeulen 2003a: 974.

50. Favell (2001: 366) argues that the asymmetric relations of power between Europe and America distort an equal exchange of ideas so that Europeans often end up uncomfortably, and often inappropriately, trying to apply American ideas to the European context.

51. In this regard, Alba (2005) suggests that the model of segmented or downward assimilation can be freed from a dependence on U.S. structural features (hardened racial boundaries and ghettoization) and reformulated to apply to second-generation exclusion in Europe.

52. Model 2003: 280–281; van Niekerk 2004.

53. Waldinger and Feliciano 2004: 380.

54. Joppke and Morawska 2003: 23–24.

55. See the articles in the recent special issue of *International Migration Review* edited by Maurice Crul and Hans Vermeulen (2003b) on the future of the second generation in six European countries.

56. France is an exception in that it introduced double jus soli in the nineteenth century: an individual born in France to an alien father born in France was a French citizen by birth (Weil 2001: 28–29).

57. In 2000, these included Belgium, Denmark, Finland, Italy, the Netherlands, and Sweden (Weil 2001: 30).

58. Alba 2005. Previously, the second generation was legally foreign at birth and had to undergo a naturalization procedure in order to acquire German citizenship. According to the 1999 law, children whose parents are foreigners acquire automatic provisional German citizenship if born in Germany and if at

least one parent has lived legally in the country for eight years. The second generation must decide by the age of 23 whether they want to retain German nationality or the nationality of their parents.

59. Engelen 2003. Pyong Gap Min and Mehdi Bozorgmehr (2003: 33) speak of European scholars privileging the role of government policies in studies of immigrant business and American scholars relegating government policy to a background variable.

60. Rath and Kloosterman 2000: 657.

61. Rath 2002; see also the articles in Kloosterman and Rath 2003.

62. For a review and synthesis of typologies and models developed on comparative welfare regimes and the implications for immigrants, see Engelen 2003, who draws heavily on Esping-Anderson 1999, among others. Several articles in a special issue of *The Netherlands Journal of Social Sciences* compare the implications of American and Dutch welfare regimes for immigrants and their descendants in New York and Amsterdam, in particular, Kloosterman 2000; Mollenkopf 2000; and van Kersbergen 2000.

63. See Engelen 2003.

64. See Alba 2005.

65. Weil (2001) argues that three main factors are responsible for this trend: the influence of democratic values, the stabilization of borders, and a shared experience with immigration and desire to facilitate the integration of the second and third generation. See also Aleinikoff and Klusmeyer (2001) on the trend to relaxing formal opposition to plural nationality. Joppke and Morawska (2003: 8) argue that de facto multiculturalism, in which states allow "immigrants *qua* individuals to find recognition and protection for their distinct cultural practices . . . has become a pervasive reality in liberal immigrant-receiving states."

66. Rath 2000: 121.

# References

Abraham, Margaret. 2000. *Speaking the Unspeakable: Marital Violence among South Asian Immigrants in the United States.* New Brunswick, N.J.: Rutgers University Press.

Alba, Richard. 1990. *Ethnic Identity: The Transformation of White America.* New Haven: Yale University Press.

———. 1999. "Immigration and the American Realities of Assimilation and Multiculturalism." *Sociological Forum* 14: 3–25.

———. 2005. "Bright vs. Blurred Boundaries: Second Generation Assimilation and Exclusion in France, Germany, and the United States." *Ethnic and Racial Studies* 28: 20–49.

Alba, Richard, and Nancy Denton. 2004. "The Old and New Landscapes of Diversity: Residential Patterns of Immigrant Minorities." In *Not Just Black and White: Historical and Contemporary Perspectives on Immigration, Race and Ethnicity in the United States,* edited by Nancy Foner and George Fredrickson. New York: Russell Sage Foundation.

Alba, Richard, Nancy Denton, Shu-yin Leung, and John R. Logan. 1995. "Neighborhood Change under Conditions of Mass Immigration: The New York City Region, 1970–1990." *International Migration Review* 29: 625–656.

Alba, Richard, and Victor Nee. 1997. "Rethinking Assimilation Theory for a New Era of Immigration." *International Migration Review* 31: 826–874.

———. 2003. *Remaking the American Mainstream.* Cambridge: Harvard University Press.

Aleinikoff, T. Alexander. 2000. "Between Principles and Politics: U.S. Citizenship Policy." In *From Migrants to Citizens: Membership in a Changing World,* edited by T. Alexander Aleinikoff and Douglas Klusmeyer. Washington, D.C.: Carnegie Endowment for International Peace.

Aleinikoff, T. Alexander, and Douglas Klusmeyer (eds.). 2000. *From Migrants to Citizens: Membership in a Changing World.* Washington, D.C.: Carnegie Endowment for International Peace.

———. 2001. *Citizenship Today: Global Perspectives and Practices.* Washington, D.C.: Carnegie Endowment for International Peace.

Alexander, Claire. 1996. *The Art of Being Black.* Oxford: Clarendon Press.

Alexander, Claire. 2002. "Beyond Black: Re-Thinking the Colour/Culture Divide." *Ethnic and Racial Studies* 25: 552–571.

Alibhai-Brown, Yasmin. 2000. "A Magic Carpet of Cultures in London." *New York Times* (Arts & Leisure Section), June 25.

Anderson, Pat. 1986. "Conclusion: Women in the Caribbean." *Social and Economic Studies* 35: 291–330.

Archdeacon, Thomas. 1983. *Becoming American.* New York: Free Press.

Arnesen, Eric. 2001. "Whiteness and the Historians' Imagination." *International Labor and Working-Class History* 60: 3–32.

Austin, Diane. 1979. "History and Symbols in Ideology: A Jamaican Example." *Man* (N.S.) 14: 497–514.

Bachrach, Deborah, and Karen Lipson. 2002. "Health Coverage for Immigrants in New York: An Update on Policy Developments and Next Steps." Field Report. New York: The Commonwealth Fund.

Back, Les. 1996. *New Ethnicities and Urban Culture: Racisms and Multiculture in Young Lives.* New York: St. Martin's Press.

Baily, Samuel. 1999. *Immigrants in the Lands of Promise: Italians in Buenos Aires and New York City, 1870–1914.* Ithaca: Cornell University Press.

Barn, Ravinder. 2001. "Caribbean Families and the Child Welfare System in Britain." In *Caribbean Families in Britain and the Trans-Atlantic World,* edited by Harry Goulbourne and Mary Chamberlain. London: Macmillan.

Barrett, James, and David Roediger. 1997. "Inbetween Peoples: Race, Nationality, and the 'New Immigrant' Working Class." *Journal of American Ethnic History* 16: 432–445.

Basch, Linda. 1987. "The Vincentians and Grenadians: The Role of Voluntary Associations in Immigrant Adaptation in New York City." In *New Immigrants in New York,* edited by Nancy Foner. New York: Columbia University Press.

———. 2001. "Transnational Social Relations and the Politics of National Identity: An Eastern Caribbean Case Study." In *Islands in the City: West Indian Migration to New York,* edited by Nancy Foner. Berkeley: University of California Press.

Basch, Linda, Nina Glick Schiller, and Cristina Szanton Blanc. 1994. *Nations Unbound: Transnational Projects, Postcolonial Predicaments, and Deterritorialized Nation- States.* Langhorne, Pa.: Gordon and Breach.

Bashi Bobb, Vilna, and Averil Clarke. 2001. "Experiencing Success: Structuring the Perception of Opportunities for West Indians." In *Islands in the City: West Indian Migration to New York,* edited by Nancy Foner. Berkeley: University of California Press.

Batchelet, Pablo. 2004. "Latin Americans Repatriate $38 Billion." *Reuters,* March 30.

Baum, Charlotte, Paula Hyman, and Sonya Michel. 1976. *Jewish Women in America.* New York: Dial.

Baumann, Gerd. 1996. *Contesting Culture: Discourses of Identity in Multi-Ethnic London.* Cambridge: Cambridge University Press.

Bean, Frank D., and Gillian Stevens. 2003. *America's Newcomers and the Dynamics of Diversity.* New York: Russell Sage Foundation.

Bendix, Reinhard. 1964. *Nation-Building and Citizenship.* New York: John Wiley.

Berger, Joseph. 2002. "Well, The Ices are Still Italian." *New York Times,* September 17.

———. 2003. "City Milestone: Number of Jews is Below Million." *New York Times,* June 16.

Berrol, Selma. 1994. *East Side/East End: Eastern European Jews in London and New York, 1870–1920.* Westport: Praeger.

Beveridge, Andrew. 2002a. "City of the Foreign-Born." *GothamGazette.com,* December.

———. 2002b. "New York's Declining Ethnics." *GothamGazette.com,* October.

Binder, Frederick M., and David M. Reimers. 1995. *All the Nations Under Heaven: An Ethnic and Racial History of New York City.* New York: Columbia University Press.

Bodnar, John. 1995. "Remembering the Immigrant Experience in American Culture." *Journal of American Ethnic History* 15: 3–27.

Bouvier, Leon. 1996. "Embracing America: A Look at Which Immigrants Become Citizens." Center Paper 11. Washington, D.C.: Center for Immigration Studies.

Breckinridge, Sophonisba. 1994 [1921]. "The Duties of the Housewife Remain Manifold and Various." In *Immigrant Women,* edited by Maxine Seller. 2nd ed. Albany: State University of New York Press.

Brettell, Caroline. 1981. "Is An Ethnic Community Inevitable? A Comparison of the Settlement Patterns of Portuguese Immigrants in Toronto and Paris." *Journal of Ethnic Studies* 9: 1–17.

———. 2000. "Urban History, Urban Anthropology, and the Study of Migration in Cities." *City and Society* 12: 129–138.

———. 2003. "Bringing the City Back In: Cities as Contexts for Incorporation." In *American Arrivals: Anthropology Engages the New Immigration,* edited by Nancy Foner. Santa Fe, N.M.: School of American Research Press.

Brettell, Caroline, and James Hollifield. 2000. "Migration Theory: Talking Across Disciplines." In *Migration Theory: Talking Across Disciplines,* edited by Caroline Brettell and James Hollifield. New York: Routledge.

Brettell, Caroline, and Rita Simon. 1986. "Immigrant Women: An Introduction."

In *International Migration: The Female Experience,* edited by Rita Simon and Caroline Brettell. Totowa, N.J.: Rowman and Allenheld.

Brimelow, Peter. 1995. *Alien Nation: Common Sense About America's Immigration Disaster.* New York: Random House.

British Sociological Association. n.d. "Anti-Racist Language: Guidance for Good Practice." Sociological Research Online. http://www.socresonline.org.uk/info/antirac.html.

Brodkin, Karen. 1998. *How Jews Became White Folks, and What That Says About Race in America.* New Brunswick, N.J.: Rutgers University Press.

Brody, David. 2001. "Charismatic History: Pros and Cons." *International Labor and Working-Class History* 60: 43–47.

Brubaker, Rogers. 1992. *Citizenship and Nationhood in France and Germany.* Cambridge: Harvard University Press.

Brumberg, Stephan. 1986. *Going to America, Going to School: The Jewish Immigrant Public School Encounter in Turn-of-the-Century New York City.* New York: Praeger.

Bryce-Laporte, Roy S. 1979. "New York City and the New Caribbean Immigrant: A Contextual Statement." *International Migration Review* 13: 214–234.

Burgess, Judith, and Meryl Gray. 1981. "Migration and Sex Roles: A Comparison of Black and Indian Trinidadians in New York City." In *Female Immigrants in the United States,* edited by Delores Mortimer and Roy S. Bryce-Laporte. Washington, D.C.: Research Institute on Immigration and Ethnic Studies.

Butterfield, Sherri-Ann. 2004. "'We're Just Black': Racial and Ethnic Identities of Second-Generation West Indians in New York." In *Becoming New Yorkers: Ethnographies of the New Second Generation,* edited by Philip Kasinitz, John H. Mollenkopf, and Mary C. Waters. New York: Russell Sage Foundation.

Byron, Margaret. 1994. *Post-War Caribbean Migration to Britain: The Unfinished Cycle.* Aldershot: Avebury.

———. 1998. "Migration, Work and Gender: The Case of Post-War Labor Migration from the Caribbean to Britain." In *Caribbean Migration: Globalised Identities,* edited by Mary Chamberlain. London: Routledge.

Cahan, Abraham. 1970 [1896]. *Yekl and Other Stories of Yiddish New York.* New York: Dover.

Camarillo, Albert M. 2004. "Black and Brown in Compton: Demographic Change, Suburban Decline, and Intergroup Relations in a South Central Los Angeles Community, 1950–2000." In *Not Just Black and White: Historical and Contemporary Perspectives on Immigration, Race, and Ethnicity in the United States,* edited by Nancy Foner and George Fredrickson. New York: Russell Sage Foundation.

Camarota, Steven A. 2002. "Immigrants in the United States—2002." *Center for Immigration Studies Backgrounder* (November 2002): 1–23.

Camarota, Steven A., and Nora McArdle. 2003. "Where Immigrants Live: An Examination of State Residency of the Foreign Born by Country of Origin in 1990 and 2000." *Center for Immigration Studies Backgrounder* (September 2003): 1–23.

Chamberlain, Mary. 2001. "Migration, the Caribbean and the Family." In *Caribbean Families in Britain and the Trans-Atlantic World,* edited by Harry Goulbourne and Mary Chamberlain. London: Macmillan Education.

Charles, Jacqueline. 2001. "West Indians Lead Black Growth." *Miami Herald,* November 21.

Cheetham, Juliet. 1972. *Social Work with Immigrants.* London: Routledge and Kegan Paul.

Chen, Hsaing-Shui. 1992. *Chinatown No More: Taiwan Immigrants in Contemporary New York.* Ithaca: Cornell University Press.

Chessum, Lorna. 2000. *From Immigrants to Ethnic Minority: Making Black Community in Britain.* Aldershot: Ashgate.

Child, Irvin. 1943. *Italian or American? The Second Generation in Conflict.* New Haven: Yale University Press.

Cinel, Dino. 1982a. "The Seasonal Emigration of Italians in the Nineteenth Century: From Internal to International Migration." *Journal of Ethnic Studies* 10: 43–68.

———. 1982b. *From Italy to San Francisco: The Immigrant Experience.* Stanford: Stanford University Press.

Cockburn, Andrew and James Ridgeway. 1982. "The Revolt of the Underclass." *Village Voice* (January): 6–12.

Cohen, Miriam. 1992. *Workshop to Office: Two Generations of Italian Women in New York City, 1900–1950.* Ithaca: Cornell University Press.

Colen, Shellee. 1986. "With Respect and Feelings: Voices of West Indian Child Care and Domestic Workers in New York City." In *All American Women: Lines That Divide, Ties That Bind,* edited by Johnetta Cole. New York: Free Press.

———. 1989. "Just a Little Respect: West Indian Domestic Workers in New York City." In *Muchachas No More: Household Workers in Latin America and the Caribbean,* edited by Elsa Chaney and Mary Garcia Castro. Philadelphia: Temple University Press.

———. 1990. "Housekeeping for the Green Card: West Indian Household Workers, the State, and Stratified Reproduction in New York." In *At Work in Homes: Household Workers in World Perspective,* edited by Roger Sanjek and Shellee Colen. Washington, D.C.: American Anthropological Association.

Conover, Ted. 1997. "The Last Best Friends Money Can Buy." *New York Times Magazine* (November 30): 124–132.

Cornell, Stephen, and Douglas Hartmann. 1998. *Ethnicity and Race.* Thousand Oaks, Calif.: Pine Forge Press.

———. 2004. "Conceptual Confusions and Divides: Race, Ethnicity, and the Study of Immigration." In *Not Just Black and White,* edited by Nancy Foner and George Fredrickson. New York: Russell Sage Foundation.

Cross, Malcolm, and Han Entzinger. 1988. "Caribbean Minorities in Britain and the Netherlands: Comparative Questions." In *Lost Illusions: Caribbean Minorities in Britain and the Netherlands,* edited by Malcolm Cross and Hans Entzinger. London: Routledge.

Crouch, Stanley. 1996. "Race is Over." *New York Times Magazine,* September 26, 170–171.

Crowder, Kyle, and Lucky Tedrow. 2001. "West Indians and the Residential Landscape of New York." In *Islands in the City,* edited by Nancy Foner. Berkeley: University of California Press.

Crul, Maurice, and Hans Vermeulen. 2003a. "The Second Generation in Europe." *International Migration Review* 37: 965–986.

——— (eds.). 2003b. Special Issue on "The Future of the Second Generation: Integration of Migrant Youth in Six European Countries." *International Migration Review* 37: 965–1144.

Daniels, Roger. 1997. *Not Like Us: Immigrants and Minorities in America, 1890–1924.* Chicago: Ivan Dee.

Das Gupta, Monisha. 2003. "Of Hardship and Hostility: The Impact of 9/11 on Taxi Drivers in New York City." Report submitted to the Social Effects Working Group on New York City's Recovery from 9/11, Russell Sage Foundation.

Davila, Arlene. 2001. "The Latin Side of Madison Avenue: Marketing and the Language That Makes Us "Hispanics." In *Mambo Montage,* edited by Agustin Lao-Montes and Arlene Davila. New York: Columbia University Press.

Davison, R. B. 1966. *Black British: Immigrants to England.* London: Oxford University Press.

Deere, Carmen Diana, et al. 1990. *In the Shadows of the Sun: Caribbean Development Alternatives and U.S. Policy.* Boulder, Co.: Westview Press.

DeGenova, Nicholas, and Ana Y. Ramos-Zayas. 2003. *Latino Crossings: Mexicans, Puerto Ricans, and the Politics of Citizenship.* London: Routledge.

DeSalvo, Louise. 2003. "Color: White/Complexion: Dark." In *Are Italians White? How Race Is Made in America,* edited by Jennifer Guglielmo and Salvatore Salerno. New York: Routledge.

DeSipio, Louis. 1998. "Building a New Foreign Policy among Friends: National Efforts to Construct Long-Term Relationships with Latin American Emigres in the United States." Paper presented at the conference States and Diasporas, Casa Italiana, Columbia University, May.

Diner, Hasia. 1997. "Between Words and Deeds: Jews and Blacks in America,

1880–1935." In *Struggles in the Promised Land: Toward a History of Black-Jewish Relations in the United States,* edited by Jack Salzman and Cornel West. New York: Oxford University Press.

———. 1995 [1977]. *In the Almost Promised Land: American Jews and Blacks, 1915–1935.* 2d ed. Baltimore: Johns Hopkins University Press.

———. 2000. *Lower East Side Memories: A Jewish Place in America.* Princeton: Princeton University Press.

Dinnerstein, Leonard. 1994. *Antisemitism in America.* New York: Oxford University Press.

Dodgson, Elyse. 1984. *Motherland: West Indian Women to Britain in the 1950s.* London: Heinemann Educational Books.

Donato, Katherine. 1992. "Understanding U.S. Immigration: Why Some Countries Send Women and Others Send Men." In *Seeking Common Ground: Multidisciplinary Studies of Immigrant Women in the United States,* edited by Donna Gabaccia. Westport, Conn.: Praeger.

Doyle, Joe. 1996. "Striking for Ireland on the New York Docks." In *The New York Irish,* edited by Ronald Bayor and Thomas Meagher. Baltimore: Johns Hopkins University Press.

Dublin, Thomas (ed.). 1996. *Becoming American, Becoming Ethnic: College Students Explore Their Roots.* Philadelphia: Temple University Press.

Dugger, Celia. 1998. "Among Young of Immigrants, Outlook Rises." *New York Times,* March 21.

Elliott, Andrea. 2001. "South Florida's Caribbean Population Has Almost Doubled." *Miami Herald,* August 6.

———. 2003. "For Mom's Cooking, 2,200 Miles Isn't Too Far." *New York Times,* August 11.

———. 2004. "For Dominicans, A New York Vote Homeward." *New York Times,* May 17.

Ellis, Mark. 2001. "A Tale of Five Cities? Trends in Immigrant and Native-Born Wages." In *Strangers at the Gate,* edited by Roger Waldinger. Berkeley: University of California Press.

Engelen, Ewald. 2003. "Conceptualizing Economic Incorporation: From 'Institutional Linkages' to 'Institutional Hybrids.'" Paper presented at a conference on Conceptual and Methodological Developments in the Study of International Migration, Princeton University, May.

Esping-Anderson, Gosta. 1999. *Social Foundations of Postindustrial Economies.* Oxford: Oxford University Press.

Espiritu, Yen Le. 1997. *Asian American Women and Men.* Thousand Oaks, Calif.: Sage Publications.

———. 2003. "Gender and Labor in Asian Immigrant Families." In *Gender and U.S. Immigration,* edited by Pierrette Hondagneu-Sotelo. Berkeley: University of California Press.

Espiritu, Yen Le. 2004. "Asian American Panethnicity: Contemporary National and Transnational Possibilities." In *Not Just Black and White: Historical and Contemporary Perspectives on Immigration, Race and Ethnicity in the United States,* edited by Nancy Foner and George Fredrickson. New York: Russell Sage Foundation.

Ewen, Elizabeth. 1985. *Immigrant Women in the Land of Dollars: Life and Culture on the Lower East Side, 1890–1925.* New York: Monthly Review Press.

Farley, Reynolds, and Richard Alba. 2002. "The New Second Generation in the United States." *International Migration Review* 36: 669–701.

Favell, Adrian. 1998. *Philosophies of Integration: Immigration and the Idea of Citizenship in France and Britain.* London: Macmillan.

———. 2001. "Integration Policy and Integration Research in Europe: A Review and Critique." In *Citizenship Today: Global Perspectives and Practices,* edited by T. Alexander Aleinikoff and Douglas Klusmeyer. Washington, D.C.: Carnegie Endowment for International Peace.

Fields, Barbara. 2003. "Of Rogues and Geldings." *American Historical Review* 108: 1397–1405.

Fitzgerald, Frances. 1979. *America Revised.* New York: Vintage.

Fitzherbert, Katrin. 1967. *West Indian Children in London.* Occasional Papers on Social Administration, Number 19. London: G. Bell and Sons.

Foerster, Robert. 1924. *The Italian Emigration of Our Times.* Cambridge: Harvard University Press.

Foley, Neil. 2004. "Straddling the Color Line: The Legal Construction of Hispanic Identity in Texas." In *Not Just Black and White: Historical and Contemporary Perspectives on Immigration, Race and Ethnicity in the United States,* edited by Nancy Foner and George Fredrickson. New York: Russell Sage Foundation.

Foner, Eric. 2001. "Response to Eric Arnesen." *International Labor and Working-Class History* 60: 57–60.

Foner, Nancy. 1973. *Status and Power in Rural Jamaica: A Study of Educational and Political Change.* New York: Teachers College Press.

———. 1977. "The Jamaicans: Cultural and Social Change among Migrants in Britain." In *Between Two Cultures: Migrants and Minorities in Britain,* edited by James L. Watson. Oxford: Basil Blackwell.

———. 1978. *Jamaica Farewell: Jamaican Migrants in London.* Berkeley: University of California Press.

———. 1983. "Jamaican Migrants: A Comparative Analysis of the New York and London Experience." Occasional Paper No. 36. New York: Center for Latin American and Caribbean Studies, New York University.

———. 1984. *Ages in Conflict: A Cross-Cultural Perspective on Inequality Between Old and Young.* New York: Columbia University Press.

————. 1985. "Race and Color: Jamaican Migrants in New York and London." *International Migration Review* 19: 708–727.

————. 1986. "Sex Roles and Sensibilities: Jamaican Women in New York and London." In *International Migration: The Female Experience,* edited by Rita Simon and Caroline Brettell. Totowa, N.J.: Rowman and Allenheld.

————. 1987. "The Jamaicans: Race and Ethnicity among Migrants in New York City." In *New Immigrants in New York,* edited by Nancy Foner. New York: Columbia University Press.

————. 1994. *The Caregiving Dilemma: Work in an American Nursing Home.* Berkeley: University of California Press.

————. 1997. "What's New About Transnationalism? New York Immigrants Today and at the Turn of the Century." *Diaspora* 6: 355–376.

————. 1998a. "Towards a Comparative Perspective on Caribbean Migration." In *Caribbean Migration: Globalised Identities,* edited by Mary Chamberlain. London: Routledge.

————. 1998b. "West Indian Identity in the Diaspora: Comparative and Historical Perspectives." *Latin American Perspectives* 25: 173–188.

————. 1998c. "Benefits and Burdens: Immigrant Women and Work in New York City." *Gender Issues* 16: 5–24.

————. 1999a. "The Immigrant Family: Cultural Legacies and Cultural Changes." In *The Handbook of International Migration,* edited by Charles Hirschman, Philip Kasinitz, and Josh DeWind. New York: Russell Sage Foundation.

————. 1999b. "Immigrant Women and Work in New York City, Then and Now." *Journal of American Ethnic History* 18: 95–113.

————. 2000. *From Ellis Island to JFK: New York's Two Great Waves of Immigration.* New Haven: Yale University Press.

————. 2001a. "West Indian Migration to New York: An Overview." In *Islands in the City: West Indian Migration to New York,* edited by Nancy Foner. Berkeley: University of California Press.

————. 2001b. "Immigrant Commitment to America, Then and Now: Myths and Realities." *Citizenship Studies* 5: 27–40.

————. 2001c. "Introduction: New Immigrants in a New New York." In *New Immigrants in New York,* edited by Nancy Foner. Rev. ed. New York: Columbia University Press.

————. 2001d. "Transnationalism Then and Now: New York Immigrants Today and at the Turn of the Twentieth Century." In *Migration, Transnationalization, and Race in a Changing New York,* edited by Hector Cordero-Guzman, Robert C. Smith, and Ramon Grosfoguel. Philadelphia: Temple University Press.

———— (ed.). 2001e. *Islands in the City: West Indian Migration to New York.* Berkeley: University of California Press.

Foner, Nancy. 2002a. "Response." Forum: Old and New Immigrants: On Nancy Foner's *From Ellis Island to JFK. Journal of American Ethnic History* 21: 102–119.

———. 2002b. "Second Generation Transnationalism, Then and Now." In *The Changing Face of Home,* edited by Peggy Levitt and Mary Waters. New York: Russell Sage Foundation.

———. 2003a. "Immigrants and African Americans: Comparative Perspectives on the New York Experience Across Time and Space." In *Host Societies and the Reception of Immigrants,* edited by Jeffrey G. Reitz. La Jolla, Calif.: Center for Comparative Immigration Studies.

———. 2003b. "Then *and* Now or Then *to* Now: Migration to New York in Contemporary and Historical Perspective." Keynote address at Immigration and Ethnic History Society Conference on Transcending Boundaries: Migration, Ethnicity and Incorporation in the Age of Globalism, New York.

Foner, Nancy, and George Fredrickson. 2004. "Immigration, Race, and Ethnicity in the United States: Social Constructions and Social Relations." In *Not Just Black and White: Historical and Contemporary Perspectives on Immigration, Race, and Ethnicity in the United States,* edited by Nancy Foner and George Fredrickson. New York: Russell Sage Foundation.

Fordham, Signithia. 1996. *Blacked Out: Dilemmas of Race, Identity, and Success at Capital High.* Chicago: University of Chicago Press.

Fordham, Signithia, and John Ogbu. 1986. "Black Students' School Success: Coping with the Burden of Acting White." *Urban Review* 18: 176–206.

Fox, Geoffrey. 1996. *Hispanic Nation.* New York: Birch Lane Press.

Fox, Richard G., and Andre Gingrich. 2002. "Introduction." In *Anthropology, By Comparison,* edited by Andre Gingrich and Richard G. Fox. London: Routledge.

Fredrickson, George M. 1997. *The Comparative Imagination: On the History of Racism, Nationalism, and Social Movements.* Berkeley: University of California Press.

———. 2002. *Racism: A Short History.* Princeton: Princeton University Press.

Freeman, Gary. 1979. *Immigrant Labor and Racial Conflict in Industrial Societies: The French and British Experiences.* Princeton: Princeton University Press.

Friedman-Kasaba, Kathie. 1996. *Memories of Migration: Gender, Ethnicity, and Work in the Lives of Jewish and Italian Women in New York, 1870–1924.* Albany: State University of New York Press.

Gabaccia, Donna. 1984. *From Sicily to Elizabeth Street.* Albany: State University of New York Press.

———. 1994. *From the Other Side: Women, Gender, and Immigrant Life in the U.S., 1820–1990.* Bloomington: Indiana University Press.

————. 1998. "Italians and Their Diasporas: Cosmopolitans, Exiles and Workers of the World." Paper presented at the conference States and Diasporas, Casa Italiana, Columbia University, May.

Gabaccia, Donna (ed.). 1992. *Seeking Common Ground: Multidisciplinary Studies of Immigrant Women in the United States.* Westport, Conn.: Greenwood Press.

Gambino, Richard. 1974. *Blood of My Blood: The Dilemma of Italian-Americans.* New York: Doubleday.

Gans, Herbert. 1999. "The Possibility of a New Racial Hierarchy in the Twenty-First Century United States." In *The Cultural Territories of Race: Black and White Boundaries,* edited by Michele Lamont. Chicago: University of Chicago Press.

Gates, Henry Louis. 1997. "Black London." *The New Yorker* (April 28): 194–205.

Gerstle, Gary. 2001. *American Crucible: Race and Nation in the Twentieth Century.* Princeton: Princeton University Press.

Gerstle, Gary, and John Mollenkopf (eds.). 2001. *E Pluribus Unum? Contemporary and Historical Perspectives on Immigrant Incorporation.* New York: Russell Sage Foundation.

Geyer, Georgie Anne. 1996. *Americans No More: The Death of American Citizenship.* New York: Atlantic Monthly Press.

Gilbertson, Greta. 1995. "Women's Labor and Enclave Employment: The Case of Dominican and Colombian Women in New York City." *International Migration Review* 19: 657–671.

Gilroy, Paul. 1993. *Small Acts: Thoughts on the Politics of Black Cultures.* London: Serpent's Tail.

Glazer, Nathan. 1999. "Comment on 'London and New York: Contrasts in British and American Models of Segregation' by Ceri Peach." *International Journal of Population Geography* 5: 319–351.

Glazer, Nathan, and Daniel Patrick Moynihan. 1970. *Beyond the Melting Pot.* 2d ed. Cambridge: MIT Press.

Gleason, Philip. 1980. "American Identity and Americanization." In *Harvard Encyclopedia of American Ethnic Groups,* edited by Stephen Thernstrom. Cambridge: Harvard University Press.

Glenn, Susan. 1990. *Daughters of the Shtetl: Life and Labor in the Immigrant Generation.* Ithaca: Cornell University Press.

Glick Schiller, Nina. 1996. "Who Are Those Guys? A Transnational Reading of the U.S. Immigrant Experience." Paper presented at Social Science Research Council Conference on Becoming American/America Becoming: International Migration to the United States, Sanibel Island, Fla.

————. 1999. "Transmigrants and Nation-States: Something Old and Something

New in the U.S. Immigrant Experience." In *The Handbook of International Migration: The American Experience,* edited by Charles Hirschman, Philip Kasinitz, and Josh DeWind. New York: Russell Sage Foundation.

Glick Schiller, Nina. 2003. "The Centrality of Ethnography in the Study of Transnational Migration: Seeing the Wetlands Instead of the Swamp." In *American Arrivals: Anthropology Engages the New Immigration,* edited by Nancy Foner. Santa Fe, N.M.: School of American Research Press.

Glick Schiller, Nina, Linda Basch, and Cristina Blanc-Szanton. 1992. "Transnationalism: A New Analytic Framework for Understanding Migration." In *Towards a Transnational Perspective on Migration,* edited by Nina Glick Schiller, Linda Basch, and Cristina Blanc-Szanton. New York: New York Academy of Sciences.

———. 1995. "From Immigrant to Transmigrant: Theorizing Transnational Migration." *Anthropological Quarterly* 68: 48–63.

Glick Schiller, Nina, and Georges Fouron. 1998. "Transnational Lives and National Identities: The Identity Politics of Haitian Immigrants." In *Transnationalism from Below,* edited by Michael P. Smith and Luis Eduardo Guarnizo. New Brunswick, N.J.: Transaction Press.

Gmelch, George. 1992. *Double Passage: The Lives of Caribbean Migrants Abroad and Back Home.* Ann Arbor: University of Michigan Press.

Godley, Andrew. 2001. *Jewish Immigrant Entrepreneurship in New York and London, 1880–1914.* New York: Palgrave.

Gold, Steven J. 2003. "Israeli and Russian Jews: Gendered Perspectives on Settlement and Return Migration." In *Gender and U.S. Immigration,* edited by Pierrette Hondagneu-Sotelo. Berkeley: University of California Press.

———. 2004. "Immigrant Entrepreneurs and Customers Throughout the 20th Century." In *Not Just Black and White: Historical and Contemporary Perspectives on Immigration, Race, and Ethnicity in the United States,* edited by Nancy Foner and George Fredrickson. New York: Russell Sage Foundation.

Goldin, Claudia. 1990. *Understanding the Gender Gap.* New York: Oxford University Press.

———. 1994. "Labor Markets in the Twentieth Century." Working Paper Series on Historical Factors in Long Run Growth No. 58. Cambridge, Mass.: National Bureau of Economic Research.

Goldberg, Barry. 1992. "Historical Reflections on Transnationalism, Race, and the American Immigrant Saga." In *Towards a Transnational Perspective on Migration,* edited by Nina Glick Schiller, Linda Basch, and Cristina Blanc-Szanton. New York: New York Academy of Science.

Goldstein, Eric. 1997. "A White Race of Another Kind: Immigrant Jews and Whiteness in the Urban North, 1914–1945." Paper presented at a meeting of the Organization of American Historians, San Francisco.

———. 1998. "Becoming Ethnic/Becoming White: Race and the Emergence of

American Jewish Ethnicity." Paper presented at a meeting of the American Historical Association, Seattle.

Gonzales, Patrisia, and Roberto Rodriguez. 2003. "The Unintended Census Race." *Hispanic Vista.com,* July 25.

Gootman, Elissa. 2003. "Old Tensions Over Immigrants Surface After Fire-bombing." *New York Times,* July 14.

Goulbourne, Harry. 2001. "Trans-Atlantic Caribbean Futures." In *Caribbean Families in Britain and the Trans-Atlantic World,* edited by Harry Goulbourne and Mary Chamberlain. London: Macmillan.

———. 2002a. *Caribbean Transnational Experience.* London: Pluto Press.

———. 2002b. Review of *Islands in the City: West Indian Migration to New York.* In *Ethnic and Racial Studies* 25: 1105–1106.

Goulbourne, Harry, and Mary Chamberlain. 2001. "Caribbean Families in the Trans-Atlantic World." In *Caribbean Families in Britain and the Trans-Atlantic World,* edited by Harry Goulbourne and Mary Chamberlain. London: Macmillan.

Graham, Pamela. 2001. "Political Incorporation and Re-Incorporation: Simultaneity in the Dominican Migrant Experience." In *Migration, Transnationalization and Race in a Changing New York,* edited by Hector Cordero-Guzman, Robert Smith, and Ramón Grosfoguel. Philadelphia: Temple University Press.

Grant, Madison. 1916. *The Passing of the Great Race.* New York: Scribner's.

Grasmuck, Sherri, and Ramón Grosfoguel. 1997. "Geopolitics, Economic Niches, and Gendered Social Capital among Recent Caribbean Immigrants in New York City." *Sociological Perspectives* 40: 339–364.

Grasmuck, Sherri, and Patricia Pessar. 1991. *Between Two Islands.* Berkeley: University of California Press.

———. 1996. "Dominicans in the United States: First and Second Generation Settlement." In *Origins and Destinies,* edited by Silvia Pedraza and Ruben Rumbaut. Belmont, Calif.: Wadsworth.

Gratton, Brian. 2002. "Race, the Children of Immigrants, and Social Science Theory." *Journal of American Ethnic History* 21: 74–84.

Green, Nancy. 2002. "Comments on Transnationalism and Diaspora." Workshop on Transnational Ties and Identities: Past and Present, Wassenar, Netherlands, November.

———. 1997. *Ready-to-Wear and Ready-to-Work: A Century of Industry and Immigrants in Paris and New York.* Durham: Duke University Press.

———. 1994. "The Comparative Method and Poststructural Structuralism—New Perspectives for Migration Studies." *Journal of American Ethnic History* 13: 3–22.

Grenier, Guillermo, and Max Castro. 2001. "Blacks and Cubans in Miami: The Negative Consequences of the Cuban Enclave on Ethnic Relations." In

*Governing American Cities: Inter-ethnic Coalitions, Competition, and Conflict,* edited by Michael Jones-Correa. New York: Russell Sage Foundation.

Grenier, Guillermo, and Lisandro Perez. 2003. *The Legacy of Exile: Cubans in the United States.* Boston: Allyn and Bacon.

Grosfoguel, Ramón. 1998. "Modes of Incorporation: Colonial Caribbean Migrants in Western Europe and the United States." In *Caribbean Migration: Globalised Identities,* edited by Mary Chamberlain. London: Routledge.

———. 2003. *Colonial Subjects: Puerto Ricans in a Global Perspective.* Berkeley: University of California Press.

Grosfoguel, Ramón, and Chloe S. Georas. 2001. "Latino Caribbean Diasporas in New York." In *Mambo Montage,* edited by Agustin Lao-Montes and Arlene Davila. New York: Columbia University Press.

Guarnizo, Luis. 1997. "On the Political Participation of Transnational Migrants: Old Practices and New Trends." Paper presented at a Social Science Research Council workshop, Immigrants, Civic Culture, and Modes of Incorporation, Santa Fe, N.M.

———. 1998. "The Rise of Transnational Social Formations: Mexican and Dominican State Responses to Transnational Migration." *Political Power and Social Theory* 12: 45–94.

———. 2001. "On the Political Participation of Transnational Migrants: Old Practices and New Trends." In *E Pluribus Unum?,* edited by Gary Gerstle and John Mollenkopf. New York: Russell Sage Foundation.

———. 2003. "The Economics of Transnational Living." *International Migration Review* 37: 666–699.

Guarnizo, Luis Eduardo, Arturo Ignacio Sanchez, and Elizabeth M. Roach. 1999. "Mistrust, Fragmented Solidarity, and Transnational Migration: Colombians in New York City and Los Angeles." *Ethnic and Racial Studies* 22: 367–396.

Guglielmo, Thomas. 2003. *White on Arrival: Italians, Race, Color, and Power in Chicago, 1890–1945.* New York: Oxford University Press.

Gurock, Jeffrey S. 1979. *When Harlem Was Jewish, 1870–1930.* New York: Columbia University Press.

Guterl, Matthew Pratt. 2001. *The Color of Race in America, 1900–1940.* Cambridge: Harvard University Press.

Hacker, Andrew. 2003. "Saved?" *The New York Review of Books,* August 14: 22–24.

Hall, Stuart. 1995. "Negotiating Caribbean Identities." *New Left Review* 218: 3–14.

———. 2000. "Old and New Identities, Old and New Ethnicities." In *Theories of Race and Racism: A Reader,* edited by Les Back and John Solomos. London: Routledge.

Halle, David. 2003a. "The New York and Los Angeles Schools." In *New York and Los Angeles*, edited by David Halle. Chicago: University of Chicago Press.

————. 2003b. "Learning from L.A." *Gothamgazette.com*, October 6.

Halle, David, Robert Gedeon, and Andrew A. Beveridge. 2003. "Residential Separation and Segregation, Racial and Latino Identity, and the Racial Composition of Each City." In *New York and Los Angeles*, edited by David Halle. Chicago: University of Chicago Press.

Halle, David, and Kevin Rafter. 2003. "Riots in New York and Los Angeles, 1935–2002." In *New York and Los Angeles*, edited by David Halle. Chicago: University of Chicago Press.

Hamermesh, Daniel S., and Frank D. Bean (eds.). 1998. *Help or Hindrance? The Economic Implications of Immigration for African Americans.* New York: Russell Sage Foundation.

Hammel, Eugene A. 1980. "The Comparative Method in Anthropological Perspective." *Comparative Studies in Society and History* 22: 145–155.

Hansen, Randall. 2000. *Citizenship and Immigration in Post-War Britain: The Institutional Origins of a Multicultural Nation.* Oxford: Oxford University Press.

Harrison, Roderick, and Claudette Bennett. 1995. "Racial and Ethnic Diversity." In *State of the Union: Volume Two, Social Trends*, edited by Reynolds Farley. New York: Russell Sage Foundation.

Haslip-Viera, Gabriel. 1996. "The Evolution of the Latino Community in New York City: Early Twentieth Century to the Present." In *Latinos in New York*, edited by Gabriel Haslip-Viera and Sherrie Baver. Notre Dame: University of Notre Dame Press.

Hattam, Victoria C. 2001. "Whiteness: Theorizing Race, Eliding Ethnicity." *International Labor and Working-Class History* 60: 61–68.

————. 2004. "Ethnicity: An American Genealogy." In *Not Just Black and White: Historical and Contemporary Perspectives on Immigration, Race, and Ethnicity in the United States*, edited by Nancy Foner and George Fredrickson. New York: Russell Sage Foundation.

Haynes, George E. 1968 [1912]. *The Negro at Work in New York City.* New York: Arno Press.

Healy, Patrick. 2003. "3 Indians Attacked on Street and the Police Call It Bias." *New York Times*, August 3.

Heinze, Andrew R. 1990. *A Search for Abundance: Jewish Immigrants, Mass Consumption, and the Search for an American Identity.* New York: Columbia University Press.

Henderson, Thomas M. 1976. *Tammany Hall and the New Immigrants: The Progressive Years.* New York: Arno Press.

Hennessy, Alistair. 1988. "Workers of the Night: West Indians of Britain." In

Lost Illusions: Caribbean Minorities in Britain and the Netherlands, edited by Malcolm Cross and Hans Entzinger. London: Routledge.

Heron, Melonie P. 2001. The Occupational Attainment of Caribbean Immigrants in the United States, Canada, and England. New York: LFB Scholarly Publishing.

Hewitt, Roger. 1986. White Talk, Black Talk: Inter-racial Friendship and Communication amongst Adolescents. London: Cambridge University Press.

Higham, John. 1955. Strangers in the Land. New Brunswick, N.J.: Rutgers University Press.

———. 1984 [1975]. Send These to Me. Baltimore: Johns Hopkins University Press.

Hintzen, Percy C. 2001. West Indian in the West: Self-Representations in an Immigrant Community. New York: New York University Press.

Hirsch, Jennifer. 2000. "En El Norte La Mujer Manda: Gender, Generation, and Geography in a Mexican Transnational Community." In Immigration Research for a New Century, edited by Nancy Foner, Rubén Rumbaut, and Steven Gold. New York: Russell Sage Foundation.

Hirschman, Charles. 2001. "The Educational Enrollment of Immigrant Youth: A Test of the Segmented Assimilation Hypothesis." Demography 38: 317–336.

Ho, Christine. 1993. "The Internationalization of Kinship and the Feminization of Caribbean Migration: The Case of Afro-Trinidadian Immigrants in Los Angeles." Human Organization 52: 32–40.

Hollifield, James F. 1992. Immigrants, Markets, and States: The Political Economy of Postwar Europe. Cambridge: Harvard University Press.

Hollinger, David. 1995. Postethnic America. New York: Basic Books.

———. 2003. "Amalgamation and Hypodescent: The Question of Ethnoracial Mixture in the History of the United States." American Historical Review 108: 1363–1390.

Holloway, Lynette. 1995. "Brokers Said to Exploit Fear to Stir Queens Home Sales." New York Times, May 5.

Hondagneu-Sotelo, Pierrette. 1994. Gendered Transitions: Mexican Experiences of Immigration. Berkeley: University of California Press.

———. 1999. "Introduction: Gender and Contemporary U.S. Immigration." American Behavioral Scientist 42: 565–576.

———. 2001. Domestica: Immigrant Workers Cleaning and Caring in the Shadows of Affluence. Berkeley: University of California Press.

———. 2003. "Gender and Immigration: A Retrospective and Introduction." In Gender and U.S. Immigration, edited by Pierrette Hondagneu-Sotelo. Berkeley: University of California Press.

Hondagneu-Sotelo, Pierrette, and Ernestine Avila. 1997. "I'm Here, but I'm There: The Meanings of Latina Transnational Motherhood." Gender and Society 11: 548–571.

Horowitz, Donald L. 1998. "Immigration and Group Relations in France and America." In *The Immigration Reader*, edited by David Jacobson. Malden, Mass.: Blackwell.

Houston, Marion, Roger Kramer, and Joan Mackin Barrett. 1984. "Female Predominance of Immigration to the United States since 1930: A First Look." *International Migration Review* 18: 908–963.

Howell, David, and Elizabeth Mueller. 1997. "The Effects on African-American Earnings: A Jobs-Level Analysis of the New York City Labor Market, 1979–1989." Working Paper no. 210. The Jerome Levy Economics Institute, Bard College.

Hulse, Carl, and Sheryl Gay Stolberg. 2003. "Democrats Say the Nation Heads 'in Wrong Direction.'" *New York Times*, January 29.

Itzigsohn, José. 2000. "Immigration and the Boundaries of Citizenship: The Institutions of Immigrants' Political Transnationalism." *International Migration Review* 34: 1126–1154.

———. 2004. "The Formation of Latino and Latina Panethnic Identities." In *Not Just Black and White: Historical and Contemporary Perspectives on Immigration, Race, and Ethnicity in the United States*, edited by Nancy Foner and George Fredrickson. New York: Russell Sage Foundation.

Itzigsohn, José, and Carlos Dore-Cabral. 2001. "The Manifold Character of Panethnicity." In *Mambo Montage: The Latinization of New York*, edited by Agustin Lao-Montes and Arlene Davila. New York: Columbia University Press.

Jacobson, Matthew. 1995. *Special Sorrows*. Cambridge: Harvard University Press.

———. 1998. *Whiteness of a Different Color: European Immigrants and the Alchemy of Race*. Cambridge: Harvard University Press.

James, Winston. 1998. *Holding Aloft the Banner of Ethiopia: Caribbean Radicalism in Early Twentieth Century America*. London: Verso.

James-Johnson, Alva. 2003. "Census 2000: Caribbean Immigrants Drawn to Retirement in South Florida." *Sun-Sentinel (Fort Lauderdale)*, May 30.

Jaynes, Gerald. 2004. "Immigration and the Social Construction of Otherness: Underclass Stigma and Intergroup Relations." In *Not Just Black and White: Historical and Contemporary Perspectives on Immigration, Race and Ethnicity in the United* States, edited by Nancy Foner and George Fredrickson. New York: Russell Sage Foundation.

Johnson Jr., James H., Walter C. Farrell, Jr., and Chandra Guinn. 1999. "Immigration Reform and the Browning of America: Tensions, Conflicts, and Community Instability in Metropolitan Los Angeles." In *The Handbook of International Migration*, edited by Charles Hirschman, Philip Kasinitz, and Josh DeWind. New York: Russell Sage Foundation.

Johnson, Kevin. 2003. "A Long Way from St. Ann's Bay." In *Be The Dream:*

*Prep for Prep Graduates Share Their Stories,* compiled by Gary Simons. Chapel Hill, N.C.: Algonquin Books of Chapel Hill.

Johnston, Ron, James Forrest, and Michael Poulsen. 2002. "Are There Ethnic Enclaves/Ghettos In English Cities?" *Urban Studies* 39: 591–618.

Jones, Trevor, Giles Barrett, and David McEvoy. 2000. "Market Potential as a Decisive Influence on the Performance of Ethnic Minority Business." In *Immigrant Businesses,* edited by Jan Rath. New York: St. Martin's Press.

Jones-Correa, Michael. 1998. *Between Two Nations: The Political Predicament of Latinos in New York City.* Ithaca: Cornell University Press.

———. 2001a. "Under Two Flags: Dual Nationality in Latin America and Its Consequences for the United States." *International Migration Review* 35: 997–1029.

——— (ed.). 2001b. *Governing American Cities: Inter-Ethnic Coalitions, Competition, and Conflict.* New York: Russell Sage Foundation.

Joppke, Christian. 1999a. *Immigration and the Nation-State: The United States, Germany, and Great Britain.* Oxford: Oxford University Press.

———. 1999b. "How Immigration Is Changing Citizenship: A Comparative View." *Ethnic and Racial Studies* 22: 629–652.

Joppke, Christian, and Ewa Morawska. 2003. "Integrating Immigrants in Liberal Nation-States: Policies and Practices." In *Toward Assimilation and Citizenship: Immigrants in Liberal Nation-States,* edited by Christian Joppke and Ewa Morawska. New York: Palgrave.

Joseph, Samuel. 1967. *Jewish Immigration to the United States: From 1881–1910.* New York: AMS Press.

Kasinitz, Philip. 1992. *Caribbean New York.* Ithaca: Cornell University Press.

———. 2000. "Children of America: The Second Generation Comes of Age." *Common Quest* 4: 32–41.

———. 2001. "Invisible No More? West Indian Americans in the Social Scientific Imagination." In *Islands in the City: West Indian Migration to New York,* edited by Nancy Foner. Berkeley: University of California Press.

———. 2004. "Race, Assimilation, and 'Second Generations,' Past and Present." In *Not Just Black and White: Historical and Contemporary Perspectives on Immigration, Race, and Ethnicity in the United States,* edited by Nancy Foner and George Fredrickson. New York: Russell Sage Foundation.

Kasinitz, Philip, Juan Battle, and Ines Miyares. 2001. "Fade to Black? The Children of West Indian Immigrants in Southern Florida." In *Ethnicities: Children of Immigrants in America,* edited by Rubén G. Rumbaut and Alejandro Portes. Berkeley: University of California Press.

Kasinitz, Philip, John Mollenkopf, and Mary C. Waters. 2002. "Becoming American/Becoming New Yorkers: Immigrant Incorporation in a Majority Minority City." *International Migration Review* 36: 1020–1036.

———— (eds.). 2004. *Becoming New Yorkers: Ethnographies of the New Second Generation.* New York: Russell Sage Foundation.

Kasinitz, Philip, and Jan Rosenberg. 1996. "Missing the Connection: Social Isolation and Employment on the Brooklyn Waterfront." *Social Problems* 43: 180–196.

Kasinitz, Philip, Mary C. Waters, John H. Mollenkopf, and Merih Anil. 2002. "Transnationalism and the Children of Immigrants in Contemporary New York." In *The Changing Face of Home: The Transnational Lives of the Second Generation,* edited by Peggy Levitt and Mary C. Waters. New York: Russell Sage Foundation.

Kasinitz, Philip, and Milton Vickerman. 1999. "West Indians/Caribbeans." In *A Nation of Peoples: A Sourcebook on America's Multicultural Heritage,* edited by Elliott Barkan. Westport, Conn.: Greenwood Press.

————. 2001. "Ethnic Niches and Racial Traps: Jamaicans in the New York Regional Economy." In *Migration, Transnationalization, and Race in a Changing New York,* edited by Hector Cordero-Guzman, Robert Smith, and Ramón Grosfoguel. Philadelphia: Temple University Press.

Kastoryano, Riva. 2002. *Negotiating Identities: States and Immigrants in France and Germany.* Princeton: Princeton University Press.

Kaufman, Kathy. 2000. "Outsourcing the Hearth: The Impact of Immigration on Labor Allocation in American Families." In *Immigration Research for a New Century,* edited by Nancy Foner, Rubén Rumbaut, and Steven Gold. New York: Russell Sage Foundation.

Keogan, Kevin. 2002. "A Sense of Place: The Politics of Immigration and the Symbolic Construction of Identity in Southern California and the New York Metropolitan Area." *Sociological Forum* 17: 223–254.

Kersbergen, Kees van. 2000. "A Caring State or a Could-not-care-less State." *Netherlands Journal of Social Sciences* 36: 159–162.

Kessler-Harris, Alice. 1982. *Out to Work.* New York: Oxford University Press.

Kessner, Thomas. 1977. *The Golden Door: Italian and Jewish Immigrant Mobility in New York City, 1880–1915.* New York: Oxford University Press.

Kessner, Thomas, and Betty Boyd Caroli. 1978. "New Immigrant Women at Work: Italians and Jews in New York City, 1880–1905." *Journal of Ethnic Studies* 5: 19–31.

Khandelwal, Madhulika S. 2003. *Becoming American, Becoming Indian: An Immigrant Community in New York.* Ithaca: Cornell University Press.

Kibria, Nazli. 2002. *Becoming Asian American: Second-Generation Chinese and Korean American Identities.* Baltimore: Johns Hopkins University Press.

Kim, Ai Ra. 1996. *Women Struggling for a New Life: The Role of Religion in the Cultural Passage from Korea to America.* Albany: State University of New York Press.

Kirschenman, Joleen, and Kathryn Neckerman. 1991. "We'd Love to Hire

Them, But—: The Meaning of Race for Employers." In *The Urban Under-class,* edited by Christopher Jencks and Paul Peterson. Washington, D.C.: Brookings Institution.

Kivisto, Peter. 2001. "Theorizing Transnational Immigration: A Critical Review of Current Efforts." *Ethnic and Racial Studies* 24: 549–577.

Kloosterman, Robert. 2000. "Waltzing Elephants: Mollenkopf's View on Assimilating Immigrants in Old and New Amsterdam." *Netherlands Journal of Social Sciences* 36: 146–150.

Kloosterman, Robert, and Jan Rath (eds.). 2003. *Immigrant Entrepreneurs: Venturing Abroad in the Age of Globalization.* Oxford: Berg.

Kolchin, Peter. 2002. "Whiteness Studies: The New History of Race in America." *Journal of American History* 89: 154–173.

Kraly, Ellen Percy. 1987. "U.S. Immigration Policy and the Immigrant Populations of New York." In *New Immigrants in New York,* edited by Nancy Foner. New York: Columbia University Press.

Kraly, Ellen Percy, and Ines Miyares. 2001. "Immigration to New York: Policy, Population and Patterns." In *New Immigrants in New York,* edited by Nancy Foner. Rev. ed. New York: Columbia University Press.

Kramer, Sydelle, and Jenny Masur (eds.). 1976. *Jewish Grandmothers.* Boston: Beacon Press.

Kurien, Prema. 2003. "Gendered Ethnicity: Creating a Hindu Indian Identity in the United States." In *Gender and U.S. Immigration,* edited by Pierrette Hondagneu-Sotelo. Berkeley: University of California Press.

Kwong, Peter. 1987. *The New Chinatown.* New York: Hill and Wang.

LaFont, Suzanne. 2000. "Gender Wars in Jamaica." *Identities* 7: 233–260.

Lamphere, Louise. 1987. *From Working Daughters to Working Mothers: Immigrant Women in a New England Industrial Community.* Ithaca: Cornell University Press.

Laslett, Peter. 1965. *The World We Have Lost.* New York: Scribners.

La Sorte, Michael. 1985. *La Merica: Images of Italian Greenhorn Experience.* Philadelphia: Temple University Press.

Lawrence, Daniel. 1974. *Black Immigrants, White Natives: A Study of Race Relations in Nottingham.* Cambridge: Cambridge University Press.

Lee, Erika. 2002. "The Chinese Exclusion Example: Race, Immigration, and American Gatekeeping, 1882–1924." *American Journal of Ethnic History* 21: 36–62.

———. 2003. *At America's Gates.* Chapel Hill: University of North Carolina Press.

Lee, Jennifer. 1998. "Cultural Brokers: Race-Based Hiring in Inner City Neighborhoods." *American Behavioral Scientist* 41: 927–937.

———. 2002. "From Civil Relations to Racial Conflict: Merchant-Customer Interactions in Urban America." *American Sociological Review* 67: 77–98.

Lessinger, Johanna. 1992. "Investing or Going Home? A Transnational Strategy among Indian Immigrants in the United States." In *Towards a Transnational Perspective on Migration,* edited by Nina Glick Schiller, Linda Basch, and Cristina Blanc-Szanton. New York: New York Academy of Sciences.

———. 1995. *From the Ganges to the Hudson.* Boston: Allyn and Bacon.

———. 2001. "Class, Race, and Success: Two Generations of Indian Americans Confront the American Dream." In *Migration, Transnationalization, and Race in a Changing New York,* edited by Hector Cordero-Guzman, Robert Smith, and Ramón Grosfoguel. Philadelphia: Temple University Press.

Levitt, Peggy. 2000. "Migrants Participate Across Borders: Toward an Understanding of Forms and Consequences." In *Immigration Research for a New Century,* edited by Nancy Foner, Rubén Rumbaut, and Steven Gold. New York: Russell Sage Foundation.

———. 2001. *The Transnational Villagers.* Berkeley: University of California Press.

———. 2002. "The Ties That Change: Relations to the Ancestral Home over the Life Cycle." In *The Changing Face of Home: The Transnational Lives of the Second Generation,* edited by Peggy Levitt and Mary C. Waters. New York: Russell Sage Foundation.

———. 2003. "Keeping Feet in Both Worlds: Transnational Practices and Immigrant Incorporation in the United States." In *Toward Assimilation and Citizenship,* edited by Christian Joppke and Ewa Morawska. New York: Palgrave.

Levitt, Peggy, Josh DeWind, and Steven Vertovec (eds.). 2003. "Transnational Migration: International Perspectives." Special Issue of *International Migration Review* 37: 565–892.

Levitt, Peggy, and Nina Glick Schiller. 2003. "Transnational Perspectives on Migration: Conceptualizing Simultaneity." Paper presented at conference on Conceptual and Methodological Developments in the Study of International Migration, Princeton University, May.

Levitt, Peggy, and Mary Waters. 2002. "Introduction." In *The Changing Face of Home: The Transnational Lives of the Second Generation,* edited by Peggy Levitt and Mary Waters. New York: Russell Sage Foundation.

Lieberson, Stanley. 1980. *A Piece of the Pie: Blacks and White Immigrants since 1880.* Berkeley: University of California Press.

Lim, Nelson. 2001. "On the Back of Blacks? Immigrants and the Fortunes of African Americans." In *Strangers at the Gates: New Immigrants in Urban America,* edited by Roger Waldinger. Berkeley: University of California Press.

Lind, Michael. 1995. "American by Invitation." *New Yorker,* April 24, 107–113.

———. 1998. "The Beige and the Black." *New York Times Magazine,* August 16, 38–39.

Lobo, Arun Peter, and Joseph Salvo. 2000. "The Role of Nativity and Ethnicity in the Residential Settlement Patterns of Blacks in New York City, 1970–1990." In *Immigration Today: Pastoral and Research Challenges,* edited by Lydio Tomasi and Mary Powers. New York: Center for Migration Studies.

Lobo, Arun Peter, Joseph Salvo, and Vicky Virgin. 1996. *The Newest New Yorkers, 1990–1994.* New York: Department of City Planning.

Logan, John R. 1997. "The Ethnic Neighborhood, 1920–1970." Working Paper no. 112. New York: Russell Sage Foundation.

———. 2003. "How Race Counts for Hispanic Americans." Report of the Lewis Mumford Center, State University of New York at Albany.

Logan, John R., and Glenn Deane. 2003. "Black Diversity in Metropolitan America." Report of the Lewis Mumford Center, State University of New York at Albany.

Logan, John, and John Mollenkopf. 2003. "People and Politics in America's Big Cities: The Challenges to Urban Democracy." Paper presented at the conference on The Immigrant Metropolis: The Dynamics of Intergenerational Mobility in Los Angeles and New York, Russell Sage Foundation.

Lopez, David, and Yen Le Espiritu. 1997. "Panethnicity in the United States: A Theoretical Framework." In *New American Destinies,* edited by Darrell Y. Hamamoto and Rudolfo D. Torres. New York: Routledge.

Lopez, Ian Haney. 1996. *White by Law: The Legal Construction of Race.* New York: New York University Press.

Lopez, Nancy. 2001. *Hopeful Girls, Troubled Boys: Race and Gender Disparity in Urban Education.* New York: Routledge.

Lowenthal, David. 1978. "West Indian Emigrants Overseas." In *Caribbean Social Relations,* edited by Colin Clarke. Monograph No. 8. Center for Latin American Studies, University of Liverpool.

Lucassen, Jan, and Rinus Penninx. 1997. *Newcomers: Immigrants and Their Descendants in the Netherlands, 1550–1995.* Amsterdam: Het Spinhuis.

Lucassen, Leo. Forthcoming. *The Immigrant Threat.* Urbana: University of Illinois Press.

———. 2002a. "Paths of Integration: Similarities and Differences in the Settlement Process of Immigrants in Europe, 1880–2000." Position paper.

———. 2002b. "Old and New Migrants in the Twentieth Century: A European Perspective." *Journal of American Ethnic History* 21: 85–101.

———. 2003. "Immigration and Paths of Integration in the Dutch Metropolitan Area, 1918–2001." Unpublished paper.

Luconi, Stefano. 2001. *From Paesani to White Ethnics: The Italian Experience in Philadelphia.* Albany: State University of New York Press.

Mahler, Sarah. 1995. *American Dreaming: Immigrant Life on the Margins.* Princeton: Princeton University Press.

————. 1996. "Bringing Gender to a Transnational Focus: Theoretical and Empirical Ideas." Unpublished manuscript.

Manning, Robert D. 1998. "Multicultural Washington, DC: The Changing Social and Economic Landscape of a Post-Industrial Metropolis." *Ethnic and Racial Studies* 21: 328–355.

Margolis, Maxine. 1998. *An Invisible Minority: Brazilians in New York City.* Boston: Allyn and Bacon.

Markowitz, Fran. 1993. *A Community in Spite of Itself: Soviet Jewish Emigres in New York.* Washington, D.C.: Smithsonian Institution Press.

Marshall, Adriana. 1987. "New Immigrants in New York's Economy." In *New Immigrants in New York,* edited by Nancy Foner. New York: Columbia University Press.

Massey, Douglas S. 1993. "Latinos, Poverty, and the Underclass: A New Agenda for Research." *Hispanic Journal of Behavioral Sciences* 15: 449–475.

Massey, Douglas S., Camille Z. Charles, Garvey F. Lundy, and Mary J. Fischer. 2003. *The Source of the River: The Social Origins of Freshmen at America's Selective Colleges and Universities.* Princeton: Princeton University Press.

Massiah, Joycelin. 1986. "Work in the Lives of Caribbean Women." *Social and Economic Studies* 35: 177–240.

Mathieu, Joan. 1998. *Zulu: An Irish Journey.* New York: Farrar, Straus, and Giroux.

Mazumdar, Sucheta. 1989. "Race and Racism: South Asians in the United States." In *Frontiers of Asian American Studies,* edited by Gail Nomura, Russell Endo, Stephen Sumida, and Russell Leong. Pullman: Washington State University Press.

McLain, Paula, and Steven Tauber. 2001. "Racial Minority Group Relations in a Multiracial Society." In *Governing American Cities: Interethnic Coalitions, Competition, and Conflict,* edited by Michael Jones-Correa. New York: Russell Sage Foundation.

McNeal, Natalie. 2003. "Broward's Jamaicans Rising in Politics." *Miami Herald,* April 6.

McNickle, Chris. 1993. *To Be Mayor of New York.* New York: Columbia University Press.

————. 1996. "When New York Was Irish, and After." In *The New York Irish,* edited by Ronald Bayor and Timothy Meagher. Baltimore: Johns Hopkins University Press.

Menjivar, Cecilia. 2003. "The Intersection of Work and Gender: Central American Immigrant Women and Employment in California." In *Gender and U.S. Immigration,* edited by Pierrette Hondagneu-Sotelo Berkeley: University of California Press.

Miles, Robert. 2000. "Apropos the Idea of 'Race' . . . Again." In *Theories of*

*Race and Racism: A Reader,* edited by Les Back and John Solomos. London: Routledge.

Min, Pyong Gap. 1996. *Caught in the Middle: Korean Communities in New York and Los Angeles.* Berkeley: University of California Press.

———. 1998. *Changes and Conflicts: Korean Immigrant Families in New York.* Boston: Allyn and Bacon.

——— (ed.). 2001. *Mass Migration to the United States: Classical and Contemporary Periods.* Walnut Creek, Calif.: Altamira.

Min, Pyong Gap, and Mehdi Bozorgmehr. 2003. "United States: The Entrepreneurial Cutting Edge." In *Immigrant Entrepreneurs: Venturing Abroad in the Age of Globalization,* edited by Robert Kloosterman and Jan Rath. Oxford: Berg.

Mindiola Jr., Tatcho, Yolanda Flores Neimann, and Nestor Rodriguez. 2002. *Black-Brown Relations and Stereotypes.* Austin: University of Texas Press.

Moch, Leslie Page. 1992. *Moving Europeans: Migration in Western Europe since 1650.* Bloomington: Indiana University Press.

Model, Suzanne. 1993. "The Ethnic Niche and the Structure of Opportunity: Immigrants and Minorities in New York City." In *The "Underclass" Debate: Views from History,* edited by Michael Katz. Princeton: Princeton University Press.

———. 1997. "An Occupational Tale of Two Cities: Minorities in London and New York." *Demography* 34: 539–550.

———. 1999. "Ethnic Inequality in England: An Analysis Based on the 1991 Census." *Ethnic and Racial Studies* 22: 966–990.

———. 2001. "Where West Indians Work." In *Islands in the City: West Indian Migration to New York,* edited by Nancy Foner. Berkeley: University of California Press.

———. 2003. "Immigrants in the Netherlands: A Review Essay." *Contemporary Sociology* 32: 277–282.

Model, Suzanne, and Gene Fisher. 2002. "Unions between Blacks and Whites: England and the U.S. Compared." *Ethnic and Racial Studies* 25: 728–754.

Model, Suzanne, Gene Fisher, and Roxane Silberman. 1999. "Black Caribbeans in Comparative Perspective." *Journal of Ethnic and Migration Studies* 25: 187–212.

Model, Suzanne, and David Ladipo. 1996. "Context and Opportunity: Minorities in New York and London." *Social Forces* 75: 485–510.

Modood, Tariq, Richard Berthoud, et al. 1997. *Ethnic Minorities in Britain: Diversity and Disadvantage.* London: Policy Studies Institute.

Mollenkopf, John. 1992. *A Phoenix in the Ashes: The Rise and Fall of the Koch Coalition in New York City Politics.* Princeton: Princeton University Press.

———. 1993. *New York City in the 1980s: A Social, Economic, and Political Atlas.* New York: Simon and Schuster.

———. 1999. "Urban Political Conflicts and Alliances: New York and Los Angeles Compared." In *The Handbook of International Migration*, edited by Charles Hirschman, Philip Kasinitz, and Josh DeWind. New York: Russell Sage Foundation.

———. 2000. "Assimilating Immigrants in Amsterdam: A Perspective from New York." *Netherlands Journal of Social Sciences* 36: 126–145.

———. 2001. "The Democratic Vote in Living Color." *New York Times*, March 14.

Mollenkopf, John, Philip Kasinitz, and Matthew Lindolm. 1995. "Profiles of Nine Immigrant Categories and Their Sub-Groups and of Island-Born Populations." In *Immigration/Migration and the CUNY Student of the Future*. New York: City University of New York.

Mollenkopf, John, David Olson, and Timothy Ross. 2001. "Immigrant Political Participation in New York and Los Angeles." In *Governing American Cities*, edited by Michael Jones-Correa. New York: Russell Sage Foundation.

Mollenkopf, John, Aviva Zeltzer-Zubida, Jennifer Holdaway, and Philip Kasinitz. n.d. "Chutes and Ladders: Educational Attainment among Young Second Generation and Native New Yorkers." Unpublished paper.

Morokvasic, Mirjana. 1984. "Birds of Passage Are Also Women." *International Migration Review* 18: 886–907.

Morawska, Eva. 1991. "Return Migration: Theoretical and Research Agenda." In *A Century of European Migrations, 1830–1930*, edited by Rudolph Vecoli and Suzanne Sinke. Urbana: University of Illinois Press.

———. 2001a. "Immigrants, Transnationalism, and Ethnicization: A Comparison of This Great Wave and the Last." In *E Pluribus Unum? Contemporary and Historical Perspectives on Immigrant Political Incorporation*, edited by Gary Gerstle and John Mollenkopf. New York: Russell Sage Foundation.

———. 2001b. "Immigrant-Black Dissensions in American Cities: An Argument for Multiple Explanations." In *Problem of the Century: Racial Stratification in the United States*, edited by Elijah Anderson and Douglas S. Massey. New York: Russell Sage Foundation.

———. 2003. "Immigrant Transnationalism and Assimilation: A Variety of Combinations and the Analytic Strategy It Suggests." In *Toward Assimilation and Citizenship*, edited by Christian Joppke and Ewa Morawska. New York: Palgrave.

Naber, Nadine. 2000. "Ambiguous Insiders: An Investigation of Arab American Identity." *Ethnic and Racial Studies* 23: 37–61.

Nadell, Pamela. 1981. "The Journey to America by Steam: The Jews of Eastern Europe in Transition." *American Jewish History* 71: 269–284.

Naison, Mark. 2004. "'It Takes a Village to Raise a Child': Growing Up in the Patterson Houses in the 1950s and Early 1960s, An Interview with Victoria Archibald Good." *Bronx County Historical Society Journal*.

Neckerman, Kathryn, Prudence Carter, and Jennifer Lee. 1999. "Segmented Assimilation and Minority Cultures of Mobility." *Ethnic and Racial Studies* 22: 945–965.

Nee, Victor. 2003. "Institutional Change and Immigrant Assimilation in the United States." In *Host Societies and the Reception of Immigrants,* edited by Jeffrey Reitz. La Jolla, Calif.: Center for Comparative Immigration Studies.

Newman, Katherine. 1999. *No Shame in My Game: The Working Poor in the Inner City.* New York: Knopf.

*New York: A Collection from Harper's Magazine.* 1991. New York: Gallery Books.

van Niekerk, Mies. 2004. "Afro-Caribbeans and Indo-Caribbeans in the Netherlands: Premigration Legacies and Social Mobility." *International Migration Review* 38: 158–183.

Noiriel, Gerald. 1999. "Immigration and National Memory in the Current French Historiography." *IMIS-Beitrage* 10: 39–56.

———. 1996. *The French Melting Pot: Immigration, Citizenship, and National Identity.* Translated by Geoffroy de Laforcade. Minneapolis: University of Minnesota Press.

Nugent, Walter. 1992. *Crossings: The Great Transatlantic Migrations, 1870–1914.* Bloomington: Indiana University Press.

Odencrantz, Louise. 1919. *Italian Women in Industry: A Study of Conditions in New York City.* New York: Russell Sage Foundation.

Ogbu, John, and Astrid Davis. 2003. *Black American Studies in an Affluent Suburb.* New York: Lawrence Erlbaum.

Okihiro, Gary. 2001. *Common Ground: Reimagining American History.* Princeton: Princeton University Press.

Olsen, Laurie. 1997. *Made in America.* New York: New Press.

Olwig, Karen Fog. 1993. "The Migration Experience: Nevisian Women at Home and Abroad." In *Women and Change in the Caribbean,* edited by Janet Momsen. London: James Currey.

———. 2001. "New York as Locality in a Global Family Network." In *Islands in the City: West Indian Migration to New York,* edited by Nancy Foner. Berkeley: University of California Press.

Orleck, Annelise. 1987. "The Soviet Jews: Life in Brighton Beach, Brooklyn." In *New Immigrants in New York,* edited by Nancy Foner. New York: Columbia University Press.

Orsi, Robert. 1990. "The Fault of Memory: 'Southern Italy' in the Imagination of Immigrants and the Lives of Their Children in Italian Harlem, 1920–1945." *Journal of Family History* 15: 135–147.

———. 1992. "The Religious Boundaries of an Inbetween People: Street *Feste* and the Problem of the Dark-Skinned Other in Italian Harlem, 1920–1990." *American Quarterly* 44: 313–347.

Osofsky, Gilbert. 1963. *Harlem: The Making of a Ghetto*. New York: Harper and Row.

Owen, David. 2001. "A Profile of Caribbean Households and Families in Great Britain." In *Caribbean Families in Britain and the Transatlantic World*, edited by Harry Goulbourne and Mary Chamberlain. London: Macmillan.

Palmer, Ransford W. 1974. "A Decade of West Indian Migration to the United States, 1962–1972: An Economic Analysis." *Social and Economic Studies* 23: 571–588.

———. 1995. *Pilgrims from the Sun: West Indian Migration to America*. New York: Twayne.

Park, Kyeyoung. 1997. *The Korean American Dream*. Ithaca: Cornell University Press.

Patterson, Orlando. 2000. "Race Over." *The New Republic* (January 10): 6.

———. 2003. "Racism's Evolution." *Contexts* 2: 61–65.

Peach, Ceri. 1995. "Profile of the Black Caribbean Population of Great Britain." In *Profile of the Ethnic Minority Populations of Great Britain*, edited by Ceri Peach. London: Office of the Population Censuses and Surveys.

———. 1998. "Trends in Levels of Caribbean Segregation, Great Britain, 1961–91." In *Caribbean Migration: Globalised Identities*, edited by Mary Chamberlain. London: Routledge.

———. 1968. *West Indian Migration to Britain: A Social Geography*. London: Oxford University Press.

Pearson, David G. 1981. *Race, Class, and Political Activism: A Study of West Indians in Britain*. Westmead: Gower.

Peiss, Kathy. 1986. *Cheap Amusements: Working Women and Leisure in Turn-of-the-Century New York*. Philadelphia: Temple University Press.

Perlmann, Joel, and Roger Waldinger. 1997. "Second Generation Decline? Children of Immigrants, Past and Present: A Reconsideration." *International Migration Review* 31: 893–923.

Perlmann, Joel, and Mary C. Waters. 2004. "Intermarriage Then and Now: Race, Generation and the Changing Meaning of Marriage." In *Not Just Black and White: Historical and Contemporary Perspectives on Immigration, Race, and Ethnicity in the United States*, edited by Nancy Foner and George Fredrickson. New York: Russell Sage Foundation.

Pessar, Patricia. 1982. "Kinship Relations of Production in the Migration Process: The Case of Dominican Emigration to the United States." Occasional Paper No. 32. New York: Center for Latin American and Caribbean Studies, New York University.

———. 1984. "The Linkage between the Household and the Workplace of Dominican Women in the United States." *International Migration Review* 18: 1188–1211.

———. 1987. "The Dominicans: Women in the Household and the Garment

Industry." In *New Immigrants in New York,* edited by Nancy Foner. New York: Columbia University Press.

Pessar, Patricia. 1995a. *A Visa for a Dream.* Boston: Allyn and Bacon.

———. 1995b. "On the Homefront and in the Workplace: Integrating Immigrant Women into Feminist Discourse." *Anthropological Quarterly* 58: 37–47.

———. 1999. "The Role of Gender, Households and Social Networks in the Migration Process: A Review and Reappraisal." In *The Handbook of International Migration,* edited by Charles Hirschman, Philip Kasinitz, and Josh DeWind. New York: Russell Sage Foundation.

Pessar, Patricia, and Pamela Graham. 2001. "Dominicans: Transnational Identities and Local Politics." In *New Immigrants in New York,* edited by Nancy Foner. Rev. ed. New York: Columbia University Press.

Portes, Alejandro. 1996. "Global Villagers: The Rise of Transnational Communities." *American Prospect* (March-April): 74–78.

———. 1997. "Immigration Theory for a New Century: Some Problems and Opportunities." *International Migration Review* 31: 799–825.

———. 1999. "Conclusion: Towards a New World—The Origins and Effects of Transnational Activities." *Ethnic and Racial Studies* 22: 463–476.

Portes, Alejandro, William Haller, and Luis Guarnizo. 2002. "Transnational Entrepreneurs: An Alternative Form of Immigrant Adaptation." *American Sociological Review* 67: 278–299.

Portes, Alejandro, and Rubén Rumbaut. 2001a. "The Forging of a New America: Lessons for Theory and Policy." In *Ethnicities,* edited by Rubén Rumbaut and Alejandro Portes. Berkeley: University of California Press.

———. 2001b. *Legacies: The Story of the Immigrant Generation.* Berkeley: University of California Press.

Portes, Alejandro, and Alex Stepick. 1992. *City on the Edge: The Transformation of Miami.* Berkeley: University of California Press.

Portes, Alejandro, and Min Zhou. 1993. "The New Second Generation: Segmented Assimilation and Its Variants among Post-1965 Immigrant Youth." *Annals of the American Academy of Political and Social Science* 530: 74–98.

Prashad, Vijay. 2000. *The Karma of Brown Folk.* Minneapolis: University of Minnesota Press.

Praszalowicz, Dorota. 2003. "Polish Migrations to Berlin: Past and Present, from 'Germanization' to Globalization." Paper presented at the Workshop on Paths of Integration, University of Osnabrueck, June.

Premdas, Ralph R. 2004. "Diaspora and Its Discontents: A Caribbean Fragment in Toronto in Quest of Cultural Recognition and Political Empowerment." *Ethnic and Racial Studies* 27: 545–561.

Prescod-Roberts, Margaret. 1980. "Bringing It All Back Home." In *Black Women: Bringing It All Back Home,* edited by Margaret Prescod-Roberts and Norma Steele. Bristol, Eng.: Falling Wall Press.

Prewitt, Kenneth. 2004. "The Census Counts, the Census Classifies." In *Not Just Black and White: Historical and Contemporary Perspectives on Immigration, Race, and Ethnicity in the United States,* edited by Nancy Foner and George Fredrickson. New York: Russell Sage Foundation.

Prieto, Yolanda. 1992. "Cuban Women in New Jersey: Gender Relations and Change." In *Seeking Common Ground,* edited by Donna Gabaccia. Westport, Conn.: Praeger.

Pryce, Ken. 1979. *Endless Pressure: A Study of West Indian Life-styles in Bristol.* London: Penguin.

Qian, Zhenchao, Sampson Lee Blair, and Stacey Ruf. 2001. "Asian American Interracial and Interethnic Marriages: Differences by Education and Nativity." *International Migration Review* 35: 557–586.

Rath, Jan. 2000. "Assimilation of Immigrants in Amsterdam and New York: A Case for International Comparative Study." *Netherlands Journal of Social Sciences* 36: 117–125.

——— (ed.). 2002. *Unravelling the Rag Trade: Immigrant Entrepreneurship in Seven World Cities.* Oxford: Berg.

Rath, Jan, and Robert Kloosterman. 2000. "Outsiders' Business: A Critical Review of Research on Immigrant Entrepreneurship." *International Migration Review* 34: 657–681.

Reid, Ira De A. 1969 [1939]. *The Negro Immigrant: His Background, Characteristics, and Social Adjustments, 1899–1937.* New York: Columbia University Press.

Reitz, Jeffrey G. 1998. *Warmth of the Welcome: The Social Causes of Economic Success for Immigrants in Different Nations and Cities.* Boulder, Colo.: Westview Press.

——— (ed.). 2003. *Host Societies and the Reception of Immigrants.* La Jolla, Calif.: Center for Comparative Immigration Studies, University of California, San Diego.

Renshon, Stanley A. 2000. "Dual Citizens in America: An Issue of Vast Proportions and Broad Significance." *Center for Immigration Studies Backgrounder,* July.

Rex, John, and Sally Tomlinson. 1979. *Colonial Immigrants in a British City: A Class Analysis.* London: Routledge and Kegan Paul.

Reynolds, Tracey. 1997. "(Mis)representing the Black (Super)woman." In *Black British Feminism: A Reader,* edited by Heidi S. Mirza. London: Routledge.

———. 2001. "Black Mothering, Paid Work and Identity." *Ethnic and Racial Studies* 24: 1046–1064.

Richmond, Anthony. 1973. *Migration and Race Relations in a British City: A Study in Bristol.* London: Oxford University Press.

Ricourt, Milagros, and Ruby Danta. 2003. *Hispanas de Queens: Latino Panethnicity in a New York City Neighborhood.* Ithaca: Cornell University Press.

Riding, Alan. 2003. "A Museum Tends the British Melting Pot." *New York Times,* June 11.

Rischin, Moses. 1962. *The Promised City: New York's Jews, 1870–1914.* Cambridge: Cambridge University Press.

Robotham, Donald. 1998. "Transnationalism in the Caribbean: Formal and Informal." *American Ethnologist* 25: 307–321.

Rodriguez, Clara. 1994. "Challenging Racial Hegemony: Puerto Ricans in the United States." In *Race,* edited by Steven Gregory and Roger Sanjek. New Brunswick, N.J.: Rutgers University Press.

———. 1996. "Racial Themes in the Literature: Puerto Ricans and Other Latinos." In *Latinos in New York,* edited by Gabriel Haslip-Viera and Sherrie Baver. Notre Dame: University of Notre Dame Press.

———. 2000. *Changing Race: Latinos, the Census, and the History of Ethnicity in the United States.* New York: New York University Press.

Rodriguez, Yolanda. 2003. "Hispanic or Latino? It All Depends." *Atlanta Journal-Constitution,* December 10.

Roediger, David. 1994. *Toward the Abolition of Whiteness.* London: Verso.

———. 2002. *Colored White: Transcending the Racial Past.* Berkeley: University of California Press.

Rogers, Reuel. 2001. "'Black Like Who?' Afro-Caribbean Immigrants, African Americans and the Politics of Group Identity." In *Islands in the City: West Indian Migration to New York,* edited by Nancy Foner. Berkeley: University of California Press.

Rohter, Larry. 1998. "Island Life Not Idyllic for Youths from U.S." *New York Times,* February 20.

Rose, E. J. B., et al. 1969. *Colour and Citizenship.* London: Oxford University Press.

Rosenblatt, Roger. 1993. "Sunset, Sunrise." *New Republic,* December 27, 20–23.

Rosenwaike, Ira. 1972. *Population History of New York City.* Syracuse: Syracuse University Press.

Ross, Edward A. 1914. *The Old World and the New.* New York: Century.

Rouse, Roger. 1995. "Thinking Through Transnationalism: Notes on the Cultural Politics of Class Relations in the Contemporary United States." *Public Culture* 7: 353–402.

Rumbaut, Rubén. 2002. "Severed or Sustained Attachments? Language, Identity, and Imagined Communities in the Post-Immigrant Generation." In *The Changing Face of Home: The Transnational Lives of the Second Generation,* edited by Peggy Levitt and Mary C. Waters. New York: Russell Sage Foundation.

Sabagh, Georges, and Mehdi Bozorgmehr. 2003. "From 'Give Me Your Poor' to 'Save Our State': New York and Los Angeles as Immigrant Cities and Regions." In *New York and Los Angeles,* edited by David Halle. Chicago: University of Chicago Press.

Salvo, Joseph, and Ronald Ortiz. 1992. *The Newest New Yorkers: An Analysis of Immigration into New York City during the 1980s.* New York: Department of City Planning.

Salzman, Avi. 2003. "A Beat Spreads from Hartford." *New York Times,* December 7.

Sanjek, Roger. 1994. "Intermarriage and the Future of Races in the United States." In *Race,* edited by Steven Gregory and Roger Sanjek. New Brunswick, N.J.: Rutgers University Press.

Sarna, Jonathan. 1981. "The Myth of No Return: Jewish Return Migration to Eastern Europe, 1881–1914." *American Jewish History* 71: 256–268.

Scheiner, Seth. 1965. *Negro Mecca: A History of the Negro in New York City, 1865–1920.* New York: New York University Press.

Schill, Michael H., Samantha Friedman, and Emily Rosenbaum. 1998. "The Housing Conditions of Immigrants in New York City." Working Paper 98-2. New York: Center for Real Estate and Urban Policy, New York University School of Law.

Schwartz, Benjamin. 1995. "The Diversity Myth: America's Leading Export." *Atlantic Monthly,* May, 57–67.

Scott, Janny. 1997. "Orphan Girls of China at Home in New York." *New York Times,* August 19.

Senior, Olive. 1991. *Working Miracles: Women's Lives in the English-Speaking Caribbean.* London: James Currey; Bloomington: Indiana University Press.

Sheridan, Mary Beth. 2003. "Many Jamaicans Find Transition Easy in D.C.: Immigrant Community Grows to No.2." *Washington Post,* February 6.

Shumsky, Neil. 1992. "'Let No Man Stop to Plunder': American Hostility to Return Migration, 1890–1924." *Journal of American Ethnic History* 11: 56–75.

Simon, Patrick. 2000. "The Mosaic Pattern: Cohabitation between Ethnic Groups in Belleville, Paris." In *Minorities in European Cities,* edited by Sophie Body-Gendrot and Marco Martiniello. London: Macmillan.

Simons, Gary. 2003. "History, Mission and Philosophy of Prep for Prep." In *Be the Dream: Prep for Prep Graduates Share Their Stories,* compiled by Gary Simons. Chapel Hill, N.C.: Algonquin Books of Chapel Hill.

Singer, Audrey. 2003. "At Home in the Nation's Capital: Immigrant Trends in Washington." Washington, D.C.: The Brookings Institution.

———. 2004. "The Rise of New Immigrant Gateways." *The Living Cities Census Series* (February). Washington, D.C.: The Brookings Institution.

Singer, Audrey, Samantha Friedman, Ivan Cheung, and Marie Price. 2001. "The World in a Zip Code: Greater Washington, D.C. as a New Region of Immigration." *Survey Series* (April). Washington, D.C.: The Brookings Institution.

Sipprelle, Susan. 2004. "Technology Connects Dominican New Yorkers to Their Homeland." *Gothamgazette.com* (April 20).

Smith, Andrew. 2003. "They Saw It Burn: ADA Lays Out Details of Firebombing at Teens' Arraignment." *Newsday,* August 12.

———. 2005. "Two Guilty Pleas and No Trial: Pair of Teens Admit Role in Torching, Gutting of Mexican Family's House in a Community That Has Been Torn by Conflict Over Immigrants." *Newsday,* March 19.

Smith, David. 1976. *The Facts of Racial Disadvantage.* London: Political and Economic Planning.

Smith, James, and Barry Edmonston (eds.). 1997. *The New Americans: Economic, Demographic, and Fiscal Effects of Immigration.* Washington, D.C.: National Academy Press.

Smith, Raymond T. 1988. *Kinship and Class in the West Indies.* Cambridge: Cambridge University Press.

Smith, Robert C. 1996. "Mexicans in New York City: Membership and Incorporation of a New Immigrant Group." In *Latinos in New York,* edited by G. Haslip Viera and Sherrie Baver. Notre Dame: University of Notre Dame Press.

———. 1998a. "Reflections on the State, Migration, and the Durability and Newness of Transnational Life: Comparative Insights from the Mexican and Italian Cases." *Soziale Welt* 12: 197–217.

———. 1998b. "Transnational Localities: Community, Technology, and the Politics of Membership within the Context of Mexico-U.S. Migration." In *Transnationalism from Below,* edited by Michael Peter Smith and Luis Eduardo Guarnizo. New Brunswick, N.J.: Transaction Press.

———. 2001. "Mexicans: Social, Educational, Economic, and Political Problems and Prospects in New York." In *New Immigrants in New York,* edited by Nancy Foner. Rev. ed. New York: Columbia University Press.

———. 2002a. "Life Course, Generation, and Social Location as Factors Shaping Second Generation Transnational Life." In *The Changing Face of Home: The Transnational Lives of the Second Generation,* edited by Peggy Levitt and Mary C. Waters. New York: Russell Sage Foundation.

———. 2002b. "Gender, Ethnicity and Race in School and Work Outcomes of Second-Generation Mexican Americans." In *Latinos: Remaking America,* edited by Marcelo Suarez-Orozco and Mariela Paez. Berkeley: University of California Press.

———. 2003. "Diasporic Memberships in Historical Perspective: Comparative Insights from the Mexican and Italian Cases." *International Migration Review* 37: 724–759.

———. 2004. "Mexican New York," Presentation at Baruch College, School of Public Affairs, City University of New York, April.

Song, Miri. 2003. *Choosing Ethnic Identity.* London: Polity.

Sontag, Deborah, and Celia Dugger. 1998. "The New Immigrant Tide: A Shuttle Between Worlds." *New York Times,* July 19.

Soto, Isa Maria. 1987. "West Indian Child Fostering: Its Role in Migrant Exchanges." In *Caribbean Life in New York City,* edited by Constance Sutton and Elsa Chaney. New York: Center for Migration Studies.

Soyer, Daniel. 1997. *Jewish Immigrant Associations and American Identity in New York, 1880–1939.* Cambridge: Harvard University Press.

Spain, Daphne, and Suzanne M. Bianchi. 1996. *Balancing Act: Motherhood, Marriage, and Employment among American Women.* New York: Russell Sage Foundation.

Speranza, Gino C. 1974 [1906]. "Political Representation of Italo-American Colonies in the Italian Parliament." In *The Italians: Social Backgrounds of an American Group,* edited by Francisco Cordasco and Eugene Bucchioni. Clifton, N.J.: Augustus M. Kelley.

Stepick, Alex. 1998. *Pride Against Prejudice: Haitians in the United States.* Boston: Allyn and Bacon.

Stepick, Alex, Guillermo Grenier, Max Castro, and Marvin Dunn. 2003. *This Land Is Our Land: Immigrants and Power in Miami.* Berkeley: University of California Press.

Stone, Karen. 1983. "Motherhood and Waged Work: West Indian, Asian, and White Mothers Compared." In *One Way Ticket: Migration and Female Labour,* edited by Annie Phizlackea. London: Routledge and Kegan Paul.

Sudbury, Julia. 2001. "(Re)constructing Multiracial Blackness: Women's Activism, Difference, and Collectivity in Britain." *Ethnic and Racial Studies* 24: 29–49.

Sutton, Constance, and Susan Makiesky. 1975. "Migration and West Indian Racial and Ethnic Consciousness." In *Migration and Development,* edited by Helen Safa and Brian duToit. The Hague: Mouton.

Takaki, Ronald. 1993. *A Different Mirror.* Boston: Little, Brown.

Tentler, Leslie Woodcock. 1979. *Wage-Earning Women.* New York: Oxford University Press.

Thomas-Hope, Elizabeth. 1992. *Explanation in Caribbean Migration.* London: Macmillan Caribbean.

Thranhardt, Dietrich. 2002. "Prophecies, Ius Soli, and Dual Citizenship: Interpreting the Changes in the German Citizenship System." Paper presented at the Workshop on Transnational Ties and Identities: Past and Present. Wassenar, Netherlands, November.

Tilove, Jonathan. 2004. "Through Immigration and Exodus, a New Melting Pot." *Newhouse News Service,* February 5.

Tizard, Barbara, and Ann Phoenix. 1993. *Black, White or Mixed Race?* London: Routledge.

Tomasi, Silvano. 1975. *Piety and Power.* New York: Center for Migration Studies.

Topp, Michael Miller. 1997. "The Transnationalism of the Italian American Left: The Lawrence Strike of 1912 and the Italian Chamber of Labor of New York City." *Journal of American Ethnic History* 17: 39–63.

———. 2003. "'It Is Providential That There are Foreigners Here': Whiteness and Masculinity in the Making of Italian Syndicalist Identity." In *Are Italians White? How Race Is Made in America,* edited by Jennifer Guglielmo and Salvatore Salerno. New York: Routledge.

Toulis, Nicole Rodriguez. 1997. *Believing Identity: Pentecostalism and the Mediation of Jamaican Ethnicity and Gender in England.* Oxford: Berg.

Tuan, Mia. 1998. *Forever Foreigners or Honorary Whites?* New Brunswick, N.J.: Rutgers University Press.

United Nations Development Program. 2003. "Human Development Indicators, 2003." New York: United Nations Development Program Report.

U.S. Commission on Civil Rights. 1992. *Civil Rights Issues Facing Asian Americans in the 1990s.* Washington, D.C.: U.S. Commission on Civil Rights.

Vaca, Nicolas C. 2004. *The Presumed Alliance: The Unspoken Conflict Between Latinos and Blacks and What It Means for America.* New York: HarperCollins.

Van Kleeck, Mary. 1913. *Artificial Flower Makers.* New York: Russell Sage Foundation.

Vecoli, Rudolph. 1969. "Prelates and Peasants: Italian Immigration and the Catholic Church." *Journal of Social History* 2: 217–268.

Vertovec, Steven. 2000. *The Hindu Diaspora: Comparative Patterns.* London: Routledge.

———. 2003. "Migrant Transnationalism and Modes of Transformation." Paper presented at a conference on Conceptual and Methodological Developments in the Study of International Migration, Princeton University, May.

———. 2004. "Cheap Calls: The Social Glue of Migrant Transnationalism." *Global Networks* 4: 219–224.

Vickerman, Milton. 1999. *Crosscurrents: West Indian Immigrants and Race.* New York: Oxford University Press.

———. 2001a. "Jamaicans: Balancing Race and Ethnicity." In *New Immigrants in New York,* edited by Nancy Foner. Rev. ed. New York: Columbia University Press.

———. 2001b. "Tweaking a Monolith: The West Indian Immigrant Encounter with 'Blackness.'" In *Islands in the City,* edited by Nancy Foner. Berkeley: University of California Press.

Waldinger, Roger. 1996a. *Still the Promised City? African Americans and New Immigrants in Postindustrial New York.* Cambridge: Harvard University Press.

———. 1996b. "From Ellis Island to LAX: Immigrant Prospects in the American City." *International Migration Review* 30: 1078–1086.

———. 1997. "Black/Immigrant Competition Re-assessed: New Evidence From Los Angeles." *Sociological Perspectives* 40: 365–386.

———. 2001a. "Strangers at the Gates." In *Strangers at the Gates: New Immigrants in Urban America,* edited by Roger Waldinger. Berkeley: University of California Press.

———. 2001b. "Conclusion: Immigration and the Remaking of Urban America." In *Strangers at the Gates: New Immigrants in Urban America,* edited by Roger Waldinger. Berkeley: University of California Press.

Waldinger, Roger, and Cynthia Feliciano. 2004. "Will the Second Generation Experience 'Downward Assimilation'? Segmented Assimilation Re-assessed." *Ethnic and Racial Studies* 27: 376–402.

Waldinger, Roger, and Jennifer Lee. 2001. "New Immigrants in Urban America." In *Strangers at the Gates: New Immigrants in Urban America,* edited by Roger Waldinger. Berkeley: University of California Press.

Waldinger, Roger, and Michael I. Lichter. 2003. *How the Other Half Works: Immigration and the Social Organization of Labor.* Berkeley: University of California Press.

Waldinger, Roger, and Joel Perlmann. 1998. "Second Generations: Past, Present and Future." *Journal of Ethnic and Migration Studies* 24: 5–24.

Waldinger, Roger, and Yenfen Tseng. 1992. "Divergent Diasporas: The Chinese Communities of New York and Los Angeles Compared." *Revue Europeene Des Migrations Internationales* 8: 91–113.

Waldinger, Roger, Howard Aldrich, Robin Ward, and Associates. 1990. *Ethnic Entrepreneurs.* Newbury Park, Calif.: Sage.

Waldman, Amy. 1998. "Old Places, New Faces: In Southern Brooklyn, Coexistence But Not Quite Community." *New York Times* (City Section), April 12.

Ward, Robin. 1988. "Caribbean Business Enterprise in Britain." In *Lost Illusions: Caribbean Minorities in Britain and the Netherlands,* edited by Malcolm Cross and Hans Entzinger. London: Routledge.

Warikoo, Natasha. 2004. "Cosmopolitan Ethnicity: Second-Generation Indo-Caribbean Identities." In *Becoming New Yorkers: Ethnographies of the New Second Generation,* edited by Philip Kasinitz, John Mollenkopf, and Mary C. Waters. New York: Russell Sage Foundation.

Waters, Mary C. 1990. *Ethnic Options: Choosing Identities in America.* Berkeley: University of California Press.

———. 1994. "Ethnic and Racial Identities of Second-Generation Black Immigrants in New York City." *International Migration Review* 28: 795–820.

———. 1996. "Optional Ethnicities? For Whites Only." In *Origins and Destinies,* edited by Silvia Pedraza and Ruben Rumbaut. Belmont, Calif.: Wadsworth.

———. 1999a. *Black Identities: West Indian Immigrant Dreams and American Realities.* Cambridge: Harvard University Press.

Waters, Mary C. 1999b. "West Indians and African Americans at Work: Structural Differences and Cultural Stereotypes." In *Immigration and Opportunity,* edited by Frank Bean and Stephanie Bell-Rose. New York: Russell Sage Foundation.

———. 2001. "Growing Up West Indian and African American: Gender and Class Differences in the Second Generation." In *Islands in the City: West Indian Migration to New York,* edited by Nancy Foner. Berkeley: University of California Press.

Watkins-Owens, Irma. 1996. *Blood Relations: Caribbean Immigrants and the Harlem Community, 1900–1930.* Bloomington: Indiana University Press.

———. 2001. "Early-Twentieth-Century Caribbean Women: Migration and Social Networks in New York City." In *Islands in the City: West Indian Migration to New York,* edited by Nancy Foner. Berkeley: University of California Press.

Weil, Patrick. 2001. "Access to Citizenship: A Comparison of Twenty-Five Nationality Laws." In *Citizenship Today: Global Perspectives and Practices,* edited by T. Alexander Aleinikoff and Douglas Klusmeyer. Washington, D.C.: Carnegie Endowment for International Peace.

Weiner, Lynn. 1985. *From Working Girl to Working Mother: The Female Labor Force in the United States, 1820–1980.* Chapel Hill: University of North Carolina Press.

West, Cornel. 1994. *Race Matters.* New York: Vintage Books.

White, Michael, Michael Dymowski, and Shilian Wang. 1994. "Ethnic Neighbors and Ethnic Myths: An Examination of Residential Segregation in 1910." In *After Ellis Island,* edited by Susan Cott Watkins. New York: Russell Sage Foundation.

Wilson, William Julius. 1996. *When Work Disappears.* New York: Knopf.

Wollenberg, Charles. 1995. "'Yellow Peril' in the Schools." In *The Asian American Educational Experience,* edited by Don Nakanishi and Tina Yamano Nishida. New York: Routledge.

Wong, Bernard. 1998. *Ethnicity and Entrepreneurship: The New Chinese Immigrants in the San Francisco Bay Area.* Boston: Allyn and Bacon.

Wong, Shawn. 1995. *American Knees.* New York: Simon and Schuster.

Worrall, Simon. 2000. "London on a Roll." *National Geographic* (June): 6–23.

Wright, Richard, and Mark Ellis. 2001. "Immigrants, the Native Born, and the Changing Division of Labor in New York City." In *New Immigrants in New York,* edited by Nancy Foner. Rev. ed. New York: Columbia University Press.

Wrigley, Julia. 1995. *Other People's Children.* New York: Basic Books.

Wyman, Mark. 1993. *Round-Trip America: The Immigrants Return to Europe, 1880–1930.* Ithaca: Cornell University Press.

Yetman, Norman. 1999. "Patterns of Ethnic Integration in America." In *Major-*

*ity and Minority: The Dynamics of Race and Ethnicity in America,* edited by Norman Yetman. Boston: Allyn and Bacon.

Zhou, Min. 1992. *Chinatown: The Socioeconomic Potential of an Urban Enclave.* Philadelphia: Temple University Press.

————. 2001. "Progress, Decline, Stagnation? The New Second Generation Comes of Age." In *Strangers at the Gates: New Immigrants in Urban America,* edited by Roger Waldinger. Berkeley: University of California Press.

————. 2003. "Contemporary Female Immigration to the United States: A Demographic Profile." In *Women Immigrants in the United States,* edited by Philippa Strum and Danielle Tarantolo. Washington, D.C.: Woodrow Wilson Center for Scholars.

Zhou, Min, and Carl Bankston. 1998. *Growing Up American.* New York: Russell Sage Foundation.

Zhou, Min, and Rebecca Kim. 2003. "A Tale of Two Metropolises: New Immigrant Chinese Communities in New York and Los Angeles." In *New York and Los Angeles,* edited by David Halle. Chicago: University of Chicago Press.

Zhou, Min, and John Logan. 1989. "Returns on Human Capital in Ethnic Enclaves: New York City's Chinatown." *American Journal of Sociology* 86: 295–319.

Zhou, Min, and Regina Nordquist. 1994. "Work and Its Place in the Lives of Immigrant Women: Garment Workers in New York City's Chinatown." *Applied Behavioral Science Review* 2: 187–211.

Zolberg, Aristide R., and Long Litt Woon. 1999. "Why Islam is Like Spanish: Cultural Incorporation in Europe and the United States." *Politics and Society* 27: 5–38.

# Index

Abraham, Margaret, 55
Affirmative action programs, 59, 119, 142, 148
African Americans in Chicago, 234n24
African Americans in New York City, 43–61; competition with immigrants, 48–49; Democratic Party politics, 45–46; demographic balance between Hispanics and African Americans, 200; distancing from, 36, 61, 195, 203, 213, 231n110; earnings, 51; education, 116; employment opportunities, 50–53; entrepreneurship, 122; Hispanics/Latinos and, 27–28, 198–201; home ownership, 116; immigrants and, 43–61; interethnic/racial conflict, 261n66; intermarriage with Jamaicans, 249n90; Irish and, 45, 49; Italians and, 46, 47–48, 59; Jamaicans, 249n90; Jews and, 36–37, 46, 47–48, 55, 59; Koreans and, 55, 195, 235n56; labor force participation rate, 121; low-skilled native blacks, 50–52; median household income, 121; middle class, 59, 120; New York's ethnoracial hierarchy, 53–54, 110; police and, 45; political influence, 46, 50; population, 44, 54; public employment, 52–53, 122; in public schools, 56; racism against, 44–45; residential patterns, 22, 46–47, 54, 116–117; rioting by, 195, 260n36; Tenderloin District riot (1900), 45; Voting Rights Act (1965),
50; West Indians and, 54, 109–110, 113–125, 129, 130, 149, 247n44
African Americans in United States: affirmative action programs, 59; color line in American society, 60; compared to immigrants, 213; demographic balance between Hispanics and African Americans, 199–200; employers' bias against, 52, 121; in the future, 205; Hispanics/Latinos and, 198–199, 215; immigrants and, 214–215, 261n50; intermarriage, 35; in Miami, 199–200; in New York City (see African Americans in New York City); northern migration, 36; residential patterns, 232n128; in Washington, D.C., 150; West Indians and, 147–150, 153–154 (see also African Americans in New York City); youth culture, 70, 236n70
Africans in London, 115, 146
Africans in New York City, 20–21, 146
Africans in Washington, D.C., 254n70
Afro-Caribbeans in Britain, 110, 132
Afro-Caribbeans in London, 110, 245n2
Afro-Caribbeans in New York City, 21, 58, 228n39
Airey-Wilson, Veronica, 151
Alba, Richard, 19, 41–42, 84, 125, 232n128, 264n51
Aleinikoff, T. Alexander, 265n65
Alexander, Claire, 115, 127, 178
*Alien Nation* (Brimelow), 214

Chinese in New York City: population (2000), 20t, 28, 193; racial slurs aimed at, 32; second generation, 81; Sunset Park, 202; women and work, 97, 100
Chinese in United States, 29, 186. *See also* Chinese in New York City
Citizenship: dual nationality, 75–76, 87; education and, 77; Europe, 220–221, 222, 265n65; France, 264n56; Germany, 220, 264n58; immigration and, 137–138; Italian, 69; Jamaicans, 133, 137–138; Jamaicans in New York City, 138; second generation, 220, 264n58; United States, 220–221; West Indians, 112, 133
City University of New York (CUNY), 141–142, 186–187, 202–203, 252n40
Civil rights movement, 37
Clarke, Averil, 125
Clarke, Una, 119
Class. *See* Social class
Cleveland, 209
Colen, Shellee, 168
Colombia, 75
Colombians in New York City, 20t, 26, 72, 202
Columbia College, 18
Comparative studies of immigration: "across space" studies, 2, 4, 7; "across time" studies, 2, 4, 7; "convergent comparisons," 2; "divergent comparisons," 6; factors in comparing groups in different urban/national destinations, 131–132; future trans-Atlantic comparisons, 223; value of, 1–5, 7, 223
Connecticut, 147t, 150–151, 254n71
Connerly, Ward, 215
Coolidge, Calvin, 15
Cornell, Stephen, 12, 15, 40
Creolization, 126
Cross, Malcolm, 140
Crouch, Stanley, 218
Cubans in Miami, 190, 192, 199

Cubans in New York City, 26, 114
Cultural racism, 217, 218
Culture, 217–218, 219
Current Population Survey data, 235n66

Dallas metropolitan area, 188t
Danielovich, Issur (Kirk Douglas), 35
Danta, Ruby, 25
Davison, R. B., 167, 168–169
De Valera, Eamon, 69
Denton, Nancy, 232n128
DeSalvo, Louise, 17
Detroit, 209
Diner, Hasia, 46, 209
Dinkins, David, 50, 119, 194
Distance from homeland, 86, 143–145
Dominican Republic: blackness in, 191; dual nationality, 75, 76; Miraflores in, 72; race in, 27; remittances from abroad, 76
Dominicans in New York City: distancing from non-Hispanic blacks, 55; dual nationality, 82; effect of American norms on marital goals, 99; female-first migration pattern, 97–98; interethnic/racial conflict, 261n66; involvement with homeland, 70, 74, 87; Jackson Heights, 202; men's contribution to household chores, 99; Miraflores.com, 72; political participation, 87, 239n75; population, 20t, 78, 190; Puerto Ricans and, 200; racial status, 26, 27, 50, 55; rioting by, 195, 260n36; second generation, 81, 83; self-employment, 72; transnationalism, 70, 72–73, 74, 81, 83, 87, 239n75; visits to parents' homeland, 83; Washington Heights, 72; women's authority in the household, 96–97; women's labor force participation rate, 95, 243n31; women's satisfaction from work, 100; working wives, 102–103
Dore-Cabral, Carlos, 55
Dotbusters, 31

Hall, Stuart, 128, 135
Halle, David, 260n36
Haller, William, 236n7
Hammel, Eugene, 225n2
*Harper's* (magazine), 16
Hartford (Connecticut), 150–151,
254n71
Hartmann, Douglas, 12, 15, 40
Harvard University, 18
Hattam, Victoria, 13, 36–37
Heron, Melonie P., 251n28
Higham, John, 210–211
Hintzen, Percy, *West Indian in the West*,
148–149
Hirsch, Jennifer, 99
"Hispanic," 114, 191, 192
Hispanics/Latinos in New York City,
23–28; affirmative action programs,
59; African Americans and, 27–28,
198–201; blackness and, 26–27; of
Caribbean origin, 191; in City University of New York, 252n40; demographic balance between Hispanics
and African Americans, 200; distancing from African Americans, 195;
divisions among, 25, 200; extended
homeland visits, 82; heterogeneity of,
190; language, 82–83; native-born
(late 1990s), 186; natives' sensitivity
to differences among nationalities,
24–25, 188; New York's ethnoracial
hierarchy, 19; panethnicity, 25, 32;
population, 24, 38, 44; Puerto Ricans,
24–25; racial status, 11, 23–24, 26,
49–50, 190, 192, 201; second generation, 59, 82; transnationalism, 88;
upper middle class, 28; working
wives, 102
Hispanics/Latinos in United States:
African Americans and, 198–199,
215; demographic balance between
Hispanics and African Americans,
199–200; intermarriage, 26, 38; in
New York City (*see* Hispanics/Latinos
in New York City); panethnicity, 32;
racial status, 27, 190–191, 192,

229n64, 232n122, 260n28; residen-
tial patterns, 26, 232n128
Historians of immigration, 3–4
Ho, Christine, 257n40
Hollifield, James, 7
Hollinger, David, 42, 85, 216
Holocaust, 208, 214
Hondagneu-Sotelo, Pierrette, 100,
156–157, 164
Housing, 17–18
Houston, 190, 192, 200
Houston metropolitan area, 188t, 190
Howard University, 149
Hybridity, 126, 201–203

Immigrant cable-television channels, 72
Immigrant men, 98–99, 101, 104
Immigrant press, 68
Immigrant women, 89–105; Asians in
New York City, 97–98; burdens
resulting from wage work, 100–103,
105; Central Americans, 99, 244n65;
changes affecting, 95, 103–105; childrearing, 101; Chinese in New York
City, 97, 100; choice of work, 100;
contribution to family income, 95;
discord with spouses, 103; Dominicans in New York City, 95, 96–98,
99, 100, 102–103; effect of American
norms on marital goals, 99; empowerment of women, 97, 104; evening
school, 242n19; female-first migration
pattern, 97–98; Filipinos in New York
City, 95; gender division of housework and child care, 104; Haitians in
New York City, 101; Hispanics/Lati-
nos in New York City, 102; household chores, 93–94, 98–99, 101, 104;
improvement in life, 96–97, 243n30;
industrial homework, 95, 104; Italians in New York City, 90–95, 103–
104; Jamaicans in London (*see* Jamaican women in London); Jamaicans in
metropolitan New York, 256n21;
Jamaicans in New York City (*see*
Jamaican women in New York City);

Social mobility, 187, 214, 220
Sociologists of immigration, 3, 5
Song, Miri, 216, 264n38
South Americans in New York City,
20t, 26, 71–72, 81, 190, 202,
261n66. *See also* Guyanese in New
York City; Trinidadians in New York
City
South Asians in New York City, 32, 55,
193, 202. *See also* Indians in New
York City
Southeast Asians in United States,
260n31
Southern Europeans in United States,
14, 15, 35, 207, 213, 231n103. *See
also* Italians in New York City
Soyer, Daniel, 79
Speranza, Gino, 62–63, 64
State University of New York (SUNY),
141
Statue of Liberty, 210–211
Statue of Liberty–Ellis Island Founda-
tion, 211
Stevens, Gillian, 39
Surinamese in Netherlands, 217
Switzerland, 208
Syncretic cultures, 126, 128–129,
201–203

Taiwanese in New York City, 98,
243n42
Taiwanese in United States, 186
Tenderloin District riot (1900), 45
Texas, 189, 190, 191, 199
"Then" *vs.* "now," 5
Thomas, W. I., 12
Thranhardt, Dietrich, 216
Topp, Michael, 13, 68
Toronto, 144, 154–155
"Trans-national America" (Bourne), 77
Transmigrants, 236n9
Transnational households, 64
Transnationalism, 62–88; aging and, 84;
airline travel, 136, 144; American
businesses, 77; assimilation and, 78,
85; benefit to immigrants, 87–88;

Brazilians in New York City, 71–72;
campaigning across borders by politicians, 68, 78; Caribbeans in Britain,
252n46; Caribbeans in New York
City, 70; Central Americans in New
York City, 70; changes in, 69–79, 85;
definition, 62–63; distance from
homeland, 86, 143–145; Dominicans
in New York City, 70, 72–73, 74, 81,
83, 87, 239n75; dual nationality, 70,
75–76; economic endeavors spanning
national borders, 72–73; economic
insecurity and, 67; Filipinos in New
York City, 71; Hispanics/Latinos in
New York City, 88; homeland governments' involvement with citizens
abroad, 69; immigrant cable-television channels, 72; immigrant press,
68; Indians in New York City, 70–71,
72, 73; involvement in homeland politics, 68, 74, 88, 151; Irish in New
York City, 68–69, 72, 79; Italians in
New York City, 63–69, 74, 79–80,
86; Italians in Philadelphia, 80,
240n94; Jamaicans in London, 144–
145; Jamaicans in London and New
York, 135–137; Jews in New York
City, 63–69, 74, 79–80, 81, 86; Koreans in New York City, 72, 74; lack of
acceptance in America, 67–68; land
purchases in the homeland, 65; legal
status and, 86–87; length of stay in
United States, 87; life course and, 87;
lobbying governments about homeland issues, 68–69, 76; Mexicans in
New York City, 71, 83, 86; nationalism among immigrants, 74–75,
76–77; in New York City, 63–88;
"old" *vs.* "new" ("then" *vs.* "now"),
69–79, 85; parental retirement patterns, 82; patriotism to United States,
84; Poles in New York City, 68;
remittances sent home, 64–65, 76, 87,
239n87; return migration, 65–68, 76,
144; scholarship concerning, 5, 63,
78–79; second generation, 79–85,

87–88; ties to homeland, 144–145, 252n46; transnational motherhood, 167–169; transportation systems, 70–71, 136, 144; visits to homeland, 66, 82, 83, 136, 137, 251n19; West Indians in New York City, 81, 82, 86, 88, 237n13, 251n19
Trinidad, 21, 23, 111
Trinidadians in New York City: college education, 255n84; empowerment of women, 97; men's contribution to household chores, 98–99; population, 20t, 254n82; self-employment, 248n55; transnationalism, 251n19; visits to homeland, 251n19
Trinidadians in United States, 250n14
Tuan, Mia, 30
Turks in Germany, 262n11
Turks in Netherlands, 217
"Twice migrants," 145, 152

"Underclass," 41, 213
Undocumented immigrants: Jamaican women in New York City, 164; Jamaican women in United States, 160; Jamaicans in New York City, 137; Los Angeles, 197; New York City, 137, 197; Proposition 187 (California, 1994), 196; West Indians in New York City, 137
United States, 206–224; citizenship, 220–221; collective memories of immigration, 207–212; future racial order, 38–42, 126, 204–205; higher education, 141–142; immigrant population, 1, 133, 138, 147t, 209, 215, 250n14, 259n1; immigrants in (see Immigrants in United States); immigration restrictions, 133, 137, 214, 263n19; U.S.-Europe comparisons, 206–224; welfare state in, 140, 221–222

Vecoli, Rudolph, 47
Vertovec, Steven, 238n47
Vickerman, Milton, 111, 118, 123–124,

125, 129, 190, 248n61, 249n90, 256n21
Vietnamese in United States, 260n31
"Visa overstayers," 137
Voting Rights Act (1965), 50, 119

Waldinger, Roger, 39, 48, 50, 52, 56, 186, 187, 188–189, 220
Washington, D.C., 149–150
Washington, D.C. metropolitan area, 188t, 189, 254n69, 254n70
Waters, Mary, 20, 22, 38, 113, 121, 123, 126, 135, 141, 143, 178, 201, 232n121, 246n24, 248n62, 251n19, 261n66, 261n68
Watkins-Owens, Irma, 237n13
Weil, Patrick, 265n65
Welfare state, 140, 221–222
West, Cornel, 215
"West Indian": in Britain, 110, 114, 246n14; to Indo-Caribbeans in Britain, 245n5; in New York City, 110, 114; as self-identification, 246n24; in this text, 21, 110
*West Indian in the West* (Hintzen), 148–149
West Indians, 109–179; Belizians as, 110; blackness, 109–114; citizenship, 112, 133; Guyanese as, 110; Jamaican women (see Jamaican women in London; Jamaican women in New York City); in London (see West Indians in London); London as destination, 146; in New York City (see West Indians in New York City); New York City as destination, 146; scholarship about, 121–122, 126, 154–155, 253n54, 253n56; in Toronto, 154–155; in Washington, D.C., 149–150
West Indians in Britain: class composition, 138–139; gender gap in educational attainment, 178; gender patterns of migration, 158–159; geographic distribution, 146; history of migration, 110, 132–133; in London

unions, 121; middle class, 150–151; in New York City (*see* West Indians in New York City); party affiliation, 151; political mobilization, 148; population, 133, 138
West Indians in Washington, D.C., 149–150
"White," 188–189
"White Hispanics," 260n28
Whiteness: future of, 38–42; groups currently thought of as not-white but not-black, 38–42; "inbetween people," 13; Italians in Chicago, 231n110; Italians in United States, 16–17, 33–37, 48; Jews in United States, 33–37, 48; money and, 111–112; as the norm, 111; "probationary whites," 13; "white by law," 14; "white," meaning of, 13–14, 39; white-nonwhite division, 39
Whites: domestic work field in London, 165; in Hartford (Connecticut), 150; index of dissimilarity between West Indians and non-Hispanic whites, 117, 255n85; intermarriage, 23, 39, 40–41, 230n79, 230n81; in New York City (*see* whites in New York City); New York's ethnoracial hierarchy, 19; oppositional behavior among, 58
Whites in New York City: in City University of New York, 252n40; native-born with two native-born parents, 185; non-Hispanic whites, 19, 117, 189, 196, 259n4; ongoing influx of Europeans, 189; political incumbents, 187
Wisconsin, 260n31
Women. *See* Immigrant women
Wong, Shawn, *American Knees,* 40
Work. *See* Employment and unemployment
World Trade Center attacks (2001), 31, 77
Wyman, Mark, 67

*Yekl* (Cahan), 64

Zangwill, Israel, 77
Zolberg, Aristide, 208, 212, 263n26

# About the Author

Nancy Foner is Distinguished Professor of Sociology at Hunter College and the Graduate Center, City University of New York. She is the author of numerous books, including *From Ellis Island to JFK: New York's Two Great Waves of Immigration* (winner of the Theodore Saloutos Book Award of the Immigration and Ethnic History Society) and *Islands in the City: West Indian Migration to New York.*